George Lang's Cuisine of Hungary

The wedding feast of King Matthias. Drawing by István Engel-Tevan.

George Lang's Cuisine of Hungary

With a new introduction
by the author

WINGS BOOKS

New York • Avenel, New Jersey

I dedicate this work
to the
sweet memory of two ladies:

GRANDMOTHER GIZELLA,
who taught my mother,
and

MY DEAR MOTHER,
who taught me the love of the kitchen.

Instead of flowers . . .

✡   ✡   ✡

This 1994 edition is published by Wings Books,
distributed by Random House Value Publishing, Inc.
40 Engelhard Avenue, Avenel, New Jersey 07001.
Originally published in New York by Atheneum in 1971.

Random House
New York • Toronto • London • Sydney • Auckland

Printed and bound in the United States of America

Library of Congress Cataloging-in-Publication Data

Lang, George, 1924-
    [Cuisine of Hungary]
    George Lang's cuisine of Hungary / George Lang.
        p.   cm.
    Reprint. Originally published: New York : Atheneum, 1971.
    Includes bibliographical references and index.
    ISBN 0-517-11868-8
    1. Cookery, Hungarian.   I. Title.   II. Title: Cuisine of Hungary.
TX723.5.H8L3   1994
641.59439—dc20   94-14864
                                                    CIP

8   7   6   5   4   3   2   1

✿ PREFACE BY JOSEPH WECHSBERG ✿

THERE may be somebody in Hungary or elsewhere who knows more than George Lang about the cuisine of Hungary, but I doubt it. This isn't the sort of statement a non-Hungarian ought to make; Hungarians, who are all members of the most closed secret society, are very strict about this. I'll stick to it. Lang's knowledge about the subject is encyclopedic and often bewildering.

On the manuscript of this book that he sent me it said "12th revised version," but that's one of Lang's rare understatements. With all the thinking and planning he's done on this book, the worrying and meditating, this must be closer to the 112th version, and there may be more. He must have written this book in an agony of ruthless self-discipline, eliminating many things he likes and cutting much of what there was left. In its present form, I believe it will be the definitive book on the cuisine of Hungary.

This is much more than a mere cookbook. It is a theoretical treatise, a cultural-culinary history of Hungary. It deals with gastronomy in the sense of Brillat-Savarin, who called gastronomy "the intelligent knowledge of whatever concerns man's nourishment." It is also a book that people will read for sheer entertainment, like a mystery novel. And, finally, there will be many who take it out into the kitchen to try one of the recipes. In due time, paprika will be sprinkled over the pages. Lang is not only something of a poet (most Hungarians are) but also a practicing cook who has no patience with gastronomic writers who poetically describe a dish without telling their readers exactly how to do it because this is much more difficult.

He is also that exception, a genuine Hungarian who doesn't think that Hungary is the beginning and the end of the universe. On our forays through the markets, shops, espressos and restaurants of Budapest, he often criticized something he didn't like. He isn't narrow-minded. The great Károly Gundel, who did for Hungarian cuisine what Carême and Escoffier did for French, once told me that "the French must always be our masters." Lang has followed the philosophy of Gundel, who created the modern renaissance of Hungarian cooking by raising it to the level of elegant, fine cuisine—making it lighter, yet retaining the characteristic elements of folklore. Gundel realized that Hungarian cooking must be Hungarian as well as Western, just as Hungary's poets want to be Hungarians *and* Westerners.

Born in Hungary and now living in New York, Lang has been able to build a bridge that ought to be crossed in both directions. This is a book that tries to explain Hungarian cooking to Hungarians and to the world-at-large. It shouldn't be read in one sitting, but should be enjoyed like a well-orchestrated meal, with time between the courses. After this book, there is no more excuse for bad Hungarian cooking. It matters little that *I* like it, but I think that Károly Gundel would have liked it.

✵ HOMAGE IN THE FORM OF A FOREWORD ✵

I'M PLEASED to write the foreword to this volume and salute the author. His extraordinary research and creativity have produced a work which deals with the entire world of gastronomy. In *The Physiology of Taste,* Brillat-Savarin said that the fate of nations depends on their eating habits. This book analyzes how eating, drinking and the practitioners of gastronomy influenced the flow of Hungarian history and vice versa.

Today we live in an era when our life is almost dominated by our diet. Scientists have proved that foods influence creativity, judgment, courage, awareness, affect our dreams, waking hours and all our physical actions and mental exercises.

Not only great pleasure, but the understanding of each other often happens at the dinner table. It even influences politics, creating an ambiance which releases built-in guards and acquired tensions. Perhaps "political gastronomy" should be practiced more often at the peace tables.

Hungarian writers contributed as much to the development of the national cuisine as did chefs or the unique quality of the ingredients. The author amply illustrates this in many areas of the book, enriching this work way beyond the level of cookery books. It is my opinion that this volume will not only be invaluable for historians, chefs and housewives alike, but it will be a vital tool in Hungary to develop the next chapter of the Hungarian kitchen. Posterity will be grateful for such a rich material and, at the same time, the present generation will be able to use brought-back-to-their-original-state, noncliché recipes with great success.

[Homage in the Form of a Foreword]

I am gratified that the world at large, the experts and home cooks alike will at last be able to learn the authentic Hungarian cooking methods and be aware of the highly developed state of our cuisine.

Through the work of George Lang, the readers will meet a person who serves the art of the kitchen and dining room with undivided intellect and, at the same time, offers his monumental work with traditional humility.

Please accept this volume with love.

JÓZSEF VENESZ
*President of the Hungarian
Chefs and Pastry Chefs Association*

✲ A NOTE OF INTENTION ✲

WRITING A COOKBOOK is not too difficult these days. All it seems to require is a pair of scissors, a pot of glue and an optimistic publisher. When I began this book in the early sixties, since I was out of glue and my scissors were dull, I decided to actually write a book about the cuisine and wines of a comparatively little-known country—Hungary. It has had the misfortune to have a reputation akin to pseudo folklore with the background music of gypsies playing into the ears of contented tourists eating the red-hot "goulash."

Of the many reasons for this book, perhaps the most important one is to show to the rest of the world that this step-child of history, located on the eternally explosive borders of East and West, of Asiatic origin and an almost surrealistic history, has an extraordinary and unique cuisine. Some of the chapters deal with the relationship among the peasant, bourgeois and aristocratic kitchens, and examine how and why Hungarian cuisines as a whole developed.

A Hungarian food historian once said that a nation's cuisine is like a Royal Crown: to last throughout the ages it has to start with a good basic structure; as the country grows so grows the Crown in its glory, with various jewels and decorations being added from time to time to its original framework.

I should mention in this freshly-baked introduction that many of our jewels were added by friends and enemies, since Hungarian cuisine was pervasively influenced throughout history by everybody who passed by during the last eleven hundred years. The painfully long list includes the Tartars, Turks, Germans, Austrians, Italians, French, Czechs, Slovaks, Serbs, Croatians and these days even the Americans to a small degree. In each instance, however, whether it was a specialty dish or a technique (like the *phyllo* pastry of Turkey, which the Hungarians turned into strudel) they magically transformed the foreign ingredients into authentic Hungarian specialties.

I have tried to search out the influences of geography, literature, climate, royal intermarriages and scores of other forces and happenings. When reading this book or cooking one of its recipes, please remember that Hungary's borderlines are made of a rubber band that have changed from time to time, and this is easily discernible in its cuisine.

Early gastronomic literature is rich with detailed descriptions of various dishes, almost exclusively dealing with the foods and tables of the nobility. Since the most characteristic and richest part of Hungarian cuisine is common people's food, particularly pre-eighteenth century, reconstruction was a painstakingly slow process. Also, because of politically motivated historical writing and nonscientific deductions and theories, most of the previous reseach had to be discarded. Sometimes libraries had to be researched extensively for a single paragraph.

There are no original creations; even one of the most expensive dishes in history, Esau's lentil pottage, must have been a variation on an earlier rendering. In this book I tried to sort out the great Hungarian specialties of the past, regardless how dim the past, combine them with the skill and applied art of cooking and pastry making, wrapped up in tradition.

To me and to non-natives alike, one of the gratifying things about the cuisine of Hungary is that while enjoying it you do not have to feel that you must have an "experience." You are not eating philosophy, but a satisfying potato dumpling made with sheep's cheese or a delicious pancake topped with apple meringue. Also, you can prepare and serve any of these dishes without the anxiety of wondering if you or your guests will measure up to the food.

Since 1990, the almost unprecedented speed of change that happened to the restaurants of Hungary is a kind of modern miracle. During the Cold War years I still remember when I was sitting in what was one of the formerly-famous pastry shops of Budapest and when I ordered a *kuglóf,* a turban-shaped coffee cake that is known in Vienna as *gugelhupf,* I noticed a dead fly inside the cake. Naturally I complained to the waiter, who shrugged his shoulders and said: "You're right, but still, Comrade, you should be reasonable about it. The majority of those dark spots are raisins." Sitting in the same *cukrászda* (pastry shop) these days you will find this delicacy all raisin, sweet butter, vanilla beans and rich chocolate.

Another thing has changed since the first of many editions of this book, a turn of events that has almost the coloration of a small miracle. In the section titled "The New Era" I wrote with admiration and affection about Károly Gundel, the greatest restaurateur Hungary has produced, and about the venerable restaurant in Budapest which still bears his name. In 1991 my friend and partner Ronald S. Lauder and I purchased this establishment which became a symbol of culinary art and refined hospitality during the past hundred years. Gundel and his chefs created many dishes during the first half of the century that achieved international fame, which I had already included in the 1971 edition of this book.

The rebirth of this fabulous institution and the achievement of creating what was recently called "one of Europe's preeminent gastronomic experiences" gives me great satisfaction, as does the fact that our chefs at Gundel have used many of the recipes in this volume.

These days the problem is not resisting temptation but finding temptation worth resisting, and I earnestly hope that for the housewives, chefs, food and wine-loving artists, writers and others of their ilk we have risen to the occasion.

George Lang
Budapest
7 February 1994

✡ CONTENTS ✡

[Contents]

✡ ILLUSTRATIONS ✡

{ Illustrations }

PART ONE

✹

A HISTORY OF
HUNGARIAN CUISINE

✹ ✹ ✹ ✹ ✹
✹ ✹ ✹
✹

✲ I ✲

THE MYSTERIOUS BEGINNINGS

IF ever the Hungarian nation behaved well in the past 1,100 years, it is probably because it would have been useless for anybody to tell them, "Go back where you came from." Nobody knew where *that* was—the Hungarians themselves still argue about it. Volumes have been written on this subject and many adventurers and explorers spent their lives trying to find the birthplace of the Magyars.

From the hundreds of hypotheses, most experts listen to the etymologists, who point out that the structure of the Hungarian language and its most ancient words are of Finno-Ugric origin. The ancient homeland of these two tribes was on the border of Europe and Asia, near the Ural Mountains. According to the earliest records, the Hungarians had lived there as hunters and fishermen around the time Christ was born. Some time later they turned to a wandering nomadic existence and this is how their contacts with the various Turkish tribes began. Many of the ancient Hungarian words are of Turkish origin, stemming not only from the 150 years of the Turkish occupation that came nine centuries later, but also from this era.

Because the shepherds needed new grazing fields for their herds and partly because they were obliged to migrate, being driven by the Pechenegs, the Hungarian tribe slowly but continuously moved south and southwest. By the fifth century after Christ we find them north of the Caucasus in the territory around the Don River. For the next two centuries they were under the influence of Bulgarians and Turks; and during the eighth and ninth centuries, when they lived under the Khazar Empire, they learned agriculture, handicrafts, commerce and wine making.

An ancient utensil which recalls their way of life is the *bogrács,* or kettle. The large cast-iron vessel, which could be held on the *szolgafa* (holding

Cast-iron kettles held by szolgafa

stick), was a basic cooking utensil of the nomad Hungarians. It hung behind the saddle even when they went on their marauding excursions.

From a variety of sources—including the so-called KUM codex (anonymous, 1303) and a tract by Ármin Vámbéry (explorer and Orientalist), János Jankó and György Almásy—a striking picture emerges of the ancients' dining habits.

The scene is a large tent somewhere around the Ob River,* with the middle open, under which is a hearth. The wooden supports of the tent are colorfully painted and decorated with ribbons, and the walls are covered with handsome woven rugs—a warm hospitable décor. Opposite the door, near the fireplace, is the head table to which the host leads his male guests. Behind it the treasures of the house are arranged—huge silver-studded leather casks, mounds of embroidered cushions and a few shiny metal chests. After the company has admired the treasures of the house, they take cushions and rugs and seat themselves in a semicircle around the hearth, discussing, no doubt, rising prices and falling neighbors. The women bring in tea and kumis (fermented horse milk) and tin ewers of warm water for handwashing.

Then comes the big moment. As in the triumphant *pièce montée* of Carême more than 1,500 years later, a pair of young lads carry in a live, struggling sheep. If the guests are properly brought up, they feel the body of the animal and make approving noises. The most desirable animal is the so-

* Western Siberia, U.S.S.R.

called "three-mothered sheep" which has not been allowed to graze until late fall and has been fed on mother's milk. (Since one mother's milk would not have been sufficient, three were necessary to supply its needs—hence the name.) After this introduction, the animal is taken out and killed according to ritual. The women and servants—in another tent—boil the sheep in an enormous kettle. Meanwhile the head, the four legs and part of the stomach are brought to the host, raw. The host singes the hides, cleans the parts, stretches the meat with the help of wooden stakes and spit-roasts them on the open fire. Toward the end, carefully, he bastes them with a saline solution. When the meat is cooked, he tears off pieces, places them on wooden trenchers and serves them to his guests, with the broth from the boiled sheep prepared by the women.

The host never ate until the guests were served—by then he was either too tired or there was no food left. This was the true beginning of Hungarian hospitality.

The dinner was usually finished with *bes-parmak* (five fingers)—finely chopped leg of mutton mixed with sheep-fat broth and kneaded into a mixture which was then made into meatballs. The name comes from the fact that it took a peculiar five-finger position to make balls out of this sticky concoction. (As with the glutinous rice of Indonesia, the ancient Hungarians learned this technique from the Chinese.) Candy and fruit were passed and the music began. Every man played the *koboz,* a three-stringed instrument, and they sang songs of ancient heroes and, naturally—being Hungarians, after all—the pangs of love.

In the ninth- and tenth-century pre-Christian Hungarian cuisine, the most important element was the soup, and its importance has not waned since, except in the Middle Ages. An overwhelming number of the soups had a sour or semisour taste, achieved by whipping in sour cream, vinegar, yogurt, horseradish and sauerkraut. Other soups they thickened with a mixture of flour, milk and egg yolk or the browned flour and fat mixture still basic to many Hungarian dishes.

One of the most interesting features of this era is the variety of techniques used to preserve meat. One method was to cook pieces of meat down to the point where they were completely dry (without, of course, burning them). Then the shepherd put his *ködmön* fur coat on the ground, skin side up, and emptied the stew meat onto it. In three or four days the sun dried the meat completely. The shepherd then put the meat into pouches made of sheep's stomachs. Whenever he wanted a meal, he simply took out some meat, added water, and brought it to a boil.

Another variation was pounding the dried cooked meat into a powder—

5

this may account in part for the Hungarian's success as a warrior. While the enemy had to stop to kill and cook animals, thus wasting valuable time, the Magyars had instant rations. According to Leo VI,* Emperor of Greece, who described the warfaring methods of the Hungarian tribes against the Byzantines, the Hungarians' food was carried by horses, while the Byzantines kept cows and oxen to provide their meat. These slower beasts alone put them at enough of a disadvantage to cause their defeat at the hands of the Hungarians.

The Hungarian tribe did not eat pork until they reached what is now Hungary, since most of the time they were associated with Moslems, or with the Khazar Kingdom which was converted to Judaism in 740. In the new country, however, they tamed the local wild boar and developed an enormous fondness for ham and every form of bacon and a very sophisticated sausage culture, which is still a very important part of the present-day cuisine.

Another basic food was *zsendice,* which is still eaten in some parts of Hungary. It was made by adding rennet to sheep's milk, and when curdled, it was strained through a bag full of holes. The result was a very creamy type of cottage cheese.

There were millet and groats in a great variety of forms, including flat baked pancakes, dumplings and breads, and later the more noble grains such as wheat and rye were used in a great many ways, most of which are still practiced today.

Fish was a very important part of the ancient Hungarians' daily fare, and its most popular mode of preparation was spit-roasting. Fish soup, without paprika, was also known, and fish as well as meat was smoked to preserve it for the winter.

Winter game hunting, too, was part of their daily routine, and words for "snow" and "shooting" come from this era, making them some of the earliest-known Hungarian words still in use today.

Peter Magister, the scribe of King Béla III at the end of the twelfth century —whose work is among the earliest written sources—records that when "our ancestors, led by Álmos, entered the fort of Hung, they gave offerings to the gods and had a four-day feast: *'fecerunt magnum aldumas.'* (They made a great ceremonial feast.)" *Aldumas,* in today's Hungarian with only one letter changed—*áldomás*—means a toast. *Aldumas* comes from *Áldozat,* meaning sacrifice, which of course was the original ritual of thanksgiving.

It is well known that certain liquids are helpful in inducing the proper mood for merry thanksgiving, and the ancient Hungarians did it with fermented horse milk, or with birch water. Ibn Fadhlan† in the tenth century

* Leo VI (the Wise), 886–912.
† Persian courier.

6

describes the white birch* into which the Hungarians bored a hole and inserted a reed or sunflower stem to collect the sap. Birch sap had about a 2-percent sugar content and fermented into a pretty powerful, slightly carbonated drink.

Hungary has always been, because of its position between East and West, overrun and invaded; and the occupiers have left indelible marks on Hungarian cuisine. Even so, the basic elements of the Magyar kitchen as we know it today were already in practice by the time the seven Magyar tribes, under the leadership of Prince Árpád, conquered their new homeland in A.D. 896.

* *Nyírfa,* which is the same family as birch.

THE FIRST FIVE HUNDRED YEARS

THE last stage of the migration of the Magyar tribes was the result of intrigues and manipulations between the Byzantine Empire and Slavic kingdoms. Forced to leave the Khazar Empire (Asiatic Turkey of today), they kept moving in a southwestern direction, reaching the Carpathian basin at the end of the ninth century. By 896 their permanent homeland was conquered.

The word Magyar, which became the name of the entire nation, was originally the name of the dominant ruling tribe. It comes from *magy,* which was another word for the Voguls; and *ar* meant "man" in Csermisz, the language that is the forerunner of Finnish. Ungarn, Hungary, Venger, Hongrois, etc., came from the ancient Russian *Ugrin*—the name by which the Hungarians were known to the Slavs.

The tribes couldn't and didn't change their way of life simply because they had arrived in what was to be their permanent homeland. In small groups they crossed the border into Byzantium, Switzerland, Germany, Italy, France —virtually across Europe—raiding and robbing, gathering treasures and slaves. But every now and then they were beaten and retreated.

A nation's ancient misfortunes sometimes provide rich material to the historians, and one of the most interesting descriptions of the hit-and-run forays is in the manuscript written by the scribe of St. Gallen monastery in 924. The God- and Hungarian-fearing monks ran away when they heard that the Asiatic barbarians were near. Only one, Brother Heribald, stayed, burning with curiosity to see the legendary horsemen. He not only survived this meeting but had a pretty good time and told his story—which can be found in the famous Ekkehard Chronicles. "Some of them set up an open fire and huge splinter-skewers and barbecued meat. They also cooked some meat in their kettles. With this they drank an unbelievable amount of wine which they brought with them. After the feast they threw beef bones at each other as the beginning of the frolics. Finally they sang, danced, wrestled and fenced in front of their leaders."

The introduction of wine making in what was to become Hungary is attributed to the Roman emperor Probus (A.D. 276–282), who thought very much like today's industrial management consultants. He wanted to maintain a large army, but he felt that the soldiers should earn their keep even in peacetime, and he set his legions to planting vineyards in Pannonia. Eventually, the local population took over the cultivation. Today the area is known as Transdanubia. Around Lake Balaton a peculiarly shaped pruning knife is still used; one can see the same shapes in various Roman museums in Italy.

Later, when the feared Huns, under the leadership of Attila, set up their headquarters in Hungary, according to some historians Attila's personal camp was in the Tokaj district,* right at the foot of the vineyards. In time of battle, the bags which usually held wine were inflated and used as pontoons by means of which Attila's soldiers crossed the river and thus took the enemy by surprise.

When the Magyar tribes arrived in the ninth century, the chroniclers report that they came in the month of September when the grapes were ready to be harvested. The Magyars were already familiar with viniculture; they had learned it in the Khazar Kingdom, and were able to take over the cultivation.

The ancient method of cooking in the open remains with the shepherds and cowherds to this very day. The ancient Magyars cooked their meat in a heavy kettle, sat around it and dipped into the *gulyás* with their wooden spoons. A table was not to be found in the villages and hamlets until the tenth century. The kettle or cooking vessel was placed on the floor (which was always pounded earth) and everyone sat on little stools around it eating with wooden spoons. This took place in wintertime in the kitchen and in the summertime in the yard. For the chieftains to eat in a dining room was a "new-fangled fashion." Tents remained their abode except in the winter months, when they moved into small wooden houses.

Then King Stephen, in his political wisdom, during his reign (1000–1038) forced the pagan Hungarians into the civilizing mold of Christianity. Monasteries were built whose duty it was to provide travelers with food and lodging. The royal house, in exchange, gave them certain rights and subsidies.

At the same time, certain landowners received a royal grant to sell wine and to lodge guests within the boundaries of their land. This revolutionary measure was actually the beginning of the tavern and inn concept. The first written record of an inn and tavern in operation is in a deed of sale dated 1279, when

* See page 102.

9

a nobleman named Ugrinus sold his land. In the detailed description of the boundaries, one part says, ". . . and leads to the borderline of Peter the Innkeeper, known as The Bald One."

One of the earliest records of the housekeeping of a monastery is the thirteenth-century manuscript from the monastery of Pannonhalma, which tells among other things that they had thirty-six cooks preparing the daily meals. From the daily expenditures we can see that the greatest expense was for sturgeon and other fish; there was no meal without fresh fruit, honey, wine and barley ale.

The monastery had several of the curious contraptions of the times such as an "eating chair" with a hole in the middle for the cooking vessel. There are areas in today's Hungary where the dining table is still called a "table chair" or "eating chair."

The monastery had an indoor and an outdoor kitchen. The indoor kitchen's three-legged iron stoves and the large kettles of the outside kitchen, in which they cooked the peppered soup stews, can be found even now in the villages.

Were this volume's subject the history of Hungary, our chronicle would discuss some thirty kings and queens in the next four centuries, the hard times that followed Stephen's reign, internal fights to gain control of the crown, royal offspring teaming up with different neighboring countries and so on. Fortunately, our interest is the gastronomic history of Hungary, so we can look at the pleasanter sides of this epoch. The Hungarian nation, always interested in food, learned and benefited from events even in these dark times. They learned a variety of Mongolian dishes including cooking mutton in its own juice (*berbécstokány*).*

The low point of this era came in 1241, when the Mongolian invasion almost totally devastated the country. After this disastrous Tartar invasion, King Béla IV imported French winegrowers who brought with them a great variety of grapes; one of these was called *froment* (wheat), probably because of the pale yellow color of the grape. This term slowly changed into *furmint*, or *furmintos*, which is the name of a still popular wine in Hungary.

Historians have found some references to chefs as early as the tenth century, but the first notable document was the recent discovery of the crest of Ferenc Eresztvényi, the court chef of King Sigismund, who was awarded a patent of nobility in 1414 by his royal employer. He was born in a village called "Noble Chef" (*Nemesszakácsi*), which supplied all royal cooks for more than two centuries. The coat of arms features a boar's head, a sturgeon on fire and a chef's hat. (I would not be surprised if it was given to the good chef instead of a raise.) Sigismund also granted privileges to the recently arrived gypsies

* See recipe on page 272.

Crest of Chef Ferenc Eresztvényi

whose music eventually became so much a part of the Hungarian dining experience.

In the Middle Ages all walks of life were controlled, prescribed and regulated. Merchants and craftsmen received permits to make and sell certain items on certain days and places. Fortunately, the statute book of Buda survived and we have a fairly complete list of licensed items sold there, which includes most of the standard milk, meat, vegetable and fruit items of today and the less customary bear meat, fox loins, wild cherries, geranium mint and green almonds.

Servants on the vast royal lands had to perform special duties such as fishing, milling or baking, and this practice helped to develop the craftsman class. Even within the same craft, three or more skills received special licenses. For instance, at the marketplace you could buy three kinds of bread, each one sold by bakers of three different ranks. The master baker baked the white bread and rolls. The "middle" baker baked the everyday bread, and the black-bread baker the cheapest, unrefined loaves. The first two types of baker could sell their products on a table or bench; the last had only the right to sell it from the ground. Anyone who didn't bake good bread was punished—the first time with a fine and the second time by a dunking in the Danube.

In the butchers' guild, several members were appointed to make sure there was enough meat in the city and to run a complete self-inspection system. Pastry making was the exclusive privilege of the pharmacists, as was the making of spiced drinks and perfumes. Trading with foreign countries began by importing spices and exporting wine and cattle on the hoof.

Rigid division is a dominant social characteristic of these times: separation between classes; between agriculture and small-craft industry; between villages and towns; between the land of the king, the church, the nobility; between the lives of the landed gentry, the patricians of commerce and craft, the landed peasants and the serfs.

Outside of waging war and playing the game of politics, as far as we can discover, the nobility occupied themselves with greyhound breeding and falconry. Like their foreign counterparts, they were more interested in the quantity of the food and wine than its quality.

A galvanic personality combined with consummate powers and noble taste will change not only the fate of his country but the taste of his countrymen as well. During Matthias I's thirty-two year regime (1458–1490) the standard of the Hungarian cuisine suddenly soared to a level rarely equaled since. It is interesting that his era coincides with a period in which Hungary was the largest, richest, most powerful in its history.

2. *The First Five Hundred Years*

The fifteen-year-old Matthias, on becoming king, personified the Greek ideal of an aristocracy of the mind and the full enjoyment of life. But this gifted and privileged youth also had something even rarer—a sense of social justice. His inquiring mind was interested in everything from astrology to printing; music was an important part of life at the court, and his illuminators created more than five hundred magnificent volumes (the *Corvina*), many of them still the ornament and pride of various national libraries today. Happily for us he had a great affinity for the pleasures of the table as well and took an active interest in the running of the royal kitchens. His favorite country was Italy, the birthplace of the Renaissance. Thus it was entirely natural that he should bring back a queen from there, the fair Beatrice, daughter of Ferrante d' Aragonia, King of Naples.

We are fortunate that the Hungarian Renaissance king had such Boswellian scribes as Marzio Galeotto and Antonio Bonfini. They recorded the remarkable and elaborate hierarchy of Matthias' kitchen and service staff. Some of the descriptions of food served have also come down to us from György Veres, who was the royal chef from 1462 onward.

The marriage of Matthias and Princess Beatrice in 1475 enriched the Hungarian cuisine with the highly civilized refinements of the Italian chefs and pastry makers she brought with her from her own country. Judging by the recipes of Matthias' court kitchen from the 1480's, she most likely owned the first printed cookbook: *De Honesta Voluptate,* published *ca.* 1474, written by Bartolommeo de' Sacchi. Not only were the various kinds of *pasta asciutta,* cheeses, pastries, ice creams, chestnut, anise, dill, caper, and other delicacies imported, but the great chefs of the Aldobrandini family in Frascati as well. Lancelotti, who was the chef and chronicler of Ippolito Aldobrandini, in a book published in 1610 mentions that Catherine de' Medici brought cooks from the Frascati castle's kitchen. Henry II's court received the same vital Italian influence King Matthias acquired about three generations earlier. In turn, the Neapolitan court apparently accepted some Hungarian dishes. Giuliano Passero in his *Giornali* gives us the account of a going-away banquet in honor of Bona Sforza, who was to marry Sigismund I, King of Poland, in 1517. The first course included "wild game, boiled and served with Hungarian soup." The high style of Italian dining, which Beatrice introduced, included *commedia dell' arte* entertainment during and after the meal, fine majolica ware on which the food was served, knives and forks from Modena and choirs to provide music during dinner.

"Food happenings" already existed in the fifteenth century. They were called *sotelties** (subtleties), although the fanciful adornments were rarely subtle. For example, one of the highlights of the wedding feast was a pâté

* Archaic English.

13

The wedding feast of King Matthias. Drawing by István Engel-Teván

course which was brought in an enormous litter, carried by six people; suddenly a gypsy lad, dressed in a red costume, jumped out of it and serenaded the newlyweds with his viol. (Gypsy music was already an essential part of the dinner—hopefully not as inseparable as in the restaurants of Hungary at the present time.)

For the wedding feast of Beatrice and Matthias, several fountains, each made of 300 pounds of silver, flowed with special wine punches, and 980 golden dishes were used to serve the wedding guests. The guests sat at large square tables and began with stewed meats of all kinds, flavored with ginger, nutmeg, pepper and other spices. Then came roast game, such as pheasant and peacock, all kinds of roast fishes, pâtés; elaborate desserts and fruit completed the meal. Young noblemen were assigned duties in connection with the dinner, carving and serving—even tasting.

Recipes for four dishes served at the court of King Matthias survive in a codex now in the Munich State Library. The carp dish at the feast was prepared as follows: First, the fish was roasted; then gingerbread and white rolls were cooked in wine and pressed through a sieve; then apple and pear added and again the whole thing puréed. Finally the roasted fish was placed in the middle of this purée and served with saffron-honey. Another dish was capon in ginger juice thickened with the dough of a white roll cooked in wine, peppered and properly salted. (The use of bread or rolls for thickening was quite common in other European cuisines as well during the Middle Ages and was a heritage of the ancient Roman cuisine.)

King Matthias' interest in food became more and more intense. According to the notes of his chronicler, whenever he traveled he carried a "veritable army of chefs" and they were often sent ahead to set up kitchens, secure local provisions, etc. For instance, when in 1480 he went to Raguza (today's Dubrovnik), he sent ahead five chefs months before, with quite a treasury, to set up the royal kitchens and to make arrangements for a herd of fattened steer to be brought there from Zagreb.

According to Marzio Galeotto, "the most popular dishes on the royal table were beef, ewe, pork, venison, hare; also duck, quail and starlings." They also had capon and pheasant, which were bred on numerous royal farms. The fact that they quite often served roast stuffed peacock indicates that the great Renaissance king did not intend to lag behind his Italian in-laws in culinary elegance, where gilded, roasted swans were the everyday fare of the aristocratic dinner tables.

Galeotto also tells us about the secrets of the style of cooking in the royal kitchens: "Every food is served in its own juices . . . goose, duck, capon, pheasant and quail, which all are plentiful; furthermore, beef, lamb, kid, pork, wild boar and different fishes always are cooked or marinated in their own juices. *Aut merguntur, aut condiuntur"* (cooked in long or short broth).

How much in the same style is today's Hungarian kitchen, which frowns upon sauces made apart from the dish itself! And, as you see in the recipe for *gulyás* (pages 270–75), it is made even today with "long" or "short" broth.

Onions became known during Matthias' reign, through the active help of his Italian queen. In one of her letters to her sister Eleanora, Beatrice says in breathless style: "Thanks for the onions and garlic sent me from Ferrara. The king could not have been more pleased if they had been pearls." From this time on the onion became the single most important vegetable in Hungary.

King Matthias' favorite fruit was the fig, also brought to Hungary by his Italian wife. The mineral water from Visegrád, famous for its purity, was piped directly into the royal palace. (This lovely little town is completely restored and well worth a visit when you are in Hungary.)

Apparently the king, whose fairy-tale-like deeds live in the folklore of the people, was very fond of cooks and cooking and many times walked into the kitchen to joke with the chefs and even help them in the preparation of some special dish, especially sturgeon.

Otto Herman, the great Hungarian naturalist who lived in the nineteenth century, has left us a description of how sturgeon was caught in the Danube. For hundreds of years the fishhook of wrought iron was about six inches long and, strangely enough, no bait was used at all. The fishermen hung about 150 hooks on very heavy flaxen rope at some distance from each other. Each hook was attached to a piece of cork so it would float. The fish would notice the piece of cork and bite into it; when he realized it was not edible he spat it out and, angry at having been tricked, began to splash the water with his tail. Usually during this tantrum some part of his body—never the mouth—got caught in the hook. So acute was the early Hungarian insight into piscine psychology that no further refinements of the method were needed—they caught all the fish they wanted, with no effort.

According to a contemporary story, at that time the Hungarian rivers and lakes were so filled with fish that there was actually more fish than water. (The characteristic Hungarian talent for hyperbole was already well developed.)

A delicacy of which Queen Beatrice was reputed to be very fond was plover eggs. Even wholesale slaughter has not succeeded in making extinct these magnificent little birds whose eggs are among the finest delicacies in the world of gastronomy. In the fifteenth- and sixteenth-century markets, in the proper season, there were often more plover eggs than chicken eggs. Even in today's Hungary, this delicacy is still fairly common.

According to accounts of the time, King Matthias requested Lodovico Sforza, the Duke of Milan, to send him a variety of domestic fowl and someone who could take care of them. These birds acclimatized themselves to such an extent that the fame of Hungarian geese, ducks, hens, and other birds slowly spread all over Europe. Today they are considered the choicest on the continent, and no English Christmas is complete without turkeys imported from Hungary.

The end of the fifteenth century was the close of the only truly independent period of Hungarian nationhood in its eleven centuries of existence. This is when cooking became an exact craft and eating turned into—at least on occasion—formalized dining. Artists and artisans produced the finest table accouterments to please all the senses. Chefs were appreciated, honored and elevated to the level of the landed gentry. The intelligentsia considered gastronomy an exciting and worthwhile hobby. The interaction of these elements created the kind of atmosphere conductive to the development of a cuisine with a unique national flavor.

Faïence platters made for the coronation of King Matthias and Queen Beatrice.
Victoria and Albert Museum, London.

THREE WORLDS, THREE CUISINES (THE SIXTEENTH AND SEVENTEENTH CENTURIES)

FOLLOWING King Matthias' death the country suffered a rapid decline, first because of inner dissension, and then because the Turks attacked the divided nation and, in 1526, at Mohács, defeated the Hungarian army, killing even the king, Louis II, on the battleground. Sixteenth- and seventeenth-century Hungary was a nation in turmoil. The country split into three sections: Transylvania became an independent principality; the western and northern parts were ruled by Ferdinand of Habsburg; the central region—the most fertile land—was under Turkish occupation. This division, however, enriched the Hungarian cuisine with new flavors and foreign cooking methods.

Some of the strange imports, particularly the Turkish, were absorbed and transformed by the strength of the Hungarian character and became part of the kitchen of the common folk. On the estates of the nobility, the quality of the cooking reached new heights enhanced by the work of the imported French chefs. The new style consolidated the ancient Asiatic heritage, King Matthias I's introduction of the Italian Renaissance, and the mellowing effect of the French kitchen; and this amalgam should be considered the foundation of the modern Hungarian cuisine.

One of the reasons the cooking was so highly developed in the medieval Hungarian nobility's household was that the chef was the supreme commander. (Today, in the White House in Washington, by contrast, the executive chef has to take orders from Civil Service ignoramuses.) The chefs had all the staff help they needed to create a perfect meal in all respects: wood carvers

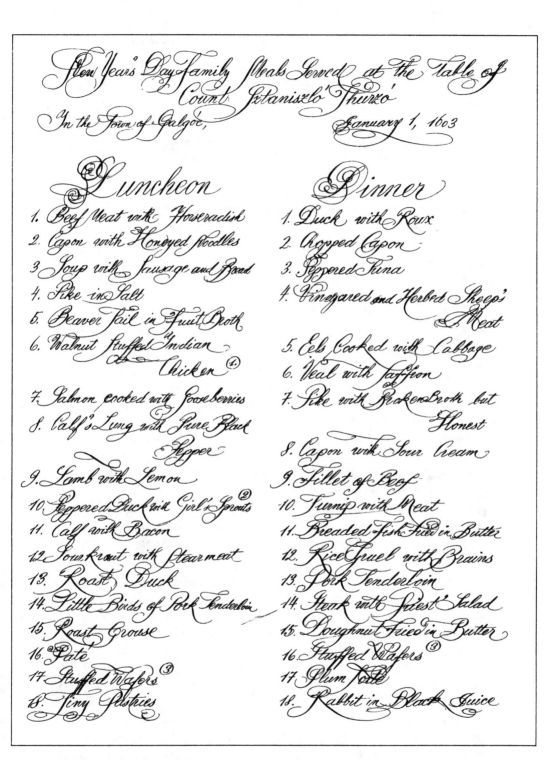

New Year's Day Family Meals Served at the Table of
Count Sztaniszló Thurzó
In the Town of Galgoc,   January 1, 1603

Luncheon

1. Beef Meat with Horseradish
2. Capon with Honeyed Noodles
3. Soup with Sausage and Bread
4. Pike in Salt
5. Beaver Tail in Fruit Broth
6. Walnut Stuffed Indian Chicken [1]
7. Salmon cooked with Gooseberries
8. Calf's Lung with Pure Black Pepper
9. Lamb with Lemon
10. Peppered Duck with Girl's Sprouts [2]
11. Calf with Bacon
12. Sourkraut with Steam meat
13. Roast Duck
14. Little Birds of Pork Tenderloin
15. Roast Grouse
16. Pate
17. Stuffed Wafers [3]
18. Tiny Pastries

Dinner

1. Duck with Roux
2. Chopped Capon
3. Peppered Tuna
4. Vinegared and Herbed Sheep's Meat
5. Eels Cooked with Cabbage
6. Veal with Saffron
7. Pike with Broken Broth but Honest
8. Capon with Sour Cream
9. Fillet of Beef
10. Turnip with Meat
11. Breaded Fish Fried in Butter
12. Rice Gruel with Brains
13. Pork Tenderloin
14. Steak with Priest' Salad
15. Doughnut Fried in Butter
16. Stuffed Wafers [3]
17. Plum Torte
18. Rabbit in Black Juice

New Year's Day family meals. Calligraphy by the author.

to make the forms for the fantastic birds and elephants used for decoration, illuminators who gilded and decorated some of the showpieces and could paint the crest of the mistress of the house on the peacock pâtés and other preparations. Impressively enough, a sixteenth-century Transylvanian head chef writes: "You need these specialists. Even though the cook may know how to do the carving or painting, it's unlikely that he would have the time to do it. . . ."

After the chef in rank came the *tálnok,* whose job was both to organize the service and to make sure that the platters were properly garnished. In some houses there was also a head spicemaker, a very oriental touch! Twelve-year-old boys started as *kukta* (called *commis* in France) and it took a minimum of twelve years and usually longer before they could become masters. The household was run by the lady of the house, whose total involvement would astonish and dismay the modern housewife.

The dining room was called curiously a "dining-castle" (*ebédlő-palota*) and had few pieces of furniture compared with its Western counterpart. Usually it had a balcony for the musicians who played during dinner. Table setting was quite simple. The *pohárnok* (a kind of steward) entered the central section of the dining room and set two places with a cloth, two plates and a loaf of bread covered with a cloth. Next to the plate he placed a spoon and this was just about the extent of the table arrangements for the lord and mistress of the house. The retinue and the guests brought their own spoons and knives. The nobility's plates were made of silver or gilded silver, often depicting mythological or hunting scenes. (The middle class used pewter plates and the rest of the people ate on pottery.)

Water pitchers were brought around and everyone rinsed his hands, then took his place. Bread was passed after they sat down. The women sat on one side of the room and the men on the other side. Either the chaplain or an old retainer got up and said grace; then the servants began with the procession of food. Wine service started with the second dish, but from there on it didn't stop.

A description we have by Count Simon Forgách, toward the end of the seventeenth century, tells that dinner was served in twelve different rooms of his palace, dividing the household into twelve separate groups. The first was the count's family, and the second consisted of the managers of the estate. The third, the maître d'hôtel and butlers; the fourth, the musicians, trumpet players and book illuminators; the fifth, the steward ("keeper of the keys"), bakers and cooks; the sixth, the hunters; the seventh, specially skilled craftsmen; the eighth, the sutlers and couriers; the ninth, the dog catcher and horse trainers, including the German blacksmith; the tenth, grooms and a Hungarian blacksmith; the eleventh, coachmen; and the twelfth, all other servants.

Looking at Hungarian history with its unequal feudal caste system, one can not help feeling that the serfs and laborers should have had no stomach at all, the "free citizens" (guildsmen, shopkeepers, etc.) needed a stomach only on holidays, and the nobility needed several stomachs for constant use. For instance, according to sixteenth-century records, for an Easter dinner a serf would have a sheep cooked in spiced water with groats. A silversmith had "blessed" calf's meat, kohlrabi with pork bone, young goose, game and a noodle dessert made with milk and sour cream.

According to the same source, the following was served at the lord's table: roast; soup with bread; game sausage; tenderloin of venison and salad; two capons sprinkled with raisins; two calves' heads; sheep fillets cooked with rice in almond milk; roast game; veal cooked with pepper; young cabbage with liver sausage; small meat tarts; cabbage with pork cutlets; hare in black sauce; whole tongue in fruit purée; capon in "harvesters' juice"; whole fish baked in salt; olives; blood sausage; ox meat; peacock with gray sauce; ham; boiled pig's head; fruit, including pomegranates;* chestnuts and sweets.

As for official banquets, the ordinance of the Free Cities separated the citizens into three categories: officials, noblemen and patricians; members of the Council of the Hundred; and, finally, all other citizens. The first group could be served ten courses at a wedding, the second one eight, the third one six; however, the last group could not serve pâté or torte. Every plate above the allowed number drew a two-*forint* fine. The dessert plates, even in the first category, couldn't contain anything but candied almonds, raisins, honey cakes, fruit; the second, only fruit and honey cake and on certain occasions "carnival" doughnuts. For the third group there were also strongly worded prohibitions —such as no coffee after the meal. At a baptism the first group could drink coffee, the other two, nothing.

The law not only prescribed the number of guests and serving personnel, but even the number of musicians. The first group could have a complete orchestra, the second up to six players, the third no more than three and only up to midnight.

In the aristocratic dining rooms soups were rarely served, and if they were, they were never thickened. Actually they did have soups, but they were served together with the meat or poultry, and the broth had a secondary, almost sauce-like function. In the commoner's kitchen meat was used as a main course and the dish was split into two courses by serving the bread-thickened broth first.

Sometimes the very same name meant two totally different foods among the two classes. In the higher-class kitchen "black soup" was made with lung,

* Imported from Italy.

21

liver and kidney, and thickened with blood, but in the lower-class kitchen it was a thinner soup made with blood and vinegar and served on toasted bread.

Hungary is a bread-eating nation and already at this age there was no meal imaginable without bread served throughout. According to an English traveler, Robert Townson*: "Lighter, whiter and better flavored bread than made here I never had nor did I ever see elsewhere such large loaves. Were I not afraid of being accused of taking advantage of the privilege of travelers, I should say they were near half a cubic yard." Then he describes a hop yeast which keeps active for as long as half a year. He was hoping that aboard ships or for armies in the field, this might be useful information.

An architect friend of mine once pointed out to me that in Italy certain building techniques were forgotten for as long as three centuries, then rediscovered. The salad course, which is only now beginning to gain popularity in Hungary, with some rare exceptions, was virtually unknown in the past two centuries. But in the sixteenth and seventeenth centuries they were fond of seasonal salads, particularly endives, lettuce, fresh raw cucumbers and chicory. Usually it was served with flax oil and wine vinegar. Another forgotten food is snail, although Gyula Illyés in a recent book† presents a vignette of how he was ridiculed by the village folk as "that person who eats snails." In past centuries it was a common food of the people, cooked either with cabbage or eaten with oil and vinegar.

Previous to the sixteenth century, desserts were no more than one tenth of the daily fare. (In the last 175 years it has changed to about one third.) Those appearing in fragments written around the end of the sixteenth century are various sweet porridges, pancakes, honey breads, strudels, doughnuts and fritters made by dipping flowers, plants and vegetables in batter.

A certain Chef Antal apparently roasted an entire ox which was stuffed as follows: a sheep inside the ox, a newborn calf inside the sheep, a capon inside the calf, and pigeon inside the capon. And only when the pigeon was as tender as butter was the ox ready to serve.

Lajos Zilahy, in his historical novel *The Dukays,* describes an ox-roasting feast based on a sixteenth-century manuscript by an unknown chef. A wedding of the lord master of the estate was one of the few occasions the village folk "ate with a big spoon, and with a big knife." As the stage is set, the hero of the "great barbecue" is introduced, the expert in the forgotten art of ox roasting.

> . . . and Master Kigyó appeared, a short little wrinkled-faced man, so small that one wondered how he managed to contain so much knowl-

---

* Townson, Robert, *Travels in Hungary* (London, 1797).
† Illyés, Gyula, *Kháron ladikján* [*On Charon's Barge*] (Budapest: Szépirodalmi, 1969).

edge. Brandishing his cherrywood stick, he issued hoarse commands from beneath his gray walrus mustache. He supervised every step in person, tested everything. He took the knives in hand, the platters, the spits, the crosspoles, and the pokers, even tasting the cakes of lard and the salt. He dismissed each item to its task with a cry of "Good enough—let 'er go!" First he skinned the ox, after explaining that the head and the hoofs must be left in place. He slit the throat to make room for the spit, which was as thick as a telegraph pole and would come out at the tail after passing under the backbone. He cut a hole into the stomach of the ox, just large enough to receive a calf, which would replace the tripe, the stomach, and the lungs. But the kidneys were left inside. When all this was done they produced a quail larded with bacon. Master Kigyó took it in his hand and looked it over.

"Did you salt it on the inside too, Julie?"

"Salt it, love—of course I did! Don't ask so many questions!"

"Good enough—let 'er go!" and Master Kigyó handed the quail to one of the assistant butchers.

They placed the quail inside a plucked capon. Good enough—let 'er go! They put the capon in the stomach of a lamb, and the lamb was nestled inside the calf. Good enough—let 'er go! Now the calf was crammed into the stomach of the ox. The poor ox had never imagined it would sometime be so pregnant.

They drove the tremendous spit through the flayed beast. And now came the most difficult part. Kontyos, the estate blacksmith, came forward with five-foot-long iron spikes under his arm. They drove these through the backbone of the ox so that they penetrated the spit and came out of the belly. It was hard work that took expert skill. It was even harder to nail the legs of the ox to its shoulder blades so it would seem to be in a reclining position—for the ox would have to be served, in its entirety, from the center of the table. Finally it was secured. Twenty strong men were needed to lift the spitted ox onto the crosspoles. There a mechanism similar to that of a grindstone would turn the beast. Of course Csengős, the estate cartwright, had fashioned a wheel for the tail end of the spit, which was long enough so that the men turning the spit would be out of range of the blazing heat. They tried the wheel, and found it worked splendidly. Good enough—let 'er go! The two-thousand-pound ox began to turn.

"All right! Light the fire! Let's move! No loitering!" But Master Kigyó did not use the ai or i sounds. What he said was, "oll rot! Lot the far!" But first the wood had to be stacked, and that took considerable finesse. The logs were placed on both sides of the crosspoles, none of them longer than the ox itself, and far enough from the meat so that it would be enveloped in heat but not touched by the flame. If only there be no wind! For if a breeze should strike up the whole arrangement would have to be moved to face it, and the whole business started from the beginning again. The horns and hoofs of the ox were wrapped in wet rags, lest they catch fire in the course of roasting. Just let the horn take fire, and then watch everyone run from the smell!

The women were melting the lard and boiling the salt in a large kettle. This mixture would be poured over the roasting ox. They were already tieing saucepans to the ends of broom handles.

"Good enough! Let 'er go!"

They lit the bonfire. The sparks began to crackle, the dry oak logs popped angrily, and the smoke whirled skyward just as it had done once upon a time in Asia, in the ancestral home. Slowly the ox began to revolve to the tune of *Ladi-ladi-lom*,* for the arms of the turners unwittingly took on the rhythm of the music.

"Tha ox" had been revolving over a tremendous heat for nearly four hours. Now it slowly came to a standstill. János Kigyó doffed his hat and clicked his heels together before Count Dupi. "Beg to report to His Excellency the Count—tha ox us done!"

They put the fire out on both sides, and removed the kettles as well to make room for the carvers. From the horns and hoofs they removed the steaming wet rags that had been periodically dampened during the roasting. Master Lusztig, the estate painter, stood with his brush and cup in hand, ready to spread gold paint on the hoofs and horns. When this was done, Master Kigyó personally tied the Dukay† seal, with its eleven-pointed coronet, between the two horns. "Good enough—let 'er go!"

Five wagon shafts were poked under the ox, and ten strong-fisted men lifted the enormous roast from the crosspoles. They put it on a wide table that Master Berecki, the estate carpenter, had made for this very purpose. The ox lay quietly on the table, its legs drawn under, like any ox when it settled down to rest, with the difference that this one had settled down to roast. And how it had been roasted! Its crackling exterior was iridescent with the most beautiful hues of rose-red and deep brown, for it had been continuously drenched with fat while it was cooking. There lay a ton of ox, with the Dukay seal on its forehead between the tremendous forked, golden horns, in Renaissance splendor.

"Bring the knives!" commanded Master Kigyó. And the women

* Popular song.
† The landlord of this estate.

brought their clothesbaskets full of kitchen knives. Now came the final embellishment: hundreds upon hundreds of knives were driven into the ox. The multitude of black knife-handles made the ox look like a quilled beast of prehistory. János Kigyó offered Count Dupi a long knife, and when he saw the Count eye the ox indecisively, he whispered into his ear: "From tha brosket, your Lordship, from tha brosket. Thot's the best!" *

Just as rare as the ox-roasting description are Hungarian cookbooks from the beginning of the sixteenth century. That's why the mysterious manuscript in the Széchényi Library of Budapest is so precious to us since it throws considerable light on Transylvanian court cooking at the beginning of the sixteenth century. The front page is missing, leaving us to speculate about the author's name, the title and the year it was written. The first half deals with Hungarian cooking methods, and the second with dietetic instructions. It contains almost seven hundred recipes.

Paprika, of course, is not mentioned, since the Turks brought it in just about that time and it had not yet become a part of the nobility's cookery. Many things were fried in oil and butter (in addition, later, to lard, which is used almost exclusively now).

No soups are included; the reason was that a huge number of the main courses were cooked and served in *hosszú-lé* (literally, long juice), a soupy liquid, as we saw some pages ago. Combined cooking methods—which is very Chinese—were quite prevalent, i.e., they often boiled the meat first after which it was roasted, or the other way around.

Cooking with wine was even more common than in France today, and the use of sour cream and vinegar was as frequent as in today's Hungary. The fact that onions were not used nearly as much as in today's cooking again may be for the same reason as the absence of stuffed cabbage and *gulyás*—they may have been a part of peasant cookery only, and thus not recorded.

An early practical joke is mentioned in the manuscript: singeing live crabs over a brandy flame in such a way that the crab was alive, but its shell grew red as though it were completely cooked. Although the author doesn't report what happened when these were served, it is not difficult to imagine the discomfiture of the guests when they tried to bite into the crabs, and the crabs bit back!

Another illuminating early Hungarian cookbook is *The Book of Mihály Szent-Benedeki*, August 10, 1601. A sample of the descriptive recipes from

* Zilahy, Lajos, *The Dukays* (New York, 1949), pages 181–84.

these two books may make you want to jump into a time machine and go back to the sixteenth and seventeenth centuries.

Capon Baked in Paper

"Cover capon with paper and sew edges," the recipe mentions; "while baking it, keep it far away from the fire so as not to burn the paper." (This probably came from the Italian kitchen, which invented the technique, at least in Europe. There is a strong possibility that it originally came from China, via Marco Polo, since the Chinese had used this technique for at least 2,000 years.)

Capon with Juniper Sauce

"Crush juniper berries in butter. Stuff and roast the capon. Gather the juice of the bird, add wine, black pepper and cinnamon, simmer it and pour sauce over the sliced roast capon."

Zoklé*

"Roast a duck, and after cutting it in pieces, cook in beef broth with onion and parsnip. Add to cooking broth saffron, black pepper, smashed garlic and ginger, thicken with egg yolks mixed with the blood of the duck."

Veal in Pastry

"Chop the veal finely, as if for sausage, and cook it with gooseberries, nutmeg and a little salt. Make a very flaky dough with butter, white flour, egg and water. Let it rest; then fold more butter into it. Make egg-shaped small tartlets, fill them with the above mixture, and cover the top with a small piece of dough. Bake the tartlets and when finished, just before serving, make a tiny incision on top of each and pour in an infusion of strong broth and honey." (Very much like *vol-au-vent*!)

Venison

"Stuff hind quarter with a mixture of bacon, beef and pork meat and spit-roast it. Put it atop a platform carrier decorated with little trees, miniature pastes, beignets, grapes, figs and colored papers. Serve as a fancy show dish."

Stuffed Sheep's Stomach

"Make stuffing with pork meat, pork blood and grapes, and braise until cooked. Prepare sauce with grated horseradish and bacon."

* The meaning of this word is lost although *lé* means sauce.

Rose Doughnut

"Make a batter of egg, flour and as much whey as necessary for right consistency. Take a fully developed white or red rose with some of the stem; wash it, and put it into a clean bowl to drain. (Make sure that there are no bugs inside flower.) Dip it into the light batter, and stand it up in plenty of hot butter to fry. Shake it every now and then to make sure its petals will stand apart as they did on the rosebush. If you add some rosewater to the batter, so much the better. Flavor with cane honey." (Was this a poetic variation of the zucchini-flower fritter they must have learned from the Italians some generations ago?)

Being a bibliophile of a sort, it always pleased me that one of the greatest Hungarian printers, Miklós Kiss de Misztótfalu (1650–1702), edited and published, at his own expense, the first Hungarian-language printed cookbook in 1695. Since the other two major works of his were the Bible and a dictionary, we can readily see that the "Hungarian Elzevir" was a man of impeccable taste. In his very-much-to-the-point introduction he offered his book to "the honest kitchens . . . without a cook," and not to the kitchens of the aristocracy "where the chefs have the knowledge to cook dishes with great taste."

Admittedly I chose one of the more puzzling and unusual dishes, although many of the stews, soups, cabbages and desserts are similar to today's recipes.

Crab Cheese

"Cook crab until half done. Remove meat and mash it in a mortar. Pour milk onto it, add two raw eggs. Mix it well and drain excess liquid, if any. Boil or steam this mixture. When cooked, take out with slotted spoon and drain it well. Mix it with a little honey and cinnamon, and chopped fresh grapes. Tie it in a clean cloth and let it drip, as when you make cream cheese. When concentrated, take it out of cloth, cut it into finger-size pieces and grill it with a little oil. Serve it with a sauce made of white wine, honey, saffron, ginger, pepper, chopped grapes."

It's difficult to imagine that less than three centuries ago, two of the now important and common ingredients of the Hungarian kitchen, tomato and paprika, were not yet known and mentioned.

Recipes such as this were the pride of the nobleman whose chef developed it and later, with the help of the master, printed it. Cooking became a favorite pastime for the nobility. An inventory of Count Miklós Bercsényi's castle in the city of Ungvár showed nine cookbooks, two of which were in manuscript.

How keenly interested the Hungarian nobility was in the quality of the

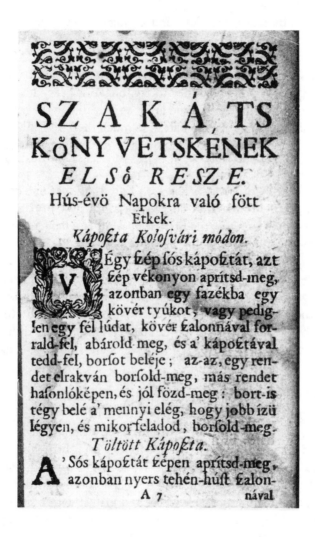

Recipe for layered cabbage, from the first printed Hungarian cookbook,
1695 (see page 27)

food is indicated in a letter which Paul Esterházy wrote to his wife October 6, 1684. He was at the military camp outside Buda, and even amidst the bustling preoccupations of the siege, he took time to write about hiring a new chef who "will be able to do all sorts of broths and displays."

But the work that gives us a panoramic view of the life and times of the seventeenth century is *Metamorphosis Transylvaniae*, a thorough study covering all areas of life from social customs to the art of cursing, from 1687 to 1736. The author, Baron Péter Apor of Al-Torja, in one chapter describes hospitality at the end of the seventeenth century. The day started with an aqua vitae flavored with cinnamon. As another breakfast apéritif, they poured brandy into a huge bowl, adding honey, figs and raisins, flaming it, and then drinking it while hot. The fruit was eaten as a delicacy afterward. For luncheon at ten and dinner at six, the foods served were not unlike those described in previous chapters, flavored with saffron and other spices, horseradish, dill, tarragon, marjoram and other palate-exciting herbs. (The famous nineteenth-century novelist Mór Jókai, reading a seventeenth-century Hungarian cookbook, said: "It seems to me that our ancestors not only wore steel outside, but lined their stomachs with it as well.") The wine was drunk from huge pails and, if a duke or a prince was present, as long as he drank, everyone had to follow suit. In some cases this must have had a disastrous mass effect. However, this is a kind of forcible emulation which nobody seemed to mind.

Baron Apor mentions an amusing folk tradition, the breakfast following the wedding dinner. Apparently everyone except the young couple had to attend this meal, which was cooked, baked and served by the maid of honor. A special *béles* (a kind of filled cake) was served, and the best man had the "honor" of cutting it up in pieces and serving it to everybody. If he was wise and experienced in these matters, instead of trying to plunge his knife in to cut it into serving pieces, he carefully took out from certain parts of the dessert such things as nails and cut-up clothing which had been baked into it. After this, amidst the laughter of the wedding guests, another day of feasting began.

Whenever the new wine fermented enough to have a "bite," they immediately started drinking it, boasting how fine and sweetly pungent it was. The old wine was drunk only by the coachmen and grooms, but even the table servants resented being given "aged" wine! Well now! Can one say anything but *de gustibus non est disputandum?* In food and wine at least, as we survey the long ruthless sweep of history, there is no such thing as absolute standards of excellence—one age's gourmandise is another's despair.

The Hungarian lawbooks of the sixteenth and seventeenth century show us the careful control of quality and prices of wines, and policing of public morality. A few excerpts:

—Priests are not allowed to enter taverns, unless they are traveling, because of the low language and immoral behavior of the citizens therein.
—Tavern-keepers who lend their place to whoring will be thrown into prison.

—There is no credit for anyone including the barkeeper. The barkeeper must give a "welcome-glass" to respectable citizens, free of charge.
—The barkeeper is forbidden to praise one wine to the detriment of others. [No commercials, please.]

It is clear from all records that Transylvania, which lived in relative peace and prosperity, was able to develop forward-looking economic policies, found important colleges, develop export-import and set up exchange programs with Western European nations. In this part of the country, as well as those under Habsburg rule, in the houses of the aristocracy the French cooking methods harmoniously blended into the ancient Hungarian cooking style. This brought forth a sophisticated cuisine, tempering the overspiced base with the subtle aspects of the French kitchen.

On the other hand, the century-and-a-half Turkish Occupation of the very center of Hungary, including parts of Transdanubia, the Great Plains and the Southern Province, was hardly the ideal condition for the peaceful development of its cuisine. The population was reduced by more than half, and where there had been flourishing villages and towns, only waterless and grassless plains with a few straggling settlements were left. Yet in these areas the ancient lineage of folk customs and cuisine was preserved in astonishing purity because of the isolation of the lowest classes and their poverty.

Some of the foods the Turks introduced into Hungary became part of the national tradition—for instance, the variety of rice pilafs served even with spit-roasted meat, the *pitah* which remained as *lángos* (ancestor of the pizza), the strudel which was brought in originally as *filo,** various honeyed drinks including the *márc,* which today is only served at village festivals.

Someone once remarked that you start from the West with pure red meat, and the farther East you go the more sophisticated and elaborate the stuffing will be; finally, when you get to the Near East there will be almost nothing but the stuffing. Many of the filled, stuffed standbys of today, like stuffed pepper, squash, kohlrabi, tomato, eggplant and grape leaves, come from the Turkish Occupation. Stuffed cabbage, however, was already known to the ancient Hungarians, and both the Italian visitors and the Turkish invaders found it when they arrived in Hungary.

The names of many Hungarian drinking and eating utensils also came from the Turkish. Several of the cooking terms such as "to knead" (*gyúr*) originated in the sixteenth century. *Bogaca* became *pogácsa* in Hungary—a kind of sweet biscuit.† On my recent visit to Turkey I found the origin of the

* The onionskin-thin pastry which is the base, for instance, of baklava.
† For recipe see pages 347–52.

Turkish food merchants in Hungary, sixteenth century

túróscsusza (egg noodles, dill, cottage cheese, sour cream, and bacon crackling, baked together) in the *borekler* or *suboregi.**

Evlia Cselebi, a Turkish traveler and diarist, gives a striking picture of life in Buda during the Turkish Occupation.

. . . people visit each other very often and the host lays a big and full table. Favorite Hungarian foods are the white bread loaf, roast chicken, the chicken *pörkölt,†* the carp *pörkölt‡* and breaded *süllő* (a small *fogas§*). The people have a great choice of beverages, including a wine called Ketkozia which has a topaz yellow color, a crystal clear liquid not to be found even on the island of Tenedos.

* For recipe, see page 369.
† For recipe, see page 276.
‡ For recipe, see page 277.
§ See page 201.

The major change the Turks made in the Hungarian cuisine was the introduction of paprika. Only the common people absorbed this innovation at the time; the nobility was not to use it until several hundred years later.

The Turks brought in many other new plants, for instance, tomato, which became very popular during this time and remained an essential part of the past three centuries of Hungarian cuisine. Cherries and sour cherries were planted for the first time and the large dark red, crisp and juicy fruit is unique in the world. (Perhaps it is worth considering a Turkish Occupation of the United States to change the lamentable quality of this fruit that one buys in the supermarket here.) Even corn of the New World came to Hungary via Turkey and for centuries was to be called "Turkish wheat."

But the most important contribution of all was coffee, which eventually became a major factor in establishing an important social and cultural phenomenon—the coffeehouse. It was there that the Hungarian literary tradition with its revolutionary poets, journalists and playwrights burgeoned and flourished for the next three hundred and sixty years.

HUNGARIAN FARMER'S ALMANAC ANNO 1674

JANUARY

The housewife should be careful not to let her chickens get fat because they won't lay eggs. You can tell that they are fat when they cluck too much. You have to seal the entrance of the beehives before snow falls because the bees get snowblindness. The lakes which have fish must have holes made in them daily after the lake freezes, so the fish won't suffocate.

FEBRUARY

Every fifth day you have to give kiln-dried beans to peacocks to make sure that they will lay eggs speedily enough.

MARCH

Put three goose eggs under the stork and when they hatch take them away from the stork. You can catch crabs with frogs' legs, and fish with your hands if you smear your feet and legs with a mixture of melted game grease and honey.

APRIL

Buy salt for the summer and put the carp into the lake.

MAY

Repair your baking oven with prepared clay.

JUNE

Catch quail in bushes; they don't go to the field until harvest time.

JULY

To bake bread from new wheat, first dry it well in the oven, then grind it and put hot stone into the dough letting it stand overnight.

AUGUST

Make jam from unripe grapes, gooseberries, with cinnamon and cloves and cane honey.

SEPTEMBER

Birdtrapping is fruitful this month. To put them away for the winter, throw away their insides and soak them overnight in cold water. Bake them, put them into a stone jar, add pepper, ginger, spices, honey and vinegar, and cover tightly.

OCTOBER

Now is the time to hunt for wild pigs in the forest.

NOVEMBER

Plant chestnuts and almond seeds.

DECEMBER

Weed out the rotten ones from the winter fruits.

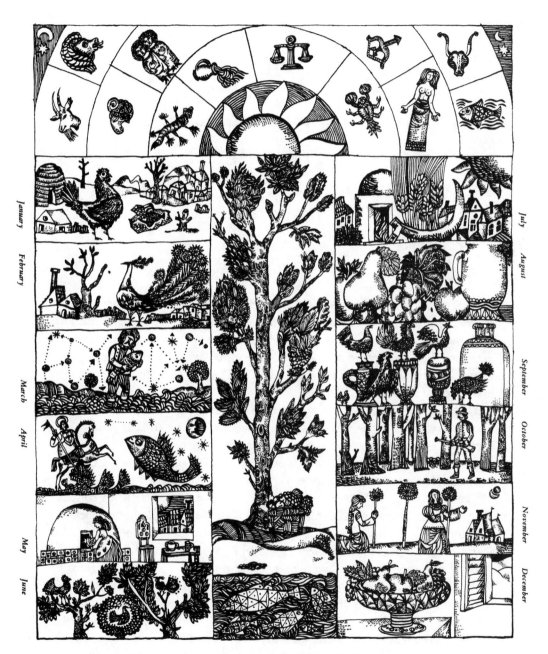

Hungarian Farmer's Almanac, newly interpreted by István Engel-Teván

✵ 4 ✵

FROM THE LIBERATION OF BUDA
TO THE
AUSTRO-HUNGARIAN MONARCHY

THE Turkish Army was defeated in 1686 at the siege of Buda and in the following few years forced to leave the entire country. When the Habsburgs took over from the Turks, extending their northern third of the country, the fact that they subjugated the nation with more finesse and culture did not change the harshness of oppression, which was relieved only by intermittent revolutions.

One of the few that almost succeeded was masterminded by the Transylvanian Ferenc Rákóczi, who was not only perhaps the wealthiest aristocrat of the seventeenth century, but also an important statesman, writer, philosopher and—above all—gourmet, a witty conversationalist, and a connoisseur of the pleasure of women and the dinner table. So it is not surprising that when he was seeking Louis XIV as an ally, as his best possible argument to convince the Sun King, he sent him barrels of Tokay wine with a diplomatic courier.

The ways of diplomacy are mysterious so we should not be too surprised to learn that as an answer Louis did not send the requested French battalions but a barrel of choice Beaujolais wine and one of the great French chefs from his royal kitchen. The revolution was lost but the disciples of Maître Vatel and the subsequent cooks he brought into Rákóczi's kitchens further influenced the Transylvanian cooking style.

The Habsburgs Germanized all walks of life: the schools, the army, the language of the officers, even the expressions and style of cooking—or at least they tried. Only the Hungarian aristocrats' kitchens remained French-oriented by imitating the Viennese court, where cooking was done by the disciples of the great La Varenne. Some of the Austrian rulers actually did it from a deeply felt sense of duty, somewhat like that of missionaries confronted with poor heathen. The books of this era are all in German and many of the dishes are also straight imports from Vienna. All this rolled off the Hungarians like water off the back of a duck—for they withstood Tartar, Turkish, German, Austrian and all other invasions, at least as far as their kitchen is concerned.

During the eighteenth century the Habsburgs used Hungary as a purely agricultural part of their empire, not allowing industry to develop at all. As far as the dining room is concerned, its effects were more good than bad because the ingredients necessary for developing a great cuisine were the main occupation of the entire nation. During this time Hungary became "the food basket of Central Europe."

All vineyards were replanted, and the quantity, quality and variety of the wines were vastly augmented and improved. By 1741, when Prince Festetich, the "King of Keszthely," was host to Empress Maria Theresa, on a wine buffet table he displayed and served three hundred different wines, casually remarking to the Empress, "These are all from the vineyards around Lake Balaton."

Prince Ferenc Rákóczi II did everything in style. In 1705 he served 366 dishes at a feast. Huge barrels were set up high enough for streams of wine to flow through pipes leading to the marketplace, where enormous tubs were filled with the noble liquid. Everyone came with cups, pots, basins, ewers— everything but a sieve—to scoop up the wines.

This was also the age of the emergence of national consciousness, the reform age, when writers, economists, statesmen and poets worked tirelessly to renew the nation and put sparkle into its cultural life. Traveling both inside the country and to foreign lands became very prevalent, and naturally contributed to the establishment of inns and restaurants, and to social life at all levels.

The many forms of Hungarian public eating and drinking developed in the eighteenth century and persist today with small changes and few additions.

Restaurants and pastry shops opened up, where nonalcoholic beverages were served with the pastries. Little boutiques (spelled *butiks*) along the Danube sold ice cream, lemonade, fruit and other refreshments. *Pálinka* (fruit brandy) drinking became popular. In 1720 the first of many dance halls (or ballrooms) opened its doors to be rented for group festivities and outfitted with special rooms for refreshments and à la carte foods.

The country inn, or *fogadó,* for overnight stops, served simple meals. Long before the Guide Michelin, stagecoaches went out of their way to stop at an inn where the innkeeper's wife was fat. This was considered a sure guarantee

Merchants traveling by stagecoach, seventeenth century

of good cooking. "At the Sign of the Innkeeper's Fat Wife" later became a common name, famous in many counties. (Let's remember we are talking about a country where as recently as my own grandfather's time no thin man could hope to be elected mayor of his village, though it is doubtful whether they had ever heard of Shakespeare's warning against a man with "a lean and hungry look.") One of the Pest hotels—if you can call a six-story building with one huge room on each floor a hotel—the Fehér Hajó (White Ship) opened in 1696. A contemporary satirical poem says that staying there for a year is like a one-year sentence. Still, it has operated for over 140 years.

The *fogadó*-style inn is still alive in a few small towns and villages of Hungary today, and it is a good idea to look for these places when you travel. The chances are that the innkeeper's wife is as fat as ever.

In the middle of the eighteenth century Thalia's wandering children found

Inside the village kocsma, *eighteenth century*

homes in several inns of Buda, including Fortuna, the predecessor of the present-day expense-account-type restaurant.

What the pub is for the English, the bar or, in some cases, tavern is for Americans, the *kocsma* used to be and to some extent still is for Hungarians: mostly a drinking place, but some food is always available. Its main attraction was a rough camaraderie, which often ended in fights, breaking up the furnishings and the participants. Patrons discussed the flow of world events and all the subjects which could be aired only in the bracing male atmosphere, seldom disturbed by women. No wonder that some *kocsmas* praised their manly comforts with a rhyme painted over the entrance:

> Here is the world's center
> If you don't believe it
> Just enter.

The *kocsma* was also often the place of traditional seasonal merrymaking. According to an 1847 copy of the magazine *Honderü* (National Amusements), the following ritual was performed for centuries in many villages on Ash Wednesday:

> The peasants make a straw-filled man's figure out of sacking, lay it out on the *kocsma's* table like a corpse, and a local who is known to be excessively fond of wine, dressed in a long white shirt, makes a long mock sermon about mortality—liberally spiced with Rabelaisian jokes and references. The pious listeners reward the "preacher" with wild laughter; then they pick up the figure and take it out to the end of the village. After this they return to the tavern and dig up bottles of wine which they had buried the year before and bury more bottles for the next year. Then the drinking and dancing start, going on until sunup the next morning.

Villagers used many party games as part of their festivities. For instance, jumping over a string while holding a pitcher of wine, trying not to spill a drop, then taking a mouthful, jumping again, drinking again, until the pitcher is empty. Or a kind of blindman's buff, where a man is blindfolded, turned round and round a barrel till dizzy, then set to hit a rooster, tied to a tree twenty paces off. Or improvising rhymes holding a five-foot pewter drinking vessel shaped like a long tube with a gourdlike swelling at the end. The name of the drinking vessel was *Floribusz,* and a folk rhyme took its name from this. After every five lines, the village minstrel had to drink and finish the refrain and the wine while standing. The center of these and many other frolics was in or around the local *kocsma.*

What the inn was for city travelers, the *csárda* was for highwaymen or any hapless traveler out on the lonely roads at night. The first record we have of one is from 1720, near the city of Kecskemét on the Great Plains. The word *csárda* was used for the first time about twenty years later in a dictionary that described it as a "guesthouse on the lowlands." (It originates from the Persian-Turkish *csardak*, meaning a hut or shed with a thatched roof.) Besides travelers, they were frequented by shepherds, cowherds, highwaymen (*betyárok*) and prostitutes. The *betyár* came because the owner usually gave him refuge and helped to hide him from the gendarmes. Deserters, runaway serfs, drovers tired of the lowlands, all found shelter, food and drink at the *csárda*. Small wonder that at least one *csárda* had as its sign a hangman's noose.

Generally a *csárda* had a "souse's" room (*korhelyszoba*) with a taproom called *kármentő* (damage-saver), where the bottles were protected by vertical bars. When the inevitable fights began, the liquor would be protected from damage by bars that could be let down from ceiling to floor. Although today this is not considered as urgent a necessity, the style has survived and is very handsome. In the larger establishments, two or three guest rooms provided overnight accommodation; in the smaller ones everybody shared the same large room. There was also a stable and a carriage house, which occasionally housed those who couldn't get into the main building. Music was provided by a cimbalom atop a barrel. The violinist sat on the *cserépkályha* (tiled stove), and the *dudás* (Hungarian piper) shared the floor with the dancing lads. The contemporary Hungarian restaurant industry has kept the name *csárda*, turning it into a charming place where a limited menu and wines are served. The buildings are appropriately rustic, mainly with thatched roofs, heavy beams and painted peasant motifs on chairs and tables. The many fishermen's *csárdas* (*halászcsárda*) specialize in fish dishes like *halászlé*,* mixed fish grill, breaded carp fillet with a sweet and sour mayonnaise, etc. A most worthwhile resurrection.

Kisvendéglő (little restaurant) was and still is generally a more citified version of the *kocsma*, with greater emphasis on food than on drinks. Mostly it is a family operation, with the wife or mother of the owner as cook. Whether it was called "The Marble Bride," "The Red Frog," "The Dandy Flea," "The Two Pistols," "The Little Pipe" or "The Seven Owls," the guests always could be sure of aromatic *pörkölt* chicken with freshly made *galuska*† (dumplings), carefully rolled strudel stuffed cabbage,‡ good wine in earthenware pitchers, a cimbalom player or a gypsy orchestra, geraniums in the window and the warm personal attention of the host.

In the summer it's a real pleasure to go to a garden restaurant or, as it's

* See recipe on page 203.
† See recipe on page 297.
‡ See recipe on page 388.

Betyárs *meeting at a* hortobágyi csárda

called in Hungary, a *zöldvendéglő*. What is a garden restaurant in Hungary? It's about ten square fathoms (each one is about 38 square feet) of blue sky; half a dozen little trees in green barrels and a couple of dozen tables and chairs; five musicians playing a waltz on a little stand; behind the kitchen window the owner's wife bustling about frying young chickens; a peddler selling oranges among the tables; one of the guests standing up to offer a toast; the enticing smell of the *székelykáposzta** floats upward; and all, everyone, quite content.

The small Hungarian restaurants—like some of their wines—don't travel well. That is the reason one has such mixed and rarely satisfactory experiences in most Hungarian restaurants outside of Hungary, from New York to Tokyo. The qualities that make the *vendéglő* unique are the raw materials, beginning with the water, the flavor of the fresh vegetables, the old-fashioned way of purchasing and cooking, where every detail is important and nearly everything is made right there. These make the *vendéglő* like a loving grandmother in every village, town and city.

Every beginning ends something. Up to this time girls learned cooking from their mothers, and restaurant cooks from masters to whom they apprenticed within the professional field. The first cookbook which broke this pattern was written by István Czifrai,† who was the cook of the Palatinate-Viceroy of Hungary (Nádorispán). A few of the recipes from this 1826 volume may prove to be very interesting and surprising, too.

Beef Meat Covered with Blood

> Cut out the bone from a piece of good beef. Pound the beef well to flatten it and rub with a mixture of salt, cloves, lemon peel, marjoram and pepper. Let it stand overnight. In the morning, remove the excess salt. Cook some diced bacon in a large roasting pan and place the beef on top of it. Cook for 15 minutes. Smother the beef with chicken or pigeon blood and continue to roast while basting with blood. When outside of meat becomes crusty, pour on a mixture of 1 part wine, 1 part vinegar and 2 parts water. Cover with wet paper, and braise for 3 hours. Serve gravy with meat.

Carrots with Kohlrabi

> After you have cleaned both, slice and cut out little moon shapes with cookie cutter. Slowly cook in butter with chopped flat parsley, making sure that it doesn't get brown. When almost finished, sprinkle with a

* See recipe on page 287.
† Or Cziffray.

Zöldvendéglő, or garden restaurant; a turn-of-the-century postcard

little flour, stir and go on simmering it. Finally, add some meat broth and a little piece of sugar, and let it cook till sauce thickens somewhat. Decorate platter with brain-sausage croutons which should be made as follows: After cooking the brain in salted water, put into cold water and peel off thin membranes. Chop fine and sauté in butter, with pepper and bread crumbs, and wet it with a little consommé. Take a biscuit, cut it in two, dip in cold water, and cover each piece with the brain mixture. Dip into egg, bread crumbs and flour, and fry until golden brown.

Stuffed Cabbage

Get some hard, but not too big, cabbages, slice off top and scoop out the middle. Chop a piece of boiled beef, onion and bacon, mix with egg and roll soaked in milk, and the very finely chopped center of the cabbages. Also mix in 2 tablespoonfuls of sour cream and herbs. Fill the cabbage cavities with this stuffing. Put back cabbage top as cover, placing it on top of filled cavity. Tie cabbage with string and cook in salted water. Pour some butter sauce on top of cabbage head when serving it.

Sauerkraut with Pike and Oysters

If the sauerkraut is too sour, wash it a few times in cold water. Put it into a pot and cover it with a liquid made of half hot water and half meat broth. Add a small piece of goose fat, and cook it an hour. In a separate frying pan, make a *roux* with goose fat and flour and add it to the sauerkraut. Add a glass of good wine to the cabbage and cook it a little more. Clean the pike, cut into pieces (but leave the head in one piece) and cook it in a little salted water. Skin it, bone it and cut it into small chunks—except the head. Put a layer of sauerkraut into a baking dish and place the head of the pike in the middle, with the liver in the mouth of the pike. Surround it with the little pieces of pike and top with some shelled oysters. Repeat these layers, making sure that the very top will be sauerkraut, again. Pour over some of the liquid from the cooked sauerkraut, and sprinkle with plenty of bread crumbs, dot with lots of butter. Put dish in oven and bake until top is nice and golden yellow. If you have no oysters, you can substitute crab tails.

White-Cooked Chickens

Take two or three quite large chickens and fill them with a good stuffing, including crawfish, and cover birds with thin sheets of salt

45

pork. Wrap the whole thing in white paper, put a skewer through, and spit-roast in such a way that they won't burn. Cook the gizzard and liver separately, together with parsnip, scallions and about two dozen chanterelle mushrooms. After it is cooked, add some spices, remove the paper and salt pork from the chickens and serve together with stuffing, making sure that the chickens remain so white that they do not even look cooked.

Capon with Snails

Salt a fine big capon and prepare to roast it to a nice brown color, but make sure it is not dry when finished. Make a golden *roux* and brown in it some bread crumbs, anchovies, parsley, lemon peel and a little onion. Pour some broth and a little vinegar on this mixture and cook it, whipping every now and then. Cook snails in wine and add them to above, and serve with roasted capon.

Calf's Leg Larded with Smoked Tongue

Take a medium-size leg, wash and salt. Cut smoked tongue, raw calf's brains and anchovies into strips, make holes in leg with knife and press them into openings. Spread the bottom of a pot with butter and three heads of sliced onions, sprinkle with new spice (paprika!) and the juice of a lemon. Place the leg on it, pour in a little wine and broth, add lemon peel and cover tightly. Cook 2 hours from both bottom and top (in oven) very slowly, and turn several times. Then take out the cooked leg, place it in another baking dish. Add chopped dill mixed with sour cream and the strained liquid from the first pot. Cook a little longer and serve.

Tenderloin of Beef Cooked in Grape Must

Salt a nice fillet of beef and cook in new must (freshly pressed grape juice before fermentation), adding some sugar, a little beef fat, carrots, knob celery (a root vegetable), parsnip, uncrushed pepper, a piece of ham, onion and some consommé. Cook the meat in this until soft, adding more must as needed. When meat is cooked strain the sauce. By this time it is a nice golden color and rather gelatinous.

Egg Sausage

Chop six hard-boiled eggs and mix with a roll soaked in milk, a little salt and chopped parsley. Melt a little butter till frothy, adding the chopped ingredients. Mix in raw eggs, heavy cream, bread crumbs. When thickened a little, make sausage shapes out of the mixture and fry them gently.

46

Plum-Wine Sherbet

Pit the ripe plums, put them in a ceramic pot and cook them in wine. When very soft, squeeze through a sieve and add sugar, lemon peel and clove. Cook again until it becomes gelatinous. Strain again and cool. Then pour into ice cream machine and while making it, keep separating ice cream from side of dish with a silver spoon so as to avoid lumps. The texture should be like good butter and it can only be made with continuous churning.

One of the most interesting chapters deals with sausages. It seems that sausage making became a shadow of its former self in all the famed sausage countries, i.e., Hungary, Czechoslovakia, Poland, Germany and Switzerland. Chef Czifrai's recipes include: capon sausage, brain sausage, pork and ham sausage with basil and tarragon, goose liver sausage with truffles and marjoram, carp or pike sausage, smoked salmon sausage, crayfish sausage cooked in milk, spit-roasted sheep sausage flavored with strong herbs, fish sausage made with pork blood, smoked pork liver sausage, capon, chicken, turkey, and veal sausage spiced with coriander, steamed and then roasted, calf's lung sausage with nutmeg, sturgeon sausage with horseradish, pork skin and ear sausage, and beef tongue sausage, etc.

A taste for simplicity cannot last long. As this frequently reprinted book clearly shows, by the beginning of the nineteenth century the cooking, even in the kitchens of the middle classes, became a rich, aromatic and complex cuisine.

The dining room of the Vigadó between 1830 and 1840

✳ *5* ✳

THE NEW ERA

IT wouldn't be too farfetched to say that Hungary specializes in winning international culinary battles and losing revolutions.

The 1848–1849 revolution ended in disaster; yet it brought major changes in the life of the people. It threw off many of the feudal chains which had paralyzed development in most fields, and speedily created new industries using the extraordinary talents of Hungarian craftsmen. Settlers from foreign lands were brought in to develop agriculture and fill the empty areas. The farmers experimented with new plants and cultivating techniques, and from the time of the reign of Empress Maria Theresa, potatoes became a staple of the people's diet.

As far as the world market and export were concerned, the problem up to the eighteenth century was that scientific methods of cultivation, harvesting, preserving, bottling, etc., were totally unknown in Hungary. Not the first, but one of the most fervent propagators of scientific viniculture was Count István Széchenyi, the man who was called the greatest Hungarian of his time even by his most serious critics. In the mid-nineteenth century, he tried to bring Hungary into the modern world singlehandedly. By building the famed chain bridge* (the first of its kind) on the Danube, he forced the nobility to pay a tax—for the first time in Hungary—each time they crossed. He founded the Hungarian Academy of Sciences, organized steamship lines on the Danube for international shipping, formed Western European-style banks and credit systems; and he founded vine-plant nurseries and training institutes and also established the wine department at the Hungarian Academy of Agriculture.

These vital steps could not have been taken before the rise of Prussia, which significantly weakened the Habsburg Empire. As a result, Franz Joseph I had

* Lánchid.

to re-establish relations with Hungary on a new foundation. The 1867 *Ausgleich,* or compromise, was the formation of the Austro-Hungarian dual monarchy in which the Hungarians became almost equal partners. With this new relative independence, important Hungarian dynasties rose up—in the restaurant and hotel industry.

Luxurious hotels such as István Főherceg (Archduke Stephen) opened a new era in Budapest, and according to foreign visitors compared favorably with the finest hotels in Vienna, Munich and Paris. The restaurateur was János Gundel, father of the great Károly Gundel. Its menu included oysters from the Adriatic Sea, hazelhen served with apple mousse, crab from Ljubljana, salmon from the Rhine, sturgeon from the Danube, as well as native Hungarian specialties.

The Angol Királynő (The Queen of England) innovated a "ladies' dining room" in 1854, probably the first one in Europe's grand hotels. Franz Liszt stayed there in 1847, and the famed gypsy of the era, Józsi Farkas, stole under his window to serenade the great man. Liszt came out, embraced the *primás** and the champagne flowed freely. Johann Strauss the elder played there during one ball season, just as his son did a quarter century later in the Savoy of London for M. Ritz.

The restaurateurs tried to design and build the ultimate in each category. The Café New York was the biggest and most sparkling coffeehouse, decorated with important frescoes and with the appearance of a castle in never-never land. The New Gundel Restaurant, which opened in 1910 in the Zoological Gardens, was ballroom size and as elegant as any in London or Paris. And the Gerbeaud pâtisserie was the Taj Mahal of them all, its high-ceilinged, gold, marble and stucco complex of giant rooms suggesting the cozy splendor of a museum or a church.

Other major cities like Szeged, Debrecen, Sopron, Győr also established comparatively large-scale dining facilities. These developments available to the moneyed class and foreign visitors made the differences between the urban and rural picture even greater. Actually what really happened was that the fabulous level of hospitality in private estates was transferred to the fine hotels and restaurants of the major cities.

In the countryside, the roadside inns got a big boost from the scheduled stops of stagecoaches, which connected the different sections and towns. A 1793 advertisement describes the "conditions of travel." As long as you left your Fido home and agreed to "smoke a first-rate tobacco in your pipe," you could spend half an hour for breakfast (two cups of coffee and bread), one hour for lunch (boiled beef and its broth, roast with salad, hot noodle dessert)

---

* The violinist leader of a gypsy orchestra.

Wine label of Lauder-Lang vineyards, based on early nineteenth-century Gundel wine label

and a short time for dinner (fricassee and roast joint with salad).

Even in the restaurants the guests had very limited choice, even though by the beginning of the 1800's menu cards were in widespread use, showing the foods available daily and their prices. But even after the introduction of this new system, almost all through the nineteenth century there were "common" tables where only "the daily special" was served.

The veritable flood of cookbooks was part of these exciting decades, and between 1870 and 1939 over four hundred books talked about the well-tempered oven. Many described the forgotten glories of the golden age of Hungarian entertaining; some offered wit and delightful anecdotes; more important, others contained fascinating descriptions of now-forgotten culinary wonders.

The eminent Hungarian novelist Lajos Zilahy kindly gave me an important Hungarian cookbook, written around 1890 by one of his ancestors, Ágnes Zilahy, called *Erdélyi konyha* (Transylvanian Kitchen). In the foreword, she explains that Count Sándor Teleki asked her to write an original Hungarian cookbook, since he always wanted to use one written by someone who "actually can cook." Thus encouraged, she wrote the cookbook but couldn't find a publisher who had enough confidence in her knowledge. At last, after eight years, it was accepted and proved so successful that it was printed in ten editions in a short time.

One of the books was specifically for housewives and mothers who were working at a job and had to leave the cooking to a maid, or do it themselves

Roasting an ox

after work. It's rather surprising that this group was large enough to account for the book's success—more likely it was valuable enough to be of interest to other housewives as well. Its publisher, Singer & Wolfner, claimed the sale (throughout the decades) of over half a million copies. Since the Hungarian-speaking population was less than 12 million at the time, this is quite a figure.

Just as in France during the same time, writers and artists became part of the culinary scene. The now defunct publication called *A Hét* (The Week) printed a fascinating volume, and, characteristically, under a *nom de plume,* in this case "Emma Asszony." Mme. "Emma" hid about two dozen of the best Hungarian novelists and poets whose second passion was cooking. The chapter on strudel quips, "According to the legend, a good goldsmith could hammer a *Körmöci arany* (the Hungarian gold florin which was minted in the town of Körmöc until 1914) so thin that a hussar and his horse could be covered with it! A good pastry cook likewise could take a handful of strudel dough and stretch it out so thin that the same hussar on his horse could be totally enveloped with the dough." Nowadays, you would have a rough time finding the hussar, and with frozen strudel dough, you might be barely able to cover the horse's hoof!

Some of the recipes were dug up by writers who worked "on location" in tiny hamlets where the indentured peasants had cooked the same way since the time of the Great Migration. A typical example is a shepherd's recipe that begins by killing the sheep on a special holiday. For dessert the guts were cleaned and boiled, stuffed with white bread soaked in milk and sugar, and roasted in the sheep's fat. Instead of the expected tortes and noodle desserts, many of the dessert recipes written for the upper-middle-class housewives or for their cooks have a distinct flair—such as a whole poached apple stuffed with cherry compote, then embedded in aspic of apple.

Many of the books on cookery specialized in pastries. For hundreds of years Hungary was referred to as the country of romance, wine and gypsy music, but perhaps the most fitting title should be: the land of ten million pastry lovers.

Although the Hungarians learned of the fancy tortes and tarts from the French at the beginning of the nineteenth century and the homestyle cakes and pastries from the Austrians about the same time, the origins of their own pastry-making craft are lost in the Middle Ages. According to fifteenth-century records, a guild existed, members of which had permits to make medicine, spiced drinks, candies and pastries. Some of the more accomplished or brave members even busied themselves with alchemy and the selling of potions and ingredients for black magic. From the Italian traveling candy makers they learned chocolate making, and from the Turks the art of the honeyed sweetmeats and Near Eastern specialties.

The first pastry shop was opened in the middle of the eighteenth century. It was called St. Sebastian Kaffee-Conditorei, and its fame endured mainly because of its beautiful serving maid, "sweet-talking Janka." The Biedermeyer era, with its musical clocks and *gemütlich* spirit and décor, stamped its charac-

Der Rosolij ist sehr gut
Erdek! er macht den Unger Frisches Blut

Hungarian public-house scene, eighteenth century

ter on Hungarian pastry shops permanently.

A perfect example is the Ruszwurm Cukrászda, which is one of the most charming places anywhere. The building, which is in the heart of Buda, a chocolate bonbon's-throw away from the *Mátyás templom* (Matthias Cathedral), originally housed a Turkish biscuit baker. Its name comes from Vilmos Ruszwurm, who started his pastry shop there in 1830. According to legend, he hid the great Hungarian poet Petőfi for forty-eight hours during the revolutionary days of 1848. By that time, his pastries were so famous that a weekly courier brought his goods to Vienna. Queen Elizabeth, the wife of Emperor

Franz Joseph I, visited there often and, when she went on trips, always took with her cakes and confectionery from this pastry shop. Above the glass showcase gilded angels stand displaying an eternal, though casual, wisdom; the clock above the doorway shows the passing of time since the glorious imperial days, and the gilded mirrors sparkle with fire, just as they did when grandfather met grandmother there. In the showcase stand some of the classic Hungarian pastries, including the Dobos Torte, the Indianer and the Rigó Jancsi. Sitting at one of the little tables at Ruszwurm one invokes the perfect atmosphere for recalling the stories of these long-ago creations.

On Christmas Day, 1896, all news about wars, catastrophes and such was overshadowed by the romantic elopement of a gypsy violinist and a princess. The gypsy *primás* (leader), Rigó Jancsi, who was born in the poor Gypsy Row of Székesfehérvár, my home town in Transdanubia, had by 1895 become the sensation of Paris. One day the beautiful, golden-haired Princess Chimay came with the prince to the elegant restaurant where Rigó Jancsi was playing. The diabolical eyes, good looks and brilliant playing of the young gypsy mesmerized the princess. From here on the story reads like a plot for a 1930 Hollywood movie: the big diamond ring the princess takes off her delicate finger and places on the gypsy violinist's hand; secret meetings; her leaving the prince and two little children and running away with the gypsy fiddler. Their wedding, finally, was conducted by a Papal Nuncio and witnessed by the American and English ambassadors. Hungary was saturated with gossip and excited speculations. Poets, short-story writers, journalists and old ladies' tongues were working overtime. One of the pastry chefs created a cake and named it Rigó Jancsi, and another created a torte under the same name. The latter became a Hungarian and later an international classic.

As a bittersweet postscript, we should mention that twenty-two years later another gypsy *primás* repeated the performance with an English countess, but the cake which was named after him, Jancsi Kiss Torta, never became a hit. The second batch of moon astronauts cause hardly a ripple and a shrug. . . .

Let's examine the birth of another great dessert *in statu nascendi* by going back to 1813, with the help of our magic pastry shop.

It was fashionable for the Hungarian aristocracy to live most of the time in Vienna and pursue some private, and often eccentric, hobby. Count Ferdinánd Pálffy purchased the Theater an der Wien that year to play the game of international producer. Unfortunately, the theater was not successful, and to popularize it the Count decided to spice up Aristophanes with jugglers. One of the acts was an East Indian magician, but the jaded Viennese did not react to this bit of showmanship either.

In desperation Count Pálffy, who was a well-known gourmet of the time,

Folk festivities in Budapest during the coronation of Franz Josef I

asked his Hungarian pastry chef to make an unusual dessert to be handed out during intermission to the people who attended the performance and remind them of the Indian in the show. Unfortunately the historians forgot to record the name of the chef and the only thing we know is the delicacy he created. He made a fist-sized doughnut and after baking it he hollowed out the center and filled it with whipped cream and covered it with chocolate. The shining dark brown sweet created an immediate sensation. The following day everyone talked not about the play but only about the new black-and-white cake, and within a week every pastry shop had in front of it a long line of people demanding to purchase the new cake. Pastry shops stopped making all their other products because no one wanted to buy anything but Indianer, the name it retains to this day.

To put it into perspective, we have to remember that although the great French chef Carême had just left Paris to work for Alexander, Emperor of Russia, desserts were still simple sweets and this was the first occasion when whipped cream was used in pastries. Since that time Hungarian chefs and housewives have made a sport out of creating new tortes, and you are likely to find in the cookbooks or on your plate a Cotton Torte, a Potato Torte, a Potato Layer Cake, a Water Torte, or even—believe it or not—a Carrot Torte.*

The only places you won't be able to order pastries in Hungary are the restaurants. While the city administration has been a bureaucratic mess for the past century or so, the departmentalization of edible sweets is admirable. Restaurants make their own hot noodle-type dessert; *csárdas* may possibly have strudel, but no other sweets. Pastries are to be found in pastry shops and espressos. There are exceptions to this rule (as to everything in our fascinating country), but you should remember this division when you are ready for dessert sampling.

Virtually all forms and varieties of pastries can be found at the grandest pastry shop in Hungary, and probably in the world. The Swiss Kugler family opened the original store in Budapest almost two hundred years ago, and it became world famous during the Gerbeaud regime. Emil Gerbeaud was justly proud of the fact that he was the only pâtissier who received the highest civilian order the Austro-Hungarian monarchy could bestow, and also the *Légion d'Honneur*. After the Second World War, the shop was nationalized (together with most other pastry shops) and named for the poet who gave his name to the square where it is located: Vörösmarty.

Perhaps the finest pastry in present-day Hungary is to be found in the pastry shop of the Grand Hotel Royal, where the Prince of the Kitchens is Zoltán Kenderessy, the most decorated contemporary Hungarian pastry chef. In view

* For Carrot Torte recipe see page 417.

of the almost "baker's dozen" gold medals he has won in international competitions, only his modesty keeps him from being crowned the World's Foremost Practitioner of the Craft of Pastry Making. I am proud to be his friend and grateful for his advice in connection with many of the recipes in this book.

Pastry's first cousin (removed once and for all) is the honey-bread craft. The literal translation of *mézeskalács* or *mézesbábos* is honey cake or honey puppets or honey dolls. These words have been in use only for the last two hundred years; until then, the Latin *dulciariorum* was the name. This is one of the oldest Hungarian crafts. It is as much a part of every village fair and holiday festival as the *török-méz* (nougatlike "Turkish honey"), *márc* (caramel-based honey drink), the carousel and the shiny penny gifts for the children. Unfortunately, very few of the craftsmen carve their own molds any more; they just keep making the traditional shapes—like the hussar, fancy heart or baby bunting, sticking a colored paper face and other decorations on the cake itself.

The themes used for these figures are either religious or popular. Religious themes include Adoration of the Magi or Nativity scenes. Sometimes, family crests and popular folk heroes are used. The different influences produced their own particular subject matter—from the baroque era came elaborate ornamental carvings and from the turn of the century, a locomotive.

Tension and release is the key to most art forms. It is also often what warm memories are made of. Not to be obscure for one minute more than is necessary, I recall a time in my childhood, at about age four, when my mother was unable to pick me up from kindergarten—there was some misunderstanding between her, the maid and a neighbor's mother. As a result, instead of going home at the usual three o'clock, I was still playing with the blocks in kindergarten at the unheard-of hour of six—growing more and more uneasy. Finally, my father picked me up. To give me a special treat—because I was shaken up by the experience, thinking that they had abandoned me—on the way home he took me to a little honey-bread maker's shop on Iskola Street and bought me a piece of honey bread and a gingerbread figure. I don't recall whether I chose a pretty girl in a hoop skirt or a soldier with a sword, but I do remember that the tension was released by the mellow cake and it was perhaps one of the sweetest experiences I ever had.

When I visited my home town after eighteen years' absence, I went back to find the little store, but it didn't exist any more; the name of the street was also changed, but the recipe can be found on page 396, with the taste I still recall.

If you love wine you must visit the French wine country, and if you like beef, Argentina will be your paradise. But for pastry lovers at large, a visit to Hungary is highly recommended because these fairy-tale pastry shops often produce extraordinary quality. The decorations of individual pieces are still little masterworks and the level almost uniformly high. There are few delights more enchanting than sitting down at a charming little lace-covered table and drinking espresso or hot chocolate with whipped cream, accompanied by a delicately decorated slice of *torta* or an endless variety of dainty *mignons* which make the Western petits fours seem like five-and-ten-cent gewgaws next to Tiffany's diamonds and precious stones.

Just as the Hungarian coffeehouse was an intellectual playground, whetstone of wit and a battleground of habitués, the pastry shop was always a haven against the cruelty of the outside world. In Hungary they still offer assorted consolations of cake and coffee, lace and legend.

It is not obligatory for every generation of any craft to have great personalities and teachers, but it helps. Fine restaurants and pastry shops, and inventive cookbooks, generally come from a handful of extraordinary restaurateurs and chefs. In the early nineteenth century, Hungary was especially fortunate in having brilliant chefs who studied and worked in France. They brought back their knowledge and applied it with a flair and subtle sense of how it could be adapted to Hungarian conditions and tastes. They were wise enough to know when less was more, and that restraint is an important virtue. Paprika and other spices were used more judiciously; the heaviness of foods reduced drastically; the almost oriental oversweetness of stews and even roasts changed. They balanced menus with more sagacity, but—and this is important—they retained the basic characteristics of the national cuisine. In fact, they raised it to a refinement and dignity so that it came to be internationally appreciated.

It was said that a chef's education begins two hundred years before he is born. Today's giants owe a great debt to three men: József Marchal, József C. Dobos and Károly Gundel; their education contained many centuries of culinary tradition.

József Marchal the elder began his career in France, where he learned the secrets of its famed cuisine. Soon his talent brought him the exalted position of *chef de cuisine* to Napoleon III. As a special emissary, as respected as an ambassador, he was sent to the Czar, and later the Russians sent him to cook at the front in the Crimean War. (It is interesting to note that Alexis Soyer, the great French chef who worked in London, was also active in the Crimean War but on the English side.)

The next step in Marchal's phenomenal career was a special mission to be chef to Archduke Albrecht during the Lombardian War. Finally, he returned to Hungary in the 1870's to become the director-chef of the National Casino in Budapest. We have a nice description of his establishment and its food in *The Gourmet's Guide to Europe,* 1908, written by Lieutenant Colonel Newn-

Cover of sheet music, Zrinyi cafehouse song

ham-Davis. He praises the "French-Hungarian" food served in the stately National Casino, which by then was 120 years old. In a quiet, high-ceilinged white room he sat near the Hungarian Minister of War and other celebrities, and when leaving, was ushered out by a porter who wore the scarlet uniform of the hussars. This is the dinner he ordered:

Somlói	Gulyás Clair
Château Margaux 1875	Fogas de Balaton à la Jean Bart
	Cuissot de Porc Frais
Moët 1884	Choucroute Farcie
	Cailles Rôties sur Canapé, Sauce Bordelaise
	Salade:
	Artichauts Frais
Tokay 1846	Túróslepény*
Szilvórium 1796	
Barackpálinka 1860	

Marchal was given the honor of creating and preparing the Coronation Dinner of 1867 for Franz Josef I, which was an unprecedented occasion for the gathering of great European chefs (among other nobility and royalty) in Budapest. Among these chefs were Clavel, Lemyra, Andremond and Pilon. Dubois and Bernard, in their *La Cuisine Classique* (Paris, 1876), described the Coronation Dinner and the menu.†

Finally, Marchal became the owner of the Angol Királynő (Queen of England), an extraordinarily luxurious Budapest hotel and restaurant, and there he trained eleven chefs, all of whom became giants in the pantheon of Hungarian cuisine. One of these was Ede Palkovics, who became the chef of the famed Sacher in Vienna at the age of twenty.

József C. Dobos, born in 1847, was proud of the fact that an ancestor on his father's side was the chef of Count Rákóczi. Toward the end of his life he opened a fabulous food specialty shop in Budapest, where he stocked over sixty different cheeses and twenty-two kinds of champagne and managed to import every rare seasonal delicacy imaginable. Famous far and wide was his showmanship, whether it was a machine of his own invention that projected a clock face on the sidewalk, or his stunt of hollowing out a fifty-kilo cheese, pouring in a magnum of the finest burgundy, leaving it in the shop window until the wine had completely soaked into the cheese, then selling pieces to the passionate epicures who flocked to buy from him. It was in this shop that he created

* Cottage cheese cake.
† Facsimile of menu on page 61.

FAMILLE ROYALE D'AUTRICHE

Consommé printanier aux quenelles de volaille.

HORS D'ŒUVRE.

Petits pâtés à la russe.
Foie-gras et caviar.

RELEVÉS.

Saumon sauce génevoise et hollandaise.
Filet de bœuf à la financière.

ENTRÉES.

Côtelettes de veau à la maréchale, petits-pois.
Chaufroix de poulets (sur socle).

ROTS.

Oisons, selle de chevreuil.

ENTREMETS.

Savarin à la macédoine de fruits.
Gelée au citron, garnie de fraises.

Diner servi par cent, à Pesth, pour le couronnement de S. M. le roi de Hongrie,
sous la direction de M. Maréchal,
avec le concours de MM. Matisse, Muller, Clavel, Lemyre, Jules Andremond,
Charles Halter, etc.

Menu of the Coronation Dinner of Franz Josef I

Rajnai lazacz apró tengeri rákokkal köritve.
Saumon du Rhin garni des ecrevisses

A salmon-and-crayfish presentation by József C. Dobos, 1875

and sold his famous *Dobos torta* in 1887. He had devised a packaging for sending this delicacy to foreign countries. Soon everybody started to imitate this cake, mostly with very bad results. This prompted him to publish the authentic recipe in 1906, donating it to the Budapest Pastry and Honey-bread Makers Guild. The sensation of the Millennium Exposition in 1896 was the Dobos Pavilion, where guess what was baked and served! One of the four major works he published is his *Hungarian-French Cookbook*. It stands as a classic.

The world remembers the anniversaries of battles and the birthdays of great composers—but what city other than Budapest would stage a full-scale festival to commemorate the seventy-fifth birthday of a torte? In 1962, *Dobos torta* had this unique honor when the Hungarian Chefs' and Pastry Chefs' Association placed a wreath on Dobos' grave to commemorate the seventy-fifth anniversary of the creation of the Dobos Torte. After this, in the Hungaria Café-Restaurant, they held a banquet, reproducing one of his great dinners; and for two days the Vörösmarty Pastry Shop sold only cakes and tortes of his creation. His grandson was presented with a heart made of traditional honey bread, and a six-foot-diameter *Dobos torta* was paraded by pastry chefs through the avenues of Budapest. Dobos died in 1924, and many of us born the same year secretly hope there is some kind of reincarnation of his culinary talents in us.

A small country like Hungary (population 10 million, and the size of Indiana) cannot have the luxury of having many specialists. Perhaps that is why you very often find a "triple threat" expert, talented in a great many fields. Károly Gundel was such a person, combining the gifts of a Ritz, an Escoffier and a Prosper Montagné. He was without a doubt the greatest restaurateur Hungary has produced.

Very often the best way to measure a man is to look at his children, and several of Károly Gundel's offspring are leaders in the restaurant and hotel industry. Ferenc is writing textbooks and teaching at the College for the Catering Industry; Károly, Jr., managed the Restaurant of the Hungarian Pavilion at the 1939 New York World's Fair; Imre is one of the curators of the Museum of Culinary Guild. They like to tell about "life with father," which must have been very eventful, since they were three of thirteen children.

"Father said that it was better to be an honest street sweeper than a dishonest king. He always felt that the restaurateur was responsible for his guests while they were in his house. Father knew the science of all parts of gastronomy, yet insisted on simple terms and believed in the gods of common sense." *Varietas-delectat* was his motto and his menus are food-illustrations of his tenet.

His perfection in all details was legendary. One of his former chefs tells this story. When a guest ordered a lobster and then sent it back, Gundel came to inspect the crustacean. When he sniffed it, he paled—the complaint was justified; the fish was "over the hill." In his restaurant this sort of thing could not happen! The best proof of a lobster's freshness is that it is still alive when it is dropped into the *court-bouillon.* This lobster surely wasn't! Immediately he went to the kitchen to fire the fish butcher. With tears in his eyes, the latter insisted that the lobster was alive when he started to cook it. Gundel, instead of losing his head, began to think of all the possibilities, and narrowed it down—like a sharp detective—to a chance that the lobster had been fed with a piece of spoiled meat. After rechecking, they found that this was exactly the case, and as a result, the fish butcher could stay. The guest, of course, was not allowed to pay the bill and was reinvited to dinner.

Károly Gundel considered his father, János, who opened his first restaurant in 1869, his master and example, and Károly's major work, *The Art of Hospitality*, was dedicated to him. At an interview on his sixtieth birthday, he recalled that at age nine he had been sent out by his father, the proprietor of the famed Archduke István Hotel, to serve rolls and water to the guests to find out whether undiluted Gundel blood ran in his veins or not. Every Gundel child was tried out this way and his reactions carefully watched. If he panicked or did not act in accordance with the elegance of the room, father János began to think in other than hotel or restaurant terms as a career for the offspring. (Most of the Gundels became well known in other fields.)

Gundel creations in the Hungarian cuisine became part of the standard repertoire, and one very often has to stop and research certain dishes to find out which Gundel one should thank for it. Károly was a Latin scholar, which came in very handy in his research into very early documents and manuscripts. His cookbook, which is translated into many languages, and his professional textbooks stand as monuments of Hungarian culinary classicism.

Born in 1883, he represented the best in the great tradition of Hungarian craftsmen. In 1912, he took over the concession of the City Park Restaurant. This is the place where he and his chefs perfected the modern Hungarian cuisine, and it has become an institution. Until the age of fifty he never took more than one week's vacation annually. He died at age seventy-four, in 1956, and it was amazing that such an extraordinary amount of work (writing books and other publications, creating and operating restaurants, being president of the Hotel-Restaurateurs Guild, helping thousands of people in the industry) could be squeezed into less than a century of living.

Aside from every superlative one can think of, when writing about Károly Gundel we must mention the very small yet meaningful gesture he made in the thirties when he refused the highest honor and title the Hungarian government could bestow on anyone, saying, "I want no official recognition that can be purchased with money as well as achievement." All of us restaurateurs should remember his tenet: "Restaurateuring is to cause pleasure, felicity and a happy state of satisfaction to your guest."

Hungary never conquered significant foreign territories, but its women's cooking and its chefs' creations triumphed with the people of faraway lands. The famed French academician Francois Coppée wrote an ode to the chef of the Hotel Hungaria for his chicken *paprikás;* Kant bragged about the mustard sauce he learned to make from his friend Count Fekete de Galántha; Dumas *père* "in ecstasy" copied recipes while visiting Hungary; Edward VII requested a Hungarian chef, and Rezső Török took this exalted position.

5. The New Era

The road from the Ural Mountains to the Carpathian Basin was not as adventurous as the one which led—in fifteen hundred years—to *fogas à la Gundel.** In reaching the New Era at the end of the nineteenth century, the cuisine absorbed along the way the influences of many cultures; developed its sons into great professionals; infused into its daughters an understanding of cooking; involved its intelligentsia in the art of gastronomy; impelled its poets to inspire the nation about the Dionysian pleasures of the table; and always, under all circumstances, retained the true national character of its cuisine.

* See recipe on page 209.

✧

PART TWO

GASTRONOMIC
PROFILES OF THE
HUNGARIAN REGIONS

✧ ✧ ✧ ✧ ✧
✧ ✧ ✧
✧

✵ 6 ✵

TRANSDANUBIA
(DUNÁNTÚL)

CURIOUSLY, "beyond the Danube" is what the atavistic Hungarians still call the section to the west of the river. Probably when the Magyar tribes came in to establish the homeland, this part was left until later, and meantime they called it "beyond the Danube."

It is a gastronomically rich section of Hungary. Almost its exact center is Balaton, which is the largest warm-water lake in Central Europe, supplying the famed *fogas* and other fishes. Here, where nature created a giant hothouse, flowers sometimes bloom even in December. Along its hundred-mile-long shore, ten thousand acres of vineyards grow some of the best wine-grapes of Hungary.

All the Balaton wines are white, characterized by a somewhat fruity flavor. The most commonly grown grape is the Riesling (which curiously enough produces only insignificant wines in Austria and Switzerland). Its nostalgic bouquet is kin to that of the mignonette flower.

Unquestionably, the most superior Balaton wine is the Badacsonyi Kéknyelű (Blue Handled) of which there is only a small quantity each year. There are two types: the "short handled" and the "long handled." The latter has an extremely small yield but extraordinary quality. The Kéknyelű is an ancient and noble grape, peculiar to the Badacsony region. The wine itself is greenish-white, has good body and a distinctive bouquet and taste.

Just as in many French wine regions, like Chablis or Montrachet, many more wines bear the labels of this area than it could possibly produce. A very small amount of real Kéknyelű ever gets commercial distribution. It is one of those minor, quiet, everyday scandals that are politely taken for granted most of the time, understandably human, normal and inevitable.

Another immigrant, the Szürkebarát, which comes from France as the Pinot Gris, found its true home in Badacsony. In France it's used mostly to make champagne. But in Hungary it becomes a pungent wine that can accompany even a roast with dignity. Its bouquet is spicy, with a darkly golden color, and the flavor is what the Italians refer to as *amabile*—rich without being actually sweet. One of the finest Hungarian wines, the Akali Muskotály, is finally available in the United States.

Not long ago, a Csopak* farmer named Imre Balogh was tilling his land when his horse tumbled into a big hole. Archeologists rushed to the scene and found a Roman wine cellar on that very spot. There were still crude stone benches along the walls and in the ceiling an opening for ventilation. In the dim quiet in which it had lain almost two thousand years, and into which Balogh's horse had unwittingly stumbled, all was nearly as it had been when the Romans also grew wine along the shores of the Balaton.

The county of Zala lies on the southern part of Transdanubia on the Croatian border, and has a mild, almost Mediterranean climate, producing the finest fruits, grapes, chestnuts and vegetables. It seems natural that Janus Pannonius, the fifteenth-century poet-churchman, wanted to found a new Athens around here. He thought the people, the climate and even the food were perfect for creating a humanistic paradise in this place already cultivated by the Roman legions. Though floods and famines have devastated it time and time again, it has always regenerated itself.

In the heart of Zala lie the fascinating villages of the provinces of Göcsej and Örség. This section has retained much of its early folk art, music, festivals and cooking. The county of Örség is certainly worth a visit on a Sunday: the costumes and the after-church dinners are marvels of traditional authenticity. These two provinces are quite similar in their cuisine, probably because of their custom of intermarriage throughout the ages.

There are many echos of ancient rites in some of the local gingerbread customs. For instance, in Göcsej, part of the baptismal celebration is eating the *fumu*—a baby figure—a reminder of the original pagan sacrifices of real infants; and the braided cake originally imitated the long coiled braids of a woman's hair. As for the *frászkarika* or "pox-hoop": when babies were sick, the parents borrowed flour from nine different places, mixed it with holy water, baked it for nine days, and gently passed the sick baby through the hoop as a symbolic plea for its healthy rebirth.

* A village in the Balaton district.

But I suspect that the health of the people of Őrség-Göcsej comes more from the unusually varied and well-balanced fare. Rich mushroom dishes are well known throughout the county; various aspics (*kocsonya*) are popular here, as is squash-seed oil for salads. Sausages, instead of being smoked as in other parts of Hungary, are stored in their own fat in crocks—a process learned, no doubt, from the Croats. Milk, which is not very commonly drunk in Hungary by adults, is an essential part of everyday fare, often taken for lunch with bread instead of soup. When broth is made (sometimes for the first course of a Sunday meal), it's always with at least three different kinds of meat. The second course is usually boiled meats, served with horseradish, tomato or sorrel sauce. The third course might be cabbage with pork and bits of bacon. This is followed by a strudel made with dilled cottage cheese or turnip with plenty of sour cream. The next service is some kind of roast meat either with prune compote, red cabbage or cucumber salad. The final serving is a cake made with jam, poppy seeds or squash seeds, or baked stuffed noodles.* Generally they drink fruit brandy before the soup, interrupted with wine to accompany the meal, then the brandy resumed ad infinitum.

So many unflattering jokes have been made about the people in this area that if you ask any villager in the district if this is Göcsej, he will probably tell you that it is the next village. Every country has its village or county which is the butt of jokes and spurious stories of comic-opera-scale confusions and ignorance. This kind of innocent lunacy is presumed about Göcsej with stories like the one about the three villagers who had to borrow a very long ladder from the next town: to get it through a thick forest, the only solution they could figure out was to cut down enough trees to make a road wide enough so they could carry the ladder through marching three abreast. This comic simplemindedness, for which Göcsej is nationally known, surely doesn't extend to its kitchen.

Since the ninth century Göcsej has guarded the southwestern section of Transdanubia, and for that reason it was highly privileged by the Hungarian kings. Perhaps it was this undisturbed wealth that made the culinary development of County Zala possible. Food descriptions from a nineteenth-century household recipe collection attest to its richness:

Turóslebbencs-leves (*Cottage-Cheese Noodle Soup*)

Stretch strudel dough and sprinkle it with farmer's cheese. Fold and cut into 2-inch pieces. Fry in lard till crisp and golden brown. (This soup garniture will have, when it is finished, a close relation to the Turkish *beurek* and was probably imported during the Turkish occu-

---

* See recipe on page 366.

pation.) To make the soup, place 1 or 2 bay leaves in salted water and when it is boiling, whip in a mixture of flour and sour cream. Reduce heat and add the fried noodles.

Hablegény-leves (Merman* Soup)

Mix 1 egg with 2 cups of milk and enough flour to make a very light dough. Pour into a baking pan and bake it in a moderate oven. Cut it up into small squares and put it aside. Bring ⅔ part milk with ⅓ part water and salt to taste to boil, then whip in some sour cream. Just before serving, place the little baked squares in the soup.

Csutrirépa-zöldség (Baby Turnip)

Slice and sauté young turnips in lard, together with some chopped flat parsley. Add a little water and cook under cover. Make a light *roux.* When light brown, mix it with salt and sour cream. Add it to the cooked vegetables. Tightly packed in small wooden barrels, it can be used during the winter to mix with noodles, or as a filling for a non-sweet strudel.

Babos káposztafőzelék (Bean and Sauerkraut Casserole)

Cook sauerkraut with tomato purée and thicken it with onion *roux.* At the same time, cook cranberry beans with pieces of smoked pork ribs. When they are done, mix them with sauerkraut.

Ecetes-zsírkaleves (Vinegary Bacon Soup)

Cook smoked meat and the skin of bacon cut in small pieces. Fry chopped onion and sprinkle it with paprika. Add it to the cooked, smoked meat in broth. Flavor it with vinegar and salt.

Lakodalmas-vertperec (Beaten Wedding Pretzel)

Mix 8 egg yolks, 1 tablespoon lard, ½ ounce plum brandy, ¼ pound sugar and finally, fold in the stiffly beaten egg whites. Add enough flour to make it easily kneadable, work it well, and shape it into pretzels. Boil them in water. Brush them with a mixture of sour cream, flour and sugar and bake in a hot oven. (The medieval name was *hőkkőnsült,* meaning "baked on heated stone," indicating the original baking method.)

From Zala County come the best crab preparations,† using the sweet, delicate river crabs found in this section of the country.

---

* A male mermaid.
† See page 210.

6. Transdanubia

Below Lake Balaton, alongside the present-day Yugoslav border lie two excellent wine-growing areas: the vineyards of Villány and Szekszárd. It will come as a shock to the winebibbers who finally, after considerable difficulty, have learned to pronounce *Egri Bikavér,* that the Bikavér of Szekszárd is often superior though lighter in body. As an old rhyme says:

Szekszárdi bikavér
Orvosságnál többet ér
Aki issza holtig él

Bulls' blood of Szekszárd
Is better than medicine.
He who drinks [it] shall live till he dies.

The blue Kadarka from which this heroic wine is made is one of the basic, typically Hungarian grapes. On the gentle hillsides around the town of Szekszárd, the blue Kadarka grape produces a very spicy, aromatic wine, with the color of the inside of a pomegranate. But the word *Kadarka* appears in a great many wine districts in Hungary. (Some etymologists insist that it comes from the Serbian word *skadar,* meaning that it originated in the city of Skutari. Others claim that it was originally Albanian (*Skadarka*), but strangely enough, there is no such wine in Albania.) In the Buda district the same grape produces a wine that is almost black. In the Great Plains it ends as a pale-pinkish wine.

Intoxicating stories drift out of the past. Franz Liszt was so fond of this wine he made frequent pilgrimages to Szekszárd, and at least one of his Rhapsodies (the "Szekszárd March") was composed under the benign influence of Kék Kadarka. According to Anselm Hüttenbremer, Schubert once "drank quite a lot of Nectar Szekszardique and falling into the proper mood took out pen and paper and began working on a piece he later named 'Die Forelle.'" Glorious associations indeed!

There is no indication that red wines were known in Hungary before King Matthias brought in Burgundy vines from France in the fifteenth century. It seems very likely that the Szekszárdi Kadarka popularized red wines in Hungary. Tastes change, but this wine has enjoyed an unflagging devotion throughout its long history. It seems always to have been not merely an accompaniment to food but an experience in itself, virile, voluptuous, yet with a certain aromatic delicacy that could not fail to attract the allegiance of poets and composers.

What the Tokay is to white wines, the Villány is to red. (In 1958 in the Budapest International Wine Competition, all of Villány's eighteen entries

73

won prizes—twelve gold and six silver.) The Villány wines are usually made half of Kadarka grapes and half of Oporto grapes. They generally contain an exceptionally high percentage of tannic acid, with a 13-percent alcohol content; and the taste can range from austere to elegant, but always distinctive.

Directly below this hilly section of Transdanubia is Ormánság, where the life of the people is simple compared with some of the richer provinces. This ethnic group has remained virtually unchanged since time immemorial, and this makes it an important part of the regional profile.

Until the twentieth century in this section of Hungary, the women did not even sit with the men at the dinner table, but stood behind, occasionally reaching over the men's shoulders to take some food from the plates; or they would sit apart, away from the table, on small stools—an unfortunate but direct survival of the ancient Hungarian table manners.

The local specialties are noteworthy for their simplicity:

White Hurka
> *Hurka* has the shape of a sausage, but is always eaten fresh and filled with a mixture where meat is of secondary importance. Here it's made with cornmeal mixed with a little bit of ground pork, stuffed in the casing, first boiled then fried.

Tied Dumpling (*Kötözött gombóc*)
> The noodle dough is stretched thin, then cut into 4-inch squares. Fried onion and cottage cheese are placed in the center and the four corners are brought together to make a kind of "bound" noodle package. It is served in a paprika essence.*

Another of their specialties is *gánica*. Only enough wheat flour is added to corn flour so that it will stick together with lard and milk, to be kneaded into a dough. After being shaped into dumplings with a spoon, it is boiled and then fried in bacon drippings with bread crumbs and paprika. It is a relative of the ancient Hungarian "five-finger dish" and the Rhode Island johnnycake.

Old-timers tell you that everyone in the Ormánság always ate "three bites of horseradish" before Easter luncheon so that if in the following year he slept outside with his mouth open, he would not have a snake crawl into it. Fortunately, this was followed by a piece of good cured ham to relieve the bite of the horseradish.

The whole of Transdanubia is studded with goose farms. I visited one a few years ago and was suddenly transported back in memory to my childhood, when I had to help my mother or the maid to stuff the geese in the back of our garden. The memory association suddenly focused on a single minute. It was

* See recipe on page 343.

seven o'clock in the morning and I was ready to go to school. My mother gave me a good-sized package, which was my *tizórai* or ten o'clock snack. With a sudden suspicion I opened it up and started to complain miserably: "Do I have to eat goose liver and green pepper again?" With a sad smile and a blushing face, I recall the crosscut of the balloonlike bread, spread with paprika, goose fat and thickly cut roast goose liver, not to mention the medium-hot, fleshy, canary-yellow-green peppers. Not only youth, but goose liver, is wasted on the young.

Some sly individual may go even further and suggest that goose liver is wasted, too, on certain other nations, who actually changed the texture and taste of goose liver, perhaps because they did not have the God-given natural materials to work with. Or perhaps they just don't know the straight and narrow path to proper preparation.

What makes the Hungarian goose liver unique? First of all, through careful crossbreeding, the size of both the goose and its liver has been increased in the past fifty years to a preternatural splendor. Very important is the type of corn that is force-fed to the goose, and what kind of earth the corn is grown in. Vital is the goose's drinking water—each farmer has his own formula of how much white clay and other natural elements he mixes with the water.

This is the biological process: When the body of the goose absorbs the maximum amount of fat, certain disorders begin to take place. The exhaustion of the whole system causes difficulty in sugar production, which in turn leads the blood to call upon fat reserves, raising considerably the fat content of the blood (when you kill this fattened goose, the blood is almost a golden yellow), which in turn delivers the fat to the liver. The goose liver is able to retain this fat in great quantity and consequently swells to abnormal proportions. Today, a three-pound liver is not uncommon.

An early document tells us of a pork and goose-liver sausage with truffles. The Hungarians also used truffles as stuffing for the goose itself. Such gastronomic refinements are astonishing from a supposedly coarse age of centuries ago.

The Hungarian variety of truffle, mostly found in the Bakony hills, is somewhat inferior to its French cousin, lacking the faint licorice odor and the rich black color. Its botanical name is *Tuber aestivum*. In a Hungarian hunting book published in 1829 by Dénes Pák, a long and detailed chapter discusses the training of truffle hounds. He suggests using the famed Hungarian sheepdog—the puli—calling it the "diver dog" (from *búvár* which means deep-sea diver).

The dog must become familiar with the smell and taste of truffles. You have a problem when you begin teaching the dog in wintertime, which is

Pigherders in the Bakony Hills

out of season for truffles. I advise you in this case to knead and roll a piece of freshly baked bread dough with ripe cheese and saturate it with an oil in which truffles were cooked. Believe me, the dog will find this buried treasure, particularly if you lead him wisely. You have to pet him and fondle him and slowly begin to bury the false truffle deeper and deeper, and Eureka! You will have a truffle hound.

Is it worth it? If beauty is in the eye of the beholder, are exquisite tastes as much a state of mind as objective fact? When I ate a young gosling stuffed with truffles, I was prepared to swear that my exquisite pleasure was more than a state of mind.

Someone asked me once what I miss the most from my childhood. Half

76

facetiously I answered: "The mineral water." Hungarians, particularly in Transdanubia, often use natural mineral waters—with which the country is generously supplied—instead of bottled soda. There are thousands of mineral springs in Hungary and at least two dozen waters are bottled commercially. Some of the best known are Mohai Ágnes, Kékkuti, Parádi Salvus, Jodaqua, Igmándi, Mira, Apenta, Hunyadi János, Ferenc József. The country is so richly endowed, in fact, that almost anywhere you start digging, you will probably strike mineral water.

Between Lake Balaton and Budapest lies Székesfehérvár, the ancient capital of St. Stephen, and the town where I was born. Just before the Second World War, our ambitious mayor decided that the quickest way to international fame for our little city was to build a spa. The most important single requirement, of course, was missing—natural hot springs. But nothing daunted the mayor, and his enthusiasm fired the town council to allot funds (some of which—claimed certain malicious tongues—were not even in the treasury) and digging was begun on a large scale. Alas, no matter how deep they dug, and in how many places, no hot springs—only magnificent natural sparkling water. As it happened, we already had several dozen local waters. At last, after several years of concentrated effort and heavy expenditure, the project was abandoned. The very next morning a huge sign appeared on the site of the latest well, reading "Here Lie One Million Pengős from the Pockets of Székesfehérvár's Citizens." The well-digging firm cursed the mayor, as they were never paid for the complete amount they demanded; the city cursed the mayor for his failure to realize his grandiose scheme; and I, a small insignificant boy, cursed my luck—the latest mineral well was so near our house that every day I had to go fill a demijohn for our midday dinner. I would not mind now walking several miles if it meant I could drink that excellent mineral water again—every day if possible.

A few miles from Székesfehérvár is the village of Mór, which was the memorable place where a friend of my father introduced me to the enjoyment of wine. I recall the thick, short glass he handed me in his vineyard and the pleasant shock which I—a seven-year-old kid—felt sipping the powerful liquid. It must have been the famous local wine, the Ezerjó, whose vines were planted about 250 years ago by German settlers. There is some argument about the meaning of *Ezerjó,* which means literally "Thousand-Good" and can be taken to signify either "wine of a thousand virtues" or "a thousand times good." It has a powerful aroma, and due to its special hard acids is white-greenish in color. The taste is fruity and rather rich. The alcohol content may be as high as 14 percent, the sugar content often as much as 3 percent.

The nearby Somló, located on the western plains of the county of Veszprém, is one of the smallest wine-growing districts of Hungary. Nevertheless, it produces several legendary wines, the very names of which are saturated with history.

Like a strange mirage, the fantastic cone shape of the extinct volcano Somlóhegy rises abruptly above the flat plain, as though out of nowhere. The volcanic soil, composed of basalt and lava, bears a striking resemblance to that of the Mediterranean vineyards, and the wines often do, too. Although the entire area consists of less than 1,000 acres, at least ten basic varieties of quality wines are grown here.

Different sections of the cone produce different wines; from the slope toward Somlóvásárhely comes a strong, pungent dessert wine. The western slope, below the ancient crumbling ruin of a castle, makes a dry wine which takes on a magnificent strawberry aroma and a dark golden color. (This one has a high iron content.) Powerful in taste, it can be drunk either as a dinner accompaniment or as a dessert wine (not unlike some of the Barsac wines of Bordeaux). These highly aromatic wines take at least four years to mature and often as many as ten.

According to a certain János Gombás (1805), the 1802 vintage of Somló wine was so strong that when lit, it would burn like brandy! Local historians tell us that the local grape inspired Berlioz to write his famous "Rákóczi March." Berlioz, visiting Somló, heard a gypsy girl violinist named Panna Cinka play her own composition, on which he later based his march. Naturally Panna had been fired to eloquency by the rich subtle local wines. What with the intoxicating interaction of native wine and music (especially gypsy music), how could Berlioz have resisted such potent chemistry? (I must add, in all honesty, that I came across at least two other explanations for the birth of Berlioz's "Rákóczi March.")

As distant and august a personage as Queen Victoria was well acquainted with Somló wine and used it to play a gentle practical joke on a fellow monarch. Once after Franz Josef I had sent her a selection of Hungarian wines—which included the wines of Somló—the Queen (who had become very fond of them) sent as a return gift to the Emperor a case of unlabeled bottles. The Emperor was delighted with the wines, but slightly puzzled because he could not identify them. The joke, of course, was on him; they were the wines of Somló, from his own realm.

Going in the northwest direction, you'll find near the Austrian border Sopron, one of the oldest cities in the country. Its baroque buildings remind you of the "era of enlightenment" when Hungary emerged from its medieval cocoon. Its wine industry, which has existed for about 1,500 years, has long been the tranquil source of both its wealth and pleasures. Sopron wines in-

clude the light red Kékfrankos, the pleasant dessert wine Veltelini, the Furmint, the Zöld Szilváni (green Sylvaner), Riesling and yellow Muskotály.
Except for the Veltelini, they all have a low alcohol content. The white wines,
pale yellow, have a delicate aroma, sometimes almost weak. The red wines are
mild enough to deserve the wine drinker's praise: "It allows itself to be drunk
all day." Alas, they do not travel.

On a leisurely ramble down the flower-decked streets of Sopron today, a
visitor notices eye-catching signs indicating the delightful cavelike basements
of old houses—called Borharapó (Wine-Biter). One may enter the cool dark
caves with their vaulted ceilings and sip wine as in the old days. The name of
the most famous is the Gyógygödör or Medicine Pit. Like the Chinese who
used to call on the chef when a case was considered medically hopeless, the
Sopron people resort to their most efficacious Sopron wines not only as a
remedy but as a preventive.

Transdanubia—with the exception of Zala, Ormánság and a few other
pockets—absorbed much of the Austrian culture, the Latin-Catholic spirit of
the Habsburgs; and throughout the centuries its cities were the advance forts
of Western civilization. The foods of Dunántúl are the base of the Hungarian
bourgeois middle-class cooking, which is much more varied but less pure
Magyar than in other parts of the country.

To a Fattened Goose

Egy tömött libához (1945)

Do my eyes deceive me? A goose of
Such mighty proportions rises in pride
before them, I almost faint in amazement.
One cannot refrain, doffing one's hat,
bow to the ground in face of such weighty
authority; come here, my darling, do not
shun me so stubbornly! Do not excite in vain
my longing imagination forever!
Fly into my lap; let me kiss and caress you!
Fly into my open mouth, heavenly vision, to roast
alive upon the tip of my burning tongue.
No finer death has ever been offered to you!
You are now the only object of my love, you,
creature of princely rank! Take pity
upon my pining for you in these days of starving,
O mightiest goose! Do not be overweening;
appreciate my simple-minded praise which
no mortal on earth has earned so fully!

JÓZSEF BERDA (*translated by Paul Tabori*)

Praise of the Delicate Wild Boletus Mushrooms

A finom tinórúgomba dicsérete (1943)

Ornament of grim forest who so often
laughed at me from behind the hiding grass:
fairy-like boletus, you—
now my enamored nose recalls
your perfumed scent and
my imagination kindles at once
if I recall: what tasty
portions I ate of your swelling and firm
flesh on those rare festival days
when sometimes you were served for a treat!

You are the year's finest gift,
the precious food of wood-roaming poor,
whom the serene Creator made in a happy mood.
You're unlimnable, beauty itself, something
only aged appetite can appreciate
when you reach our table.
My eyes' and palate's joy, mostly fleshy
dish whom my teeth chew in piety,
feeling while eating the taste and scent
of most majestic woods in my mouth which
has already tasted so many noble flavors.

JÓZSEF BERDA (*translated by Paul Tabori*)

Open air market at Pest, 1859

✿ 7 ✿

BUDAPEST

BUDAPEST has been called by one of its knowledgeable citizens a "Janus-faced city." It is, at the same time, the oldest and youngest metropolis of Europe. Oldest because, called Aquincum, it was the capital of Pannonia, an eastern province of the Roman Empire, and already had 100,000 people living there 2,000 years ago. It is also the youngest major European city because the three cities, Buda, Pest and Óbuda, were not united until 1873.

The split personality, the "two faces," expresses itself in its cuisine, too. Buda is the home of the most elegant, old-fashioned Biedermeyer and Baroque restaurants. The older section, Óbuda, still has tiny restaurants with outdoor gardens and simple kitchens to fit its surroundings. Large contemporary eating places, hotels and buffets fill many corners of Pest.

The Danube, which cuts the city in half, is still full of fish, despite intense shipping activity; and you see many amateur fishermen eagerly perching on its steps.

You can find nearly all of Hungary's regional cooking in Budapest. Just as in Paris you can eat a Burgundian dinner, a Lyonnais lunch and an Alsatian supper in a brasserie—in Budapest you can have a Kalocsa fish *csárda* luncheon, a Transylvanian game dinner and, after the opera, specialties from the Great Plains. But since we deal with the past, to understand the present, we should examine the origins of one of the most important and characteristic features of Budapest: the coffeehouse.

Legends, folk tales and hearsay color the origin of the first coffeehouses in most countries. A controversial hero of Vienna's claim to establishing the first coffeehouse in Europe was one Frantz George Koltschitzky, reputedly a Polish nobleman who lived in Vienna. His romantic tale was a greater testimony to his genius for public relations than his actual contribution to coffeehouse history.

The Italians insist that the first coffeehouse in Europe opened in Venice in 1645, but the evidence is inconclusive. It would probably startle Viennese, Italians and Hungarians to hear that the English believe *theirs* the first such establishment in Christendom! A Greek named Pasqua Rosee opened the first coffeehouse in London in 1652. But even before that, in 1650, a man named Jacob opened a coffeehouse in Oxford, at the "Angel in the Parish of St. Peter." A certain redoubtable lady named Dorothy Jones opened one in Boston in 1670; and a few years later, there were coffeehouses in Boston, Philadelphia, New York, Marseilles, Hamburg and throughout Europe. In spite of the lively opposition which coffee invariably aroused wherever it was introduced, within a short time hundreds, even thousands of coffeehouses sprang up and became part of public life.

By 1541, during the Turkish Occupation, there were *Kahva Hanes* (coffeehouses) in several sections of Buda, Óbuda and Pest. A gentleman named Balázs, or Blasius, opened what was supposedly the first Hungarian coffeehouse in Buda in 1714.* For this, the coffeehouse owners' guild honors him as their quasi-patron saint.

* Fifty-one years before the first restaurant opened in Paris.

Improvised food stands in front of the National Museum, 1855

7. Budapest

Early Hungarian coffeehouses were much like the Turkish ones, and did not become characteristically Hungarian for a long time. Noisy, full of thick smoke and bargaining merchants, they provided a meeting place for different nationalities and were really extensions of an Eastern marketplace. During the Turkish Occupation, from about 1535 on, the new drink had been brewed and sold at improvised stands by itinerant vendors, shadow puppeteers, brandy distillers, itinerant dancing masters, musicians and traveling fireworks-makers. Many of the Balkan vendors had learned to make coffee in Turkish villages. There is an intriguing account of their methods in the memoirs of Count Marsigli, an Italian who was a prisoner of the Turks from 1683 to 1685:

. . . The coffee powder must be fine enough to pass through the finest sieve. Water and coffee, in the ratio of ten to one (best proportion for making a perfect coffee drink), are placed in a silver canister, then returned to a very slow fire for the duration of three paternosters. He who likes delicate tastes should add a little sugar, cedar-bark or violet root to the coffee, which sweetens it and makes it aromatic. Coffee made in this way will clear the mind and keep the stomach in order. It will also be very useful for those unfortunates who overuse opium.

In the Turkish villages the coffee vendor had traditionally been a sort of mobile community center. He would choose a centrally located spot, string up rush matting from an old mulberry tree for a windbreaker, rub two stones together to make a fire, then brew his coffee. Around him, the waiting customers sat in a semicircle or on benches placed against the houses on either side of the street. Nearby a wandering barber squatted, ready to shave heads, Turkish fashion. The Medah Baba, or traveling storyteller and living-newspaper, brought vital news and gossip—an essential function in those days when few people could read. But it was the coffee vendor who was the center of interest and the reason for the "instant shopping center."

Certain features of these primitive forerunners survived coffeehouse transplantation to Pest and Buda. For instance, when coffeehouses became an established part of the two cities' lives, the barbershop was always next door. In addition to the ever-ready supply of live tale-bearers, newspapers from all over the world hung on racks for customers to read at leisure.

Blasius' early coffeehouse offered, in addition to coffee and tobacco, a place to play chess, an early form of billiards and various card games. Clay pipes, used with personal "reeds," were rented to the customers. Although gambling, card games and even bets for "anything over two shillings" were barred from early London coffeehouses as too likely to encourage "disputation and dissen-

85

sion," in Hungary (which was very much accustomed to disputation and dissension) they became as much a part of coffeehouse life as the pungent brew
itself.

The coffeehouse never completely lost its Eastern flavor, but slowly developed a new pattern of leisure which began to take on a distinctively Hungarian character. A few parts Turkish marketplace, plus a few parts friendly
(though passionate) gambling *à la française,* plus the Viennese "club" atmosphere, plus the special Hungarian talent for barbed wit, intricate practical
jokes, wild schemes and visionary dreamers, produced a place where *luft-
existence* (making a living "out of air") and genuine greatness could flourish
side by side. In the succeeding two hundred years, if any Hungarian became
either famous or infamous he was likely to be a habitué, or a descendant of a
habitué, of Hungarian coffeehouses.

Although coffeehouses existed in most European cities from the eighteenth
century onwards, the Budapest coffeehouses with their insidiously free spirit
were unique. The growth of the coffeehouse tradition, in fact, became closely
intertwined with the cultural, political and literary life of the nation. The best
in literature, music and theater, along with gorgeously elaborate practical
jokes and marvelous supper dishes, were born within its four walls.

To *Homo caffeaticus*—that peculiarly Budapest specimen—the coffeehouse
was not merely his club but his home, his refuge and his castle; he virtually
lived there. The coffeehouse was the "guildhall of philosophers" and coffee
itself the "drink of the creative intelligentsia."

But there were other heady potions brewed there besides coffee—such as a
will to revolution. In 1848, from the Café Pilvax to the barricades was a
short, straight road lined with poetry and burning nationalism. It was there at
the Pilvax in the middle of the nineteenth century that Petőfi, perhaps the
greatest poet Hungary ever produced, met with his friends, the leading writers
of the day; and it was there he wrote the stirring national ballad which as
much as anything started the 1848 Revolution.

At the very beginning, coffeehouses served only coffee and tobacco. Gradually, however, the bill of fare expanded to include hot chocolate, tea, sweet
wafers and ice cream. In those early coffeehouses everybody sat together at
long, wide tables. Few people realize that the origin of "table d'hôte" is the
host's or innkeeper's table. He sat at the head of the long common table, with
the guests ranged along the two sides. Servants kept a small table, or *guéridon*
(from French *guérir*—to aid) alongside the great table, to aid their service.

Some unknown genius in the eighteenth century suddenly realized the advantages of using *la petite table* or *guéridon,* and dispensing with the large
tables altogether! More people could squeeze into the same space, guests could

86

Sign for a café, 1840, named after the famous Hungarian hero Miklós Zrinyi

choose those they wished to sit with, and since practically no food was served, very little table space was necessary anyway. Thus the little coffeehouse table was born.

Much later, the famous literary cafés had round marble tables with wrought iron legs. (Naturally, circular tables were ideal for reading aloud new works to a circle of interested listeners.) Coffeehouses for ordinary mortals had square tables with solid mahogany legs.

There were more changes in store. Not only the bill of fare, but the ambiance began to expand. Someone thought how nice it would be to remove a wall in fine weather—and lo, the garden-coffeehouse became a reality. Then, with the addition of the ubiquitous gypsy musicians, music enlivened the scene. Coffeehouses became less family oriented and more like night clubs. Soon they decided to compete with restaurants. Much to the dismay of the restaurateurs' guild, in 1827 coffeehouses began to serve cold meats, sausages, cheese, pâtés and other foods.

Next the coffeehouse owners, inevitably, realized there was a growing demand for a late supper. After all, in other European countries a man finished work at six o'clock and then dined at home or at his club. But in Budapest, with its lively night life, he would merely have an afternoon snack at six o'clock, then go off to a cabaret, theater or concert. By eleven he was really hungry and ready for a substantial dinner. The coffeehouses saw their duty clearly: anxious to compete with restaurants for supper business, they, too, added a hot kitchen. Now a man might order dishes of every description— nearly anything one could desire.

During this era, the coffeehouses came full circle: the erstwhile *guéridon*, now covered with a tablecloth, at last became a dinner table! From then on, with complete hot and cold menus, coffeehouses could satisfy every appetite at almost any hour. Which was just as well—since some people never seemed to go home at all.

At the height of coffeehouse culture in its great days, many cafés contained a group of little kingdoms—each literary luminary held court at his own table. Somehow amidst the noise, thick smoke, chatter and distraction, magazines were edited; and poems, stories, plays and novels were written. Against a running counterpoint of arguments, incredibly elaborate word games and refined verbal warfare, journalists, poets and playwrights turned out an astonishing amount of enduring work. In the coffeehouse salons composers like Lehár and Kálmán played their latest scores; melodies which would become internationally famous were heard there for the first time.

That benevolent dignitary, the headwaiter, presided over each establishment as father confessor and unofficial banker, loaning an *ötös* (five-spot) to a hungry writer when necessary; meanwhile, of course, addressing him with undiminished respect. Writers knew they could count on the headwaiter's ready credit, as well as the reassuring aroma of fresh *zsemle** and good coffee, and the stimulating acerbic banter of their confrères. (Karinthy, the great Hungarian humorist, once defined the coffeehouse succinctly as a "place where writers go to drink coffee and eat each other.")

Members of other professions gathered at their own coffeehouses. At the Actors' Market (the Pannonia Kávéház) provincial and unemployed actors waited to see theater directors (many of whom had traveling troupes) hoping for employment. In one corner, an actor declaimed the soliloquy from *Hamlet;* in another, a soprano sang the Countess' entrance from a Jacobi operetta.

For writers, the coffeehouse was their *mise en scène* as well as their home. They drew on the rich fund of lives and characters that moved through these intensely alive social centers: the foppish, monocled Count . . . the old Shylock with a heart of eight-carat gold . . . the voluptuous blonde cashier . . . the would-be poet who was heir to the fertilizer fortune . . . all the little sparrows of the city . . . the girl who rode horseback on a Methuselah of champagne . . . Miklós, Champion Eater of the World, for whom the question was not how many portions he could eat, but how many were available, the only man to have a double-size chair at the coffeehouse and special double sheets at the steambath next door, and who once defended his title by eating a strudel of forty feet—the width of the coffeehouse . . . Berci, the professional love-letter carrier . . . the coffeehouse waiter, whose side job it was to trim off the edges of the playing cards when they got worn and greasy . . .

These and dozens of others furnished countless plays and novels with heroes, heroines and supporting characters. These plays and novels have already outlasted the revolutions.

At the Café Orczy, businessmen arranged every kind of commercial activity from buying and selling tobacco, feathers (for comforters) or false witnesses, to top-level business deals. At the Café King Mátyás, the pig-dealers gathered; at another, the butchers. Still others catered to folk musicians, horse trainers, circus artists or students. Indeed, every legitimate and illegitimate activity found a home in its own coffeehouse.

The mere fact that some patrons never achieved solvency did not in the least impair their status. A man might be a genius without being able to make a living—that was acknowledged. Nowhere was a finer line drawn between respectable occupations and petty rackets—in fact, it was altogether imperceptible.

A businessman's routine included at least three visits to his coffeehouse

* Hard rolls.

Poet in the Café, *drawing by Guncser of the writer Frigyes Karinthy*

every day. (Naturally, if he did a good deal of business there, his visits tended to overlap.) He would arrive first between eight and nine o'clock in the morning to read all the papers over his morning coffee. Then around three in the afternoon he came for his "small black." (At this point, shortly after lunch, retired patrons would nap peacefully in their chairs for a few hours.) In the evening at nine or ten he met his friends there and devoted himself to social life.

Probably the most celebrated coffeehouse of all was the Café New York. In Hungary, when a letter was addressed simply to "New York," it was usually delivered first to the Café New York, on the sound assumption that it was probably intended for someone there anyway.

Coffeehouse scene, turn of the century

Besides, who could be sure that the other New York really existed? About the Café New York there could be no doubt whatever—not only was it the most famous coffeehouse of all, it was undoubtedly the giant of the breed. All the most important and famous writers worked and spent their time there.

Oddly enough, this elaborate coffeehouse was originally financed by an American insurance company. What a long way from the itinerant coffee vendors! As much money, care and talent went into its creation—with post-Baroque columns, neoclassic frescoes and gilded ornaments—as into an opera house. It became the unofficial forum for artists, writers, and influential patrons, and its pre-eminence was unchallenged during the golden age of the coffeehouse.

A larger body of legend has grown up about Molnár, one of the Café New York's habitués, than almost any other single writer. A fan once pleaded with him to meet a dentist friend who had been Molnár's faithful admirer for years. "Tell him," snapped Molnár, "my circle at the New York is complete. I'll let him know when somebody dies."

The beloved theatrical producer, magazine editor, bon vivant, wit and lover of life—my late friend Sándor Ince—was devoted to the pleasures of the table and to the New York while he still lived in Budapest. One day he invited all his friends to a lavish buffet which consisted entirely of the finest Hungarian appetizers, in glorious abundance. Delighted guests found an enormous turntable awaiting them at the Café New York.

On the bottom level were:

Crab Salad as in Zala (*Zalai ráksaláta*) *
Stuffed Morels (*Töltött kucsmagomba*) *
Suckling Pig in Aspic (*Malackocsonya*) *
Green Pepper Stuffed with Meat Salad (*Hideg töltöttpaprika*) *
Goose Crackling Biscuits (*Libatepertő*) *

The second level offered:

Calf's Brains with Eggs (*Velő tojással*) *
Hot Cheese Crackers (*Sajtos izelitö*) *
Stuffed Eggs in Pastry (*Tésztában sült töltött tojás*) *
Mushroom Strudel (*Gombás rétes*) *
Knob Celery Salad (*Zellersaláta*) *
Goose Liver (*Libamáj*) *
Lecsó *

On the third level, circling serenely, were:

Bottles of Alka-Seltzer, Bromo-Seltzer, Brioschi, bicarbonate of soda, etc.

Once Sándor told me what he called "the saddest coffeehouse story." This woeful tale of self-punishment happened at the Café Otthon (what a lovely name for a coffeehouse: the Home Café!).

Every morning Kázmér Kázméry, who cherished his reputation as a mean man, would go to Franciscans' Square to shoo away the pigeons. Then he retired to his "home," the Café Otthon, to play baccarat, as was his custom every day. Usually he was careful not to lose more than four or five forints at a time. But once, caught in a losing streak, he dropped a thousand forints at the table. Utterly disgusted with himself, he decided on a self-punishment so severe he would never forget it. "Let me have fifty forints," he demanded gruffly of the *fizető-pincér* (cashier-headwaiter). With this, he went to Dobos' delicacy shop and bought a fine take-home dinner with all his favorites, starting with duck paté,* stuffed eggs Casino,* croquette *à la palota*,* homemade sausage,* little ham crescents,* beet salad Gellért* and ending with Gerbeaud slice* and Tokaji Aszú.

Back at his hotel, he asked room service to send up their finest linens, glassware and silver. After the waiter had set the table with silver candlesticks, fresh flowers and Bohemian lead crystal goblets, he carefully laid out all the exquisite foods. Then he lit the candles. "Is that satisfactory, sir?" he asked.

* See recipe section for all these recipes.

92

Then, "Sir, sir, have you gone crazy?" For Kázmér Kázméry, after surveying the magnificent, tempting feast, swept everything to the floor. Then he rushed to the little window that opened on the airshaft and, while the waiter watched in horror, threw everything out, cursing himself loudly, "You stupid fool! Oh, oh, duck pâté, glorious sausage, Gerbeaud slice, Tokaji Aszú! Out, out! away with everything! Idiot! Cretin! Maybe this'll teach you to throw away all your money on gambling!"

Coffeehouses were so segregated by types that it's most unlikely that Kázmér Kázméry ever heard of the Café Mókus (squirrel) in ancient Buda (Óbuda—now on the outskirts) which had three distinct kinds of patrons. First the regular, then those who paid either on odd or even days only (though they were there regularly every day) and the third category who didn't pay at all. This third group demanded even more attention and respect than anybody else, so no one would guess that the management was "papering the house." With their elegant manners and aristocratic monocles, they added "tone."

The coffeehouse was in the banquet business, too. Poor people who wanted to invite the whole neighborhood to a wedding but couldn't afford even cold cuts, would serve coffee and *mákos tekercs** for all, in one of the private rooms or in the coffeehouse itself. Such an affair was called a "milk wedding." As the highlight, a professional reader would read aloud to the assembled guests the list of wedding gifts. Judging by the list, one would have thought this was a royal wedding, such were the astounding jewels and other riches. But what really happened was that for a modest extra fee the reader "embroidered" a little—and when it came to imagination, no expense was spared. Thus the present of a rolling pin was magically transformed into a signed Louis XIV ebony masterpiece. The simplest object became an heirloom. Since everything sounded better graced with a French name, even the reader himself was called, elegantly, M. Chamaisse.

A certain freeloader, who happened to wander in while a reading was in progress at one such "milk wedding," was utterly disgusted by the pretensions of the gift list. Adjusting his monocle disdainfully, he complained to the manager, "Really, if you insist on letting in such low-class people, you're going to lose the better people like me. Do you realize I can trace my ancestry back to St. Stephen?"

The manager smiled apologetically and murmured, "Well, my dear fellow, times are hard. I'd rather have a plain cow that gives milk than a pedigreed ass that doesn't."

In spite of political and social upheavals, the "steadies" lived, loved and laughed in the world of the coffeehouse, and even a world war was only a

* See recipe section.

93

distant murmur beyond its walls. Some faces disappeared for years, perhaps forever, but coffeehouse life went on exactly as it always had. If people came back, they were accepted matter-of-factly, as though they had never been away.

One such habitué, Imre Kálmán, the famed operetta composer, was a prisoner for years in a Russian prison camp during World War I. When he got back to Budapest, the first thing he did, naturally, was to visit the Café New York. When he walked in, the headwaiter called out casually, "The usual coffee-in-a-cup for Mr. Kálmán." (It was fashionable, then, to drink coffee in a glass, but the waiter remembered that Mr. Kálmán preferred the old-fashioned cup.) Nobody thought it necessary to mention that this was the first time in five years the headwaiter had laid eyes on him. The world outside might not have existed at all. The only true reality was the coffeehouse itself.

What a curiously complete, self-contained little world it was! For its faithful habitués it was workshop, womb, refuge, court and battlefield. There the elders of the tribe thrashed out the problems of the world, undisturbed, and the younger struggled for entry and jockeyed for status.

Social magnet, intellectual playground, whetstone of wit, goad and comfort —it was full of kindness, laughter, cruelty and the assorted consolations of work, love, pastry, coffee, literature and legend. The marble-topped tables, crystal chandeliers and great plate-glass windows are still there. But this special world has all but vanished into nostalgic history, except perhaps for an occasional, elegantly dressed, carefully barbered old gentleman wandering into his old habitat. The golden, bittersweet world of coffeehouse society has vanished forever.

Ave atque—vale.

Outdoor terrace of a Budapest café, about 1910

☆ 8 ☆

NORTHERN HUNGARY
(ÉSZAK—MAGYARORSZÁG)

FROM the Danube above Budapest, up to the border of the Soviet Union, the scene is picturesque: rolling countryside covered with forests and the ruins of a castle perched on a hilltop; in the valleys colorful little villages and ancient towns.

In the northern valleys of the Mátra hills live the Palóc people, one of the most complex and ethnically pure groups in the entire country. Many of the villages have remained as they were in medieval times, their food, customs and clothing a direct link with the Hungarian past.

The three Kabar tribes of the Khazars joined the Hungarians in the ninth century and came to present-day Hungary with them. The entire group lived almost exclusively by hunting and later were named by the local Slavs *Polovetz,* meaning "hunter." The Hungarians changed this into the name they are known by today: *Palóc.*

The Hungarians, from the ninth to the fifteenth centuries, used outdoor open-fire cookery to a great extent. A description of the "baked in ashes" technique used in the Palóc area barely forty years ago reads like a Stone-Age document:

When the rye is almost ripe but can still be squeezed between the fingers, the woman of the house cuts down as much as she needs, takes it home on her back and, on the so-called fire bench, makes a fire from dried twigs, singes the rye sheaf until the seeds pucker and the rest burns. Then what remains she pulverizes in a wooden trough, blows off the skin, salts the rest and powders it in a wooden mortar and pestle. She kneads this mass with a little water and makes fist-size balls of it, baking them over the fire. If one large pancake is made from the mass and it is put directly on the ashes, it becomes a legendary ash-baked *pogácsa,* which every Hungarian child learns about from countless folktales.

The next stage of development was baking on a heated greased stone block and combining the mixture with potatoes.

Other ancient customs prevail, too: the collecting and eating of bird eggs, for instance. (An interesting sidelight: the Palóc people even fed their pigs on bird eggs and fish.) Preserving fish through smoking, drying and salting, to be put away for the lean years, was started in the early days of the kingdom. So was the drying and smoking of farmer's cheese, wrapped in paper. This custom still prevails in certain variations in northern Hungary. The Palóc make sausage shapes out of the tightly wrapped cheese, and after smoking it they hang it from the so-called "master beam."

They like to add a unique touch to important occasions. The Palóc "Joy Cake," made for weddings, is an elaborately braided yeast dough, shaped in such a way that in the center of a giant pretzel there is space for a bottle filled with honeyed brandy.

The beech and pine forests of the Mátra are among the best hunting preserves in Europe, especially for deer, wild boar and the curved-horn mouflon.

Another colorful jewel in northern Hungary is the Matyóföld. Around the town of Mezőkövesd and the village of Boldog (Happy), the people must have been very insistent when God gave out artistic talents. The flowing sleeves of the young lads; the headdresses of the girls, often outshining Balinese tiaras; the dazzling aprons worn by both men and women; the decoration of the eating utensils, tablecloths, kitchens and just about everything which surrounds them, reminds one of the *Bauhaus Manifesto,* which stated that art should not be in museums but part of our daily lives.

The reconstructed Gothic-Baroque town of Eger is the home of the Egri Bikavér—the famous "Bulls' Blood." This wine is celebrated in colorful legends, owing at least in part to its fanciful name. It is doubtful that in medieval times bulls' blood was actually added to the wine to give it its dark black-red color. There are other explanations—all entertaining although just as questionable. For instance, one popular tale tells of a Turkish soldier who was caught drunk by the Turkish Occupation authorities. As Moslems are forbidden to drink wine, the local pasha condemned the soldier to die. The soldier's last request was that he might talk with the pasha personally.

"Sire," he said, "this was not an alcoholic beverage but the blood of a bull which I drank. As my last request on earth, I implore you to taste it."

97

The pasha could not refuse such a wish and reluctantly tasted the brew. Thereupon, he not only pardoned the soldier—so the story goes—but drank eternal brotherhood with him. Such was the power of the Egri Bikavér! Although the fable is amusing, it probably has very little to do with the origin of the name, which may simply have been a poetic reference to its color.

The three grapes used for the wine are the Kadarka (70 percent), Burgundy (15 percent) and Médoc Noir (15 percent). Certain vintages can be aged even longer than the French burgundies, and they acquire a "nose" that is a cross between cloves and vanilla.

Other Eger wines are the white dessert wine Leányka (Dear Little Girl) and the Egri Kadarka-Siller.

At the time of the Turkish Occupation, intricate underground passages were secretly cut into the soft volcanic rock by Eger's inhabitants. Later, wine cellars were added, which turned out to be ideal for keeping and maturing wine. Visiting these wine cellars and tasting a glass of wine is a memorable experience.

"It was a fine holiday—the city fathers of Eger decided the date of the harvest for the end of September. The forests were turning red and so were the grapes in the vineyards. The city divided itself into two sections; while one part harvested, the other stayed in the city to guard the houses." So goes a description by the chronicler of the City of Eger in the eighteenth century.

Up to this time, during grape harvest even court activities were suspended. In some towns as much as half of the population made a living out of viniculture: young and old joined in the work. Since those days, very little has changed on wine harvest day in the small Hungarian vineyards, even though in the large State cooperatives mechanization is the order of the day.

The whole family, including the old people and distant kinsmen, goes to the vineyards. Some families don't hire help; their neighbors with their relatives from far and near pitch in. Everyone comes with a big basket to help gather the grapes, and the same basket is used to take home grapes. No one idles: not the mistress of the house, whose pink plump hands never know work during the year; nor the doctor of medicine or law; nor the priest, whose hand, accustomed only to bless and be kissed, seizes the buckets to pick the grapes during harvest. Yet it is a holiday, because no one supervises the picking—nobody works more or faster than he wants to. The women gather the grapes, the men prepare the wine tubs, scouring the barrels with boiling water and walnut leaves. Anyone who drops a grape has to pick it up and special care is taken not to drop dry leaves into the *puttony* (bucket), because they tend to soak up the must.

When the grape tub is filled, the wine master washes his feet with warm

Grape harvest festivities

water, rolls up his trousers and jumps into the treading tub to stomp on the grapes. The contraption is a very simple one: A hole is dug in the earth and a wooden tub placed in it; on top of this is placed another tub with holes in the bottom. This second tub is kept filled with grapes; as one batch is pressed, new ones are added. On top of the grapes a loose-woven sacklike material—something like burlap—is laid for the treaders to stamp on. Usually they are offered a glass of good wine to improve their mood for "dancing"; and as they continue, people around them keep urging them on to an even wilder tempo.

The *törkö* (*marc* in French—the skins, seeds and stems of pressed grapes) is continuously removed and resqueezed in a wooden press. The experts keep sniffing the must, making judgments and remarks. The barrels slowly fill with must. It's quite a trick to make bungs for them out of grass! Then the horse-drawn wagons arrive to pick up the barrels. If the weather is warm, they take out the bung and put in a "pipe" made of the dry stem of the sunflower plant, which in Hungary grows ten feet tall. A couple of feet of stem are inserted into the hole and the rest bent outside. Thus on warm days the must can ferment and still be transported; for at least the keg does not explode when, on the bad roads, the must is shaken.

Nearby, the women are cooking mutton stew with millet (*juhhúsos kása*),* and after a prayer by the master of the vineyard, everyone sits down at the long tables to eat. Wine, of course, accompanies this welcome repast for the tired troops; and the children drink the still mild, sweet must. Lunch over, everyone returns to work, an occasional song lightening their labors.

At sundown, they finish the work and start the real festivities—eating, drinking, dancing, guns popping, bagpipes sounding, practical jokes—allowing themselves more freedom than at any other time of the year. Young men put live frogs down the backs of girls' dresses; fireworks, homemade noise-makers, even little cannon are pressed into service for revelry. The vineyard owner keeps offering wine to the guests, friends and workmen and getting fancy replies such as, "I don't drink wine—only the juice of the grapes." The wine-press houses are like free restaurants, vying with each other to attract friends and strangers.

It is an ancient custom that the harvesters, when finished, weave either an enormous wreath or a huge cluster of grape leaves and grapes which is usually carried on decorated poles by four or more persons.† The procession consists of a band followed by the harvesters, then the couple that finished gathering grapes last; finally come two flag bearers, flanked by girls dressed in white with grape leaves in their hair. The pole bearers also wear elaborate grape wreaths.

* See recipe on page 257.
† See illustration on page 99.

Sometimes the *vincellér* (wine master or overseer) dons a fancy hat, hangs a grape wreath on his right arm, and holds in his left hand a *szüretifa* (harvest cane), a walking stick decorated with grapes and flowers. The entire procession, including the harvesters, proceeds from the hill vineyard to the vintner, singing, shouting and stopping every now and then to accept a glass of wine offered to them. Finally, they arrive at the vintner's village home; and the *vincellér*, lifting his hat, delivers a short, flowery speech, giving the wreath to the mistress of the house and the cane to the master. In some villages, they hang the grape-cluster in the ceiling of the "White Room," after which the *mulatás* (merrymaking) really gets under way in earnest. Often the harvest starts by "capturing" the boss (currently, the head of the cooperative) and tying him up with young shoots of the grapevine. He is released only if he pays the ransom by serving wine to everyone.

Humorous contests color the festivities, for instance, the vineyard-watchman play, which goes like this: The garden of the restaurant, or the yard where the festivities take place, is transformed into a vineyard by hanging grapes. Half of the men become the watchmen and the other half fill the role of *betyár* (highway robbers), who try to steal the grapes. If they are caught, a fake court metes out the sentences.

Many of the dances are clever enough to have been choreographed by Balanchine. My favorite is the Hoop Dance, which uses the metal hoops of the barrels with great imagination. The customs represented in these dances are often an acting out of proud or kidding quotations from the past, such as those that ridicule Turkish figures or Habsburg soldiers.

In other villages the harvesters parade on horseback and four husky lads carry the "wine king," sitting on a litter made of wine barrels. Oddly, the wine king is always a little boy with a paper crown on his head, a moustache made of corn husks and a beard of the sheepskin *suba,* or cape.

At nightfall, the gypsies arrive and start playing the *hallgató*—the slow, quiet songs. Later on they will play the fast, furious *csárdás* for dancing. One traditional slow one goes like this:

> The grapes will soon be ripe
> And the vines will be orphaned
> You will be orphaned too my little angel
> Because I must march with the Army.

Many vineyard owners sell their own wine in the villages or towns. If the wine comes from garden vineyards, the sign outside the vineyard owner's door is a pine branch. If, however, it comes from the hill vineyards, ivy is put outside the door. Since Budapest itself has no grape harvest, restaurants and taverns, to let the population know that the new wine is available, display colored paper and other insignia on their shingles and in their windows, and there is a carnival atmosphere in the streets.

Out of the four main ingredients prescribed for happiness, according to an old Hungarian slogan—wine, wheat, peace and a beautiful wife—wine is mentioned first. Until quite recently, the entire country's welfare depended on the quality and quantity of the grape and wheat harvest. The harvesting was a loud, colorful, important festival, and happily it still retains the same joyous spirit throughout the country.

Perhaps Hungary has the only national anthem that contains a stanza thanking God for its country's wines. The 1823 poem by Ferenc Kölcsey that became the national anthem contains the lines:

> On the grapevines of Tokaj
> Thou dripped nectar . . .

In fact, the whole history of Hungary is interwoven with its complex culture of wines, and nowhere is this more evident than around the hills of Tokaj, which lie in the northeastern part of Hungary near the Czechoslovakian border. Tokaj's history is rich in melodrama, intrigue and adventure. It produces, of course, the most famous of all Hungarian wines since the fifth century, yet it became world famous only in the sixteenth century—thanks to a papal pun.

The Council of Trent in 1551 was one of the most important and well-publicized events of the century. Every nation sent ranking dignitaries, and the whole world watched and waited breathlessly while key theological questions were hotly debated (for instance, how many angels could dance on the head of a pin?). In the evenings, delegates were feted at lavish dinners. One night, at a dinner where the finest Italian and French wines were served, the Hungarian representative—the Bishop of Pécs—proudly placed a Tokay wine from Tállya on the table for the Pope to taste. Pope Julius III was so delighted by the new wine that he instantly improvised a pun in pentameter: *Summum Pontificem Talia Vino decent.* Now *Talia* can mean either "that sort" or the name of the town from which the wine came. Thus the pun meant either, "This type of wine belongs at the papal table" or "The wine from Tállya belongs at the papal table." Both meanings were highly flattering to the new wine. Endorsement from high places was at least as effective in those days as it is now. The fame of the Tállya wine began to spread.

Eighteenth-century engraving of Tokaj

What was there about Tokay wines that inspired papal puns? (Or was it simply a mild form of pontifical one-upmanship?) At any rate, when Benedict XIV received a sample from Empress Maria Theresa, he promptly punned: *"Benedicta sit terra quae te germinavit, benedicta mulier, qui te misit, benedictus ego qui te bibo."* Or, "Blessed be the land which grew you, blessed be the lady who sent you, and I am blessed, too, who drinks you." (The pun here involves his name, Benedict, which also means "blessed.")

Since we are presenting worthy recommendations, we should not leave out the gentleman with the impeccable pedigree, Monsieur Voltaire, who said:

> . . . *Et du Tokai la liqueur jaunissante*
> *En chatouillant les fibres de cerveaux*
> *Y porte un feu qui s'exhale en bons mots*
> *Aussi brillants que la liqueur légère*
> *Qui monte et saute et mousse au bord du verre* . . .

And the yellowish liqueur of Tokay,
While caressing the fibers of the brain,
Carries a fire that generates witticism

As dazzling as the liqueur is light,
Which rises and leaps and sparkles at the edge of the glass . . .

In medieval times, when people spoke of Tokaj, they said, "It begins with a tent, and ends with a tent." The two "tents" were the twin volcanic cones which flanked each end of the seventeen-mile chain of gentle hills. In between lies a characteristically Hungarian wine-growing district, producing wines as unique and flavorful as the country itself. Naturally everybody wanted to claim the name of "Tokay," and for centuries bitter controversies raged over precisely which villages had the right to call their wines *Tokaj* (or "Tokay," as it is called outside of Hungary). Two counties in the northeastern part of Hungary claimed the Tokaj vineyards. At last all controversy was settled once and for all when the twenty-five villages of the *Tokaj-Hegyalja* ("at the feet of the hill") were granted the right to use the name.

A certain mysticism and hyperbole has crept into descriptions of the magical volcanic soil. King Matthias Corvinus' chronicler, Marzio Galeotto, to whom we owe thanks for many fascinating accounts of the period, wrote in his work, *Epitome Rerum Hungaricorum*, that the earth of the Tokaj hills contained gold! (In point of fact the vine itself does have golden tendrils as thick as straw.) He was not the only observer to be dazzled. A naïve German naturalist claimed he found "gold seeds" in the Tokaj grapes. Later, when Paracelsus, the famous Swiss alchemist, visited Hungary, he failed to find any gold in or around the grapes, but he wrote, "The Tokaj grapevine is the most magnificent product of weather, soil and minerals—certainly worth its weight in gold."

A certain Thomas McMullen, who published a *Handbook of Wines* in 1852 in New York, writes somewhat disapprovingly of the fantastically high prices people were willing to pay for Tokay as an "example of the caprice of taste or fashion in wine." An ex-emperor of Austria was known to pay as high as seven ducats a bottle, and at the Marquis of Queensberry's sale in London, the Tokay from his cellars "realized the extravagant sum of $50 per bottle—about $10 per glass!" (This in 1852, when the dollar certainly had many times the buying power of today. These bottles, by the way, held only a bit more than a pint!)

The legends of Tokay flavor and its efficacy as elixir and medicine are so numerous that it is impossible to discount them all. Mr. McMullen claimed that the Tokay wines

when new, are of a brownish-yellow color, and exhale an odor which has been compared to the smell of the pumpernickel. It has so peculiar a flavor of the aromatic kind, and is so luscious that the taste is not easily forgotten; it also has a slight harshness, perceptible to the palate, which is highly esteemed in some parts of Europe—its durability is very great, some of it having kept good for a century. It is highly odoriferous.

The legendary *aszúbor* can last as long as two or three hundred years. *Bor* means wine in Hungarian. *Aszú* is an ancient word for the long drying on the vine which produces a "noble rot" (*pourriture noble*). Homer described this transformation in the Odyssey.

The *Botrytis cinerea* fungus attacks the grape in the warm, humid air, and it shrivels into a kind of raisin. During this process, part of the acidity disappears, and a strange, richly fruity flavor develops, along with a miraculous aroma. (The Rheingau vineyards are also famous for this grape and the wine produced from it.) The local poet-philosophers explain that the remnants of the summer heat are caught between the two ranges of the Carpathian Mountains, so the region gets a long, lingering Indian summer that ripens the *aszú* grapes.

The vintage is delayed as long as possible, so the fruit may attain its fullest ripeness. The harvest officially begins on October 28, Simon Judas Day, and ends at the very beginning of December, often under snow. By that time, a great number of the grapes have become shriveled or half dried. (These are called *Trockenbeeren* in German.) The *aszúbor* is a combination of regular Tokay wine and *aszú* grape, which fortifies and gives the wine its heavy, luscious quality. Its strength depends on how many caskfuls of *aszú* grapes are added to barrels of ordinary must. (Generally the relation is three to five.) Naturally, the quality will also depend·on the quality of the *aszú* grape itself, the must, and other vintage factors.

When the wine was produced from a perfect vintage, the Tokaj vintners would always mark the wine barrels with the initials C.O.S. This signified *Colorem, Odorem et Saporem*—still today the best capsule definition of the ingredients of a good wine. There are six basic types of Tokay (all but the last named signify techniques): (1) Aszú, (2) Szamorodni, (3) Forditás, (4) Máslás, (5) Eszencia, (6) Ordinárium.

This is how the *aszúbor* is made: First the grapes are collected in butts or portable casks; each of these—called a *puttony*—holds about six gallons. Then the casks of *aszú* grapes are added to the barrels of ordinary must, and the grapes are trampled by young girls in the time-honored manner: heavy-footed and lighthearted, with much singing and gaiety. (Local wags quip that girls will be fired only if they sit down on the job.) The completely liquid mass, called *aszú* dough, is then collected, put into another vat, and a certain amount of must poured over it—depending on how many *puttonyos* of wine there will be. There it stays from twelve to forty-eight hours (depending on the weather) and is thoroughly stirred several times a day. Then the workers pour it into fine-meshed sacks and again trample on it; the liquid flows into barrels below. Finally, the long fermentation is allowed to begin in these barrels, a process which, because of the high sugar content of the *aszú,* may take as long as several years.

The Tokaj vintners developed a special barrel—called the *Gönci hordó*—which holds about thirty-five gallons. Some airspace is always left at the top of the barrel; perhaps this accounts for the fresh fragrance of pumpernickel exuded by the new wine.

Tokaj Aszú was first made in 1650 in the vineyards of Zsuzsanna Loránt-ffy, the widow of the Prince of Transylvania. (The Prince's family name—he was George Rákóczi—is familiar to Westerners largely because of Berlioz's "Rákóczi March.") The whole process has hardly changed at all since then.

No one knows why this particular wine can last as long as two hundred years, but this miracle is unquestionably true. In the 1930's the Fukier Company of Warsaw owned over three hundred bottles of the 1706 vintage. A wine blender in the Tokaj state cellars once told me that he had tasted a Tokay wine from the pre-phylloxera* year of 1874—when nature probably wanted to show off her glory before going into eclipse. He recalled it as an almost supernatural experience; oddly enough, it had the aroma of chocolate!

Szamorodni wine is made from grape clusters containing both *aszú* and ordinary grapes, pressed together. The Szamorodni wine, unfortunately, is likely to be somewhat uneven, since in some years the number of grapes within the cluster which become *aszú* is very low. The taste may range from very sweet and heavy to almost dry.

The dry Szamorodni, when perfect, is the classic of all dry wines. Its superb qualities develop during a lengthy aging in barrels, which, as in the case of the Aszú, takes several years. The wine, during this period, gradually becomes thinner, its acidity increases and the sugar content can no longer cover inferior characteristics, if any. That is why it is so difficult to produce a perfect dry Szamorodni. Golden brown in color, the dry Szamorodni taste is a cross between St. John's bread and the crust of fine, fresh yeast cake.

Tokay Fordítás gets its name from an archaic word meaning "turning-in." When the girls have finished trampling the *aszú* grapes, the men "turn-in" (pour) the leftover *marc* (husks) into a huge vat, and pour ordinary Tokay over it. After mixing the whole brew well, they leave it alone for five hours,

* Phylloxera is a plant louse that devastated the European vineyards beginning in the 1860's. This pest made its destructive way into Hungary around 1875.

then place it in trampling sacks (as with the *aszúbor*) and press the dripping mass again. This procedure can produce good wine, although not of the same quality as an Aszú.

Tokaj Máslás derives from an archaic word for "copy." The same process is followed as for the Fordítás, but young wine is substituted for must. For hundreds of years both Fordítás and Máslás have been favorites of the Poles, and almost the whole yearly vintage is bought by Poland.

Either in a year when the grape has no *aszú,* or else by simply using clusters from which the *aszú* grapes have been removed, the vintners make a table wine called Ordinárium, which is usually a little rough, slightly spicy and decidedly on the ordinary side.

Some sage once remarked that all great pleasures must be diluted slightly lest their intensity render them unbearable. This unknown philosopher probably never tasted the Eszencia, which is the essence of essences, being made of nothing but *aszú* grapes. The sugar content is so high it sometimes takes five years to ferment.

Unlike the other types, the Eszencia is never trampled. The collected *aszú* grapes are tenderly placed in a vat, at the bottom of which is a small opening usually fitted with a goose quill. Through this tiny aperture, the natural weight of the heavy grapes presses the sweet liquid—drop by drop—through the quill into a basin. The syrupy liquor thus collected contains about 50 percent sugar. When it finally becomes wine, in its own sweet time, the alcohol content will still be only about 6 to 8 percent. After at least twenty-five years, the Eszencia becomes a concentrated elixir, guaranteed to gild a winter afternoon with a rare interior glow.

That worthy wine merchant, Charles Walter Berry, has written with both reverence and a quaintly extravagant enthusiasm in his *Viniana* of the myriad wonders of "Essence of Tokay," as he calls it:

"It has been borne in upon me in a very convincing manner that this wine has a most wonderful effect in cases of extreme illness. As you will perceive it has a minimum of alcohol, yet I can assure you that it contains as its hidden virtue a maximum nourishment. . . . it should be jealously hoarded up for use in cases of illness, pulmonary troubles in particular." He then goes on to declare that the venerable old Pope Leo XIII lingered on to such a great age mostly because of the famous Essence, sent directly to him by the Austrian Emperor. "I believe I am correct in saying that for the last six or eight weeks, nothing passed his lips save this immortal liquor." He also declares that King Edward VII, whose coronation had to be postponed because of illness, was completely restored by the Tokay. He then, quite immoderately, quotes from letters he has received from sufferers who have assured him that the Tokay cured patients afflicted with such varied ills as diabetes, gangrene, dangerous confinements, senility, lung trouble—even a child dying of double pneumonia.

This "most cherished possession of Emperors, Kings and Princes" is one of the

> indescribable mysteries of Nature. All I can tell you is that it is rich in phosphates of magnesia and lime, besides which it contains ethers and other valuable properties. . . . I am no chemist. All that I am telling you is, I can assure you, from personal experience. . . . A medical man, and a friend who had sneered at the suggestion to try this wine in a case of extreme illness, actually put a little in a man's mouth, a patient who was none other than his father-in-law, when he really had come to the conclusion that he had passed away. My friend told me afterwards that the effect was like an electric shock—the old man is alive today, and believe me, this is no fairy tale.

And so on, all from the astonished pen of Mr. Berry. He also ventured a lugubrious prediction: "It is sad to think," he wrote in 1929, "that there is very little probability of the Essence of Tokay being made in the future, the celebrated estates belonging to the Royal and Imperial House and others . . . having passed into other and very different hands."

Fortunately, his pessimism was unwarranted—the Eszencia continues to be produced, despite wars, revolutions, and innumerable changes of fortune; the immortal liquor survives, though it rarely reaches the retail market.

Since today's taste has swung to dry wines, the full-bodied dessert wines have been rather neglected. But fashions being fickle, fortune may eventually again favor the Hungarians when sweet wines and fruity wines become, as they were for hundreds of years, the preferred dinner beverage.

It is pleasant to imagine this year's vintage sweetening the future, several hundred years from now, when other certitudes have long since crumbled to dust.

Pious Words in Praise of Wine

Borocskát dicsérő ájtatos szavak (1941)

Stomach-healing
All spice little wine,
I draw from you now
the Holy Ghost's fire,
like a pious soul draws
peace after prayer.
On this hot summer day
when I'm sodden with sweat,
during the rich meal only you
quench my beastly thirst,
you cool my glowing forehead,
you aid happy digestion
by your tongue-tingling taste.
I feel already how gay
and light I become both
in body and soul, all compassion
for the world—a man who
pardons everybody.
Only a quietly carousing, pleasuring
friend can praise you so steadfastly:
stay with me always, on my table
be the most festive ornament
and when I die at last,
upon my coffin I want a keg
filled with you for consolation,
so that on Resurrection Day
I should have something to fill my glass
if a good-tempered God should by
any chance seat me at His table.

JÓZSEF BERDA (*translated by Paul Tabori*)

�֍ 9 �֍

TRANSYLVANIA
(ERDÉLY)

TRANSYLVANIA has been inhabited by Rumanians, Hungarians and Germans for many, many years. It depends on which "commercial" you read: according to one theory, it was originally Rumanian because of the Roman legionnaires who stayed there and founded their kingdom. The Hungarians have equally attractive theories, which, of course, change with the political winds. The Germans who came from Alsace and were called *szász* probably arrived in the twelfth century, but even this is debatable because Germanic tribes existed there before the Hungarians arrived in the ninth century.

It would be difficult to argue the point, however, that the *székely* people, as Hungarian Transylvanians are called, are the most colorful and gastronomically interesting group in the area. Their origin is lost in the mist of the chaotic eighth to eleventh centuries, but they are probably descendants of Hun-Bulgarian tribes. Quite different in looks, in life-style and even in dialect from the rest of the Hungarians, living in forests and mountains populated with fairy-tale images, they are droll and fantastic figures. They live in a world that is one part reality, one part poetry and one part self-created mythology. You can "feel" them instantly listening to much of the music of Bartók; and if you are fortunate enough to hear the great cellist Janos Starker play Kodály's *Solo Sonata,* you will instantly understand the spirit of the *székely* people. Even though they share the same ideas about cooking as the rest of Hungary, because of their special historical and geographical advantages and no doubt unusual talents, they have developed and kept a remarkable culinary entity. To my mind, it's the most interesting part of the Hungarian kitchen.

Transylvania today is part of Rumania (since the 1920 Treaty of Trianon). With the wholesale nationalistic trend prevalent in today's Rumania, I am

Transylvanian peasant girl in front of carved portal

afraid the Hungarian-Transylvanian-*székely* folk art and cuisine may soon disappear.

The ingredients used for cooking are often different from those found in the heart of Hungary, and so are the resulting dishes. Cottage cheese, sour cream and even the meat have a different taste in Transylvania. The main difference is caused by herbs and spices like tarragon and *csombor* (summer savory), which are used almost as freely in Transylvania as paprika is used in central Hungary.

Sheep herding is one of the most important parts of the husbandry, and as you'll see in the Transylvanian recipes, sheep's cheese can be used in just about any part of the meal. A special stew called *tokány** is of Rumanian origin and has innumerable variations, as does *puliszka*† (a cornmeal porridge). Flax, eaten as a vegetable and flavored with sour cream and lemon, is just as typically Transylvanian as the various grape leaves stuffed with meats and vegetables.

Similar conditions produce similar results. Wherever there were forests, the people came up with a cross-cut of the tree to be used as a platter (trencher). In Transylvania, the *fatányéros* or wooden platter is a glorified mixed grill. The only vegetable addition is *cika,*‡ the core of the cabbage head pickled together with sauerkraut and served as part of the wooden platter presentation.§

The "Baking Bell," which was made from pottery or sheet metal, is also of Transylvanian origin. One name for it was *bujdosó,* or "fugitive," probably because each village had only a few, which were passed from house to house as they were needed. This baking bell was hung directly over the fire. When both the fire and the bell were hot enough for baking, the food was placed on a grill on the fire, or on a stone over the fire, and covered with the bell: a portable oven that really worked.

In a few Transylvanian coffeehouses you can still get buffalo milk with your coffee. It is worthwhile to try this rich, creamlike milk with a high butterfat content.

Two Transylvanian desserts that became national favorites are the *vargabéles*|| and the chimney cake.¶ Another cake specialty is the *ordás-lepény,* made from a yeast dough with a very thick stuffing of farmer's cheese, sour cream and dill, with a latticework of strips of dough decorating its top.

* See recipe on page 280.
† See recipe on page 303.
‡ See recipe on page 282.
§ See description on page 115.
|| See recipe on page 387.
¶ See recipe on page 398.

9. Transylvania

The very intelligent approach of the Transylvanians to cooking resulted in the most detailed descriptions of foods, methods and celebrations in all Hungarian literature. All types of festivities have been recorded in great detail for the past several hundred years, including an unusual and colorful part of the Transylvanian wedding ceremony, the giving away of the *prémes* (furry twig). It was also called a "bridal cake tree," *menyasszonykalácsfa,* or "life tree," or *életfa.* Everything placed on it symbolically expressed a good wish for the young couple. The curious name "furry twig" probably originated from the very elaborate decorations—frogs, braids and such, imitating the designs with which the holiday dresses were decorated—that trimmed the tree.

The preliminaries started with the picking of just the right size and shape branch, always done by the men. The important thing was to have a main or central post with many branches going upwards, almost like an umbrella which was turned inside out by the strong winds. The men cleaned it, took off the bark and gave it to the womenfolk.

The next step was making the base or "new skin" for the *prémes,* a fritter-type dough, the *csöröge,** which was stretched out quite thick and cut into strips, which were wrapped around the branch completely covering it. Or the branch could be dipped in a pancake dough, a heavy *palacsinta appareil.* If the branch was of a manageable size, it was fried in a big iron or pottery kettle; but if it was very large, it was put into the oven and dry-roasted with the cakes.

A large cake served as a base for the tree. Then came the decorations made of colored ribbons, little fruits, ring-shaped cakes and all kinds of frills made by both adults and children. Sometimes the more artistic families kneaded heads and arms out of the dough, and sticking them into the strategic places made the piece look like a human being. A pouch might be hung on this figure, to be filled with money intended for the bride. For this elaborate showpiece, variations were virtually unlimited: a boy or a girl figure or both; tree leaves made from the dough and attached to the twigs; little roses; a harvest of small gifts.

Usually it was brought to the bride's house on the morning of the marriage together with the other wedding gifts. A lucky bride might receive as many as fifteen or twenty *prémes.* These contraptions played an important part in the procession to the new home of the newlyweds. Folk poetry had a field day and the rhymes which were supposed to accompany this gift were plentiful. Some of the elaborate and formalized rituals put the medieval Spanish court's etiquette to shame.

At the end of the wedding dinner, the *prémes* were put on a table and

* See recipe on page 359.

Bridal cake tree, an interpretation by István Engel-Teván

everyone broke off a twig and ate the crust happily. But the more sentimental brides kept the prettier ones for many years. Too bad this colorful practice has largely disappeared.

A much more essential, though brutal, ritual, that of the killing of the pig (*disznótor*), is still very much with the Transylvanians and virtually with all provincial households in Hungary. The fattening of the pig starts in the summer and is completed by December or January. These are the months generally for the *disznótor*. *Tor* is an ancient Hungarian word meaning the wake held for the dead. Strangely enough, this ritual is called "the pig wake."

Early in the morning before the activity begins, it is traditional to drink hot, spiced, honeyed wine with *kalács** (a kind of coffeecake), or *pogácsa.*† Then comes the actual killing of the pig. By eleven o'clock, when it is time for breakfast, everybody is ready to feast on sour potato or chicken soup, a *paprikás* made from the brains of the porker (just as the ancient hunters made it), roast pork fillet with pickles or a layered cabbage as in Kolozsvár,‡ and golden dumpling cake,§ all accompanied, of course, by wine.

The Honorable Pig's earthly remains are carefully ground, cut up, shaped into sausages, and made into many forms and textures by the men. The women finish melting the lard while the men visit the nearby wine cellars, taking with them, naturally, some of the fresh sausages and *hurkas* (liver‖ and blood sausages), a bit of the roast and some doughnuts. After proper sampling and criticism of the wines, they fill a few demijohns and return to the house in time for dinner.

A long table is laid with crusty, balloon-like breads, pickled peppers, cabbage salad,¶ paprika of varying strengths (from coarse and hot to sweet), and the meal begins. First comes a soup made of the pig's snout or of the traditional *orja;*§ then the ears with horseradish, the lean part of the porker steamed with fresh cabbage, a variety of roasts from different parts and at least half a dozen kinds of fresh sausages. Everybody drinks and sings traditional folk songs, sometimes to the accompaniment of gypsy musicians—crying with laughter and laughing with tears—telling the "wine-born" truth about things important and dreaming curly fibs about unimportant ones.

Practical jokes spice the proceedings. Here is one story that I heard from the father of a girlfriend in the city of Arad: A Sámuel Pap, swineherder, was always hungry. During a big wedding feast, his neighbor noticed that he kept

* See recipe on page 396.
† See recipe on page 347.
‡ See recipe on page 289.
§ See recipe on page 399.
‖ See recipe on page 232.
¶ See recipe on page 331.
*§ See recipe on page 160.

Designs for Transylvanian portals

putting pieces of roast chicken and pretzels into his pocket. The neighbor took a big demijohn of wine and promptly started pouring it into the same pocket. When the screaming and laughing subsided he announced: "Since Sámuel Pap keeps his pocket well fed, it is only fair that I should keep it well supplied with drinks." The wine was dripping all night from his pocket, but all was forgiven.

At midnight everybody helps to hang the meat, sides of bacon, ham and sausages in the smokehouse. The sausages are sometimes very sophisticated and subtle-tasting, flavored with juniper berries, wine, marjoram and caraway seeds. The next morning, samples are sent to the neighbors and relatives, while at home everybody eats the *disznókocsonya** (pork in aspic) sprinkled with crudely crushed cherry peppers.

In the restaurants of Budapest or other cities, a simplified basic *disznótor* can be ordered, usually consisting of several kinds of fresh sausages and perhaps a *flekken,*† with a garnishing of peppered rice and assorted pickled vegetables.

The beginning of the winter is still signaled, not by the calendar or even the falling snow, but by *Feri,* the waiter, who writes on the menu of the local restaurant the exciting words: *Minden nap disznótor:* "Pig-killing mixed grill —available every day."

* See recipe on page 187.
† See recipe on page 226.

In Praise of a Sow
(Ars Poetica)

Egy anyadiszno dicsérete (1957)

Your Grace, Your Most Gracious Majesty!
thus I courted the four-hundred-pound sow,
when grunting she approached me—
Love's passion's fine work raises us
to human dignity; but a handsome porker
can also be praised by the poet's art!

JÓZSEF BERDA (*translated by Paul Tabori*)

* IO *

THE GREAT HUNGARIAN PLAIN
(NAGY-ALFÖLD)

ABOUT two-thirds of that part of Hungary lying east of the Danube is called the *Alföld,* or the Great Plains, and generally referred to by uninitiated foreign travel writers as the *Puszta.* The original meaning of the word *puszta* is "barren," which was true of the region many hundred years ago, but no longer. It is now a rich agricultural area, growing rice, wheat, barley, corn and fruit, and producing the Hungarian *vin ordinaire.* In a few sections of this tabletop-flat region you will still find herdsmen dressed in broad-brimmed hats and embroidered, silver-buttoned capes, carrying enormous, carved whips that are used to control the animals; or shepherds wearing their sheepskin *suba* with the wildly shaggy fur on the outside.

In Hungary, village settlements are the rule for the peasants; but in the Great Plains, the *tanyavilág* or homestead system of settlements, developed during the sixteenth- and seventeenth-century Turkish Occupation, to a great degree still exists today. The peasants fled the Turks during these unsafe times, leaving the unprotected plains villages and entering the relative safety of the towns. The villages decayed and have never been rebuilt, as the peasants stayed in the towns. Since their grazing and cultivation land was quite a distance away, the men would spend months in their fields in temporary shelters. A few years later the sons would join them; then the whole family moved there and soon began a farmstead, the *tanya.* Life was lonely and isolated in these outposts, the children's education was neglected and the grownups lost touch with the outside world. For this reason they have farmed, dressed, spoken and eaten the same way for the last two hundred and fifty years. In the last fifty years, irrigation, planting junipers to guard against the wind, and

Life on the puszta, *1855*

binding the sand with grapevines have made this once barren land a huge wheat and fruit basket.

The first geographic unit of the Great Plains is the land between the rivers Danube and Tisza, often called the orchard of Hungary. There are sections here, particularly near the river Tisza, which are supposed to be so fertile you can stick a dry branch into the earth and next spring find it budding. Anyway, this is what the local *Háry János** tells us.

Jules Romains, visiting this area, wrote: "The French traveler suddenly feels that he is in Brie, fifty kilometers from Porte de Vincennes. . . . Then suddenly from the train window I noticed a fat sheep flock and a strange, almost ancient, shepherd. I kept looking at the flock until I discovered that those were not sheep but pigs. Peculiar! The first time I ever saw curly-haired pigs."

Visiting Kecskemét in the springtime and seeing one and a half million

* Hero of Zoltán Kodály's opera about the retired, bragging mercenary full of tall stories.

apricot trees in flower makes it difficult to believe that the peasants struggled hard to conquer this territory, winning it away from Nature. To arrest the wind-blown sands, which sometimes changed the topography overnight, they planted grapes, acacia trees, sunflowers and, eventually, apricots, cherries, tomatoes, cucumbers, green peppers and other vegetables.

Only very recently has it come to light that on the sands of the Alföld, during the first century of the kingdom, Hungarians had already cultivated vineyards and fruit orchards—which were totally ruined during the Turkish Occupation. Replanting began in the eighteenth century, culminating and succeeding in the twentieth. In this superhuman work of virtually recreating the terrain, many foreign experts helped, especially the Swiss, János Mathiasz, who developed forty-four muscatel strains and seventy white and red varieties of table and wine grapes.

Alföld winegrowers make a somewhat soft, pleasant, fresh table wine, but every now and then, a well-balanced, quite full-bodied wine is produced, suitable to accompany good roasts. Mostly the Olasz Rizling, Kövidinka, Szlankamenka, Mézesfehér and the red Kadarka grapes are used. The latter give the well-known Siller wine. (A few of these "sand wines" are similar to another faraway sand wine, that of Gascony in France.) Most of these wines are for Hungarian consumption, but at least two are exported: Zsengődi Rizling and the Pusztamirgesi Kadarka.

The phylloxera destroyed a great part of the Hungarian vineyards, but these plant lice were not happy in the sandy soil. Thus, during the destructive years, the Alföld vineyards had just as rich a harvest as before.

The wines of the Great Plains are often drunk mixed with mineral water or club soda and the catalogue of variations is long and full of social subtleties. *Fröccs* (a squirt) consists of two parts wine and one part soda. *Kisfröccs* (little squirt) is the same drink, but only a small (eight-ounce) glass of it, and *hosszúlépés* (long step) is two parts soda to one of wine. *Házmester* (janitor) is usually served in a large (sixteen-ounce) stein, mixing three parts wine to two parts soda. There are several other variations—the lowliest is *piszkos víz* (dirty water). When a man was really down on his luck, he would take a glass in which wine had been served and fill it with soda water. Enjoyment depended on the strength of his imagination rather than the finesse of his taste buds.

The distilling of fruit brandies in the vicinity of Kecskemét is as widespread as bourbon making in Kentucky. The most popular varieties are apricot and plum. Green walnut, cherry, sour cherry, peach and blackberry brandies are made in lesser quantities. (Brandy making was started by some unknown Arabs in the fourteenth century, luckily far too late for Mohammed to have

Scene from a country inn

banned it. Thus, the Turks could drink it without fear of ending up in hell.)

Probably the best-known brandy is the world-famous *barackpálinka,* or apricot brandy. Like most great "made" specialty items, it is a happy marriage of raw materials and technique. Two kinds of apricots are used: the so-called *kajszi* and the *rakovszky,* a rounded, juicy, fuzzy-skinned fruit with a characteristically lush flavor and aroma. Continuous tasting and adjustment take place during the complicated process of distillation. The degree of ripeness of the fruit is vitally important. If the apricots are not ripe enough, a considerable amount of methyl alcohol forms; and if they are overripe, aldehydes spoil the taste. During distillation, crushed pits are added in the ratio of 1 percent, which creates the characteristic taste qualities of Hungarian apricot brandy.

After distillation, the brandy is put into oaken barrels for at least a year before bottling, in order to eliminate "scratchiness." The bottle, which is highly individual, may be a copy of an ancient Hungarian handmade bottle called the *fütyülő* (whistler), or a fine Herend porcelain *kulacs* (canteen).

Cognac may be the "refined lady" most suited to accompany you to an elegant dinner, but on a cold winter morning on the farm, starting the day with a piece of roast bacon and a slice of crusty, toasted bread, you would prefer the ripe peasant beauty of a Hungarian fruit brandy. It would warm you up and give you strength to start the day.

The *Puszta* (Great Plains) of Bugac, near Kecskemét, and its historic *csárda* are still not far removed from the distant past. When you visit there, if you're lucky, you'll catch one of the men roasting bacon. It would be hard to find a type of bacon that the Hungarian does not like. As the local saying goes, the breakfast consists of bread with bacon, the lunch is bacon with bread, and the dinner is a combination of the two. And when he has a chance to roast it, it becomes real holiday fare. As a child I heard the story about the boss who asks the shivering gypsy: "What do you want to do more—eat or get warm?" The shrewd answer, "I want to roast bacon." Bacon roasting became almost a ritual, with the dogma and formalized customs of a religious ceremony.

First, a level place must be found. Then wood and twigs are gathered and a fire built. While the fire is kindling, the man selects wood for spits, sharpening both ends. One end, for the bacon, will have a longer point and the bark taken off. The other end will be sharpened slantwise for sticking into the earth should he wish to stop the roasting for some reason. He then cuts two slices of bread lengthwise. Considering the size and shape of a Hungarian country bread loaf, we should mention that the length of the "slices" will be well over a foot, and the thickness will be about seven inches—not quite like the bread one puts into the toaster, west of Hungary. He now starts toasting the giant cuts of bread by propping them up near the fire.

Meantime, he cuts off a half pound of bacon in an oblong shape, puts it on the wooden spit making sure that the end of the stick does not protrude. Holding the spit in his left hand, he makes short, half-inch scores in the bacon with great care. He also makes three incisions lengthwise so that the side of the bacon will be nice and "checkered." He turns over the bread and toasts the other side. He then cuts the opposite side of the bacon the same way. He makes a deep cut in the skin of the bacon (which is always left on, as you can see on page 161) and this part of the ritual is finished. He takes a seat on a log, and holding the toasted bread, he begins to roast the bacon over the fire very slowly, moving it from left to right. By now the fire should have burned down and have no flame. The bacon begins to sizzle and the drippings fall heavily into the embers. The fire picks up and flames. Our man now takes the toast with his left hand and stretches it toward the fire and holds the bacon on the skewer with his right hand directly over it so that the drippings will fall onto the toast. When the bacon shrinks to the size of his palm and starts to glitter, he bites into it and tastes it, then continues roasting. The incisions begin to open up, and the flow of the drippings increases. He leans the skewer at an

Wine drinking in a hortobágyi csárda; *an early postcard*

angle so that the fat continuously drips onto the bread. With the point of a knife he pricks the bacon and squeezes it to get more of the fat out. Now the bacon is beautifully red and ready to eat. (To allow it to get black is a shame; no one likes to eat "gypsy," as burned bacon is called.) He sticks the spit into the earth, gets up and stretches himself. He cuts some more bread, cleans a big onion, pulls out the skewer from the earth and pours a little water from a pitcher onto the bacon to wash off any ashes. He places the bacon on the bread, pulls out the skewer and slowly, deliberately, with an unhurried dignity, starts eating. His right hand holds his knife, alternately cutting off little pieces of the bread, onion and bacon, which are held between different fingers of his left hand. It is quite amazing how clean his hands remain.

It sounds simple? Perhaps it is if you do everything properly. But it is very easy to get a smoky, unpleasant-tasting bacon, and even easier to drop the bacon into the fire or get burned with the red-hot, dripping fat. The love of rituals, order, and a place for everything and everything in its place, helps the Hungarian country folk to make a royal feast out of such simple pleasures as eating bacon with bread.

Not far from the Bugac Puszta is Kiskunság, which is not a geographic unit, but an ethnic-historic one. The Kuns are of Turkish origin and lived around the Dnieper River when they fled from the invading Mongol armies in the thirteenth century. They became Hungarians and retained their own virtues and mores to a remarkable degree. In "Little Cumania" the men, until recently, worked almost exclusively as shepherds.

The conquering tribes of Chief Árpád dried their kettle-cooked meat as an early form of preserving, and the Kun shepherds dry-braise their sheep meat in an identical manner, even in the second half of the twentieth century. Early pagan sacrificial rites are suggested in fragments of their cuisine, such as cakes baked in animal shapes.*

Just as in other parts of the country, cabbage is shredded, pickled and put away in barrels for the winter as sauerkraut, but here the same process is also done with cucumbers. During the winter a favorite one-dish meal is ham soup made with this sour-pickle-slaw.

The Kuns are very fond of potatoes in all forms and vary their use imaginatively. For instance, potato-barley with smoked sausage and potato pancakes† are brought to perfection and eaten often. A lot of people come to the Kunság from Budapest just to eat the *bürgepaprikás*‡ praised by presidents and peasants, poets and pedants alike. *Gomolya*, a fresh sheep's cheese, is an almost everyday food of the shepherds. It would be fascinating to chart the routes of dishes throughout the ages and countries, and find out, for example, how *gomolya* got to the United States as *smearcase* (a Pennsylvania Dutch cheese) or vice versa.

Everything is strictly organized in the kitchen: there is a beechwood spoon for each purpose—to make porridge, stir bread starter, mix *roux,* scoop grapes, bake lentils (they don't eat them whole) or taste with. Even the shape of the ceramic pot differs according to its use: for honey, lard, flour, sour cream, etc.

This is a patriarchal society, and the men who run it insist on a tightly composed order in their day-to-day life. They accept no changes other than those of the seasons. Sons want to eat the same dishes that their fathers ate, served in the same way, with the identical utensils. Since the land of Kiskunság and its people are poor, their everyday meal is short and plain, yet "red letter days" are almost Baroque in their color, richness and ornamentation.

In the southern part of Alföld, on the banks of the Tisza River, lies Hun-

* See gastronomic map.
† See recipe on page 304.
‡ See recipe on page 275.

Fish barbecuing on the Tisza River

gary's "second city," Szeged, an interesting and likeable combination of refined urbanity and direct contact with the earth. It really isn't large, compared to Budapest's two million population, but it's one of the four cities with more than 150,000 inhabitants. It is considered the capital of salami and paprika making; at the same time, it has some of the most elegant restaurants and pastry shops, and one of the greatest summer theater seasons in Europe. Supported by the river Tisza, its fish cuisine is unparalleled in all of Hungary, as evidenced by tasting their famed Fisherman's Broth.* Decidedly, it is a good eating country.

There is something about paprika itself that makes it synonymous with "Hungarian." "Fiery," "spicy," "temperamental"—all these adjectives suggest both paprika and the Hungarian national character. Paprika is to the Hungarian cuisine as wit is to its conversation—not just a superficial garnish, but an integral element, a very special and unique flavor instantly recognizable.

The transformation of paprika into this vital element of Hungarian cuisine is a curious and fascinating story. Like the meeting of two people who seemed fated to fall in love, the marriage of paprika and Hungarian cooking was almost predestined.

* See recipe on page 203.

10. *The Great Hungarian Plain*

Where did paprika come from? There are many hypotheses. . . .

It came from the slopes of the Himalayas (where it probably put hair on the Abominable Snowman) . . . Columbus brought it to Europe from America, along with potatoes . . . it came from Central Africa . . . the Greek gods first used it for snuff on Mount Olympus . . . it came from India. . . .

In the first century A.D., Nero's celebrated personal physician, Dioscorides, in his famous *De Materia Medica,* described a *piper longum rotundum*—which sounds astonishingly like paprika. Was it paprika, or something similar? We shall probably never know for certain, as there is no record of it after that until Columbus' momentous voyage to the New World.

The first written record of paprika as we know it appears in letters that Chanca, Columbus' ship surgeon, wrote to his friend Hernández, court surgeon to King Philip of Spain. Chanca described "Indian pepper" growing in the New World as a "very attractive, ornamental plant which may prove medically useful." He mentioned, offhandedly, that the natives used this Indian pepper as a condiment.

Although Chanca managed to bring back some of these interesting plants from America, for a long time paprika remained only a botanical curiosity. (In Cardinal Lippay's gardens near Esztergom it grew next to the rare aloe, which flowers only once every hundred years.)

However, by the end of the sixteenth century a flourishing paprika culture had grown up in the Iberian peninsula. Clusius, the famous court botanist of Emperor Maximilian, described it in his book *Capsici Historia* in 1593: "In Castilia, gardeners and housewives grow this capsicum of Indian-American pepper, though with difficulty. There are many varieties, and it is very generally used as a seasoning agent. . . ." It also grew, he reported, in Moravia and the eastern parts of Europe. All this is solid evidence that Columbus introduced paprika to Europe, or at least that paprika appeared there only after his Western voyages.

Was it always the same plant which was known in the past five centuries by such an astonishing number of names: *Piper Indicum, Cardomomum Arabicum, Piper Indianum, Piper Bresilianum, Capsicum vol potius Americum, Peruvianum,* etc.?

Now every historian tends to be a "cautious carouser"—that is, he would like to be strikingly original, but at the same time historically accurate. To make sure I am not neglecting any legitimate claim, this is the time to mention that several learned authorities, including Károly Gundel, felt that the Spanish pimiento paprika indeed came to Spain via Columbus, but that the Hungarian *capsicum* paprika arrived in Hungary from India via Persia, and was brought in by the Turks at the beginning of the sixteenth century. The main support for this "India" theory is simply that just about everybody called paprika "Indian pepper" for several hundred years, and one botanist (D. Jacobi Theodore Tabarnaemontani, of Basel), in a herbarium published in 1731, flatly declared that it came from India. It gives an extra dimension to the already confused picture, that "Indian" to the early botanists probably meant American or Central American Indian.

Livingstone reported that paprika had been growing wild since ancient times in East India, Abyssinia and Central Africa. There is no evidence that anyone else noticed.

Amid this welter of conflicting evidence, we are sure of only one thing: before Columbus, paprika was unknown in Europe. For all intents and purposes, therefore, let us consider paprika a delightful fringe benefit of Columbus' discovery of America.

After the Italians introduced paprika to their country (from Spain), the Turks, who had many contacts with the Italians, took the seeds from Italy to the Balkans, then part of the vast Ottoman domain. In the sixteenth century the Turkish Empire included Bulgaria as well as most of Hungary in its realm. The Bulgarians, known as the "gardeners of Europe," have always been famous for being able to make almost anything bloom. Having learned to cultivate paprika from the seeds given them by the Turks, many Bulgarian gardeners emigrated to Hungary during the sixteenth century, partly attracted by the far more favorable soil and climate, and partly fleeing the Turks. Also, some Bulgarians were forced to serve in the Turkish army; others were servants of the Turkish officers. This is the source of most of the mistaken scholarly conclusions about the Turkish role. There is ample evidence that the Bulgarians brought paprika to Hungary and started its cultivation.

The origin of the word paprika is the Latin *piper* (pepper). In the Slavic language, its diminutive is *pepperke* or *piperka,* which evolved into *peprika* and finally, *paprika.* This again supports the claim of scientists who believe the Bulgarians brought paprika to Hungary before the Turks. By a fitting irony, paprika became, in its adopted home, more characteristically Hungarian than it had ever been before.

A folk legend dating from the Turkish Occupation retells a bittersweet tale of the infancy of Hungarian paprika. Once upon a time, there was a Hungarian girl named Ilona, "so beautiful that had she been a statue, all would have worshipped her as a holy image." Ilona was in love with a young Hungarian, but Mehmed Pasha, Chief of the Turkish Army occupying Buda, kidnapped her for his harem.

In the harem gardens, Ilona saw paprika and learned the secrets of its cultivation. Every night she escaped through a secret underground passage and

Fishermen from the Tisza River area, mid-nineteenth century

went to meet her lover. After a while, she began to smuggle out the little paprika plants to him. Thus, the townsfolk of Buda were able to start growing paprika. Eventually, a small group of Hungarian warriors surprised the Turks by invading the castle through this underground passage disclosed to them by Ilona. In the meantime, paprika growing had spread to the southern hills beyond Buda.

Just what is paprika? As mysterious as its origins, as difficult as its cultivation, the nomenclature is twice as baffling and confusing.

When a Hungarian says "paprika," it means only the ground spice (and it's also referred to as "red paprika"). "Green paprika" refers to the fresh vegetable; if it is red-ripe, it is generally called a "tomato paprika." Fortunately, black pepper has a name of its own (*bors*). In English, it is a little more complicated. The vegetable itself is called "green pepper" (or, with a prefix of the variety, such as bell-, banana-, etc.). The peppercorn is known as "black pepper," the spice paprika as "red pepper." And if you want the fresh, ripe, red vegetable, you'd better point! Or ask for a "red green pepper, please."

In Hungary there are two basic categories of paprika: first, those grown for eating fresh, cooked or marinated; and second, those destined to be dried, ground into powder and used as a condiment.

Hereafter, we shall refer to the first category as an eating paprika, and to the second as a spice paprika, without discussing the several types of spice paprika. Paprika, all alone, will only mean the ground spice itself.

Whew! All clear?

The spice paprika plant is a branchy, annual shrub, sixteen to twenty-four inches in height. Its fruit is three to five inches long and one to one and one-half inches wide, and its green-yellow cone-shaped pod turns red when it is ripe. The *Capsicum* genus is a member of the potato family (Solanaceae) and thus is related to tobacco, tomatoes and potatoes—all three of which, by the way, originated in the Americas.

As paprika growing took hold toward the end of the sixteenth and the beginning of the seventeenth century, the red pod began to be widely used as a spice. Shepherds added it to their kettle *gulyás* (*bográcsgulyás**), fishermen to their fish stew. (In 1604, a Hungarian dictionary listed it, for the first time, as "Turkish pepper, *piper indicum."* The word "paprika" didn't appear until 1775, when J. Csapó, in his *Herbarium,* called it "paprika garden pepper.")

Townspeople sprinkled their bacon with paprika, made of crudely crushed "cherry paprika," † and added it to a variety of dishes, mixing it with sour cream. The landed gentry were slower to realize its virtues. At last they, too, recognized that not only was paprika cheaper than black pepper, but it stimulated the appetite and had a most delightful character of its own. They also began to appreciate that paprika grows in hundreds of varieties from very hot to sugar sweet, with colors ranging from green to yellow, purple to red, and textures from delicate to one-quarter-inch-thick flesh.

Hungary was unquestionably the first to use powdered paprika in pure form, unmixed with anything else. In Turkey, Central and South America it was only used whole, added to other foods. The Spaniards mixed it with other spices, kneading it into a kind of flat pancake, which they dried in the oven and then ground. In India it was only one of the ingredients in their countless curry variations. Somewhere along the line the Hungarians hit on the holy trinity of lard, onion and pure ground paprika. This simple combination became the base of virtually unlimited taste combinations.

---

* See recipe on page 273.
† Similar to the American cherry pepper.

10. *The Great Hungarian Plain*

There are a great number of documents indicating that paprika was becoming popular with all classes. Naturally, it was the hot paprika that drew the most attention from foreign travelers. At the end of the eighteenth century a visiting nobleman, Count Hoffmanseg, wrote to his sister: "For the first time I tasted this Turkish pepper, which here is called paprika, when the stuffing of the cabbage was seasoned with it. It stings terribly, but not for long, and then pleasantly warms the stomach!"

At about the same time, a Capuchin priest, Ubaldis, mentions it among Hungarian sins—*"Condimentum Ciborum est una Rubra Bestia, vocant Bobriga; sed mordet sicuti jobulus"* ("The spice of their food is some sort of red beast called paprika—it certainly bites like the devil").

In its slow climb to acceptance as a national treasure, paprika rose from the lowest classes, through the broad masses of peasants and fishermen, to the townspeople and gentry. The nobility was the very last to acknowledge paprika, probably because it did not stem from aristocratic tradition. Eighteenth-century records are full of recipes for pâté made with turtle meat or pheasant cooked with crayfish, and other rare delicacies. But not till 1844 did Paprikás Chicken appear on a menu of the National Casino, the exclusive club of the Hungarian House of Lords. The fact that it was a favorite dish of the beautiful and popular Queen Elizabeth (Franz Josef I's consort), who often visited Hungary, from 1860 until her assassination, probably won over the Hungarian aristocracy finally.

A queen couldn't be wrong! Paprika's victory was complete. In shaping the cuisine of Hungary, it was itself transformed. It had now become utterly Hungarian.

No less a personage than Escoffier himself introduced paprika to the *grande cuisine* of France. Escoffier brought it from Szeged, and served it in Monte Carlo in 1879, in *Gulyas Hongrois* and *Poulet au Paprika*.

But the very first time paprika turned up in a recipe in a printed cookbook was much earlier—in 1817. Printed in Vienna, the cookbook was the work of one F. G. Zenker, chef of Prince Schwarzenberg. He listed paprika in his recipe for Chicken Fricassee in Indian Style; but judging by the way he described it, even to this learned gastronomic authority paprika was still a startling novelty.

The earliest of "modern" Hungarian cookbooks—that is, with recipes in fairly easy-to-follow form—was probably István Czifrai's* (written with the help of the viceroy's chef). The first edition was published in the early 1820's. But it was not until the third edition (1829) that paprika appeared in two famous and characteristic Hungarian dishes. The first dish, *halász-hal* or

* See page 43.

131

Decorating gingerbread   *Master honey-bread maker with his molds*

kevert halétel (fisherman's soup or mixed fish dish), is the famous *Szegedi halászle** (fisherman's soup of Szeged). Paprika, of course, is an essential ingredient of this glorious Hungarian fish soup. The other notable "first" is the *paprikás csirke†* (Paprikás Chicken), which became one of the most popular dishes not only in Hungary, but the whole world. Here are the actual recipes as they then appeared:

Fisherman's Broth

"Clean a variety of fishes like carp, *fogas,* sheatfish, perch and pike. Let them stand in salt about half an hour. Cut them into pieces. Make a little *roux,* add a halved onion and a mixture of red wine and water. Add also parsley, a paprika pod, scallion, a little tarragon, grated lemon peel and new spice. [This is the ground paprika powder.] Cook it well. [Note: This must be a special version for the aristoc-

* See recipe on page 203.
† See recipe on page 278.

racy's table; the fisherman's own had no *roux* or wine.] Place fish in above liquid and cook it slowly. When it is cooked, put on platter and strain the sauce over it. Decorate the edge of the platter with triangles of toast made of rolls."

Paprikás Chicken

"Take two or more chickens and cut them up into pieces. Melt a piece of lard in a copper pot. Put in paprika, clove and onion and cook slowly. Then add the chicken pieces, pour a little meat broth over them, and begin cooking. Sprinkle with a spoonful of flour, add sour cream and sprinkle with paprika. Cook a little longer and then serve."

The taste of these dishes will depend to a great degree on the quality (and freshness) of the paprika itself. As even the earliest observers noticed, spice paprika is exceedingly difficult to grow. It isn't surprising how many religious festivals are connected with phases of its cultivation—man sorely felt the need of divine help. For instance, the prescribed time to set the precious plant seeds in lukewarm water is St. Gregory's Day, at the beginning of March. The water must be changed every day for seven days. Then the seeds are tenderly transferred to the top of the stove to keep warm, and a few days later sown in hothouse beds. During the ensuing seven weeks from seed to plant, the spice paprika plant requires more loving care and earnest prayer than a sickly baby.

When the time arrives for the outdoor planting, the whole village organizes itself for the complex and physically demanding rites; there must be precise coordination between those who drill the holes, those who actually do the planting, seated on tiny stools, and the people who follow behind with watering cans. When and how much water should they give the tiny sprouts? This judgment, a combination of knowledge and intuition, will be decisive in the life of the plant.

During June and July the developing paprika needs warmth, rain and sunshine in about equal proportions. The harvest begins September 8, on the feast of the Nativity of the Holy Virgin, every phase of which is brilliantly colorful. It is a sort of combination of medieval festival, husking bee and vast block party. Everybody is involved. After the villagers have picked the spice paprikas, they pile them into carts and bring them, looking like mountainous heaps of deep red jewels, to the village. There the village maidens string the flawless paprikas into tight, eight-foot-long garlands and hang them under the eaves of each house to dry. But first the girls sit in a circle examining each paprika to make sure it is perfect, while they gossip, improvise stories or repeat favorite old tales and folk songs that have been handed down from generation to generation.

Their own livelihood figures in one tale about the great King Matthias and the pretty daughter of a paprika grower. She was, so the story runs, so clever that her fame reached the king's ears and he sent for the girl to test her. First he asked her to spin a golden thread from cotton yarn in the royal attic. The girl answered demurely, "I will be happy to weave the golden thread, if the king will make a golden spindle from my father's fenceposts."

"Here are a hundred glass jars with holes. Can you patch the holes?" the king inquired next.

"Sire," replied the wily maiden, "I beg you to turn the jars inside out first— since patches must always be mended on the wrong side!"

"Well," said King Matthias, "I can see you stood close to God when he was giving out brains. My last question is this: Can you bring me something, and *not* bring me something at the same time?"

The girl asked permission to withdraw. The next day she returned carrying two sieves.

"Here, Sire," she said, "is what you have asked." As the king lifted the top sieve, a pigeon escaped and flew away. The mission was fulfilled. The king gave the clever girl a magnificent dowry and a noble husband to help spend it. Ever since, at every harvest, the village girls stringing together the spice paprikas with their six-inch-long needles retell this story as they work and wonder if that was the end of the affair between the pretty daughter and the king.

When they have finished the garlands, they hang up the paprikas under the eaves, solidly covering the upper half of the house under the roof with a brilliant fringe. During the next few weeks, in the mild fall weather, the spice paprikas slowly dry until they are so brittle they click in the breeze like hundreds of high-pitched castanets.

Up until the late nineteenth century the Hungarian peasants finished the drying of the pods in special earthenware ovens. Then they crushed the spice paprikas by treading (as in wine making), and pressed them through a sieve or pounded them to powder in large mortars.

Eventually, somebody developed a laboriously operated great wooden mortar with a two-armed lever. This contraption, named the *külü*, was very difficult to operate, but enabled them to produce a much finer powder. Then the expert millers along the banks of the river Tisza, who had ground only grain in their water mills, began to grind paprika. But though the slow-moving millstones of the Tisza ground exceedingly fine, nobody as yet knew how to control the pungency of the paprika.

There was a historic breakthrough in 1859 when the ingenious Pálffy brothers, in the city of Szeged, invented a technique of removing the veins and seeds and milling the dried and tempered pods in a tubular machine. Until

134

about twenty years ago, when a new and highly mechanized system was introduced, the same technique was used in all factories. With this process, they created something entirely new—the mild "noble-sweet-rose" paprika. At last, you no longer had to be Hungarian to enjoy (while suffering) the fiery enchantment of hot paprika. This "new spice" contained almost no capsaicin, the substance that produces the tongue-stinging "heat" in the hot seasoning. The capsaicin, and thus the pungency, can be controlled, depending on how much of the veins and seeds remain inside to be ground up with the rest. The more you leave to be milled, the hotter the paprika will be.

The new, tamed paprika was an immediate sensation. Its popularity spread all over the world, with amazing speed. Of course, it was "born" at a fortuitous moment: because of the Napoleonic war, the flow of pepper from the East had been cut off. Paprika was a natural substitute, and people soon began to realize that the "tamed fire" of paprika was both more interesting and more stimulating than black pepper—and cheaper as well!

The paprika growers, a proud and tenacious lot, many of whose descendants still run the modern processing factories, kept trying for finer selection and cross-fertilization, an unending search for paragons of paprika. About twenty years ago they perfected a subspecies of the *Capsicum annuum L. var. lingum Szegedense* which, even with its veins and seeds, is sweet throughout. By using it alone or in mixture with hotter types, the paprika industry markets the following six categories: exquisite delicate (*különleges*), delicate, noble sweet (*édesnemes*), semi-sweet (*félédes*), rose (*rózsa*) and hot (*erős*). (It is interesting to note a linguistic somersault: "sweet" in this case means lack of spiciness.)

No matter how mechanized and automated the paprika processing factories become, the judgment of the millmaster still does and probably always will play a decisive part in the whole process. Paprika must be heated during the grinding—but not too much or it will scorch; each lot has a different texture and moisture content. These factors, and others having to do with color, smell and taste, prompt a hundred vital decisions the millmaster must make to turn out exactly the right kind of paprika. Mechanized it may be, but in spite of scientific and industrial aids, it will remain an art relying on years of experience and intuition.

The zeal for continuous improvement, cross-fertilization and paprika development shows no signs of abating. Scientists study its effects; growers work out ways of improving its color properties, creating new, ever more subtle tastes, and increasing the yield.

Some, though not all, of this discovery is post facto. For instance, the scientists' definition of ideal conditions for growing paprika includes all kinds of

Nineteenth-century drawing of a shepherd

finicky requirements: an average daily temperature of 63 degrees Fahrenheit from spring through fall, a minimum of two thousand hours of sunshine yearly, two and one-half inches a month of rain in June and July, a certain felicitous mixture of chemicals and minerals in the soil—and so on. And where are all these requirements exactly fulfilled? You guessed it! Precisely in certain southern regions of Hungary famous for paprika—particularly around Szeged, Kalocsa, Cegléd, and Szentes. (Kalocsa, by the way, is fast becoming the new paprika-center of Hungary.)

From the beginning of the eighteenth century paprika was considered an effective fever preventative in the Balkan Peninsula, and Jamaicans drank a paprika concoction to cure malaria. The favorite peasant's medicine on the *puszta* was brandy with paprika; he took it for everything from swamp fever and stomachache to toothache. In Szeged and its environs, people sprinkled paprika on a wound (in lieu of iodine) so it would heal quickly without infection.

The first man to do extensive experiments on the effect of paprika on the body was Dr. Endre Hőgyes in 1873. He found that the capsaicin, taken from paprika, stimulates mucous membranes of the mouth and stomach, and paprika itself enhances gastric secretions, causes strong peristalsis and thus aids digestion.

Next Dr. L. Berkessy, of Szeged University, conducted extensive tests and found that functioning of the stomach was accelerated and intensified by paprika. Good for the appetite, good for the digestion—and still other miracles were noticed. For instance, people used paprika plasters for boils, and night-blindness was cured with paprika tea. Professor László Cholnoky proved that there is so much carotene in paprika that even the vitamin A-loaded carrot cannot compete with it. (It is well known that vitamin A deficiency can cause night-blindness; hence the effectiveness of paprika broth.) Three or four grams of Hungarian paprika satisfy the daily adult vitamin A requirement since a single gram contains 430 to 1,320 units of the vitamin. For centuries, scientists could not understand how the Hungarian peasant or shepherd could live on bacon, bread and paprika alone and remain perfectly healthy. Twentieth-century biochemistry showed that paprika is a veritable storehouse of assorted vitamins, and Professor Szent-Györgyi discovered that the red-ripe green pepper is the richest single source of vitamin C! He obtained the first substantial quantity from Hungarian paprika, which contains five or six times as much vitamin C as citrus fruit. (One milligram of lemon or orange juice contains .5 milligram of vitamin C; the same quantity of the juice of red-ripe Hungarian green pepper is saturated with 21 to 34 milligrams of vitamin C.)

Another boon: paprika is also rich in vitamin P, a vital remedy in illnesses of the blood system. There is even some vitamin B_1 and B_2 in Hungarian paprika—and who knows what else? It is perfectly clear that science has not yet exhausted the beneficent possibilities of the paprika!

A nation's heroes give us vital glimpses of a nation's character. The Spaniard idolizes the greatest bullfighter; nineteenth-century America revered Horatio Alger; Italians idolize Caruso. Who could be a more appropriate hero for Hungarians than Nobel Prize-winning Professor Albert Szent-Györgyi? For he proved that Hungarian paprika is a prime source of vitamin C. By giving scientific justification to a long-standing romance (and naming the vitamin which he found in Hungarian paprika "ascorbic acid"), he earned a special place in the hearts of all native and honorary Hungarians.

Giant Peppers

Óriás-paprikák (1954)

You speak now and you sing now,
mounds of peppers with smiling bellies,
who traveled here from the fat soil of Cegléd
speak and sing of the fine freedom
of industrious toil! May you always
swell like this in plenitude and rise;
let the essence of taste pour from you!
If our brave work thus brightens us
neither our body nor our soul shall ever ail.

JÓZSEF BERDA (*translated by Paul Tabori*)

South of Szeged is a part of Croatia called Bácska-Bánát, presently part of the Yugoslav Republic. The natural watering system of the rivers Danube, Tisza, Dráva and Száva make it a flowering garden of Eden. Its rich culinary past, when a seven-day wedding feast was common, is a combination of Croatian, Serbian and Hungarian elements. You'll find some of the dishes from this area in the recipe section. Candidly, I think that the Hungarian cuisine received more from its Serbian neighbors (including such a basic preparation as the *lecsó**) than the other way around.

The northeastern part of the Alföld on the Czechoslovak border is Nyírség; it is as lean and poor as the others are fertile and rich. Just like the Hortobágy, this area is covered with sand, but *this* sand is not "golden." In their poverty the people developed ingenious substitutes for hard-to-come-by foods like meat, eggs and flour.

Being poor creates certain limitations. Limitations, however, often stimulate masterpieces. The windows of Chartres Cathedral are so extraordinary—they say—because the local artisans had access to only a very limited variety of colored lead glass, and imagination became the essential ingredient.

In Japan, poverty—through the spirit of Buddhism—is a virtue. To live simply and by inexpensive basic materials is much more laudable than a limitless use of all the riches of the sea and the land. For instance, they created several hundred variations of soybean dishes and transformed the mundane

* See recipe on page 315.

139

world of everyday eating into the realm of artistry. When dining in a Zen temple you will not notice the lack of meat. As a matter of fact, the exquisite taste and presentation will make it one of the memorable events of your life, even though it will be all based on a few plants and roots.

Some individuals go to pieces in poverty. There are others who take deprivation as a challenge and use their energy and ability to get out of this degrading state. Hungarians see no virtue in poverty and try to make the best of a temporary or permanent indigence. They feel that God supports only the rich man with a stake; the poor man must carve his own.

Amerigo Tot, the great Hungarian sculptor presently living in Rome, comes from a small village. When he was a child, his whole family would sometimes sit under a big tree in the yard where the neighbors could observe them, but could not see that they were ladling nothing into their soup plates from a tureen, so no one would think that they were starving. This sort of pride and vanity, combined with a peculiarly ingenious thinking process, produced some very interesting foods and drinks. Toward the end of the eighteenth century, Parmentier won a competition "to find a plant that can replace cereals in time of famine." Poor Hungarian households should have his image right next to Christ's since potatoes have saved many families from starvation in the past two centuries.

The frying of onion in bacon or lard, adding paprika to it, is about as simple a culinary process as one will find anywhere. However, many a poor Hungarian farmer's wife is able to control the subtle differences in this process so that the various plain dishes using this as a foundation will taste like anything from fish to meat with many variations in between. Thus, a plain paprika potato can taste like a meat and vegetable casserole, and a millet porridge (*Köleskása*) like a fish specialty.

A Hungarian housewife would be angered at a French or Western European cookbook's direction on stock, basic to making a soup. She might feel like a Scotsman toward the American system of conspicuous consumption. Fresh, pure water is what she uses, never any meat and rarely even bones, and yet she is able to make an onion broth with garlic toast that tastes better than most fancy soups in expensive restaurants. Offals are used as substitutes for meat in some kitchens, but a Hungarian lung stew in a lemon sauce became a national favorite.* Pork crackling or the nose and the ears of the pigs all became delicacies when the simple Hungarian household got through with them.

Poverty, of course, is a very relative term, and entire provinces in Hungary probably would object to the notion that eating potatoes without meat is a sign of poverty. The people of the Nyírség (and some other counties) had to

* See recipe on page 241.

catch, cook and live on sparrows, crows and gophers. They had to grind tree barks into a kind of flour and bake bread with it, and on very special "red letter days" make a "chestnut" purée out of mashed beans to celebrate an important event. Not only did they have to rub chicory beans against coffee beans, dropping the chicory beans into the water to make coffee, but at times even the substitute became scarce and they had to rub the chicory beans against some kind of wild plant and use the latter to make coffee. (During World War II, I tried everything to quiet my demanding stomach, but I did not find a pancake made of dried corncob flour very satisfactory.)

There is a craving for sweets after a while, not only by children, but by grownups, too. In Hungary, there are, unfortunately, no maple trees, but there is a kind of white birch (*nyírfa*) which gives out a sweet sap, and the poor people learned to boil this down and make a few desserts from it. (This tree gave its name to the province.) Fortunately apples in the county Szabolcs and plums in the Szatmár area are the finest in the country and plentiful. The latter are made into the powerful and famous Szatmári plum brandy.

Flowers were another food source for the poor, particularly the buds and even the sprouts. (The most unlikely bedfellows: Hungarian poor people's food and the recherché esoterica of flower-cookery. . . .)

Unfortunately, the Hungarian people have had a longer span to develop their imaginative substitutes than the proverbial seven lean years. The past one thousand years, according to a study compiled by Antal Réthly, have included one hundred years of famine.

The little they have—on occasion—they save and hold on to, with the wisdom of many generations. That is why the saying goes: when a Hungarian peasant eats chicken, either the peasant is sick or the chicken.

Curnonsky, the great French food writer, said that a nation's gastronomical level should be examined by tasting both the products of the best private kitchens and restaurants and the dishes from the kitchens of the poor. Somewhere in the middle, one will find the true level of gastronomy.

The Free City of Debrecen must be set apart and paid homage. The "Calvinist Rome" lies east of the river Tisza in the northern part of the Great Plains, near the border of Transylvania, and has always been known as the home of the "independent, thick-necked Hungarians." Their independence comes naturally. The surrounding county got its name (Hajdúság) from the sixteenth-century armed cowboys (*hajdúk*) whose main occupation was the driving of animals from the grazing lands to the marketplace. When the

Mid-nineteenth-century watermelon market

Habsburg oppression became unbearable, the *hajdúk* formed bands that waged war on the government forces, often victoriously. After one such blitzkrieg in 1606, Prince Bocskay gave them land and the privileges of nobility. The largest city of the Hajdú region was Debrecen, later the center of the Reformation in Hungary.

From many small pieces of information found on my recent visit to Debrecen, an interesting picture emerges of the middle-class life of the craftsmen. Most of the time they had one- or two-dish meals, the first course being a soup and the second often combining the virtues of a main course and a dessert (such as a hot, sweet noodle dish or cakes made with honey). When it came to entertaining they were extraordinarily hospitable, and it was sometimes difficult not to eat more than one wanted, or to leave the table sober.

One of the most charming little tales describes a special *decretum* (document), which had to be filled out by the host-to-be and given to the guests-to-be, indicating that a guest could get up from the table any time he desired and could stop eating and drinking if he had had enough. In possession of such a license, he was able with great pleasure to visit a friend's house knowing that he could always pull out the signed document insisting on the "freedom of getting away."

I read somewhere that round-bottomed, stemless glasses were of sixteenth-century English origin and were devised to make sure that everyone finished his drink, since the glasses could not be stood up on the table. At the risk of sounding like a boastful chauvinist, I state that this invention of questionable value doubtlessly emerged for the first time in Debrecen in the late fifteenth century. At least I have never seen an earlier claim for it.

According to an old menu manuscript recently unearthed, to lay a solid foundation for a wedding dinner, a proud *Debrecener* of a century and a half ago would set a table with the following:

Fowl Soup with White Raisins* and Snail-Shaped Noodles
Hajdú Cabbage†
Suckling Pig Pörkölt
Turkey Capon roasted whole and served with Plum Compote
Pork Tenderloin
Honey Cake‡
Fresh Fruit
Black Coffee

At weddings they served "two and a half" meals. The first came directly after the church wedding, about two o'clock. This lasted until about seven o'clock, when the dancing began. After nine o'clock they brought around *café au lait* with freshly made hot pretzels and plain cake. At midnight they set the table again and ate cold roast, ham and freshly fried doughnuts.

For name-day feasts, paprika chicken and cheese strudel are musts, and this is what I ate on April 24, St. George's Day.

Near Debrecen, between the Tisza River and the Nyírség, is the famous Hortobágy Puszta. Its 75,000 acres lie as flat as a stretched, endless sheet. The vast expanses are broken up only by herds of cattle, snow-white oxen with

* See recipe on page 171.
† See recipe on page 284.
‡ See recipe on page 396.

*A sweep-pole well. A white cloth is pulled up into the air to call
the shepherds and herdsmen to meals.*

horns three feet long, flocks of sheep tended by herdsmen in wide-brimmed
hats and huge sheepskin capes, near-wild horses, ancient burial places, *csárdas*
underneath the gold-laced clouds and the ever-present sweep-pole wells.* The
shadoofs (as Webster calls them) look like enormous letter T's written by
giants. They consist of two poles twenty (or more) feet long. The vertical
pole is fixed in the ground and the other one is pivoted to it near one end,
having its shorter end weighted. A bucket hangs from its longer end; thus, it
operates as a well-sweep. It is as common a sight in Hortobágy as windmills
are in Holland.

While the scenery seems exotic to the tourist, to the "people of the *puszta*"
(as Illyés† called the Hungarians in his classic volume of the same title), it is
the last remnant of the solitude and silence of nature that the conquering
ancestors must have found. The Hortobágy has inspired writers, artists and
poets throughout the centuries, and perhaps Petőfi,‡ who was born around
here, should be quoted: "[Its] perspective is infinite, like the forehead of God.
It must take longer for the sun to travel its route, which is covered with the
blue glass bubble of the sky."

The people of the Great Plains—the peasants in the villages and garden

* See illustration above.
† The greatest living Hungarian poet.
‡ Great Hungarian poet-patriot (1823–1849).

*Saltcellars made of gourd and bone.
A wooden canteen called a* csobolyó.

cities, the shepherds, the fishermen, the descendants of the serfs, the artisans—they are the people of songs and fairy tales, of pagan and Christian ceremonies celebrating the important events of their lives. Even the shepherds are inspired here and become artists. An engraved bone or gourd saltcellar or a *csobolyó* (wooden canteen) is a minor masterpiece, and a wooden knife handle in a few hours of carving becomes museum perfect.

Only their food remains unadorned, simple and honest; it has never turned "bourgeois" as in the towns of other regions. In the Hajdú province (of which Hortobágy is a part), the kitchen is formed by the available ingredients and the prevailing conditions. There are no meals without some form of noodles: in soup (*lebbencs*),* main course (grated noodles)† or dessert (*túrós-csusza*).‡ Most meats will be barbecued or stewed; all parts of the animal are used, even the sheep's head;§ wild ducks and geese and other game birds are as

* See recipe on page 168.
† See recipe on page 302.
‡ See recipe on page 369.
§ See recipe on page 173.

145

common for the traditional stews as chicken in other parts of Hungary. The cooking is—to be sure—on the fatty and spicy side, just as it has been throughout the ages.

It is a long time since the Magyar tribes gave up their homeland in the steppe. Since then, Tartars, Turks, Slavs, Germans and others have tried to change the face and substance of the Great Plains to their image. But the proud heritage of the Asian character accepted very little from the invading forces. The aroma of the *gulyás* boiling in the cowboys' kettles still lingers like a sparkling ribbon amidst the thousand smells of the field, just as it did around the Ob River a thousand years ago, and the cuisine of the Great Plains represents an almost unbroken line of ten centuries of Magyar tradition.

Mutton Stew

Birkapörkölt (1961)

Proud dish of the Kunság, true miracle
spiced with dense-thick red wine—
to taste and eat you demands the smacking of lips!
Your enjoyment makes us burp as if
we heard charming baaing from the Great Beyond!
You thunderously plead for a drink that's
thirst-quenching, digestion-aiding; you are
so delicate, such a heavenly-earthly blessing
only the pagan god of elect bellies
can bestow upon us.

JÓZSEF BERDA (*translated by Paul Tabori*)

Drawing by István Engel-Teván

The definitive goose, by Milton Glaser

PART THREE

✡

RECIPES

✡ ✡ ✡ ✡
✡ ✡ ✡
✡

A visiting Englishman asked me the secret of the Hungarian cuisine. I told him:

"It's sweet onion, noble paprika, unmatched bacon, the very best sour cream and a thousand years of experience."

✡ ✡

Life is too short to cook improper Hungarian food.

✡ ✡

In a culinary contest, God is always on the side of the cook with the better recipes.

—ANONYMOUS TWENTIETH-CENTURY RESTAURATEUR

A FEW CAUTIONARY NOTES

MANY of the recipes that I have chosen to assemble are little known or even completely unknown to Hungarian housewives because a valuable part of the repertoire has been forgotten. Perhaps only a tenth of existing Hungarian recipes are currently in use. Many recipes had to be omitted simply because there wasn't space. Those dishes that came from foreign cuisines and were not "Hungarianized" throughout decades or centuries were left out. Categories that have secondary importance in Hungary—sauces, salads and such—were given less emphasis.

Many of the recipes are regional specialties. Generally speaking, in Hungary today about 75 percent of the regional dishes are cooked and served throughout the country. About 25 percent can be found only in the areas where they originated. Another thing about regional cuisine: For over a thousand years Hungary contained geographic areas which, after the Treaty of Trianon in 1920, became parts of Czechoslovakia, Rumania, Yugoslavia and Austria. Although these areas don't belong to Hungary anymore, parts of their food culture are so much a part of the Hungarian experience that some of those dishes had to be included to avoid giving only a partial picture of Hungarian cookery.

Other recipes are the creations of individuals. These manmade little marvels can be considered as the basis of Hungarian *grande cuisine.* I hesitate to use this term because, like the word "classic," it can mean various things to various people. At times it seems to signify the old and venerable recipes that have lasted through ages; sometimes the term is used to indicate a specific style or period. In this collection the dishes I consider as Hungarian *grande cuisine* use Hungarian ingredients and have a Hungarian quality, while the techniques of the international *grande cuisine* are used in preparation. They were created by "culinary demigods," and many of them have not only survived in Hungary, but also have become part of our collective Western culture.

These recipes have been collected from many sources. As a result they do not conform to the standard of being consistently planned for the same number of servings. Most recipes still make the portions given in the original sources, and I did not change this during testing. Then, too, some dishes cannot be made satisfactorily in small quantities. Even though I have given a suggested number of servings, this cannot be considered as fixed. A dish can be used in more than one way, or the other dishes in the menu might influence the size of servings. The appetites of the guests will be a factor, too.

In Hungary, as in most Central and Eastern European nations, until very recently every girl learned cooking from her mother as part of her general upbringing and education. When she made a special torte, she did look in a book to make sure of the ingredients and measurements, but the techniques and procedures were known through experience. Consequently, recipes in Hungarian cookbooks were, and are, little more than chefs' reminders. I have tried to keep a balance and mention technical details in each recipe while still presuming a certain amount of cooking knowledge on the part of the reader. There are many recipes here which an intelligent twelve-year-old could prepare perfectly, but one must hope for experience with recipes for noodles, pancakes, pastry and a few of the other preparations.

Don't worry about such measurements as the exact size of the onion, tomato, potato; whether to use one or two teaspoons of lard to start an onion frying; whether to flavor with one or two pinches of tarragon—these variables will not make too much of a difference. This does not mean that you can add (as they do in Germany) brown sauce to the paprika chicken, or make a *pörkölt* with butter, and hope to have an authentic flavor. Follow the method exactly before you start to make your own version. However, when it comes to noodle making or baking, you must keep to the given formulas. Even then you may have problems: flours of different brands act dissimilarly; the size of the eggs you use makes a difference; the quality of the butter and its water content might alter your final product. In all recipes using flour, I eliminated sifting. The flour was poured directly into a measuring cup, then the sides of the cup were knocked twice and a knife evened the top.

An easy way to start an argument is to ask two musicians their opinion about the "authentic" Bach style. The same controversy exists about, for instance, the "definitive" *sauce grand veneur* (once I found twenty-three different nineteenth-century recipes for this). One could argue about recipes in this collection, too—whether one should put flour into layered cabbage, paprika into *tokány,* and so on. We can disagree about the definitive version, but just about everybody will agree as to what is inaccurate, a blunder or a sham. Most people have a culinary fancy about their favorite dishes. Some, like the novelist Julius Krúdy, may make an overnight hansom trip on the spur of the moment when the powerful image of Fowl Soup Újházy Style (page 170) comes to them. (Krúdy was on the way home, remembering a little restaurant in a town forty miles away, when he made the driver turn onto the highway toward the heavenly dining room which served the—for him—perfect version.)

Hungarians don't easily accept new ideas (eating raw tomatoes in my childhood was unheard of), and surely they don't allow heresy concerning the traditional dishes. Even a culinary pope—if there were one—would not be considered infallible and allowed to put sour cream into *gulyás!*

The one fundamental I'd like to convey to the reader is the average Hungarian's pleasure in eating. For him fulfillment does not come from expensive champagne, truffles and complicated concoctions. Happiness, for him, is to enjoy in the flavor of the meat the freshness of the mountain springs, the perfume of the meadows and forests; to taste in the wine the flowering of the vines and the joy of the grape-trampling girls at the autumn harvest.

When you are "eating Hungarian," please remember these few observations. Cook some of these recipes for dinner tonight; it isn't wise to put off till tomorrow what you can enjoy today!

✷ II ✷

SOUPS
(LEVESEK)

ACCORDING to the rules of the French kitchen, you're not supposed to start *déjeuner* with a soup course. In Hungary it is different; there soup is an essential part of the midday meal.

If Brillat-Savarin's thought that the discovery of a new dish creates more happiness for mankind than the discovery of a star is true, Hungary should be a deliriously happy nation where soups are concerned. There is continuous innovation going on, while the traditional repertoire is kept lovingly and dutifully intact. You will find soups which are complete meals, soups which soothe, soups which excite the palate and soups which are essential parts of wedding days or similarly important events.

Cold soups, which became popular only in the 1920's in the United States and are barely known even today in other parts of Europe, were already at the turn of the century an integral part of Hungarian summer menus.

You may sample other dishes at Hungarian tables which may not be to your liking, but it is difficult to imagine the same experience with soups. Just as—according to a former professor of mine—the secret of the abundance of good Hungarian string instrumentalists is that they have a well-developed "sound sense," it is most probable that Hungarian housewives and cooks are either born with or develop a keen "soup sense."

In Hungary thickened soups are called, with limited logic, "brown soups," and their common characteristic is that they are thickened or "bound." To illustrate the different methods, let's take a vegetable soup and the various ways a Hungarian cook would give body to it.

11. *Soups*

A. The cut vegetables are cooked in water or stock; when the vegetables are almost done, the soup is thickened with *roux,* and vegetables and thickening are finished together.

B. The vegetables are cooked first in butter or fat together with a little onion until half done, then sprinkled lightly with flour, then cooked a little longer in water or vegetable stock until done.

C. The vegetables are cooked in butter or fat with a little onion until half done, then broth or water is added. Just before the soup is completely cooked, *roux* is incorporated and the soup is cooked for a few more minutes.

In each case the soup will have a different taste. The first method will not provide as good-tasting a soup as the second or third method, because the hot fat will release certain tastes from the mixed vegetables which will not come out when they are cooked in liquid. Also the fat releases certain coloring agents, particularly from carrots, which lend a beautiful color to vegetable soup. The second method will give a better-tasting soup, but because it is thickened with flour sprinkling, the taste that comes from browned flour will be missing. The best method is the third one.

There are certain soups which can be prepared with either method, such as mushroom, potato or pea soups. There are also soups which can be prepared only with one or the other method.

Vegetable soups in which the basic ingredient needs longer cooking, such as the various bean soups, should be thickened only at the very end. In a Hungarian kitchen puréed soups are thickened in several ways. Cream soups are purées with heavy cream or sour cream mixed with egg yolk added just before serving. Make certain not to boil a cream soup after you have added the egg-yolk and cream mixture, lest it curdle. Cold fruit soups are thickened with warmed flour.

A curious change in the meaning of words developed in the West after frozen and canned foods became part of the everyday menus. We now call "fresh" any vegetables that are not canned or frozen. It is sad to observe, and even sadder to eat, most of these "fresh" vegetables today; they are often not terribly good to start with, but with the waiting periods in various warehouses, the transportation time and the time lapses in stores or supermarkets where the poor, shriveled things are displayed, such produce becomes less desirable than a first-rate frozen product. You can follow these recipes faithfully, but the result will not be laudable unless the vegetables used are *"fresh* fresh," and not the miserable facsimiles generally available. The simple methods of Hungarian soup making (no stocks generally, no fancy spices, no cognac or sherry or other taste crutches) produced soups as good as those from any nation's kitchen, because of the fine vegetables of the land and the foolproof methods faithfully followed.

Hungarians do not like mysteries where their stomachs are concerned. Housewives may keep the secret of a great short-dough formula but no unknown ingredients will find their way into soups, sauces, stews, etc. The Hungarian poet Sándor Petőfi wrote a poem, well known in Hungary, which starts with a lover addressing his beloved, *"Minek nevezzelek?"* (What shall I call you?) Whenever a Hungarian *feinschmecker* is faced with a mysterious or phony soup he usually wryly remarks, "This is a Petőfi soup."

WHITE TOMATO SOUP

Fehér paradicsomleves　　　　　　　　　8 *servings*

8 cups strong chicken broth　　½ teaspoon salt
8 very ripe medium-sized
　　tomatoes, peeled

1. Combine the broth and peeled whole tomatoes. Add salt.
2. Simmer gently for 1 hour.
3. Remove the tomato pulp and strain the broth. The soup should remain clear. Adjust salt if necessary. Serve in cups.

NOTE: *If you have transparent cups (glass or crystal), this is a perfect soup to show them off.*

HERB SOUP

Füvesleves　　　　　　　　　6 *servings*

1 teaspoon fresh marjoram
　　leaves
1 teaspoon fresh thyme leaves
1 tablespoon 1-inch pieces of
　　chives
1 teaspoon chopped fresh
　　applemint
⅛ pound (4 tablespoons)
　　sweet butter

1 tablespoon flour
1 teaspoon salt
Sprinkling of black pepper
3 egg yolks
1 tablespoon sour cream
3 hard rolls, cut into halves
　　and toasted

1. Cook all herbs in half of the butter for 2 or 3 minutes. Sprinkle with flour, then stir and cook for another 4 minutes. Put it aside.

2. Pour 6 cups water into a pot and bring to a slow simmer. Add salt and pepper.

3. Mix the egg yolks and sour cream and remaining butter, softened, and whip into the simmering soup. Cook the soup over low heat, stirring, until it thickens. Add herbs and simmer another few minutes.

4. Place half of a toasted roll in a soup plate and ladle soup over it.

NOTE: *This is a recipe from Gyula Vasváry, master chef of the 1820's.*

SAGE SOUP

Szágóleves   *4 servings*

2 tablespoons minced fresh   Lemon juice
  sage   2 cups dry red wine
1 teaspoon grated lemon rind   1 cinnamon stick
2 tablespoons sugar (to be
  adjusted)

1. Boil sage and lemon rind in 3 cups water for about 30 minutes. Strain.

2. Add sugar, lemon juice to taste and wine, and bring to a boil.

3. Put the cinnamon stick in a soup tureen and pour soup over. Serve in cups.

NOTE: *This is a spiced drink as much as a soup. I have tried it as a winter drink and it easily competes with the traditional hot wine punches.*
This is another recipe recorded by Vasváry.

FRESH DILL SOUP

Friss kaporleves   *6 servings*

2 tablespoons butter   Salt
1 tablespoon flour   ½ cup sour cream
2 tablespoons minced dill   1 tablespoon lemon juice

1. Make a *roux* with the butter and flour, and slowly cook it till golden brown.

2. Add dill, stir it well, and immediately pour in ½ cup cold water and whip till smooth. Add 3½ cups water and salt to taste, and cook the soup for about 10 minutes.

3. Mix sour cream with lemon juice and put in the soup tureen. (Eliminate lemon juice if the soup is too sour for your taste.) Pour soup over.

4. Serve with Potato Dumplings (page 179). Cook these dumplings in the fresh dill soup for 5 minutes.

NOTE: *This is a Transdanubian recipe which brings back to me taste-memories from my childhood.*

MILK SOUP

Tejleves   4 to 6 servings

4 cups milk   ½ teaspoon salt
2 cups water   Soup Noodles (page 178)
1 tablespoon sugar

1. Bring milk, water, sugar and salt to a boil.
2. Put the prepared noodles into soup and boil for 3 to 4 minutes.

NOTE: *The war of salty versus sweet in soups and stews is a considerable one in different households. For instance, my mother reversed the salt and sugar ratio, thus making a salty milk soup. I must confess, however, that in this case the "sweets" are in the majority.*

You may also use boiled little new potatoes instead of noodles in this soup.

SPAWN SOUP FOR LENT

Böjti halikraleves   8 servings

2 carrots   Pinch of paprika
2 parsnips   ½ pound fish fillet, cut into
2 medium-sized onions   small pieces
1 small knob celery   1 fish head
1 teaspoon salt   1 pound spawn (fish roe)
2 bay leaves   2 tablespoons white-wine
5 black peppercorns   vinegar
1 tablespoon butter   ¼ cup sour cream
1 tablespoon flour

1. Peel vegetables and cut into small pieces, and together with salt, bay leaves and peppercorns cook them in 2 quarts water till they are almost soft.
2. Meantime make a *roux* with butter and flour; cook it for only a few

minutes, leaving it very light. Add paprika and whip ½ cup cold water into the *roux*.

3. Pour *roux* into the vegetable mixture and bring again to a boil. Reduce heat to a simmer.

4. Add fish pieces and fish head, and simmer soup for 10 minutes. Add spawn and cook for another 5 minutes.

5. Pour in the vinegar; just before serving stir in the sour cream. Adjust salt and vinegar to your taste.

NOTE: *During Lent most Hungarians eat a lot of fish. Almost always there are little bits of fish meat, fish bones, fish heads left over, and that's the time when this soup would be a good beginning for a Lenten meal.*

SOUSE'S SOUP

Korhelyleves   *8 servings*

1 pound sauerkraut
2 tablespoons bacon drippings
   from smoked bacon
2 tablespoons flour
1 small onion, minced
1 tablespoon paprika

½ pound smoked sausage,
   sliced thin
3 tablespoons sour cream
Salt

1. Squeeze sauerkraut well and save the juice.
2. Cook sauerkraut in 2 quarts water till it softens.
3. Meantime, heat bacon drippings in a frying pan, add flour, and stir and fry until the mixture is light beige. Then add the onion and cook for another 5 minutes.
4. Take off the heat, stir in paprika, and immediately add 1 cup cold water and whip until smooth.
5. Pour reserved sauerkraut juice into a soup pot; add flour and onion mixture, the sliced sausage and the cooked sauerkraut. Cook for 10 to 15 minutes.
6. In a soup tureen mix the sour cream and a cup of the hot sauerkraut broth. Add salt if needed. Adjust the taste of the soup to make sure that it is quite sour (somewhat like the hot and sour soup of the Szechuan cooking), and pour into the tureen. Mix with the sour cream and serve.

NOTE: *This soup is generally served in the wee hours of the morning to revive the guests in a private home or restaurant after an all-night party. It is guaranteed to perk up all the tired, dizzy and confused senses more than the "prairie oysters" used in the United States. This traditional soup can be*

made in several different ways, but two things must be common to the varia-
tions: the soup must be slightly fatty and have a very sharp taste.

Another way to make it is first to cook pörkölt *(page 271) and use the*
broth in which a lot of different sausages were cooked instead of water; then
add the cooked sour cream, some cooked rice and sliced sausages.

ORJA SOUP

Orjaleves   *8 to 12 servings*

1 pound beef bones	2 carrots
1½ pounds beef flank	1 parsnip
Salt	2 knob celery
1 medium-sized onion, diced	1 kohlrabi
1 garlic clove	1 leek, washed and sliced
1 tablespoon paprika	Pinch of saffron
8 peppercorns	Few leaves of knob celery and
1 clove	flat parsley, diced
2-pound section of pork head	7 ounces flour
2-pound section of pork	1 egg
backbone	

1. Wash beef bones and cook bones and beef flank in 3 quarts cold water
with 1 tablespoon salt. Let the beef cook for 30 minutes, then add onion,
garlic, paprika, peppercorns and clove and continue boiling for an additional
hour.

2. Put 3 quarts of water in a separate pot and carefully put in the clean
pork head section and boil for 4 minutes. Take it out, rinse, and put aside until
beef has cooked. Then add pork head and backbone to the beef. Cook till
done.

3. Meantime peel vegetables and cut into long strips. Take out 2 cups of
the boiling meat broth and cook the vegetables in it.

4. Add saffron to the vegetables together with the celery and parsley leaves.

5. Meantime make a dough with the flour and egg and roll it as thin as
possible. Cut it into 3-inch-wide strips and roll each strip in a spiral onto a
rolling pin. Slide each spiral off onto a baking sheet and dry in a 200°F. oven
for about 10 minutes.

6. Take soup from the heat and remove meat and bones. Take pork meat
off the bones and cut into little pieces. (The boiled flank can be used as a main
course or saved for another occasion.)

7. Skim soup to remove fat. Lift out vegetables and set aside. Strain broth

through a double layer of cheesecloth. Just before serving, cook the spiral noodles in the broth.

8. Put pork in a soup tureen, add the cooked vegetables, and pour broth with noodles on top.

NOTE: *This soup is generally cooked and eaten on pig harvest day. The pork is sliced in such a manner that a fairly meaty backbone (orja) remains, and this is where the name comes from. On these occasions dozens of people work and celebrate (see page 115). They usually take a huge kettle and cook the whole cleaned pig's head and backbone in soup, leaving out the beef. Obviously, this is the kind of soup that has to be made in large quantities.*

CARAWAY SOUP WITH GARLIC CROUTONS

Köménymagos leves foghagymás kockákkal   6 servings

2 tablespoons lard or bacon drippings	1 egg
	Salt
1 tablespoon caraway seeds	1 tablespoon butter
2 tablespoons flour	1 garlic clove
1½ quarts cold water	2 slices of white bread

1. Heat fat and cook caraway seeds for 1 minute to make them pop.
2. Add flour and make a dark *roux*, making sure that it does not burn.
3. Add water and whip. Cook for 15 to 20 minutes. Strain the mixture, put it back into the pot, and bring to a boil.
4. Beat the egg till foamy and whip it into the simmering soup. Adjust salt.
5. Meantime melt butter. Rub garlic on both sides of bread and dice the bread. Add dice to hot butter. Shake the pan for a couple of minutes and place it in a 500°F. oven to toast the croutons.
6. Serve croutons separately at table so they won't get soggy in the soup.

NOTE: *In most Hungarian families, when the housewife has to make ends meet, the egg would be eliminated and lard would be used instead of butter. This is a perfect example of the Hungarian talent for making a delicious dish out of meager ingredients.*

CREAM OF SPINACH SOUP

Spenót krémleves   *8 servings*

2 pounds spinach, well washed	4 tablespoons chicken fat 6 tablespoons flour
1 teaspoon salt	2 cups light cream
2 large onions, minced or grated	4 hard-boiled eggs, sliced Bacon crumbles (optional)

1. Cook the spinach in 2 quarts water with the salt for 5 minutes.
2. Strain; save the water. Rub spinach to a pulp through a strainer or purée in a blender.
3. Brown onions in fat, add the flour, and blend. Cook for a few more minutes.
4. Stir in 1 cup of the cool spinach liquid and cook, stirring, until thick and smooth. Add the remaining liquid and the puréed spinach. Heat to boiling.
5. Remove from heat and blend in the cream. Garnish with the egg slices and crumbled crisp bacon.

CREAM OF PEARL BARLEY SOUP

Árpagyöngy krémleves   *6 servings*

1 pound pork and veal bones	1 tablespoon flour
2 carrots, peeled and sliced	⅓ cup milk
1 parsnip, peeled and sliced	Salt
½ cup uncooked pearl barley	⅓ cup heavy cream
3 tablespoons butter, clarified	1 egg yolk

1. In a 3-quart soup pot cook the bones and vegetables in 1½ quarts water for about 2 hours. Keep skimming the broth to remove impurities.
2. Strain. Add enough water to bring the amount to 1½ quarts again.
3. Add barley to the broth and cook until it is soft.
4. Make a *roux* with clarified butter and flour. Cook the *roux* over low heat, stirring constantly, but do not let it become dark. This should be a light *roux*.
5. Stir ⅓ cup cold water and ⅓ cup cold milk into the *roux* and whip till smooth.
6. Pour thickening into soup and simmer it for 10 minutes.
7. Purée the soup in a blender or through a sieve. Adjust salt to taste.

8. Mix cream with egg yolk and put it in a soup tureen. Just before serving pour hot creamed soup over.

NOTE: *In most nineteenth-century Hungarian cookbooks you will find this as a suggested dish for invalids. I find it most soothing even when I am perfectly fit, particularly on a cold winter day.*

CREAM OF CHESTNUT SOUP

Gesztenye krémleves   6 *to 8 servings*

¾ pound chestnuts
1 parsnip, peeled and
  chopped fine
2 young carrots, peeled and
  chopped fine
1 small knob celery, peeled
  and chopped fine
½ pound lean veal, cut into
  ¼-inch cubes

⅛ pound (4 tablespoons)
  sweet butter
1 teaspoon salt
¼ teaspoon pepper
½ cup heavy cream
2 egg yolks

1. Cook the chestnuts, shell them, and purée them.
2. Brown chopped vegetables with the meat in butter and cook over low heat for 10 minutes.
3. Add 5 cups water, the salt and pepper, and cook the soup over low heat until vegetables and meat are done.
4. Mix puréed chestnuts into cooked soup and boil for another 5 minutes.
5. Mix heavy cream with egg yolks, and whip into the soup. Adjust salt.

CREAM OF LIVER SOUP

Májkrém leves   6 *to 8 servings*

⅓ pound calf's liver
1 small onion, grated
1 tablespoon and 1 teaspoon
  lard
Pinch of salt
½ cup white wine (optional)
1½ quarts meat or chicken
  broth or stock

Pinch of black pepper
1 tablespoon flour
1 egg yolk
¼ cup heavy cream
Croutons made of 3 slices
  of bread

1. Put liver through the finest holes of a meat grinder.

2. Sauté onion in 1 tablespoon hot lard for a few minutes, then add ground liver and salt. Cover and cook over very, very low heat for 5 minutes. Add wine and let it simmer for another few minutes.

3. Meantime, bring meat or chicken broth to a simmer. Add liver mixture and pepper.

4. In a separate frying pan make *roux* with 1 teaspoon lard and the flour. Stir and cook for a few minutes, but do not brown. Add ¼ cup cold water. Whip the thickening, then mix it into the simmering soup. Cook over low heat for 10 more minutes.

5. Strain the soup through cheesecloth. Mix egg yolk into cream and whip it into the simmering strained soup. Adjust taste and serve immediately. Serve croutons separately.

NOTE: *In peasant houses this soup is made with pork liver and is served without straining. On the other hand, in elegant restaurants they sometimes add a teaspoon of cognac.*

LENTIL SOUP WITH PARTRIDGE

Lencseleves fogolyhússal   *4 to 6 servings*

2 partridges	1 knob celery, peeled
1 cup lentils	¼ pound smoked bacon
6 cups chicken broth	2 tablespoons flour
1 pound veal bones	1 small onion, chopped
1 medium-sized carrot, peeled	½ teaspoon prepared mustard
1 parsnip, peeled	⅓ cup heavy cream

1. Soak partridges in cold water for 3 or 4 hours.

2. Place the lentils in a large soup pot with chicken broth, veal bones, carrot, parsnip and knob celery. Slowly bring to a boil.

3. Cut smoked bacon into small dice and render fat. With slotted spoon remove the cracklings and set them aside.

4. Dry the partridges. Very quickly brown the whole birds in the bacon drippings, giving them some color. Remove partridges and place in soup pot with lentils.

5. Make a *roux* with the same fat used to brown the partridges and the flour and onion. Add ½ cup cold water and whip till smooth.

6. When partridges and lentils are done (about 2 hours depending on age of the birds), add liquefied *roux*. Cook for an additional 10 minutes.

7. Take out partridges and bone them. Replace meat chunks in soup. Just before serving, whip mustard and cream into the soup.

NOTE: *Partridge can be one of the toughest birds in the world. This is a good way to serve it when otherwise it would make a very tough roast.*

QUAIL SOUP

Becsinált fogolyleves   *6 servings*

3 quail
1 tablespoon butter
1 tablespoon lard or bacon
   drippings
2 carrots, sliced
1 small onion, sliced
1 cup shelled peas
4 mushroom caps (if possible
   Boletus), sliced

2 tablespoons flour
1 teaspoon chopped flat
   parsley
Pinch of salt
6 cups quail broth, or meat
   stock or water
¼ cup sour cream

1. Clean the quail and cut into serving pieces.
2. In a heavy-lidded soup pot melt butter and lard. Brown the quail very rapidly for a few minutes; then add vegetables and mushrooms and ½ cup water.
3. Cook slowly, covered, until water almost disappears. By this time, quail should be quite done.
4. Add flour, parsley and salt; stir well. Add quail broth or meat stock or water; bring to a boil. Cook over very low heat for a few more minutes.
5. Just before serving mix in the sour cream. Serve liver dumplings or marrow dumplings in the soup.

HARE SOUP FROM NORTHERN HUNGARY

Felvidéki finom nyúlleves   *8 to 10 servings*

Head, neck, kidney, heart,
   lung and liver of 1 hare
1 parsnip
1 knob celery
1 kohlrabi
1 carrot
Pinch of caraway seeds

Salt
2 tablespoons lard
1 small onion, minced
1 garlic clove, crushed
6 black peppercorns, crushed
1 tablespoon flour
¼ cup uncooked rice

1. Do not wash the hare parts much; try to retain some of the blood. Put all the parts except the liver in a 4-quart pot with 3 quarts water, and bring to a boil. Skim well.

2. Peel the vegetables except onion and cut into small dice. Add to pot with caraway seeds and 1 tablespoon salt. Keep heat very low and let soup simmer.

3. Melt lard in a frying pan. Add minced onion, crushed garlic and the hare liver, cut into 1-inch dice. Sprinkle with crushed black pepper. Brown onion and liver fast, then dust with flour. Stir well and cook for a few minutes more. Add a ladle of broth from the soup pot. Stir well, and pour all into the soup pot.

4. Put rice into the soup pot and cook till it is done. Adjust salt.

NOTE: *As a variation you can add some lemon juice. In other parts of Hungary cooks whip lemon juice with sour cream at the last minute.*

Provincial cooking, unlike grande cuisine, *must be based on wise, economical use of every part of the raw ingredient, in this case the hare. After you have made a good roast of the rest of the hare, instead of discarding the leftover parts, you can make this excellent soup from them.*

SERBIAN BEAN SOUP

Szerb bableves 6 servings

½ pound dried white beans
2 or 3 pounds beef and veal
  bones
2 carrots, peeled and sliced
1 parsnip, peeled
1 tablespoon salt
Little Dumplings (page 178)
1 tablespoon lard

1 small onion, minced
2 tablespoons flour
3 garlic cloves, chopped and
  mashed
1 tablespoon hot paprika
1 cup yogurt
1 teaspoon white vinegar

1. Soak beans in 1 quart cold water the night before you plan to make soup. Next day, drain beans and put aside.

2. Put 2 quarts water in a large soup pot and in it cook bones and vegetables with salt over low heat for 2 hours. Strain, and save liquid.

3. Put drained beans into the reserved liquid; add enough water to bring the amount back to 2 quarts. Cook covered over low heat till beans are done.

4. Make little dumplings (*galuska*) and put aside.

5. Melt the lard in a frying pan. Wilt onion in it, then mix in the flour and cook over very low heat till the mixture is light brown.

6. Remove from heat and mix in mashed garlic and paprika. Whip in ½ cup cold water. Add to the almost ready bean soup and cook the soup over very low heat for at least 10 minutes longer.

7. Just before serving, mix in yogurt and vinegar, adjust salt, and mix in little dumplings.

NOTE: *This southern Hungarian dish probably appears in Serbian cookbooks as a Serbian dish, where I hope it is titled "Hungarian Bean Soup." It should be spicy (use hot paprika or mix mild paprika with cayenne) and piquant-sour.*

BEAN SOUP À LA JÓKAI

Jókai bableves   *8 servings*

2 smoked pig's feet
½ pound smoked pork ribs
1 knob celery, peeled and diced
¼ pound fresh shell beans (see Note)
1 medium-sized onion, peeled and chopped
1 tablespoon lard

1 tablespoon chopped flat parsley
1 tablespoon flour
½ tablespoon paprika
1 garlic clove, mashed
½ pound smoked pork sausage
Salt
2 tablespoons sour cream

1. Cook smoked pig's feet and pork ribs in 2 quarts water till the meat comes off the bones. Bone them, and put meat pieces aside.

2. Add the diced knob celery and the beans to the meat broth, and cook till beans are done.

3. Meantime, fry onion in lard over low heat. When onion is wilted, add chopped parsley and flour and make a brown *roux* over the lowest heat possible. Stir often to prevent burning.

4. When the *roux* is light brown, mix in paprika and garlic; immediately add 1 cup of cold water. Whip till smooth, then pour into the cooked beans.

5. Add smoked sausage and ½ tablespoon salt. Simmer for 10 more minutes.

6. Cut smoked meats into small pieces, and add to the soup. Adjust salt. Add the sour cream.

7. Serve with Little Pinched Dumplings, *csipetke* (page 178).

NOTE: *The best time to make this soup is when fresh shell beans are available. However, the soup can be made with the usual dried beans, too. Almost any type can be used—cranberry or pinto beans, for instance. If you use dried beans, soak them overnight first.*

Smoked pork rib and smoked pig's feet are generally sold in the United States in Southern-style butcher shops. Any part of pork can be used.

BEEF DUMPLING SOUP AS IN LŐCSE

Lőcsei marhagombócleves   *8 servings*

Beef Dumplings as in Lőcse
  (page 180)
1 teaspoon salt
2 egg yolks

6 cups beef broth
1 tablespoon lemon juice
1 tablespoon minced flat
  parsley

1. Make the dumplings. Bring 4 cups water to a boil with the salt, and cook dumplings over very low heat for 20 to 25 minutes. Stir the water carefully several times.

2. Lift the dumplings from the water with a slotted spoon and place them in a soup tureen. Keep the water at a simmer.

3. Beat the egg yolks, then whip them into the simmering water. Add the beef broth, lemon juice and parsley. Pour the soup over the dumplings in the tureen.

LEBBENCS SOUP

Lebbencsleves   *8 servings*

½ cup flour
1 egg
Salt
1 pound potatoes, peeled
2 quarts broth or water
¼ pound smoked bacon,
  diced

1 small onion, minced
1 green pepper, cut into thin
  slices
1 tablespoon paprika
1 medium-sized tomato,
  peeled and chopped

1. Knead the flour, egg and a pinch of salt into a hard dough. Roll it very thin and let it dry for about 2 hours. By that time the texture of this dough should be almost like a stiff blotting paper.

2. Cut potatoes into ½-inch cubes and cook them in 2 quarts broth or water for about 10 minutes.

3. In a heavy soup pot, fry diced bacon over low heat. Remove the fried

little crackling pieces and set aside.

4. Put into remaining fat the onion and broken chips of the dough. (Shapes of the dough chips will resemble uneven segments of a broken slate.) Brown the onion and noodle pieces together over low heat for 5 to 10 minutes.

5. Add 1 teaspoon salt, the green pepper, potatoes with their liquid, paprika, tomato and, finally, the crackling pieces.

6. Cook everything gently until potatoes and noodle pieces are done, which should be another 5 to 10 minutes. Adjust salt.

NOTE: *This is an ancient soup, common in the farm kitchens of the Great Plains.*

PALÓC SOUP

Palócleves   *8 servings*

3 slices bacon
1 medium-sized onion, minced
2 pounds boned lean lamb, cut into ¼-inch dice
Pinch of caraway seeds
1 tablespoon paprika
1 garlic clove, mashed
1 pound young green beans, cut into 1-inch pieces
2 tablespoons salt

1 tablespoon flour
1 tablespoon lard
1 pound potatoes, peeled and diced
½ bay leaf
Pinch of black pepper
¾ cup sour cream
1 tablespoon chopped flat parsley

1. Cut the bacon into small pieces and fry in a saucepan until it releases enough fat to fry the onion. Add the onion and fry for 5 minutes.

2. Put lamb in the pot and add ¼ cup water, the caraway seeds, paprika and garlic. Cook covered over very low heat until done. Stir often, and add a little water every now and then to prevent burning.

3. In the meantime cook cut green beans in 2 cups water with ½ teaspoon salt until they are tender but still somewhat crunchy. Save the cooking liquid.

4. Make a *roux* with flour and lard and cook it to a golden-brown color. Dilute it with 1 cup cold water and add to meat in pot.

5. Cook potatoes with bay leaf and ½ teaspoon salt in 1½ quarts water until they are done but not soft.

6. Pour both potatoes and beans with their cooking liquid into the meat pot. Add enough water to make 2 quarts. Add salt to taste, about 1 tablespoon,

and the pepper. Bring to a slow boil and cook for an additional 10 minutes.

7. Adjust seasoning and mix in sour cream. Put in soup tureen and sprinkle with parsley.

NOTE: *János Gundel created this soup for Mikszáth, the famed "Hungarian Mark Twain," in a private dining room of the István Főherceg Hotel (see page 49) in 1892. Mikszáth wrote a book about the Palóc people, inhabitants of northeast Hungary (see page 96), which became a treasured classic of Hungarian literature. One day he challenged the restaurateur to cook something for him that was different. Gundel rose to the challenge and made a soup which is basically a mutton gulyás, but by adding a lot of fresh green beans he changed its character completely. His son Károly "revived" his father's specialty in the mid-1930's.*

FOWL SOUP, ÚJHÁZI STYLE

Újházi tyúkleves 8 to 10 servings

1 fowl, 3 to 5 pounds
6 black peppercorns
1 tablespoon salt
1 small onion, chopped
2 garlic cloves, crushed
1 medium-sized tomato, peeled, chopped and seeded
1 thin slice of fresh ginger root
3 small young carrots, peeled
2 young parsnips, peeled
1 knob celery, peeled and sliced
½ cup shelled fresh peas
½ head of cauliflower, broken into flowerets
1 small green pepper, diced
¼ pound mushrooms, peeled and sliced
Soup Noodles (page 178)

1. Cut the cleaned fowl into 8 pieces. Place in a soup pot with 3 quarts cold water, peppercorns and salt. Slowly bring to a boil.

2. Just before the liquid starts to boil, add ¼ cup cold water. Repeat this once more. Each time you will have a lot of scum on top, which should be carefully removed with a ladle.

3. Add onion, garlic, tomato and ginger root. Cook over very low heat, just below boiling point, for 45 minutes.

4. Add whole carrots and parsnips, the knob celery, peas and cauliflower. Cook for another hour, again making sure that soup never boils.

5. About 10 minutes before you decide that the fowl will be done, add green pepper and mushrooms.

6. Make noodles and cook.

7. Adjust saltiness of soup and add cooked noodles. Before serving, remove the slice of ginger root.

NOTE: *This soup was named after a famous nineteenth-century actor, Ede Újházi, and it is a Hungarian version of the French poule au pot. Újházi used a rooster for the soup, to give it the concentrated flavor he wanted to achieve.*

Depending on the age of the fowl, soup will have to be cooked less or more. Generally you should figure on about 1½ hours of cooking time. However, if the fowl saw Franz Josef in short pants, you may have to increase it to 2 hours.

In some parts of Transdanubia the housewife browns carrots and onion in chicken fat to color the soup to an intense yellow. Up to the nineteenth century a touch of saffron was added for the same purpose.

Another trick they use in some houses is dry-browning half onions with their skins, on top of the stove or in a frying pan without fat. By adding this to the soup you get a very golden liquid.

The inner core (about the size of an orange) of Savoy cabbage is optional and you will find it in many recipes, but I feel its taste is too pronounced and overwhelms the rest. You may, however, want to try it once.

Another possibility is to put 1 pound of good beef flank in the water and cook it for 1 hour, then proceed with the recipe. According to some contemporary reports, this is how the amateur chef-actor did it.

If you want to add marrowbones, salt the open ends of the bones to keep the marrow from coming out during cooking.

FOWL SOUP WITH WHITE RAISINS

Mazsolás tyúkhúsleves   8 servings

1 fat, 4- or 5-pound fowl or pullet

Bouquet of a few sprigs of flat parsley and the greens from a knob celery, tied together

1 tablespoon salt

1 parsnip, peeled

1 knob celery, whole, peeled

3 carrots, peeled and sliced

1 small onion, peeled

1 cup white raisins

5 pieces of cube sugar

2 lemons, peeled and halved

1 cup sweet or fruity white wine

1 tablespoon chicken fat

2 tablespoons flour

¼ cup sour cream

1. Put the bird in a large pot with 3 to 4 quarts water, together with the bouquet of greens and the salt. Bring the water nearly to a boil and just before it starts to simmer add a little cold water to delay boiling. Skim off scum and repeat this procedure twice.

2. Add washed, peeled vegetables and cook slowly for about 2 hours, until the fowl is tender.

3. When the bird is cooked, take it out and remove the meat from bones. Cut the meat into chunks and put aside.

4. In a separate pot cook the raisins, sugar and peeled lemons in the white wine for 10 minutes. Discard lemons.

5. Discard all vegetables but carrots and strain soup through cheesecloth. Add meat chunks and the raisin-wine mixture to the strained broth.

6. Make a light *roux* of chicken fat and flour. Add ½ cup cold water and stir it well. Pour thickening into the soup, and boil for another 5 minutes.

7. Remove the soup from the heat and stir in sour cream. Adjust salt and sugar. Serve in extra large soup plates.

NOTE: *This is a traditional wedding soup in the city of Debrecen. This recipe comes from a local housewife, Mrs. János Szathmáry. Although usually served as a first course, this soup, followed by a substantial dessert, can constitute luncheon.*

GUINEA HEN POTAGE AS IN CSURGÓ

Csurgói gyöngytyúkleves   8 servings

¾ pound veal and beef bones	1 parsnip, peeled and diced
1 turnip, peeled and sliced	1 small onion, diced
1 knob celery, peeled and sliced	2 tablespoons bacon drippings
1 bunch flat parsley, minced	1 guinea hen, 4 pounds
	1 teaspoon paprika
1 small onion, peeled and halved	¼ teaspoon caraway seeds
	Pinch of grated nutmeg
Salt	½ cup dry white wine
¼ teaspoon peppercorns	1 tablespoon brandy
2 carrots, peeled and diced	Pepper

1. Put the veal bones, turnip, knob celery, parsley and halved onion into 2 quarts of cold water. Add 1 tablespoon salt and the peppercorns. Just before the water starts to simmer add ¼ cup cold water and skim off impurities. Repeat twice before you allow the broth to simmer slowly for 1 hour. Strain. Discard the bones, but save the vegetables.

2. Cook the diced carrots, parsnip and onion, covered, in melted bacon drippings for about 20 minutes.

3. Add the breast and legs of the guinea hen. Cook for a few minutes on each side, then add paprika, caraway seeds and nutmeg. After cooking slowly for 2 more minutes, pour in wine, brandy and strained broth. Cook until the guinea hen is done.

4. Bone the meat and cut into small bite-sized pieces; return meat to the soup. Add the vegetables saved from the broth. Adjust salt and pepper. Sprinkle top of soup with parsley and serve in a soup tureen.

SHEPHERD'S SOUP AS IN DEBRECEN

Debreceni bárányfejleves   *6 to 8 servings*

Head, neck, lungs and liver of 1 lamb	double-smoked bacon with skin on
Salt	1 tablespoon bacon drippings
½ teaspoon pepper	1 tablespoon flour
1 carrot	1 teaspoon paprika
1 parsnip	1 tablespoon minced flat parsley
1 kohlrabi	2 hard-boiled eggs
1 thick slice (2 ounces) of	

1. Put the lamb head, neck and lungs in a large pot of salted water, and bring to a boil. Add pepper. Reduce heat immediately and skim.

2. Peel and dice the vegetables and add to the lamb with the bacon slice. Cook till the meat comes off the bone.

3. Add the liver for the last 10 minutes of cooking.

4. Take all the meats from the pot. Remove and discard the bones and cut the meats into pieces.

5. In a heavy casserole heat the bacon drippings. Add flour and stir the *roux,* then cook to a golden brown. Remove from heat, and stir in paprika and parsley. Then add 1 cup cold water and whip till smooth.

6. Put the casserole back over low heat and pour in the broth and vegetables that the meat cooked in. Put back the boned meat. Bring soup to a slow simmer and adjust salt and pepper.

7. Slice hard-boiled eggs. Place them in a soup tureen, pour the soup over them, and serve. Or add eggs to the casserole you cooked the soup in and serve in the casserole.

NOTE: *Debrecen is the "capital" of the lowlands, where even today shepherds live as people did before the age of the Industrial Revolution. This recipe is a refined city version of the shepherds' soup. They generally take the same parts of the lamb, place them in a big kettle over an open fire, and cook the soup with onion, paprika and whatever vegetables they can find. The one must is always a big chunk of smoked bacon; for a non-Hungarian this bacon cooked in soup is definitely an acquired taste. The shepherds leave the sheep's head and neck in the soup, but I do not recommend this for the squeamish.*

SOUR-CHERRY SOUP, HUNGARIAN STYLE

Meggykeszőce   *6 to 8 servings*

2 tablespoons flour
1 cup sour cream
Pinch of salt
1 teaspoon confectioners' sugar

1 pound fresh sour cherries,
   pitted
¾ cup granulated sugar

1. Stir flour with sour cream, salt and confectioners' sugar till smooth.

2. Meantime cook sour cherries in 1½ quarts water with granulated sugar till done.

3. Take 2 ladlefuls of liquid from the cherry pot and add to the flour mixture; stir for a few minutes.

4. Pour the mixture back into the soup and simmer for 5 minutes. Cover the soup and let it cool that way; this way it won't develop a skin. Adjust salt.

NOTE: *In some parts of Hungary this is called sour-cherry* cibere. *In other parts, however, they claim that this word should only be used for a cold soup made of beets. The name* meggykeszőce *was already used in the seventeenth century and is recorded in a manuscript of that century together with this recipe.*

You must have fresh sour cherries to make this soup. Do not make it with canned fruit.

GOOSEBERRY SOUP

Egresleves   *6 servings*

1 pound gooseberries, cleaned
   (no stems)
¼ to ½ cup sugar
2 thin round slices of lemon

½ cup sweet white wine
½ cup sour cream
1 tablespoon flour

1. Cook gooseberries with sugar and lemon slices in 5 cups water and the wine until berries are done. Depending on the age of the fruit, this can take from 10 to 30 minutes.

2. Meantime, mix sour cream and flour. Add a ladleful of the hot broth and whip the mixture to a smooth paste.

3. Pour the paste into the cooked fruit and liquid. Turn off heat but let the soup stand for a few minutes before serving.

NOTE: *Start with ¼ cup sugar and adjust it later. The acidity content of gooseberries varies.*

CHILLED CREAM OF DILLED SQUASH

Hideg kapros tökleves   *6 servings*

1 small onion, sliced	1 medium-sized potato
1 celery rib, chopped	1½ quarts beef stock
1 carrot, chopped	4 dill sprigs, leaves only,
¼ cup butter	chopped
2 yellow crookneck squash,	¾ cup heavy cream
each about ¾ pound	Salt and pepper

1. Sauté onion, celery and carrot in butter until soft but not browned.

2. Peel squash and potato. Cut into ½-inch dice; discard squash seeds. Add to stock, with sautéed vegetables, and cook until squash is tender, about 30 minutes.

3. Strain, and force vegetables through a sieve into the liquid. Add the chopped dill and simmer for 2 minutes.

4. Mix in cream, and adjust seasoning to taste. Chill. Serve in chilled soup cups.

PEACH IN CHAMPAGNE SOUP

Hideg őszibarackleves, pezsgővel   *6 servings*

8 very ripe peaches	½ bottle champagne
2 tablespoons plus 1 cup sugar	½ cup white Riesling wine

1. Peel the peaches; halve 3 peaches and sprinkle with 2 tablespoons sugar; set aside. Dice the rest of the peaches.

2. Crack peach pits, take out inner seeds, and peel. Crush the seeds in a mortar.

3. Add the diced peaches to the seeds and mash together or purée in a blender. Add 1 cup sugar, mix, and force through a sieve.

4. Add champagne and Riesling and gently stir, taking care not to release too many of the bubbles.

5. Place ½ peach in each soup cup (use crystal cups), and fill with puréed peaches and wine.

NOTE: *Adjust sugar to the sweetness of the peaches.*

✳ 12 ✳

SOUP GARNISHES
(LEVESBE VALÓK)

FRENCH cuisine is famous for making innumerable variations on a single idea. For instance, the so-called *royales,* custardlike little diamonds, are probably made in at least fifty different flavors and colors. This is not in the character of the Hungarian kitchen. Hungarians do make many soup garnishes, but each stands on its own, quite unrelated to other kinds. The exception to this is noodle garnitures. Many shapes of noodles for soup are made by cutting, pinching, grating or rolling the dough. One ancient soup noodle is the "snail." The dough is rolled into snail shapes on a grooved wooden or ceramic strip. In the villages during winter months it is a social event when cooks get together to make these snail noodles, which will last throughout the year.

KNEADED DOUGHS

Pile sifted flour on a kneading board. Make a small nest in the center and break eggs into it; add as much water as needed to make the dough neither too soft nor too hard when kneaded (see exact recipes). Add salt before kneading. Work the dough well to make sure it is completely smooth. Then make small loaves and knead them well, individually. Leave in loaf forms, oiling very lightly at the top, and cover with a cloth. Let the loaves rest for 10 to 15 minutes.

Sprinkle the kneading board with flour, and roll the loaves to the thinness that is right for the purpose. When the dough is stretched to the proper thinness, lightly sprinkle with flour and let it dry for 5 minutes.

If you use this dough as a soup noodle, then eliminate water. You can roll dough very thin and cut it into vermicelli-like shapes or squares. If you leave it thicker, you can tear off little pieces to make the traditional Hungarian *csipetke,* but you must dip your hand into flour as you work to prevent sticking. Do not pile *csipetke* on top of each other because they will stick in the warmth of the kitchen.

SOUP NOODLES

Laskatészta levesbe   *4 to 6 servings*

½ cup flour   Salt
1 egg

1. Knead a hard dough from flour, egg and a pinch of salt. Roll it out very thin and cut thin vermicelli noodles.
2. Bring 3 quarts water and 2 tablespoons salt to a boil. Cook noodles in rapidly boiling water for 3 minutes, or until done. Drain and rinse with cold water.

LITTLE DUMPLINGS

Galuska, levesbe   *2 servings*

1 egg   Pinch of salt
3 tablespoons flour   1 teaspoon of vegetable oil

1. Mix the egg with flour and salt.
2. Spoon the mixture into boiling soup, using ¼ teaspoon at a time. Cook in the soup for 2 or 3 minutes just before serving.

LITTLE PINCHED DUMPLINGS

Csipetke   *About 2-3 servings*

½ cup flour   Salt
1 egg   Flour

1. Make a hard dough by kneading the ½ cup flour and egg for about 5 minutes. Let the dough rest for 15 minutes.
2. Cut the dough into 6 pieces and roll each to finger thickness. You will get about a 6-inch length from each.

3. Bring 4 quarts water with 1 tablespoon salt to a boil. Sprinkle a little flour on the dough and pinch off little pieces. Drop them into the boiling water. Use thumb and index fingers to pinch off the pieces.

4. Boil the dumplings till they come to the surface, then sample one to make sure it's cooked through.

NOTE: *You may drop the* csipetke *directly into goulash soup, bean soup, or any other soup you use it for.*

Joseph Wechsberg once said that the real experts can tell not only if the cook was left-handed, but can even identify by the shape of the dumpling the person who pinched off the csipetke.

POTATO DUMPLINGS

Krumplis gombóc   *4 to 6 servings*

2 medium-sized potatoes   1 egg
1 tablespoon butter   Pinch of salt
1 heaping tablespoon flour

1. Boil unpeeled potatoes in 2 quarts water. When done, peel them and purée while still warm.

2. Add butter, flour, egg and salt. Mix the dough and knead it well.

3. With a spoon cut off pieces of dough. Flour your hands and roll the pieces into round dumplings.

4. Drop dumplings into boiling soup and cook for about 5 minutes, until tender.

CHICKEN-LIVER DUMPLINGS

Májgombóc, levesbe   *18 to 20 walnut-
                            sized dumplings*

2 chicken livers   ½ tablespoon minced flat
2 eggs   parsley
2 tablespoons melted chicken   Salt
    fat   ½ cup white bread crumbs
Pinch of pepper   1 tablespoon flour

1. Place chicken livers on a wooden board and scrape them with a knife, making a pulp of the livers, or chop in a blender. Place pulp in a mixing bowl.

2. Add eggs, chicken fat, pepper, parsley and a little salt; mix well. Add bread crumbs and flour and mix further. Let the batter rest for 1 to 2 hours before poaching it.

3. After the soup is ready, make little balls out of the liver mixture: wet your palms and roll about 1 teaspoon of the mixture between the palms.

4. Cook balls in the soup over very low heat for 10 minutes.

NOTE: *If chicken livers are small, you can increase the amount to 3 chicken livers.*

Bread crumbs are generally taken for granted. The Hungarian housewife always saves white bread and rolls, scrapes off and discards the crusts, then pounds these leftover dry pieces whenever she needs bread crumbs.

BEEF DUMPLINGS AS IN LŐCSE

Lőcsei marhagombócok　　　　　*10 to 12 walnut-sized dumplings*

½ pound lean beef (top round, top sirloin, etc.), ground twice
2 large potatoes, peeled and grated

1 egg
1 tablespoon flour
1 tablespoon semolina
Salt and pepper

1. Mix meat, potatoes, egg, flour, semolina, and a little salt and pepper. When thoroughly mixed, make walnut-sized dumplings.

2. Bring 1 quart of water to a boil with 1 teaspoon salt. Drop dumplings into the boiling water and cook over very low heat for 20 to 25 minutes. Stir carefully several times.

NOTE: *These dumplings can be used separately for any soup. Also, they can be sautéed with bacon and served as a separate course.*

LITTLE POCKETS FILLED WITH CALF'S LUNG

Tüdőtáska levesbe　　　　　*6 to 8 servings*

1 cup flour
1 egg
Pinch of salt
Calf's-Lung Filling (see below)

1 egg mixed with 1 teaspoon water (for egg wash)

1. Make a dough out of the flour, 1 egg, ¼ cup water and the salt. Knead, then let the dough rest for 10 minutes.

2. Stretch dough into a thin sheet and cut into halves.

3. On half of the dough place teaspoons of the filling, at intervals of 1½ inches, in the same way you would make ravioli. Brush the spaces in between the mounds of filling with the egg wash.

4. Gently place the other half of the dough on top and push down in the spaces around the filling. Cut around the mounds of filling with a ravioli cutter. The little squares should be quite even.

5. Place pockets in salted boiling water and cook for about 5 minutes. Do not put too many in the water at once because they will stick together. For a more refined taste, boil them in a meat broth.

CALF'S-LUNG FILLING

Borjútüdő töltelék

¼ pound calf's lung	Pinch of white pepper
¼ medium-sized onion	½ teaspoon minced flat parsley
1 tablespoon lard or chicken fat	1 egg
Pinch of salt	

1. Cook lung in salted water for 30 minutes. Drain and grind.

2. Chop onion very, very fine and cook it in the lard over very low heat until it is quite limp and most of the moisture has cooked away.

3. Add ground calf's lung with salt, pepper and parsley, and cook for a few minutes to blend the flavors.

4. Take the mixture off the heat and add the egg; mix well. Use the filling when it is cool.

NOTE: *This noodle dough can be used with a variety of fillings—ground liver, chicken, veal, pork, and so on.*

Do not boil Little Pockets in the soup you will serve them in, because a large quantity of the soup would be soaked up during the process.

Poor families in Hungary always use the water in which the noodles were cooked, and flavor it somehow, serving it as a soup by itself.

SEMOLINA DUMPLINGS

Daragombóc   *12 walnut-sized dumplings*

1 egg	2 quarts beef or chicken broth
Pinch of salt	or salted water
½ cup semolina	

1. You must boil this dumpling mixture immediately after you make it. Mix together well, for about 3 minutes, the egg, salt and semolina.

2. Bring broth or water to a boil. Dip a teaspoon into the boiling liquid, then cut ½ spoonful from dumpling mixture and gently drop it into the pot. Continue with the rest of the mixture. These dumplings should be about the size of almonds when you drop them into the broth. They will swell to walnut size while cooking.

3. Reduce heat to low. Cook dumplings for about 10 minutes.

NOTE: *I have over 50 recipes for this soup dumpling, but this is the most sure-fire formula, through the courtesy of Mrs. Jenny Stratford.*

Hungarian semolina is much coarser than other kinds. If you find some, purchase it; it will make a better dumpling.

THIMBLE DOUGHNUTS

Gyűszűfánk   *6 to 8 servings*

1 cup flour	Pinch of salt
2 eggs	1 cup lard

1. Make a semihard dough by kneading flour, eggs and salt on a floured board. If eggs are extra large you may have to add a little more flour. Roll dough till it is knife-edge thin.

2. Wipe flour from the dough with a barely damp cloth and fold sheet in half. It will stick together.

3. Take a thimble and press into the dough, making as many tiny circles as possible.

4. Heat lard in a frying pan. Turn heat down to low. (Hot lard will not spatter if you put a bit of salt into it.) Fry the thimbles for 1 or 2 minutes, turning once. Remove with a slotted spoon and drain on triple-thick paper toweling.

NOTE: *These are very good homemade noodles for almost any soup. You can also serve them separately so guests can help themselves.*

FRIED SOUP PEAS

Rántott borsó   *6 to 8 servings*

1 egg	Pinch of salt
½ cup flour	1 cup lard or chicken fat
⅓ cup milk	

1. Mix egg, flour, milk and salt till smooth.

2. Bring lard to frying temperature in a large frying pan (just before smoking), then turn down to low heat.

3. Use a sieve with large holes; little by little drip the batter through the holes into the frying pan, making sure the drops do not fall on top of each other but rather next to each other.

4. Immediately move the "peas" with a wooden fork or spatula with a long blade to prevent sticking. Separate them if they clump together. Turn them till they are light brown, then remove with a slotted spoon onto heavy paper toweling.

NOTE: *In Hungary special equipment is used to make this soup garniture. The batter can be pushed through pastry tubes or separated with tiny demitasse spoons. However, the easiest and fastest method is the one described.*

If you make the "peas" hours before serving, heat them up in the oven for a few minutes till they are hot and crisp.

TRICKLED SOUP NOODLES

Csurgatott tészta levesbe   *about 8 servings*

2 eggs   ½ cup flour
Pinch of salt

1. Mix eggs, 2 tablespoons water and the salt in a bowl. Add flour and stir with a wooden spoon till the mixture is completely blended.

2. Dip a metal or plastic funnel with a small opening (about the thickness of a strand of spaghetti) into hot water. Cover the opening with your index finger and pour in the semiliquid batter.

3. Remove your finger and let the batter trickle into boiling soup. Reduce heat to a simmer and cook the noodles for 5 minutes.

NOTE: *Although these are used for all types of soups in Hungary, don't use them for clear soups if you like to keep the soup clear; rather, use them for potages and such.*

✶ 13 ✶

APPETIZERS
(ELŐÉTELEK)

ONLY in the dining rooms of the aristocrats and the very well-to-do would we find the kind of dinner menu that starts with an appetizer, or where an appetizer follows the soup, either instead of or in addition to a fish course. Hence there are few recipes for such preparations. However, many dishes in addition to those identified as appetizers, even vegetable preparations, can be used as appetizers in a traditional Hungarian menu. See pages 306 to 330.

STUFFED EGGS CASINO

Töltött kaszinótojás majonézes salátával   *10 servings*

10 eggs, boiled until very hard	1 teaspoon salt
1 tablespoon butter, softened	Pinch of white pepper
1 tablespoon sour cream	20 rolled anchovy fillets stuffed
1 tablespoon prepared	with capers
Düsseldorf-style mustard	Vegetable Salad (see below)

1. Shell cold hard-boiled eggs and cut lengthwise into halves.

2. Purée yolks and mix well with softened butter, sour cream, mustard, salt and pepper.

3. Fill egg whites, smooth tops to even mounds, and decorate each half with an anchovy.

4. Arrange eggs on top of vegetable salad.

NOTE: *The name of this dish is an abbreviation of the National Casino, where this was served as an appetizer in the middle of the nineteenth cen-*

tury (see page 58). Although this recipe may seem similar to stuffed eggs with salade à la russe, *the actual dish is distinctively different.*

VEGETABLE SALAD

Zöldségsaláta

½ pound green beans, sliced
2 young carrots, peeled and diced
½ cup shelled peas
1 small knob celery, peeled and diced
Salt
6 raw egg yolks

1 tablespoon prepared Düsseldorf-style mustard
2 tablespoons sugar
3 tablespoons lemon juice
2 cups sour cream
½ sour apple, peeled and diced
1 medium-sized semisour pickle, peeled and chopped

1. Cook vegetables with ½ teaspoon salt in as little water as possible in a covered pot.

2. Strain and cool (broth may be saved to make vegetable soup).

3. Mix raw egg yolks with mustard, sugar, lemon juice, sour cream, and a pinch of salt. Cook over very low heat or in the top part of a double boiler while whipping all the time. When the sauce starts bubbling, take it off the heat.

4. Add cooked vegetables, chopped apple and chopped pickle. Mix, and chill.

5. Put salad on a large serving platter and top with stuffed eggs.

NOTE: *Use as an appetizer or a luncheon dish. In Hungary, vegetable salad is sometimes served to accompany cold ham or duckling.*

Mustard can be replaced by ½ teaspoon minced fresh or marinated tarragon leaves.

All vegetables must be fresh.

DUCK PÂTÉ À LA SZATHMÁRY

Kacsapástétom   *4 to 6 servings*

¾ cup minced onions
2 to 3 tablespoons plus ¼ pound lard or duck fat
8 ounces raw duck livers
12 ounces cooked meat (chicken, beef, veal, pork)

6 ounces unsalted butter, at room temperature
1 to 2 tablespoons Spice Mixture (see next page)
2 tablespoons good brandy or Cognac

185

1. Sauté onions in 2 to 3 tablespoons of the lard or duck fat until very limp, but do not brown.

2. Add livers to onions. Raise heat and sauté livers until last trace of pink disappears from the thickest part of each liver. Cool.

3. Grind cooked meat three times. Any roasted, broiled, boiled, baked, braised or fried meat is good—chicken with skin, duck, turkey, pork, veal or beef—but do not use any lamb or mutton. Grind liver and onion mixture three times.

4. Put liver and onion mixture, ground meat, unsalted butter and remaining lard in a large mixer bowl. Mix with electric mixer on slow speed until fluffy.

5. Add spice mixture and brandy. Correct seasoning; add more salt and spice if needed. Chill. Serve with pickles and crusty bread.

SPICE MIXTURE

1 tablespoon powdered bay leaf	1 teaspoon ground cloves
1 tablespoon dried thyme	½ teaspoon ground allspice
1 tablespoon ground mace	1 teaspoon ground white
1 tablespoon dried rosemary	pepper
1 tablespoon dried basil	2 teaspoons paprika
2 tablespoons ground cinnamon	1 cup fine table salt

1. Mix all ingredients well in a spice mortar. If you have no mortar put them all in a deep bowl and crush with the bottom of a cup.

2. Sift through a fine sieve three times; crush again what remains in the sieve until everything goes through. Store it in a very well-sealed jar, refrigerated.

NOTE: *By the courtesy of my friend and colleague Louis Szathmáry.*

LIPTÓ CHEESE SPREAD

Körözött juhtúró

½ pound Liptó sheep's-milk cheese	½ teaspoon prepared mustard
¼ pound lightly salted butter, softened	½ teaspoon pounded caraway seeds
1 teaspoon paprika	1 small onion, grated
	½ teaspoon anchovy paste

1. Sieve the cheese and mix it with softened butter and all other ingredients till the spread is light red in color and evenly mixed. Refrigerate.

2. Serve with wedges of good, crusty bread or toast, accompanied by young radishes, green peppers or scallions.

NOTE: *The cheese which is the base of the spread originally came from a north Hungarian area called Liptó. The Austrians, who make a similar mixture, call the spread itself Liptauer or, more correctly,* Liptauer, garniert. *Since in Hungary* Liptó *is only the name of the cheese itself, this causes undue mixups in non-Hungarian recipes. If you are unable to buy the real sheep's-milk cheese, a very similar product called Brindza, which comes from Rumania, can generally be purchased in the better cheese stores.*

The basic musts are the sheep's-milk cheese, paprika, onion and caraway seeds. All the other ingredients are optional.

In my home town I would not eat this cheese spread at my friend's house because her mother also put capers and sardines in the mixture.

In aristocratic houses and at the National Casino the spread was served topped with Beluga caviar, which makes a very good combination, particularly if you get tired of eating caviar in the traditional way.

Trieste, on the Adriatic, was part of the Austro-Hungarian Empire until the Treaty of Trianon in 1920, but even then it had a strong Italian food influence. The same cheese spread was made in Trieste with Gorgonzola cheese substituting for the sheep's-milk cheese and Mascarpone, a fresh cream cheese, substituting for the butter.

ASPIC OF PORK

Disznókocsonya   6 to 8 servings

1 pork head	Salt
1 pork tongue	10 whole peppercorns
1 pig's knuckle	3 garlic cloves, mashed
2 pig's feet	2 egg whites

1. Cut meat into pieces and put in a large pot with enough water to cover. Salt lightly. Add peppercorns and cook, covered, till the meat easily comes off the bones. During cooking skim off foam and scum several times.

2. Remove meat and debone. Cut everything into ½-inch dice or small pieces. Because of the different textures you will not be able to cut it evenly.

3. Take fat off the broth remaining in the pot. Add garlic to the broth and boil till broth is reduced by half.

4. Beat the egg whites and mix into the broth. Keep stirring over heat for about 5 minutes while egg whites harden and gather the impurities in the broth. When foam hardens, remove all scum. Turn down heat to lowest and simmer for an additional 10 minutes. Strain broth through a triple layer of cheesecloth which has been rinsed in cold water.

5. Use individual soup plates or molds or one large mold (a pâté form or any other type). Place some of the meat in individual molds or the one large mold. Strain enough broth over meat to cover completely. After the broth cools, place it in the refrigerator to jell.

NOTE: *Many Hungarian houswives add 1 tablespoon paprika to the broth. Do not add any gelatin unless you want to play ball with the leftovers.*

HOT CHEESE CRACKERS

Sajtos izelítő   *30 paired crackers*

¾ cup flour   3 tablespoons sour cream
½ pound lightly salted butter   ½ teaspoon paprika
½ pound Swiss cheese, grated   Salt

1. Mix the flour and half of the butter till the mixture forms crumbs. Add half of the cheese, 2 tablespoons of the sour cream, the paprika and a little salt. Knead dough well, then let it rest in the refrigerator for a couple of hours.

2. Preheat oven to 350°F. Stretch the dough to a sheet ¼ inch thick. Cut pieces with a small round cookie cutter.

3. Bake the rounds in the preheated oven for 12 to 15 minutes.

4. Mix remaining butter, cheese and sour cream and spread a ¼-inch layer on the cooled biscuits. Place a second biscuit on top, making little sandwiches out of them.

NOTE: *If you are not serving these immediately, do not assemble the "sandwiches." Before serving, place the dough rounds in a 150°F. oven for 10 minutes, then fill as above.*

You may use this filling in puff-pastry cakes or tubes. Fill them with a pastry bag.

HOT CHEESE APPETIZERS

Sajtos tekercsek és kockák   *30 or 40 pieces*

Puff Pastry (page 430)   ½ cup grated Swiss cheese
1 egg, beaten

1. Preheat oven to 400°F. Stretch finished puff pastry to a sheet ¼ inch thick. Cut into halves.

2. Here are two ways to shape appetizers; you can cut the dough in many other shapes. Cut one portion into 2-inch squares. Brush surfaces with beaten egg, and sprinkle with some of the cheese.

3. Cut the other portion into strips 6 inches long and 1 inch wide. Put 2 strips together to make an ✕, then twist each end from the center out to make a spiral. Place the spirals on a baking sheet, brush with beaten egg, and sprinkle with grated cheese.

4. Bake both pastries in the preheated oven for 10 to 15 minutes, until the pastry has a nice color.

NOTE: *This is one of many cheese pastry appetizers that Hungarian housewives make to accompany wine.*

CONGRESSMAN'S CHEESE DOUGHNUT

Sajtos képviselőfánk   makes about 20 doughnuts

1 cup milk	7 egg yolks
5 tablespoons butter	Pinch of salt
1 cup flour	

1. Bring milk and butter to a boil. Remove from heat and stir in the flour, mixing until mixture is smooth. Cool.

2. When mixture is lukewarm, stir in six of the egg yolks, one by one, mixing well after each addition. Form walnut-sized pieces of the dough and place two inches apart on a greased and floured baking sheet. Brush each with beaten egg yolk.

3. Bake at 375°F. for 30 minutes, or until golden brown and dry in the centers.

4. Hollow out center and fill with Lipto Cheese Spread (see page 186) or goose liver pate.

LITTLE HAM CRESCENTS

Sonkás kiflicskék   *24 crescents*

Puff Pastry (page 430)   Pinch of white pepper
½ cup ground boiled ham   Few tarragon leaves, chopped
1 whole egg   1 egg yolk, beaten
1 tablespoon sour cream

1. Preheat oven to 400°F. Stretch finished puff pastry to a very thin sheet. Cut into 4-inch squares.
2. Mix ham, whole egg, sour cream, pepper and tarragon.
3. Put ½ teaspoon on one corner of each square. Roll up each filled square like a crescent; bend the ends slightly. Brush tops with beaten egg yolk.
4. Bake for 12 to 15 minutes, until light brown in color. Serve as a hot hors d'oeuvre or to accompany soup.

LAYERED HAM TORTE

Réteges sonkatorta   *6 to 8 servings*

1 pound boiled ham without   2 tablespoons sour cream
  bones   ½ tablespoon black pepper
1 white roll   Puff Pastry (page 430)
½ cup milk   1 whole egg (for glaze), beaten
4 eggs, separated

1. Grind ham very fine; put it through the machine twice.
2. Soak the roll in milk, squeeze it, and force through a sieve or purée in a blender.
3. Add puréed roll to ham together with egg yolks, sour cream and pepper.
4. Beat egg whites till stiff and fold into ham mixture. Mix well but gently.
5. Preheat oven to 375°F. Stretch prepared puff pastry into a very thin sheet. Line a 9-inch round torte pan, 2½ inches high, with two thirds of the dough.
6. Place ham filling in the pastry-lined pan. Cover filling with remaining dough, making it fit the pan.
7. Brush the top with beaten egg, and gently prick holes in a few places. Bake in the preheated oven for 50 minutes.

WILTED CABBAGE IN PASTRY SQUARES

Töltött leveles tészta   about 16 pieces

2 pounds fresh cabbage
Salt
4 tablespoons lightly salted
  butter
½ tablespoon sugar

½ teaspoon freshly ground
  black pepper
Puff Pastry (page 430)
1 egg, beaten

1. Chop cabbage very fine and sprinkle with 2 tablespoons salt. Mix well and let it stand for 2 to 3 hours.
2. Squeeze cabbage well to remove all liquid extracted by the salt.
3. Melt butter in a casserole. Stir in the sugar and carefully brown it, making sure it does not burn.
4. Add cabbage, pepper and salt to taste. Stir well and cook until cabbage becomes golden brown. Stir frequently. This process should take 15 to 20 minutes. Do not cover.
5. Preheat oven to 375°F. Stretch prepared puff pastry into a thin sheet and cut it into 4-inch squares.
6. Brush edges of the squares with beaten egg and place 1 teaspoon of the cabbage mixture in the center of each square. Fold over, pressing edges together. Brush tops of the little pockets with more of the beaten egg.
7. Place squares on a baking sheet and bake in the preheated oven for 15 minutes. Serve as an appetizer or as the main course for a luncheon.

SCRAMBLED EGGS AND CALF'S BRAINS

Velö tojással   4 servings

1 pound calf's brains
1 medium-sized onion, minced
2 tablespoons butter
½ teaspoon white pepper

½ teaspoon paprika
3 eggs
Salt (about 1 teaspoon)

1. Soak brains in cold water and peel off membrane. Drop brains into boiling water for 1 minute, then remove.
2. Dry brains and scrape with a knife, reducing them to a rough pulp.
3. Cook onion in butter over low heat for about 10 minutes.
4. Add pepper, paprika and brains to the onion. Cook covered over very low heat for about 10 minutes.

5. Beat eggs as for scrambling. Just before serving mix in with brains, making a soft scrambled egg out of the mixture. Be sure to mix brains and eggs well. The texture should be almost like a creamy risotto, not like *hard* scrambled eggs. Add salt to taste.

NOTE: *This is a traditional appetizer in Hungary, sometimes served on a slice of toast.*

SCRAMBLED EGGS WITH EGGPLANT

Rántotta törökparadicsommal   *10 to 12 servings*

4 tablespoons butter	Pinch of ground mace
3 small or 2 medium-sized	Pinch of pepper
eggplants, diced	10 eggs
1 garlic clove, mashed	Salt
1 teaspoon minced dillweed	

1. Melt butter and sauté diced eggplants. When soft, add garlic and cook for a few minutes more.

2. Sprinkle with dillweed, mace and pepper.

3. Beat the eggs lightly and add salt to taste. Mix eggs into eggplant and cook until eggs are scrambled.

NOTE: *This Bulgarian-influenced dish is still part of the everyday repertoire in southern Hungary. Sometimes it is made with onion and tomato purée, without garlic and dill.*

Rántotta, or scrambled eggs, and all the variations are popular in all Hungarian kitchens since time immemorial. Gyula Illyés told me that the word originated in medieval times when the verb rantani, *without the acute accent on the first* a, *simply meant to fry or cook something fast.*

STACK OF SCRAMBLED EGGS

Búbos rántotta   *2 appetizer servings,*
     or 1 luncheon serving

1 slice smoked bacon, ½	1 tablespoon sour cream
inch thick	1 tablespoon milk
2 slices rye bread	Pinch of salt
1 tablespoon lard	1 teaspoon paprika
2 eggs	1 teaspoon chopped chives

1. Dice the smoked bacon and rye bread to crouton size.

2. Start frying the bacon. When it has released some fat, add bread croutons and fry them till golden brown. Heat should be low otherwise the bread will burn before bacon has released enough fat.

3. When croutons are crisp and diced bacon has formed fairly crisp cracklings, remove both with a slotted spoon and place on absorbent paper.

4. Strain the bacon fat to remove any little crumbs of bread that will burn, or use 1 tablespoon lard instead. Heat whichever fat you are using.

5. Whip eggs with sour cream, milk and salt. When the fat is hot, put in the croutons and cracklings. Immediately pour in the eggs. Stir very fast and try to make a mound out of each portion. Sprinkle with paprika and chopped chives.

FISH MILT OMELET AS IN CEGLÉD

Ceglédi haltejlepény   *4 to 6 servings*

¾ pound fish milt	2 tablespoons butter
Pinch of marjoram	5 eggs
Salt	1 tablespoon minced flat parsley

1. Gently scrape off the fish milt and cook it, together with the marjoram and a sprinkling of salt, in hot butter for 5 or 6 minutes.

2. At this point beat eggs well and pour them on top of the fish milt. Cook the eggs very slowly for a few minutes, almost like making an egg pancake. The top should remain moist.

3. Gently slide the omelet out of the pan and roll it up. Top with parsley and serve.

4. Cut slices of this roulade for individual portions.

NOTE: *An unusual and excellent fish course. It must be made at the very last minute, just as you would an omelet or a* frittata.

BAKED EGG FROTH

Habjában sült tojás   *1 serving*

2 eggs	3 tablespoons sweet butter,
Pinch of salt	melted

1. Break eggs and separate yolks. Leave each yolk in a half shell.
2. Salt egg whites and whip till stiff.

3. Spoon half of beaten whites into a mound to form a nest. Press an egg-shell into the center of the mound to form a hollow. Then pour egg yolk into the hollow. Place the nest in hot butter already sizzling in an omelet pan.

4. Proceed with the second egg. Be sure there is a little space between the mounds. When the froth is firm, gently turn it upside down, or place in a 400°F. oven, till top is cooked.

5. Serve on a thin slice of toast.

NOTE: *You may also put these egg froths into attractive ovenproof platters or individual shirred-egg dishes and bake them in the oven for about 10 minutes.*

Or put the stiff egg whites into a buttered round ovenproof dish and pour whipped egg yolks into the middle so that when you serve, the dish looks like a single giant shirred egg.

STUFFED EGG IN PASTRY

Tésztában sült töltött tojás　　　　　*10 servings*

1¼ cups flour	½ teaspoon salt
7 ounces butter	10 Stuffed Eggs (see below)
2 egg yolks	1 whole egg (for glaze)
⅓ cup sour cream	

1. Mix flour with butter until the mixture forms crumbs. Then add the egg yolks, sour cream and salt. Knead very quickly. Do not work the dough for more than a few minutes. Shape into a loaf, cover, and put in the refrigerator.

2. Preheat oven to 350°F. Place dough on a floured board and stretch it to a thin sheet. Using a 1½-inch biscuit cutter, make 10 circles. Put them aside. From remaining dough make 10 squares each big enough to cover a whole egg, about 6 inches square.

3. Place a stuffed egg in the center of each square of dough, and wrap tightly.

4. Beat the whole egg with 1 teaspoon water. Using a feather brush, apply the glaze to the dough packages, particularly to the tops. Place the little dough circles on the tops; they will stick if you have used enough egg glaze.

5. Place pastries in the preheated oven for 15 to 20 minutes, or until golden brown. Serve with Tartar Sauce (page 338).

STUFFED EGGS

Töltött tojás

10 eggs, hard cooked	1 teaspoon prepared mustard
1 roll	1 teaspoon minced parsley
½ cup milk	Salt and pepper
6 tablespoons butter, softened	

1. Cut off a slice from the top of each egg just large enough to be able to take out the yolk.

2. Soak the roll in the milk, squeeze it, and force through a sieve or purée in a blender. Mix with softened butter, mustard, parsley, and salt and pepper to taste. Mix in the yolks until the stuffing is smooth, then stuff into the whites and put back the slice you cut off.

SAUCE VARIATION: *Mix 1 teaspoon paprika well with 1 tablespoon milk, then mix with 1 cup sour cream. Add a little salt if you like.*

NOTE: *This makes a suitable luncheon course if you serve it with a leafy salad.*

EGGS À LA METTERNICH

Tojás à la Metternich   6 servings

¾ pound lean veal	Pinch of ground cardamom
1 slice smoked bacon	2 tablespoons bread crumbs
7 eggs	4 tablespoons lard
Pinch of pepper	1 tablespoon vinegar
Pinch of marjoram	1 tablespoon salt

SAUCE

3 egg yolks	Pinch of salt
2 tablespoons fine olive oil	1 tablespoon sugar
1 tablespoon prepared mustard	1 tablespoon chopped parsley

1. Grind veal and bacon twice, then mix with 1 egg, the pepper, marjoram, cardamom and bread crumbs. Divide into 6 parts. Form a flat biscuit shape out of each part.

2. Heat lard in a frying pan, and brown the meat patties on both sides.

Reduce heat and cook on both sides for 3 or 4 minutes to make sure the meat cooks through but is not overdone.

3. Bring to a boil 2 quarts water, the vinegar and salt. Swirl water with a spoon and in the eye of the whirlpool gently drop in, one by one, the remaining 6 whole eggs, shelled. This will cook eggs in such a way that the whites will surround the yolks completely. Cook eggs for 3 or 4 minutes. Remove eggs with a slotted spoon and put in cold water for a few seconds. Drain.

4. Put 1 egg on top of each meat patty. Place patties in a greased baking dish, and put it in a 250°F. oven to keep warm while you make the sauce.

5. Place egg yolks in the top part of a double boiler. Over steaming water add olive oil, drop by drop, beating constantly. Add mustard, salt and sugar when egg begins to coagulate. Finally put in chopped parsley. Keep beating till the sauce becomes thick.

6. Take baking dish from oven, spoon sauce on top of each egg, and serve immediately.

NOTE: *An elegant luncheon dish when accompanied with a crisp salad.*

This was on the menu of several very elegant Hungarian hotels around the turn of the century. Whether it was originated by Hungarian chefs in Vienna or by Viennese chefs in Budapest is hard to tell, but it is one of the few instances where the duality of the monarchy worked well.

MUSHROOM FRITTERS

Bundás csiperkegomba   *1 to 2 dozen fritters, depending on size of mushrooms*

1½ pounds mushrooms	2 eggs, separated
2 tablespoons lemon juice	2 tablespoons vegetable oil
Salt and pepper	1 cup milk
2 tablespoons plus ¾ cup flour	1 cup lard for frying

1. Remove stems of mushrooms. Wipe mushrooms with a damp cloth. Do not wash them!

2. Bring 1 quart water with the lemon juice to a boil. Cook mushrooms in it for 2 minutes. Drain mushrooms and wipe them with a clean cloth. (Discard cooking liquid.)

3. Sprinkle mushrooms with salt and pepper, then dip them into 2 tablespoons flour.

4. Make a thick pancake batter with egg yolks, vegetable oil, milk and ¾

196

cup flour. Whip egg whites stiff. With a rubber spatula, very carefully fold whites into the batter.

5. Dip mushrooms into batter and fry in hot lard. Remove them with a slotted spoon.

NOTE: *Mushrooms are very fragile. Do not overboil or overfry them. And God forbid soaking them in water!*

This is a simple first course, but the texture contrast of thick pancake dough and tender mushroom makes a pleasant surprise.

CHEESE DOUGHNUTS

Sajtos fánk   *5 dozen small doughnuts*

3½ cups milk
2 tablespoons butter
¾ cup farina
Salt
1 cup freshly grated Parmesan
   cheese

3 eggs
2 cups vegetable or flower-seed
   oil for frying

1. Mix together the milk, butter, farina and a pinch of salt. Cook for 3 minutes.

2. Remove from heat and mix in half of the grated cheese. Let the mixture cool for 10 minutes.

3. Add eggs, one by one, beating after each addition.

4. Butter a baking sheet and pour the mass on top of it, spreading it to ½-inch thickness.

5. Cut it to any shape you desire; often the batter is cut into 2-inch rounds.

6. Put oil in a deep fryer; when it is smoking, reduce heat and start frying the little doughnuts. If you put in too many at one time, they will stick together. Fry them for 1 or 2 minutes on each side, until golden brown.

7. Remove doughnuts from the pan with a slotted spoon, and place them on a double layer of paper towels to drain.

8. Dredge the little doughnuts with the rest of the grated cheese, and serve immediately.

NOTE: *Cut the batter into long finger shapes to serve with a good green salad as a luncheon dish. Or make smaller doughnuts, and serve as an accompaniment with strong consommé.*

HAM IN WINTER COAT

Sonka télikabátban   *6 appetizer servings, or 2 or 3 luncheon servings*

3 slices boiled ham, ⅛ inch thick
½ cup flour
1 egg
¼ cup milk
¼ teaspoon salt
1 cup lard or oil

1. Cut each ham slice into halves, making 6 slices each about 4 inches square.

2. Stir together flour, egg, milk, ¼ cup water and salt until you get a smooth mixture. Let the batter stand for 1 hour.

3. Use the batter only just before you are ready to serve, and fry the slices only when guests are already seated. This must be served crisp and hot and just out of the fat.

4. Heat the lard or oil to high temperature in a frying pan.

5. Dip ham slices into batter and fry them over low heat, turning when golden brown and crispy.

NOTE: *For a luncheon dish, serve with a cucumber salad or a beet and onion salad.*

Ham in Fur Coat is the same recipe as this, with one added step. After you have dipped ham slices into batter, dip them into small bread dice and then fry them. The texture is more interesting, but you must continuously remove from the frying pan little pieces of bread that have fallen from the batter coating, lest you have a lot of burned bits and a burned taste in your dish.

SMOKED GOOSE-BREAST PUDDING

Füstölt libamellfelfújt   *8 servings*

4 tablespoons goose or chicken fat
4 tablespoons flour
8 eggs, separated
1½ cups ground or fine-chopped smoked goose breast
Fat for greasing mold
2 tablespoons bread crumbs

1. Mix fat, flour and ⅔ cup water till smooth. Cook the mixture till it becomes a thick paste. Cool it.

2. When cooled, mix paste with egg yolks, then add the ground goose breast.

3. Whip the egg whites to a stiff foam and carefully fold into the first mixture, using a rubber spatula.

4. Grease a pudding mold and sprinkle it with bread crumbs. Fill the mold with the mixture to about three quarters full. Put on a tight cover.

5. Fill a 4-quart pot half full of water. Set pudding mold in the pot and cook for 1 hour. If by chance the water evaporates before pudding is done, add *hot* water to the water bath.

6. When cooked, unmold the pudding to serve it.

NOTE: *This pudding can be a first course or a luncheon or supper dish. Serve with a mushroom sauce made with goose fat.*

In a late nineteenth-century cookbook written by a Hungarian countess, this dish was served as an accompaniment to roast goose. It is more interesting than its English cousin, Yorkshire pudding.

CALF'S-LIVER PUDDING WITH ANCHOVY SAUCE

Borjumájpudding ajókamártással   8 servings

1 pound calf's liver	1 hard white roll
1 small onion, minced	½ bay leaf, crushed
2 tablespoons lard	Salt and pepper
¼ pound smoked bacon, chopped fine	4 eggs, separated
	Butter (for greasing mold)

1. Skin the liver, grind it, then force through a strainer or purée in a blender.

2. Wilt onion in lard and add puréed liver and chopped bacon. Cook over low heat for 5 minutes. Remove from heat.

3. Soak roll in water, squeeze it, then shred it and add to the cooked liver mixture. Also mix in the bay leaf and salt and pepper to taste. Add egg yolks and stir well.

4. Whip egg whites till they peak, then very gently mix them into the liver mixture.

5. Butter the pudding form and fill it with the mixture to three quarters full. Cover tightly.

6. Fill a 4-quart pot half full of hot water and stand the closed pudding mold in it. Steam for 1 hour and 15 minutes. If you must add water to the water bath, make sure it's *boiling*.

7. Serve with Anchovy Sauce (page 343), or plain, as a first course, or for a luncheon, accompanied with a salad.

STUFFED PANCAKES À LA HORTOBÁGY

Hortobágyi húsos palacsinták　　　　　　　*6 servings*

1 pound lean veal, diced
2 medium-sized onions, chopped fine
1 teaspoon salt
1 tablespoon lard

1½ cups sour cream
12 pancakes (see Basic Pancakes, page 372)
¼ cup flour
1 tablespoon paprika

1. Sauté diced veal, onions and salt in lard for 5 minutes.
2. Cover and cook for 5 more minutes.
3. Remove most of the juices from the pan and reserve.
4. Add 2 tablespoons sour cream to the veal and simmer for about 30 minutes.
5. Fill pancakes with the cooked veal and roll. Put pancakes on a serving casserole.
6. Mix remaining sour cream with flour and add reserved pan juices and the paprika. Bring to a simmer.
7. Strain over pancakes and serve immediately.

NOTE: *If you have leftover Paprika Chicken (page 278), bone it, cut it into 1-inch pieces, and use that for a filling.*

✴ 14 ✴

FISH
(HAL)

LET'S face it—fish cookery is not the richest part of the Hungarian kitchen. At the better restaurants you will find *süllő* and *fogas,* possibly pike, *harcsa* and a great many versions of carp. *Kecsege,* a kind of small sturgeon, is also fairly common. But, all in all, the kinds of fish that are found in Lake Balaton and the two major rivers, the Danube and the Tisza, provide a very limited supply compared to, let's say, the Mediterranean species. The cooking methods are also fairly limited, even though I have tried to search out the forgotten and the offbeat.

Crustaceans are limited to the small crab, a fresh-water crayfish, ranging in size from very small to quite large. Generally this is made into a fine soup.

According to Gyula Illyés, as a child he had seen his neighborhood brook in Transylvania flooding the land and the fish washed up on the banks, lying there just waiting to be picked up and cooked. Peasants and workmen were desperately hungry and yet nobody would touch the fish. On the other hand, alongside the big rivers and lakes people lived on fish, and methods were developed special to their regions.

Today there are half a dozen fishes, and perhaps eight or ten very special preparations exist, but these are to be found on virtually all menus. In a way it's like the joke about life in Hungary: "Everything's forbidden, but what is not forbidden is compulsory."

The famous *fogas* (*Luciopera sandra,* a pike-perch) is only *fogas* if over 1½ kilograms (about 3¼ pounds). Smaller fish of the species are called *süllő.* In the Danube *fogas* swims against the flow, which makes the flesh of the river variety tougher.

Balaton *fogas* is flaky; the more "layered" the more valuable it is considered. The scales are silvery and the flesh is pure white. The flavor is lightly nutty, almost like a very young chicken which has been fed on nuts and trout. This predatory fish has green-gray coloring on its back, becoming silvery white toward the stomach, and is decorated with darker stripes starting from the back.

A slightly different variety is known in various countries. The French call it *sandre;* the Germans, *Zander.* The Russian variety is called *soudak, bershik* or *sekret;* this one sometimes reaches 15 to 20 pounds.

For decades, noted scientists argued whether the species in Balaton was a totally different fish or perhaps related to the salmon family. Finally the great naturalist Otto Hermann ended the argument by proving that it belongs to the same family but is a species found only in Lake Balaton and unknown anywhere else. The reason its flesh becomes snow white is that it eats exclusively smaller fishes whose meat is also very white. Its spawning season is April and May, and a *fogas* places an average of 40,000 fish eggs per year. Only about one third of these will develop because, together with other fish eggs, the *fogas* eats some of its own as well. After the first year the fish that is called *süllő* reaches almost 2 pounds in size, sometimes even a little over that. *Fogas* itself is always 2 years old or older.

In the beginning of the nineteenth century, some idiots came up with the idea of draining Lake Balaton, and the great patriot István Széchenyi came to its defense. In his *Steamshipping on the Balaton* he said: "Even if you execute this plan, it would be a crime to destroy the most Hungarian fish, the king of the sweet-water fishes. For this alone, Balaton deserves not to be wiped out as a modern Carthage."

Harcsa (*Silurus glanis,* a sheatfish or a large catfish) is the robber baron of the rivers, sometimes reaching 7 feet in length and 200 to 300 pounds in weight.

Other common fishes are *márna* (barbel), *őn* (balin), *gárda* (razorfish), *compó* (tench), *kárász* (crucian), *kecsege* (sterlet), and *söregtok* (another fish of the salmon family).

14. Fish

FISHERMAN'S BROTH

Halászlé   *8 to 10 servings*

1 whole live carp, 5 to 6
  pounds, or a section of
  similar weight
Salt
3 or 4 medium-sized onions
  (about 1 pound), chopped
  fine

2 tablespoons paprika
1 green pepper, cut across in
  very thin slices

1. Carp should be alive when you buy it. Ask fishman to bone carp, remove its skin, and cut meat into 4- or 5-inch chunks. Be sure he gives you the skin and bones. Also, make sure you purchase female carp with a lot of roe; purchase extra milt. If you buy a male fish with milt, purchase extra roe. Do not wash the inside of the fish; the blood makes the dish tasty.

2. Boil skin, bones and head of the carp in 2 quarts water with 1 teaspoon salt for about 20 minutes. Strain the broth.

3. Cook the onions in the fish broth for about 30 minutes. Force the onions through a sieve or purée in a blender and put back in the broth.

4. In a 4-quart soup or stew kettle place pieces of fish next to each other. Pour the onion broth over the fish. Add as much water as necessary to cover fish.

5. Bring liquid to a boil; add 1 tablespoon salt, the paprika and green pepper. Cook for about 10 minutes. Do not stir, but shake the pot.

6. Add the roe and milt and cook for an additional 4 or 5 minutes. Let the soup stand for 5 minutes before serving.

7. Serve as a one-dish luncheon, or as a late-night supper dish, or for the soup and fish courses of a dinner.

NOTE: *In the city of Szeged 4 or 5 different types of fish are used in addition to carp. None of these fishes is available in Western Europe or North America. Generally, they belong to the families of catfish, pike, sturgeon, tench, brill, etc. You may add some small fishes (provided you can get small fishes with taste; smelts, for instance, have very little taste when boiled). Add the fish to the chopped onion and cook them together. Then purée onions and fish through a sieve or in a blender and use this broth as a base for the soup.*

There are many variations on this theme in different parts of the country. One of the most interesting eliminates paprika, thickens the broth with a mixture of walnut paste and flour, and flavors it with lemon juice and a touch of sugar. Another variation cooks the broth with a lot of diced vegetables like parsnips, carrots, kohlrabi, knob celery and potatoes, and flavors the soup with dill.

With this very simple recipe, however, you can make a fish soup-stew that is equal to cacciucco, bouillabaisse, meurette, fish chowder, *or any of the specialties of other nations.*

SERBIAN CARP

Rácponty   *about 6 servings*

1 pound potatoes	1 large onion, sliced thin
¼ pound smoked bacon	2 green peppers, sliced thin
2 pounds carp fillet, cut into	1 medium-sized tomato, peeled
3-inch chunks	and sliced
¼ pound butter	1 tablespoon flour
1 teaspoon salt	1 cup sour cream
1 tablespoon paprika	

1. Boil potatoes in their skins. Peel and slice them.

2. Cut smoked bacon into little sticks. Make an incision in each fish chunk, and insert the bacon pieces into them.

3. Butter a baking-serving casserole thickly. Place potato slices on the bottom of the casserole, add a layer of the fish, and sprinkle with salt and paprika. Cover with onion slices, green pepper slices and finally with tomato slices.

4. Melt remaining butter and pour on top of the casserole. Bake in a 375°F. oven for 30 minutes.

5. Mix flour with sour cream, and spread it over the top of the half-finished casserole. Put back into oven for 20 to 30 minutes more.

NOTE: *This dish can also be made with whole carp.*

THE DEVELOPMENT OF A RECIPE

It's fascinating to watch the development of an idea through 400 years. Rarely do we have a chance to play this game in connection with a recipe, but here you have such a chance.

1. Fish in Sour Cream, from a cookbook in manuscript by an unknown chef in the early 1600's.

"Salt a fish and let it stand. Then wash out the salt, pepper it and strain some sour cream over it. Also throw some tarragon leaves, saffron and ginger on it too. This is how you should cook it together. When its time comes, serve it."

2. *Harcsa* or Carp with Sour Cream, from a Hungarian-French cookbook by C. József Dobos, about 1890.

"When you have cleaned the fish carefully and cut it into slices, bake it in the oven. Take it out of the pan, put it into serving casserole, cover it with sour cream, capers, and bring it very slowly to a boil. Serve it with its sauce."

3. And finally, a recipe of József Venesz, the doyen of Hungarian chefs, dated 1954.

CARP IN SOUR CREAM WITH WILD MUSHROOMS

Tejfeles ponty erdei gombával   *8 to 10 servings*

5 pounds carp, weighed after cleaning	1 tablespoon chopped flat parsley
Salt and pepper	1 cup dry white wine
4 tablespoons sweet butter	1 cup sour cream
½ pound wild mushrooms, sliced	¼ cup heavy cream
1 medium-sized onion, chopped fine	1 tablespoon flour

1. Cut the cleaned carp into serving pieces, sprinkle with salt and pepper, and place in a baking pan with the butter.

2. Sprinkle with mushrooms, onion and parsley. Pour wine over the fish, and cover with a buttered paper.

3. Cook in a 375°F. oven for about 15 minutes or more.

4. When carp is about done, pour a mixture of sour cream, heavy cream and flour over it.

5. Bring to a simmer; adjust salt to taste. Serve with buttered steamed new potatoes.

NOTE: *Even if we haven't improved in ethical matters over the past 400 years, it would seem that in affairs culinary, at least, we have made large strides.*

In 1962 Master Chef Venesz created a magnificent dish and named it Süllő à la George Lang. *The four-page detailed recipe is suitable only for the kitchen of a first-class restaurant, but perhaps you'll enjoy reading a description of it from the* Hungarian Chef's Dictionary: "Poach fish fillets in a

Riesling wine fumet *mixed with a little consommé; thicken with butter-roux and mix with crawfish butter and heavy cream. Add chopped dill and tiny button mushrooms. Cover fish with this sauce, surround with crawfish* pörkölt *and garnish with puff pastry tartelettes filled with cream of dill."*

CARP IN BUNDLE AS IN VERSENY

Versenyi batyus ponty   *4 to 6 servings*

2¼ pounds carp fillet, cut in 1   1 tablespoon paprika
  piece   4 tablespoons butter, clarified
Salt   Butter Dough (see below)
3 tablespoons flour

1. Preheat oven to 375°F. Salt fish and roll it in a mixture of flour and paprika. Shake off excess.

2. Heat clarified butter in frying pan, reduce heat to low, and very slowly fry fish on both sides.

3. Line an oblong ovenproof casserole (9 by 6 inches) with a sheet of butter dough.

4. Place fish in the center and fold the dough over and around fish. Brush the dough with egg white.

5. Bake the fish in the preheated oven for 40 to 45 minutes. Serve with Horseradish Sour-Cream Sauce (page 341).

NOTE: *If the fish fillet is in 2 or 3 pieces, cut the dough to the same number of pieces to cover each fillet individually. Try to make the pieces even in size.*

BUTTER DOUGH

Vajas tészta

¼ pound sweet butter   ½ tablespoon salt
1¼ cups flour   1 tablespoon sour cream
1 egg yolk

1. Mix butter and flour until the mixture forms crumbs. (To make even crumbs, many housewives in Hungary slice the butter with a sharp knife or in a vegetable slicer.) Add egg yolk, salt and sour cream. Knead the mixture to make a dough. Wrap dough in wax paper and put in the refrigerator for a minimum of 1 hour.

2. Remove dough from refrigerator and roll and stretch it between pieces of wax paper to make a thin dough sheet.

This dough is suitable for wrapping ham, sausage, etc.

PIKE COOKED IN HORSERADISH CREAM

Csuka tejfeles tormával   *about 8 servings*

1 carrot, peeled and sliced thin
1 knob celery, peeled and sliced
    thin
1 parsnip, peeled and sliced thin
1 medium-sized onion, sliced
1 tablespoon salt
6 peppercorns
Bouquet of parsley and celery
    greens

1 pike, 4 or 5 pounds, cleaned
    and gutted
1 tablespoon flour
¾ cup sour cream
4 tablespoons sweet butter
1 medium-sized horseradish,
    peeled and freshly grated
    (about 1 cup)

1. In a fish poacher cook all vegetables, salt, peppercorns and the herb bouquet in 1 quart water for 1 hour.

2. Place fish in slowly simmering vegetable broth and cook it very slowly for about 20 minutes, or until it is barely done. Flesh of fish must remain quite firm.

3. Remove fish and keep it warm. Strain broth and reduce it by half.

4. Mix flour with sour cream and butter. Add grated horseradish, then whip it into the boiling reduced liquid. Lower the heat and simmer for 2 minutes. Pour the sauce over fish, and serve.

NOTE: *This is an eighteenth-century recipe, with very few changes.*

WALNUT PIKE

Diós csuka   *5 or 6 servings*

2½ to 3 pounds pike
Salt
1 medium-sized onion, sliced
2 carrots, peeled and sliced
1 parsnip, peeled and sliced
1 small knob celery, peeled and
    sliced

¾ cup sour cream
2 tablespoons flour
1 teaspoon sugar
Pinch of white pepper
½ cup ground walnuts

1. Cut fish across into 3-inch sections. Salt it and put in refrigerator.

2. Cook the sliced vegetables in 3 cups water till done; remove with slotted spoon.

3. Place fish in 2 cups of the vegetable broth and cook it over low heat for about 20 minutes. Remove fish and reserve the broth.

4. Mix sour cream with flour. At the end of the cooking period whip the mixture into the reserved broth to make a sauce.

5. Adjust flavor with sugar, pepper and salt to taste. Add ground walnuts. Simmer over low heat for 2 minutes.

6. Place fish slices on a serving platter. Put sliced vegetables on top and pour sauce over it.

NOTE: *Hungarian pike is very similar to pike-perch or walleye pike.*

If the sauce is too liquid, add ground walnuts to the fish slices, add vegetables on top, and add just enough of the liquid to sauce the dish properly.

PIKE-PERCH COOKED WHOLE

Fogas, egészben sütve   4 or 5 servings

1 *fogas*, 3 to 4 pounds	1 cup sour cream
6 ounces smoked bacon strips	½ cup heavy cream
Salt	1 teaspoon paprika
¼ pound butter, clarified	1 tablespoon flour
1 small onion, minced	

1. Scale and gut the fish. Wash fish.

2. Make incisions in both sides of the fish and lard it with smoked bacon strips. Make 4 or 5 incisions across the back of fish to allow for stretching during baking. Salt the inside and outside.

3. Place the fish in a casserole with three quarters of the butter. Bake in a 400°F. oven for 10 to 15 minutes. Remove fish from pan and keep it hot.

4. Add onion to the butter in the pan and slowly wilt it on top of the stove. Mix in the sour cream and heavy cream. Bring to a slow simmer and add paprika.

5. Mix flour with remaining butter and add to the simmering cream, whipping it rapidly. The sauce should be thickened in a few minutes. If too thick add additional heavy cream. If not thick enough add additional flour and butter mixture. Strain the sauce and serve in a sauceboat.

PIKE-PERCH À LA GUNDEL

Fogas Gundel módra   *4 servings*

2 to 2½ pounds *fogas*   Salt
½ cup flour   Pinch of pepper
4 eggs   ¾ pound potatoes
1 cup white bread crumbs   Pinch of ground mace
10 tablespoons sweet butter   2 cups Cream Sauce with
1½ pounds spinach   Grated Cheese (page 342)

1. Cut fish across to make serving portions. Dip portions into flour, then into an egg wash made of 2 eggs, finally into the bread crumbs.

2. Fry in 7 tablespoons of the butter till golden brown. Rather undercook them than overcook. Reserve the butter.

3. Wash the spinach 3 times, cook in salted water, and drain. Add pepper and purée the spinach; there should be 1½ cups. Take 2 tablespoons of the butter in which the fish was cooked and mix it with puréed spinach.

4. Cook potatoes in salted water; peel them and rice them while warm. Add the other 2 eggs, 2 tablespoons butter and the mace; mix well.

5. Grease an ovenproof platter with remaining 1 tablespoon of butter. Make a potato border around the edge of the platter with potatoes piped from a pastry tube. Spread spinach purée in middle of platter. Place fried fish on top of spinach bed. Cover everything except the potato border with the sauce. Brown under the broiler for a few minutes.

NOTE: *Like most dishes that Károly Gundel created, this is based on French classic repertoire, yet with a Hungarian twist. I have seen two versions of this. Since he is no longer alive I cannot ask him which is the correct one, and I got different opinions from some of his people still around. In one, the spinach is puréed as above. In the other it is very gently poached and the whole leaves are placed under the fish. I really don't think it matters much since it will break in the service anyway. You may substitute pike or salmon-trout for fogas.*

FISH SAUSAGE AS IN RÁBAKÖZ

Rábaközi halkolbász   *2 to 4 servings*

1 white roll	Dash of pepper
½ cup milk	¼ teaspoon salt
¾ pound fish fillet, ground or chopped	¼ cup flour
	¼ cup bread crumbs
2 eggs	½ cup lard
1 tablespoon minced flat parsley	

1. Use a firm-fleshed fish, and make sure that it is not ground too fine. Soak the white roll in milk, squeeze it, and shred it. Mix the ground or chopped fish with the roll, one of the eggs, the parsley, pepper and salt.

2. Make sausage shapes out of the fish mixture, about 6 inches long and 1 inch thick.

3. Mix the flour, remaining egg and bread crumbs. Roll the fish sausages in the egg mixture and put them aside.

4. Heat lard in frying pan; when hot reduce heat to low and very slowly fry the fish sausages, turning them to cook on all sides. Drain them on paper towels. Sprinkle more salt on the sausages if necessary. Serve with mustard sauce.

NOTE: *If you have sausage casings, you can fill them with the fish mixture and eliminate breading.*

In seventeenth-century Hungarian cookbooks, this was made with saffron.

CRAB SALAD AS IN ZALA

Zalai ráksaláta   *4 servings*

40 small Hungarian crabs (freshwater crayfish)	Pinch of white pepper
4 green peppers, diced	½ teaspoon paprika
2 medium-sized ripe tomatoes, peeled and seeded	Salt
	¼ cup olive oil
2 tablespoons tarragon vinegar	4 hard-boiled eggs, separated
1 tablespoon grated onion	1 tablespoon minced parsley

1. Before cooking the crabs, scrub them well, then soak them in cold water for 1 hour. Change the water several times.

2. Pull out the center wing at end of the tail and most of the innards with it.

3. Steam or boil crabs for 5 to 10 minutes. Shell them; take meat out in lumps, if possible. Let cool.

4. Bring diced green pepper to a boil, drain, and add to crab meat. Also add the tomatoes, diced.

5. Whip vinegar with grated onion, pepper, paprika, and salt to taste. Drop by drop add olive oil, making a foamy mixture.

6. Sieve egg yolks and whip into dressing.

7. Place crab-meat mixture in a crystal or silver dish on ice. Pour dressing over it, and sprinkle it with fine-chopped egg white and minced parsley.

❖ 15 ❖

POULTRY
(SZÁRNYAS)

POULTRY dishes are very important on the Hungarian menu. Fortunately, in Hungary the chicken is still not mass-produced, nor are ducks, geese or turkeys. Turkey in some regions is stuffed with walnuts and coriander, or with corn mixed with tarragon. The roasts made of these birds have a beguilingly piquant taste.

Duckling was called by a nineteenth-century gourmand "the stupidest bird in the world because one duckling's meat is not enough for two and too much for one." However, when a duck is roasted with sprigs of marjoram in its belly one may overcome the old handicap and finish it all with a bottle of red wine from Villány.

Pigeon is very popular in many areas of Hungary, and just about any chicken preparation in this book could be applied to pigeon. Since the bird is smaller and more tender than chicken, the cooking time must be reduced.

CHICKEN FRICASSEE

Csirkebecsinált   *6 servings*

1 fowl, 3½ to 4 pounds, cut into 16 pieces	1 knob celery, peeled and diced
1 medium-sized onion, minced	3 young carrots, sliced thin
½ teaspoon salt	1 tablespoon chopped flat parsley
¼ tablespoon white pepper	2 cups chicken broth or water
1 teaspoon sugar	2 tablespoons flour

1. Render chicken fat in a heavy casserole until most of the fat is melted. In 1 tablespoon of the fat slowly wilt onion until limp, about 15 minutes.

2. Dry chicken pieces. Set aside breasts and liver, and cook the rest of the pieces together with onion in a covered pan for 5 minutes. Don't let the onion burn.

3. Add salt, pepper, sugar, knob celery, carrots, parsley and the chicken broth or water. Cook covered over very low heat for 25 minutes.

4. Add breasts and liver and cook for another 10 minutes.

5. In a separate bowl mix flour with 3 tablespoons cold water until mixture is smooth. Take a ladleful of liquid from the pot, whip it well with flour-water mixture, and finally pour entire mixture into the pot. Simmer over very low heat for 5 to 10 more minutes.

NOTE: *When making the same preparation with veal, stir in a few table-spoons of sour cream just before serving.*

You may also add cut green beans and peas if young vegetables are available. Add more flour if you like it thicker.

CHICKEN AND EGG BARLEY CASSEROLE AS IN OROSHÁZA

Orosházi tarhonyás csirke   8 *servings*

1 fowl, 4 to 5 pounds	3 tablespoons lard
1 parsnip	2 tablespoons paprika
1 celery rib	1 pound goose livers (or duck
1 carrot	or chicken livers)
1 whole small onion	Pinch of white pepper
1 pound Egg Barley,	Pörkölt Broth (page 271)
Homemade (page 296)	

1. Preheat oven to 375°F. Cut bird into 10 or 12 pieces. Scrape parsnip, celery and carrot and cut into pieces.

2. Cook cut vegetables, whole onion and chicken pieces in 2 quarts water. Do not overcook the bird.

3. Take the meat from the bones and put it aside. Put bones into broth and continue simmering the broth until you need it for egg barley, then strain.

4. Brown egg barley in 1 tablespoon lard, stirring constantly. Add the strained broth and 1 tablespoon paprika, and cook till done.

5. Cut livers into chunks, sprinkle with pepper, and brown in 1 tablespoon lard for 4 or 5 minutes.

6. Mix remaining lard and paprika and spread on bottom and sides of an

ovenproof serving casserole. Mix egg barley, chicken and liver and put in the casserole. Put it in the preheated oven for 10 to 15 minutes.

7. Serve the chicken from the casserole and ladle broth as a sauce on each individual serving.

CHICKEN AND APPLE CASSEROLE

Csirkebecsinált almával   *4 servings*

1 chicken, 3 pounds, cut into stewing pieces	Salt
2 carrots	4 green or sour apples
2 parsnips	1 tablespoon sugar
1 small onion	½ cup sour cream
	2 tablespoons flour

1. Get a nice yellow-colored, plump chicken and not one that looks as if it died of starvation. Put chicken pieces in 2 quarts water in a large pot and bring to a boil. Skim.

2. Peel and trim vegetables and cut into chunks. Add to the chicken with 1 teaspoon salt. Cook very slowly till chicken is done.

3. Peel apples, core them, and cut into quarters. Put half of the chicken broth in a separate pot. In it cook the apple quarters with the sugar till they are almost soft.

4. Mix sour cream with flour and add to the apples. Stir and simmer for 2 more minutes.

5. Add chicken pieces and cook slowly for another 5 minutes. Adjust sugar and salt to taste according to the sourness of the apples.

6. Mix the cooked vegetables with the apple and chicken, or serve them separately.

CHICKEN COOKED IN BADACSONYI WINE

Badacsonyi borban sült csirke   *4 servings*

3 scallions	1 chicken, 3 pounds
4 tablespoons butter	¼ cup Marc or Slivovitz
3 ounces double-smoked bacon, diced	¼ pound mushrooms, sliced
2 bay leaves	2 cups dry Badacsonyi wine
1 teaspoon chopped fresh tarragon, or ½ teaspoon dried	Salt

1. Chop scallions and sauté them in butter till wilted.

2. In a heavy Dutch oven or similar pot render diced bacon. Add cooked scallions and butter, bay leaves and tarragon. Add chicken and Marc; stir. Cook covered over very low heat for 10 minutes.

3. Add sliced mushrooms and wine. Add salt to taste. Cook till liquid is gone. If necessary, add a little more wine, but when the dish is finished there should be very little liquid left; all of it should be absorbed by the chicken.

4. Remove any unnecessary fat and serve the chicken with steamed rice.

NOTE: *Although mushrooms should not usually be cooked for more than 10 minutes, in this case more time is needed to get the mushroom taste into the chicken.*

ALMOND-STUFFED CHICKEN

Mandulával töltött csirke   *6 servings*

¼ pound blanched almonds	1 teaspoon salt
3 rolls	Tiny bit of grated fresh or
½ cup milk	ground gingerroot
3 whole eggs	3 chickens, 1½ pounds each
6 tablespoons butter, softened	Chicken fat

1. Preheat oven to 375°F. Cut almonds into lengthwise slices. Soak the rolls in the milk; squeeze them and force through a sieve.

2. Mix soaked crumbs with eggs, softened butter, salt, gingerroot and almonds.

3. Stuff the chicken cavities with this mixture, and secure openings with string or sewing. Pat the chickens dry and brush skins with chicken fat. Grease bottom of roasting pan with fat.

4. Bake the chickens in the preheated oven for about 1 hour.

5. After about 10 minutes in the oven, sprinkle with a few tablespoons water. Repeat this once or twice. During the last 10 minutes, baste the birds with their own juices several times.

6. Serve with roast potatoes and Lettuce Leaves in Vinegar Dressing (page 331).

NOTE: *To blanch almonds, bring them to a boil, cool them, and pull off skins. Ideally, Hungarian housewives make this stuffing when the fresh almonds are just harvested, and the mellow yet pungent flavor permeates the flesh of the chickens and gives an unusual taste and aroma to this dish.*

A good chicken will have a lot of extra fat. Render it to get your chicken fat.

STUFFED CHICKEN FOR PASSOVER

Húsvéti töltött csirke   6 to 8 *servings*

1 fat fowl, 4 to 4½ pounds	Salt and pepper
3 whole pieces of matzo	2 eggs
½ small onion, chopped fine	2 tablespoons crushed matzo
¾ cup rendered chicken fat	1 medium-sized very ripe
4 chicken livers, very carefully	tomato, cut into pieces
cleaned	1 medium-sized onion, sliced
1 tablespoon chopped parsley	1 green pepper, sliced
¼ pound mushrooms, chopped	1 garlic clove, mashed

1. Soak chicken in salted ice-cold water for 1 hour. Soak matzo in luke-warm water till soft, then squeeze till dry.

2. Cook chopped onion, covered, in 2 tablespoons of the chicken fat; do not brown. After 5 minutes add chicken livers, parsley and mushrooms. Cook, covered, for another 5 minutes. Let the mixture cool.

3. Add squeezed matzo and put the whole mixture through the grinder. Add salt and pepper to taste. Add eggs and bread crumbs and mix well. Let the stuffing rest for a couple of hours.

4. Mix in 6 tablespoons chicken fat.

5. Remove chicken from ice-cold water, wipe it well inside and outside, and salt it. Fill with the stuffing. Sew up the opening.

6. Spread 2 tablespoons of chicken fat on the bottom of a baking pan. Put in tomato, sliced onion and green pepper. Add garlic, a sprinkle of salt and ¼ cup water. Spread remaining 2 tablespoons fat on top of the chicken, put the chicken in the pan, cover the pan, and cook the chicken on top of the stove over low heat. Baste often.

7. Preheat oven to 475°F. When the chicken is done, take it out of the pan and keep it warm. Put vegetables through a sieve or blender to make a sauce.

8. Put chicken back in the pan and place it in the preheated oven for about 10 minutes to make it brown and crisp.

9. Serve the sauce separately. Accompany with egg noodles, boiled and then sautéed in chicken fat for a few minutes, or rice.

NOTE: *This matzo-stuffed chicken is Jewish family fare during Passover holidays. The stuffing is so different from the usual bread-based kind that, regardless of religion or time of year, you should try it. If you are able, put some of the stuffing under the skin of the bird.*

DUCKLING IN RICE AS IN ALFÖLD

Alföldi rizses kacsa   *4 servings*

Breasts of 2 ducklings
¼ pound rendered duck or
  goose fat
1 small onion, chopped fine
1 small knob celery, peeled and
  sliced
1 small parsnip, peeled and
  sliced
1 small carrot, peeled and
  sliced
¼ pound mushrooms
¾ pound uncooked rice (1½
  cups)

1 tablespoon chopped flat
  parsley
½ pound shelled young peas
1 teaspoon salt
½ teaspoon freshly ground
  pepper
½ teaspoon chopped fresh
  marjoram, or a good pinch
  of dried marjoram
Livers of 2 ducklings, sautéed

1. Preheat oven to 375°F. Pull off the skin of the duck breasts, then bone them. Cut meat into 1-inch squares.

2. In a heavy Dutch oven melt half of the fat and wilt the onion in it.

3. Add duck meat and sliced vegetables to the onion and sauté for a couple of minutes. Add 1 tablespoon water and cover. Cook the duck; keep adding tablespoons of water until duck is cooked. Do not have a lot of liquid at any time.

4. If mushrooms are small buttons, leave them whole; if larger, cut into pieces.

5. In a second pot melt the rest of the fat. Add mushrooms, rice, parsley and peas, and cook over medium heat for a few minutes. Stir and cook over low heat for a few more minutes till the ingredients are coated with fat.

6. Add rice mixture to cooked duck meat, together with salt, pepper and marjoram. Add 2 cups water and bring to a boil under a heavy tight-fitting lid.

7. Bake in the preheated oven for 25 minutes.

8. Place the duck and rice on a serving platter and decorate it with sautéed duck livers and duck cracklings made out of the fat (see page 351).

NOTE: *In the provinces this dish would be sprinkled with a little duck fat just before serving; however, I don't think many people in the United States would like this.*

    Alföld, the famed Hungarian lowland, has been producing its own rice for the past few decades, and many rice dishes, including this one, were developed there.

If the peas are not very young, or the so-called early June peas, they must be precooked for about 10 minutes.

GOOSE DRUMSTICK WITH BARLEY AND BEANS

Libacomb ricsettel   *10 to 12 servings*

1 pound uncooked dried small
   white beans
1 pound uncooked barley
6 goose drumsticks, about 1
   pound each
1 large onion
1 kohlrabi

2 carrots
2 parsnips
½ cup lard
1 tablespoon paprika
½ tablespoon pepper
2 garlic cloves, crushed
Salt

1. The night before you plan to cook this, wash beans and barley. Put them into a 5- or 6-quart pot to soak overnight. Cover them with enough water so there will be 3 or 4 inches over the top of beans and barley.

2. The following day add drumsticks to beans and barley. Peel the vegetables and cut into chunks. Add vegetables, lard, paprika, pepper, crushed garlic, and salt to taste to the beans. Add enough water to cover everything. (During the night most of the water will be soaked up by beans and barley.)

3. Bring the liquid to a boil on top of the stove; stir it a few times. Cover and place in a 325° F. oven for 4 or 5 hours.

4. Look at the pot every hour or so; if necessary add a little water. When beans and barley are cooked, drumsticks will be ready, and the liquid should have been all absorbed, just as in a *risotto*.

NOTE: *This is a preparation that unquestionably came from Austria.*

ROAST GOOSE LIVER

Sült libamáj   *4 servings*

1 goose liver, 1 to 2 pounds
2 cups milk
Salt

1 tablespoon goose fat
1 small onion, cut into halves
1 teaspoon paprika

1. Wash liver well. Soak it in milk for 1 hour.
2. Take liver from milk and dry it. Sprinkle with salt.

3. Bring the goose fat to a high temperature in a small roasting pan. Put liver into pan and brown it quickly on all sides.

4. Add ¼ cup water, the halved onion and a little more salt. Cover pan. Bake in a 400°F. oven till liquid is evaporated, which is generally at the time when liver is roasted rare.

5. Uncover the roasting pan. Increase oven temperature to 500°F., and let the liver brown for a few minutes.

6. Transfer liver to a serving platter. Mix paprika with the hot fat remaining in the pan; stir it fast, then strain over the liver.

7. Cool the liver, then put in refrigerator if you want to serve it as a cold appetizer. Or serve it immediately as a hot first course or a main course.

VARIATION: *Soak liver in water instead of milk. Chop 1 garlic clove fine. Sprinkle it with salt and pepper and mash it with the flat side of a knife until it becomes a paste. Make 3 incisions in the liver and put some of the garlic paste in each incision. Roast as above.*

NOTE: *Since the size of the liver varies in these specially fattened geese, the quantity of water to be poured into the roasting pan and also the roasting time will vary accordingly.*

CAULIFLOWER WITH GOOSE LIVER À LA WESSELÉNYI

Karfiol libamájjal à la Wesselényi   *4 to 6 servings*

1 pound fresh liver of a fattened goose	1 tablespoon goose fat
1 teaspoon salt	3 egg yolks, beaten
1 large head of cauliflower	4 tablespoons butter, melted
2 cups chicken broth	2 tablespoons sour cream

1. Roast the goose liver with ½ teaspoon salt until it is rare (see page 218). This will take about 15 minutes in a 400°F. oven. It is necessary to have the liver rare for this recipe.

2. Meantime, break flowerets off the cauliflower stalk. Cook both the stalk and flowerets in chicken broth until done.

3. Put flowerets aside; rub stalk through a sieve, or purée in a blender.

4. Grease a serving-baking casserole with goose fat. Place drained flowerets on bottom of casserole. Slice the liver and place slices evenly on top of the flowerets.

5. Mix the puréed cauliflower stalk with the egg yolks. Drip in the melted

butter little by little, whipping the mixture as you do. Whip in the sour cream and remaining ½ teaspoon salt.

6. Pour the sauce over the goose-liver slices. Bake the casserole in a 375 °F. oven for 10 to 15 minutes. Serve it in the same dish.

NOTE: *If you cannot obtain fresh goose liver, do not try this recipe with the canned variety unless you can buy a whole, uncooked liver packed in water.*

STUFFED GOOSE NECK

Töltött libanyak   *6 appetizer servings, or 4*
main-course servings

1 small onion, chopped fine	2 eggs
4 tablespoons goose fat	1 teaspoon paprika
1 hard roll	Salt and pepper
½ cup milk or water	½ pound goose liver
1 pound goose meat, diced	1 whole large goose neck

1. Wilt chopped onion in 2 tablespoons goose fat over very low heat.

2. Soak roll in milk or water. Squeeze it well.

3. Mix the wilted onion, diced goose, soaked squeezed roll, eggs, paprika, 1 teaspoon salt and a pinch of pepper. Put through the grinder twice, using the smaller holes.

4. Dice goose liver and gently mix it with the rest of the stuffing. Taste and add more salt if necessary.

5. Remove neck from its skin and sew the narrower end of the skin to make a kind of stocking out of it.

6. Put in the stuffing mixture and sew up the other end too.

7. Heat remaining 2 tablespoons goose fat in a pot or frying pan with a cover. Turn heat to lowest and add the stuffed neck. Cover, and cook it slowly till it is done.

8. For the last 10 minutes take off cover and turn up heat to brown both sides.

9. Serve hot or cold. Slice it like a sausage. Serve as a hot appetizer, as a luncheon dish, or as a garnish for roast goose. If served as a luncheon dish, accompany with pickles or a salad.

VARIATIONS: *Hard-boil 2 more eggs, cut lengthwise into quarters, and arrange them with stuffing.*

Mix ½ pound ground veal or ½ pound ground lean pork with ½ pound goose meat. Generally the goose meat used is scraped from the giblets and the bones, but you can also add some chicken meat to it.

BREADED TURKEY CUTLETS

Rántott pulykamell-szeletek   4 servings

8 slices of turkey breast, about
  ¼ pound each
1 tablespoon salt
½ cup flour

2 eggs
1 cup white bread crumbs
1 cup lard or clarified butter

1. When removing breast from turkey try to keep it intact; then pull off the outer skin and cut out the tendons. Cut even slices. Place each slice between 2 pieces of wax paper. With a wooden board flatten each slice to ¼-inch thickness or even thinner.

2. Mix salt with flour. Beat the eggs with 1 tablespoon water.

3. Dip the slices into flour, eggs, then bread crumbs.

4. Heat fat in a frying pan and very quickly fry cutlets on each side till they become very light golden in color.

5. Serve them with Vintner's Rice (page 330) and Cabbage Salad (page 331).

NOTE: *Turkey has been very popular in Hungary since the days of King Matthias in the fifteenth century (see page 17), when it was called "Indian Rooster." Sometimes it is used like a fat fowl to make soup with, but generally the roasted or stuffed birds differ very little from other nations' preparations.*

CHOLENT

Sólet   8 servings

1 pound uncooked dried small
  white beans
2 tablespoons goose fat
1 large onion, chopped fine
2 garlic cloves, crushed
2 tablespoons flour
1 tablespoon paprika

1 pound smoked beef breast
½ hindquarter of smoked or
  fresh goose
4 unbroken eggs, in shells
Pinch of pepper
Salt

221

1. The night before you plan to serve this dish, soak the washed beans in 1½ quarts water.

2. Next day melt the goose fat in a 5- or 6-quart heavy Dutch oven 6 inches deep, or in an enamelware casserole with a lid. Sauté onion and garlic in it over low heat for a few minutes.

3. Add flour and paprika, mix, and sauté for a few more minutes. Add 2 cups cold water; stir till there are no lumps.

4. Pour in the soaked beans together with the soaking water; stir well. Bring to a boil. Add meat pieces and the eggs still in their shells. When the mixture starts boiling turn heat very low. Cover and cook for about 2 hours.

5. If you need more water, add some, but no more than ½ cup at a time. Add pepper and salt to taste.

6. When done, slice the meat. Shell the eggs and slice into halves. Place meat slices on top of the beans and halved eggs and serve.

VARIATION: *Mash garlic, fat and paprika together; put in with the soaked beans and liquid. When the mixture starts boiling add onion, meat and eggs. Try both methods.*

The amount of meat can be increased according to the requirements. Stuffed Goose Neck (see page 220) is often added.

NOTE: *Originally, this dish was cooked in the oven or at the neighborhood baker's, but it took twice as long as the approximately 3 hours on top of the stove. Traditionally it should be cooked by a dry-heat method.*

Before placing the casserole in the oven or sending it to the neighborhood baker, the housewife sealed the opening of the casserole with a mixture of water and flour, or she tied triple layers of cheesecloth around the top and then put on the cover, securing it with strings.

The curious name of this dish puzzled food historians for a long time. According to Molly Bar David, the Israeli author, this dish was originally made with chick-peas instead of beans, olive oil instead of goose fat, and lamb instead of goose or beef. Since it had to be kept hot from Friday night to Saturday when it was a traditional Sabbath luncheon meal, it was called hamim, *meaning hot. As the Jews left Palestine they brought this name to various countries, and in France they simply translated it to the French* chaud *and then, of course, down through the usual process of changes it became* chaudlet, solet, cholent, *etc., etc., in different countries. According to others, however, the answer is much simpler: In Yiddish* shul-ente *means the conclusion of the synagogue services, which is exactly when this dish was served.*

According to one story, the Jewish rabbi and the Catholic priest were very friendly in a village in Hungary. The priest complained to the rabbi that he was unable to sleep and the latter suggested the solet *recipe as a cure for insomnia. A few days later they met again, and to the eager question of the rabbi came the rueful answer from the priest: "I understand how you fall asleep from this dish, but what puzzles me is: How do you get up?"*

Barley was added, according to the famous Hungarian food expert Emil Turós, because it has a tendency to absorb fat and the goose certainly had plenty to absorb. Another trick he mentions, if you are cooking the dish on top of the stove, is to take off the cover about 15 minutes before serving and put the casserole in a 500°F. oven. When it starts browning and becomes crusty, crush down the crust into the juicy bean casserole; then allow a crust to form a second time.

The closer you traveled toward Vienna, the less beans and more barley you found in the solet; when you arrived in Vienna you ate only barley with goose legs and peas.

✸ 16 ✸

PORK AND BACON
(SERTÉSHÚSOK ÉS SZALONNÁK)

PERHAPS the extraordinary quality of pork in Hungary contributed to the popularity of dishes made with pork, or perhaps it was the other way around. The fact is that what beef is to Argentina and veal to Italy, pork is to Hungary.

You have already seen that the statement about the importance of bacon, onion and paprika to Hungarian cooking is more than an arbitrary theory. The American housewife, who knows only the difference between brand names of sliced, cooked-cured bacon, will be surprised to learn that there are more than twenty categories of bacon in Hungary, and within each category several variations.

The best bacon comes from female animals which have just reached maturity and optimum weights. Although almost the entire porker is covered with some kind of bacon fat, the choice parts come from the stomach, back and neck. To conserve the bacon slabs, salting or marinating or smoking is used. For salted bacon the pork is cut to the desirable sizes, rubbed with coarsely ground salt and stacked on wooden lattice boards. It is stored in a dark cool place for 2 weeks; after that the same process is repeated. This is called a "dry marination." Meat conserved this way can be kept under refrigeration for 4 to 6 months. It is used generally as a base for smoked and paprika bacon.

Smoked bacon can be "bread bacon," "fine bacon" (*csemege*) or "paprika bacon." To make smoked bacon, salt is washed off the conserved slab after the 4- to 6-week cure, then the meat is cut to the size required, hung in a smoke-house and smoked till yellow-golden in color.

Paprika bacon is made with a preparation of paprika mixed with water in proportions of 1 pound paprika to 3 quarts water. The salt bacon is dipped into this mixture, dried for a few days, then finally smoked in a not too hot smokehouse for 15 to 20 hours.

The so-called *abált* (corned) bacon is generally rubbed with salt and stored for a few days, then placed in a saline solution heavily flavored with garlic for 5 days. It is then cooked for a couple of hours, depending on the thickness of the bacon. For the *csécsi* variety, the bacon is covered with paprika; for the Transylvanian kind, it is smoked over cold smoke till light brown.

If you use the meaty ribs you get a *kolozsvári* bacon; often the bones are removed, and the meaty slab will be in one big square piece. *Kolozsvári* bacon is similar to Transylvanian and both are cured in the same way, although the latter is cut into strips 5 by 14 inches.

Kassai bacon is soaked in a garlic-flavored saline solution. It is then washed in warm water, then salt cured, finally cut into 4-inch-wide strips as long as the side. The strips are coated with fresh beef blood and paprika (1 pound paprika to 3 quarts beef blood), then smoked in a hot smokehouse to almost dry-burn the coating on the bacon.

Roast bacon is made of salt-cured stomach bacon. The salt is washed off; the meat is cut into 6-inch strips and scored, but not too deeply, in parallel lines ½ inch apart. The strips are then soaked in milk, and finally fried in enough fat to cover the bacon completely.

English bacon is made from the rack part of the pork, with the bones carefully removed. It is processed with dry salt, then put through wet curing. It is dried for a few days, then smoked. This is a fairly close cousin of the so-called Canadian bacon.

SOUP AND MEAT, POLISH STYLE

Lengyeles leves és hús   4 to 6 servings

1 pound lean pork
1 bay leaf
1 teaspoon salt
1 medium-sized onion, peeled
  and halved

½ teaspoon black peppercorns
1½ pounds fresh pork sausage
2 medium-sized beets, peeled
  and diced
⅓ cup sour cream

1. Put 7 cups water into a 4- to 6-quart soup pot. Add the pork, bay leaf, salt and onion. Tie peppercorns in a cheesecloth or muslin bag and add. Put lid on halfway and a cook the pork for 1½ hours.

2. Remove peppercorns, onion and bay leaf. Put in the sausages. Finish cooking till meat and sausages are done.

3. Meantime cook the diced beets in ½ cup water. When done there should be about ½ of the liquid left; if not, add enough water to make ¼ cup liquid.

4. Mix sour cream with cooked beets and ¼ cup liquid till the sauce is pale purple and smooth. Add a ladleful of the meat cooking liquid and mix it further. Adjust salt.

5. Pour beet mixture into a soup tureen and ladle in enough broth from the meat to give sufficient soup for the table.

6. Serve sausage and meat separately as the next course, with steamed potatoes and grated horseradish.

NOTE: *In the sixteenth century, Poland had a Hungarian king and hero, Báthory, and the cultural and gastronomic exchange was influential for both countries. This soup was probably first made in that period.*

POTTED PORK TENDERLOIN AS IN VILLÁNY

Villányi sertésszelet   *6 to 8 servings*

1 tablespoon bacon drippings	1½ teaspoons paprika
1 loin of pork, about 6 pounds, boned	2 tablespoons lemon juice
	1 bay leaf
2 small carrots, sliced	1 cup Hungarian red wine
2 small parsnips, sliced	6 dried juniper berries
2 small green peppers, sliced	Pinch of salt
2 small tomatoes, chopped	

1. Preheat oven to 500°F. Heat drippings in a casserole and brown the pork quickly and evenly for about 15 minutes.

2. Add remaining ingredients and cover. Reduce heat to 350°F. and cook the pork for 3 to 4 hours, or until done.

3. Remove meat to serving platter and slice. Force sauce and vegetables through a sieve and pour over meat.

PORK FLEKKEN

Sertésflekken   *4 to 6 servings*

2 pounds loin of pork	¼ cup flour
1 teaspoon salt	2 tablespoons lard

1. Wipe the meat but do not wash it. Skin the meat and cut it into 6 slices. Flatten them, then sprinkle with salt and roll in flour.

2. Melt lard in a frying pan and sauté the meat rapidly over high heat until brown.

3. Decorate the edge of a wooden platter with shredded sauerkraut in a lettuce cup, small pickled cucumbers, green pepper rings. Pile fried thin-sliced potatoes in the middle of the platter. Lay the slices of meat on top of the potatoes.

VARIATIONS: *One of the specialties from the city of Debrecen: Make the pork flekken, put on a serving platter, and cover with* Lecsó *(page 314). Finally sprinkle thin slices of cooked smoked sausage on top.*

Another variation, which can also be used for beef or veal scallops: Slice onions paper-thin. Stack up the raw meat slices with layers of onion, freshly crushed black pepper and parsley leaves between the meat layers. Weight the layers and let them stand for 3 hours. Discard everything but the meat. Salt the meat and sauté it.

NOTE: *In Transylvania this dish was cooked over charcoal and basted with Paprika Essence (page 343) several times during the process. If you have an outdoor barbecue, it is a fine change from the usual beefsteak.*

STUFFED PORK, CEGLÉD COWBOY'S STYLE

Ceglédi csikóspecsenye   *4 servings*

8 very thin boneless pork
   cutlets, about 1¼ pounds
3 tablespoons lard
1 medium-sized onion, peeled
   and minced
¼ pound lean pork
¼ pound pork liver

¼ cup uncooked rice
1 egg
¼ teaspoon pepper
Salt
Thin strips of double smoked
   bacon

1. Pound the pork cutlets very thin, in the style of a veal cutlet prepared for *scaloppine.*

2. In a frying pan heat 1 tablespoon of the lard and wilt the onion over very low heat for about 15 minutes.

3. Meantime, grind lean pork and pork liver and add it to onion. Stir, cook for a few minutes longer, then add 1 tablespoon water.

4. Cover, and cook over very low heat for about 30 minutes, or until done. Stir every now and then.

5. Cook rice in ½ cup water for 15 minutes. Mix rice and egg with the meat and liver mixture. Add the pepper and salt to taste.

6. Place 4 pork cutlets on a flat surface. Divide the stuffing evenly among the slices. Cover with the other 4 slices. With a larding needle and the long strips of bacon in the place of thread, sew up the edges of the stuffed meat pockets.

7. Melt remaining 2 tablespoons lard in a large frying pan. Fry stuffed pork slices very fast on both sides. When they are brown, add ½ cup water and cook till liquid evaporates and finally meat is browned in remaining fat. Serve with rice and Spiced Red Cabbage (page 318).

NOTE: *Larding needles are not all of the same size. If the eye of the needle is small, obviously the bacon strip must be cut to fit it. Threading the strips of bacon is not easy. If you want to eliminate this, you can hold the pockets together if you press the edges together firmly and handle them with care when cooking and turning.*

The ideal cut for this dish is leg of pork, but you may use a boned rack if it is cut in such a way that you can open up the slice and pound it into a thin cutlet.

STUFFED PORK FROM ORMÁNSÁG

Ormánsági töltött sertésdagadó　　　　　　6 *servings*

1 *dagadó* (see Note)	1 small onion, minced
2 rolls	1 garlic clove, crushed
½ cup milk	Pinch of pepper or marjoram
¼ pound pork liver	½ tablespoon paprika
¼ pound smoked bacon	2 eggs
¼ pound lard (8 tablespoons)	Salt

1. Preheat oven to 350°F. Bone the *dagadó*. With a sharp knife open up center so you can fill it with stuffing.

2. Make the stuffing. Soak rolls in the milk. Squeeze them and rice them.

3. Put liver and bacon through the largest holes of a meat grinder and add the ground mixture to the milk-roll purée.

4. Heat 4 tablespoons of the lard and brown the minced onion. Then add garlic, pepper or marjoram, and paprika.

5. Remove from heat and mix in the eggs till completely amalgamated. Then add ground liver and mix it again. Add salt to taste.

6. Stuff meat and sew up opening. Melt the rest of the lard. Place stuffed meat in a baking pan and pour hot lard over it; sprinkle 2 tablespoons water on top.

7. Cover the pan and put in the preheated oven. Bake for 2 to 2½ hours,

basting every now and then. Add a little more water if needed. For last 10 minutes increase heat to 450°F. to crisp outside of meat.

NOTE: Dagadó *is a part of the pork which is not an American butcher's cut. Just below the ribs toward the stomach there is a meaty section which can puff somewhat like a corned beef. This is where the name (which in Hungarian means "something which swells") comes from. This part in Southern cooking is called the belly bacon or end of pork belly. However, the Hungarian cut retains also the meaty part. This can be opened and stuffed. In Hungary, particularly in the country, this is still a common cut. When finished it looks like an improved version of a stuffed breast of veal.*

STUFFED FRESH PICKLES

Töltött kovászos uborka   *4 servings*

½ pound roast lean pork	2 tablespoons butter
½ pound roast veal	1 cup pickle juice
1 egg	½ tablespoon flour
Salt	2 tablespoons sour cream
8 pickles, each 6 inches long	1 tablespoon chopped fresh dill

1. Grind the meats very well at least twice. Mix with the egg and salt to taste.

2. Peel the pickles, then slice lengthwise into halves. Very carefully scrape and cut out the insides to make a kind of boat of each pickle half.

3. Stuff each boat with some of the meat mixture. Put the boats together in pairs and tie them with white thread.

4. In a braising pot bring the butter and pickle juice to a boil. Place the stuffed pickles in the pot, cover the pot, and cook over low heat for 20 minutes.

5. In a mixing bowl stir together the flour and sour cream. Add the liquid remaining in the braising pot. Add chopped dill. Pour thickened mixture back into the pot with the stuffed pickles, and cook, covered, over very low heat for 10 to 15 minutes.

6. Very carefully remove the threads from the pickles and serve them as whole stuffed pickles together with the sauce and steamed new potatoes.

NOTE: *A little "pickleology": There are two basic types of marinated cucumbers or, as they are commonly called, pickles: (1) those made with vinegar, which will last for at least 1 year; (2) those made with natural marination, with some type of yeast process.*

This dish is based on what in American delicatessens are called "semi-sour pickles," but you may try it sometime with a more sour variety. At times you can find them in supermarkets under the label "kosher-type dill pickle." Use these if you have to, but do not make this dish with the ordinary vinegar-cured pickle.

If you want to make this with your own pickles, see page 336.

HEAD AND TAIL OF PORK WITH HORSERADISH

Tormás feje-farka   8 servings

4 pounds pork, knuckle and part of head and tail
2 tablespoons salt
1 teaspoon pepper
2 tablespoons paprika
1 large onion, cut into chunks

2 garlic cloves, crushed
2 parsnips, peeled and sliced
2 carrots, peeled and sliced
1 knob celery, peeled and sliced
1 horseradish root, peeled and grated

1. Cut up the pieces of head, knuckle and tail. Bring to a boil in 2 quarts water. Discard the water and again bring to a boil in 2 quarts of water. Remove foam.

2. Add salt, pepper, paprika, onion and garlic. Cook over low heat for 30 minutes.

3. Add sliced vegetables and cook until everything is done.

4. Serve as a soup-stew, with broth, vegetables and meat all together. In separate little dishes serve the grated horseradish.

NOTE: *This recipe is based on descriptions of Hungarian meals served between the thirteenth and seventeenth centuries. Sometimes saffron and ginger were added, but the dish was also served as above.*

PIG'S FEET AS IN BRASSÓ

Brassói sertéscsülök   4 servings

2 pig's feet with the knuckles, or 1 pork shank
3 tablespoons lard
2 medium-sized onions, chopped
Pinch of caraway seeds
1 garlic clove, crushed

1 tablespoon paprika
2 pounds sauerkraut
1 tablespoon flour
1 ½ cups sour cream
1 tablespoon chopped fresh dill
Salt

230

16. Pork and Bacon

1. Have butcher split the pig's feet. Preheat oven to 450°F. Wash and dry pork. Put it in a large baking pan. Melt the lard and pour it over meat. Put pork in the oven for 20 minutes, till golden brown outside although still raw inside.

2. Remove meat from baking pan and place pan on top of stove over very low heat. Fry onions in the fat remaining in the baking pan.

3. Add caraway seeds, garlic and 1 cup water. Mix in paprika. Put back the meat, cover, and return to the oven. Reduce heat to 300°F. and bake for 40 minutes. If necessary add some more water; at any rate baste it several times.

4. Meantime cook sauerkraut with a little water till it is done.

5. Mix flour with sour cream and chopped dill and stir it into cooked sauerkraut. Cook over low heat for an additional 5 to 10 minutes.

6. Remove cooked meat from oven. Cut meat into serving pieces and season with salt to taste.

7. Arrange sauerkraut on the bottom of an attractive oval fireproof serving casserole. Place meat on top of sauerkraut. Cover the casserole and put in the oven for 5 minutes more before serving.

HOMEMADE SAUSAGE

Házi kolbász　　　　　　　　*8 to 10 servings*

4 pounds pork, not too lean	1 tablespoon paprika
3 garlic cloves, crushed	Pinch of ground cloves
2 tablespoons salt	3 yards of sausage casing
1 teaspoon black pepper	

1. Chop the pork into very small pieces, or grind through the large holes of a meat grinder.

2. Mix in garlic, salt, pepper, paprika and cloves.

3. Carefully wash the sausage casing. Fill with the ground mixture. Use a simple sausage-filling contraption, or the ¾-inch opening of a pastry tube. Tie the ends with string.

4. Grease the bottom of a baking pan or casserole and place the whole sausage on this. Bake in a 350°F. oven until sausage is gleaming red.

NOTE: *Sausage making is a real craft in the Hungarian provinces (see pages 115–17). This recipe is a simplified version, but it is still authentic tasting.*

Sausage casings generally can be purchased in German or Hungarian butcher shops.

A variation that is served at the Rondella Wine Taster in Budapest adds the grated rind of 1 lemon to the sausage mixture.

HOT LIVER SAUSAGE

Májas hurka   *8 servings*

½ pound fat pork
2 pounds pork liver
2 pounds pork lung
2 tablespoons salt
1 cup uncooked rice
2½ cups beef broth
2 large onions, peeled and
  minced

½ pound lard
1 tablespoon pepper
Good pinch of dried marjoram
3 yards of sausage casing, about
  1½ inches in diameter

1. In a large pot cook fat pork, and lung, together with 1 tablespoon salt, until tender.

2. Meantime cook rice in the beef broth for about 20 minutes.

3. Cook minced onions in lard; cover the pan, and do not brown the onions.

4. Cut the cooked liver into small pieces, add to onions, and cook covered for 10 minutes longer. Let cool, then drain liver and onions from the lard.

5. Add liver and onions to cooked meat and lung. Put all through the smallest holes of a meat grinder. Mix with cooked rice, pepper, remaining 1 tablespoon salt and the marjoram.

6. Carefully wash the sausage casing. Stuff the ground mixture into the casing. Tie it well.

7. Cook the whole sausage in plenty of water for 10 to 15 minutes.

8. You can eat the sausage at this point, but I advise you to fry it or bake it slowly till skin becomes golden brown.

NOTE: *This recipe, like that for the Homemade Sausage (page 231), is adapted from one that is used at Hungarian pig killings (see page 115).*

PRUNE STEW, GREAT PLAINS STYLE

Aszalt szilva, alföldi módra   *4 servings*

1 pound sun-dried prunes
1 pound smoked sausage, cut
  into 1-inch pieces

1 round slice of lemon
4 tablespoons sour cream
1 teaspoon flour

1. Cook prunes in 2 cups water for 5 minutes. When soft enough to remove pits, do so.

2. Put prunes back into water; add sausage pieces and lemon slice. Cook

until prunes are almost cooked.

3. Mix sour cream and flour, dilute with a little of the cooking liquid, and whip. Pour sour-cream mixture into pot. Simmer for 5 minutes longer and serve.

VARIATION: *Replace sausage with diced smoked pork tenderloin; cook it in ½ cup water with juice of 1 lemon, juice of 1 orange, grated rind of ¼ lemon, grated rind of ¼ orange, 1 teaspoon sugar and 1 tablespoon wine vinegar. When pork is almost done, add dried prunes and cook until dish is completely finished.*

NOTE: *Reading the variation in a nineteenth-century cookbook reminded me of a similar dish: Elizabeth David writes engagingly about her special trip to Tours to eat* porc aux pruneaux *made with little pork* noisettes *and prunes.*

In today's Hungarian cooking there is little indication of the prevalence of fruit with meat cookery, so common up to the turn of the century.

The original recipe reads: "Add clean water to prunes . . ." I was amused when I read it the first time some 20 years ago, but as time and water reserves pass I am begininng to see the point. From Eredeti magyar alföldi szakácskönyv (Original Hungarian Great Plains Cookbook), *Szolnok, 1897.*

SLICED PORK LIVER AS IN DEBRECEN

Debreceni sertésmáj-szeletek   *6 to 8 servings*

¼ pound smoked bacon
½ pound lard
1 pound pork loin, cut into
   ¼-inch dice
¼ pound smoked sausage,
   sliced thin
10 medium-sized mushrooms,
   sliced

2 medium-sized garlic pickles,
   cut into thin round slices
1 carrot, peeled and chopped
2 pounds pork liver, cut into 8
   slices
¼ cup dry white wine

1. Cut the bacon into ¼-inch dice. Fry until the pieces are crisp cracklings. Lift out the cracklings and set aside.

2. Heat 1 tablespoon of the lard in a cooking pot to frying temperature. Add diced pork loin and cook and stir it over high heat for about 5 minutes.

3. Add sausage, mushrooms, pickles and chopped carrot. Cover with a tight-fitting lid and cook over very low heat till the mixture is completely done.

Add a little water if necessary but make sure that when the filling is finished there will be almost no liquid left.

4. Heat the rest of the lard in a frying pan. Fry liver slices on both sides for a few minutes. The process should be very fast otherwise pork liver has a tendency to be tough.

5. Put liver slices on a serving platter with equal amounts of the cooked filling on each slice.

6. Pour out lard from frying pan, put pan back over heat, and pour in wine. When it boils, which should be within seconds, sprinkle it over liver preparation. (This last step is optional, in case you don't like the wine taste.)

7. Sprinkle the reserved bacon cracklings over the liver and filling. Serve Baked Egg Barley (page 297) as accompaniment.

ASPIC OF SUCKLING PIG

Malackocsonya   *5 to 8 servings*

2½ pounds suckling pig (skin, 3 garlic cloves
 tail, head, hooves), cubed Pinch of white pepper
2 medium-sized onions   1 teaspoon paprika
2 carrots, sliced   2 teaspoons salt

1. Put suckling-pig cubes into 2 quarts water and bring to a boil. Discard water. Wash off meat in cold water. Add another 2 quarts cold water and all the other ingredients.

2. Cook for about 3 hours, or until meat becomes soft. Particularly in the beginning, keep skimming the surface to make sure that the broth will be clear when finished.

3. Divide meat into soup plates or molds and strain the broth over it. This can be used as an appetizer or a supper dish. Use molds of the appropriate size for the purpose.

4. Cool the aspic, then place in refrigerator to chill. Sprinkle with a little additional paprika.

NOTE: *If you want to be absolutely sure to have a properly jelled dish, add a piece of veal bone when you cook the pork.*

If you serve this aspic with a formal meal (instead of as rustic fare accompanied by good crusty potato bread, pickled peppers, and a pitcher of beer), put it into glass dishes, which will enhance its attractive, transparent quality.

❊ 17 ❊

VEAL
(BORJÚ)

VEAL FRICASSEE WITH EARLY PEAS

Cukorborsós borjúhús   *4 servings*

1 pound leg of veal, cut into
   serving pieces
1 small onion, minced
2 tablespoons sweet butter
1 pound fresh young green peas

1 tablespoon sugar
½ teaspoon salt
1 tablespoon chopped parsley
1 tablespoon flour

1. Mix meat with onion and cook in 1 tablespoon melted butter over low heat for about 20 minutes.

2. Add enough water to barely cover, put a heavy lid on the pot, and cook until done.

3. In a separate casserole melt 1 tablespoon butter and add peas, sugar, salt and parsley. Start cooking over low heat. After about 5 minutes add a little water. Do not cover the pot, because when peas are cooked there should be no liquid left in the pot.

4. Add flour, stir, and cook for 2 more minutes.

5. Mix peas with meat and its juice and simmer over very low heat for 1 or 2 more minutes.

NOTE: *My mother used to add 1 cup of cooked fine-chopped kohlrabi; try that for a taste change.*

You may use broth or stock instead of water to get a stronger flavor, but I prefer water, which never overpowers the taste of the tender young peas.

VEAL SCALLOPS À LA MAGYARÓVÁR

Borjúszeletek magyaróvári módra　　　　　*6 servings*

6 veal scallops, about ⅓ pound
  each
1 pound fresh mushrooms
1 teaspoon salt
½ teaspoon black pepper
1 cup flour

2 tablespoons lard
3 tablespoons butter
6 slices of boiled him
6 very thin slices of Gruyère
  cheese

1. Have veal scallops cut on the bias from the thick part of the leg; they should be about ⅜ inch thick. Pound the scallops to an even ¼-inch thickness. Cut ½-inch incisions along the sides to prevent curling.

2. Remove stems from mushrooms and grind mushroom caps to a fine purée. (Use the stems for another recipe.)

3. Sprinkle veal slices with salt and pepper and dip into flour; shake off excess flour.

4. Heat lard in a frying pan until smoking hot. Sauté scallops for a few minutes on each side, till golden pink.

5. Melt 1 tablespoon butter in a separate pan and add mushroom purée. Stir over heat for a few minutes to heat slightly.

6. Spread remaining butter on a heatproof glass baking platter, and place veal scallops on the bottom. Spread top of each with some mushroom purée, and cover with a slice of ham. Top the ham with a cheese slice.

7. Place scallops in a 450°F. oven until cheese melts. Serve with *risotto* made with puréed tomatoes and fresh peas and with natural veal gravy.

NOTE: *This recipe was served at the Restaurant Hongrois at the Brussels World's Fair. The name comes from the cheese used in the dish, which is made in the city of Magyaróvár.*

STUFFED VEAL CUTLETS

Borjúszelet töltve　　　　　*4 servings*

4 slices of veal cut from the leg,
  about ¼ pound each
½ pound roast pork, ground
  fine
1 tablespoon chopped flat
  parsley
Salt and pepper

2 tablespoons lard
½ medium-sized onion,
  chopped fine
½ tablespoon paprika
1 tablespoon lemon juice
3 tablespoons sour cream

1. Pound the veal cutlets, without tearing them, till they are thin.

2. Mix ground roast pork with chopped parsley and salt and pepper to taste.

3. Spread pork mixture evenly on top of veal slices. Roll slices into roulades and tie them with white thread.

4. Bring lard to frying temperature in a heavy braising pot, and brown meat in it on all sides. This should take a few minutes.

5. Add chopped onion and cook for another 5 minutes.

6. Sprinkle with paprika, then pour in ½ cup water. Cook roulades, covered, over very low heat until meat is done. Keep adding water, little by little, to make sure that when roulades are cooked there will be no liquid left, only the fat and juice of the meat.

7. Sprinkle lemon juice on top, shake pot gently, and turn off heat. Place roulades on a serving platter.

8. Pour off fat from pot and put sour cream into pot. Stir and scrape the pot with a wooden spoon, to mix scrapings into the sour cream. Spoon the flavored cream over the roulades.

NOTE: *In Hungary, particularly in country kitchens, sour cream would be mixed with fat. The world of dieting has not yet reached there.*

STUFFED BREAST OF VEAL BOURGEOISE

Töltött borjúszegy városiasan   6 servings

3 stale rolls, or 8 slices of stale white bread	1 tablespoon chopped flat parsley
1 cup milk	Salt
4 tablespoons lard	¼ teaspoon pepper
3 eggs	3 pounds breast of veal
¼ small onion, peeled and grated	

1. Make a stuffing: Remove crusts from rolls or bread, then soak in milk. When rolls or bread are soft, squeeze them and add to them 2 tablespoons of the lard, the eggs, grated onion, chopped parsley, 1 tablespoon salt and the pepper. Mix well. Adjust salt if necessary. Let stand for a few hours.

2. Preheat oven to 375°F. Cut a pocket in the meat. Wash and dry meat. Salt it on all sides and fill the opening with the stuffing. Sew the opening together. Brush meat with remaining 2 tablespoons lard.

3. Pour ½ cup water in a baking dish and put in the meat. Cover it and bake in the preheated oven for 2½ hours, or until tender. Every 30 minutes turn the

meat and baste it. Toward the end carefully test the unfilled section with a fork, to check if it is done. If necessary add a little water to make sure that the meat is always cooking in steam and won't dry out.

4. For the last 10 minutes increase heat to 425°F. so the meat will become crisp on the outside.

5. Let the veal stand for 10 minutes before slicing. The taste will be better, and it will be easier to slice.

BREADED VEAL KNUCKLES

Rántott borjúláb   2 *large servings, or*
4 *average servings*

2 veal knuckles	1 teaspoon freshly ground
1 carrot	pepper
1 parsnip	2 eggs
1 small knob celery	½ cup flour
1 small onion	½ cup bread crumbs
1 tablespoon lemon juice	1 cup oil or lard
Salt	

1. Have butcher clean and split each veal knuckle.

2. Peel all vegetables and cut into small pieces.

3. Bring 2 quarts water with the lemon juice, 1 tablespoon salt and the pepper to a boil. Add veal and vegetable pieces and cook until meat comes off bones, 1 to 1½ hours.

4. Discard bones and dry meat on absorbent kitchen towels. Cut meat into large chunks.

5. Whip eggs with ½ teaspoon salt. Dip meat first into flour, next into beaten eggs, then into bread crumbs.

6. Bring oil or lard to frying temperature, reduce heat to very low, and fry the breaded meat pieces till they are golden brown. Serve with Tartar Sauce (page 338).

NOTE: *For a country-style meal, keep the meat in as large chunks as possible.*

A thrifty Hungarian housewife would make a soup from the liquid in which the meat cooked. She would thicken it with roux, *adjust the seasoning, add a little sour cream, and serve it as a first course before the breaded veal shank.*

VEAL CHOPS À LA GUNDEL

Borjúborda Gundel módra   *6 servings*

½ pound spinach
Salt
½ pound lard
6 veal chops, ¼ pound each
2 whole eggs
¼ pound flour
1 cup bread crumbs
¼ pound mushrooms
7 tablespoons butter

2 cups milk
2 extra egg yolks
¼ pound Parmesan cheese,
    freshly grated
Pinch of grated nutmeg
Pepper
¼ pound boiled ham, sliced
Potato Cream (page 328)

1. Preheat oven to 350°F. Wash spinach in several waters and cook it in salted water for about 5 minutes. Rinse it with cold water and dry it between absorbent kitchen towels.

2. Grease a fireproof casserole with a little of the lard and line it with spinach leaves.

3. Pound the chops well. Sprinkle them with salt. Beat the whole eggs with 1 teaspoon water. Dip chops into flour, next into beaten eggs, finally into bread crumbs.

4. Heat the rest of the lard to frying temperature and in it brown veal chops on both sides. Put browned chops on top of spinach layer.

5. If mushrooms are large, cut into pieces. Leave small mushrooms whole. Cook mushrooms in 2 tablespoons of the butter in a separate frying pan, covered, for 5 minutes. Sprinkle the mushrooms on top of chops.

6. With 3 tablespoons butter and 2 tablespoons flour make a *roux*. When *roux* is light brown, dilute it with the milk and whip till smooth. Turn off heat.

7. Whip in the egg yolks, 2 tablespoons of the cheese, the nutmeg and salt and pepper to taste.

8. Arrange ham slices on top of mushrooms. Pour the thickened sauce over the ham. Sprinkle with the rest of the cheese and bread crumbs. Melt remaining 2 tablespoons butter and sprinkle on top of crumbs.

9. Spoon potatoes into a pastry tube fitted with a star-shaped No. 8 tip. Pipe a potato border around the casserole.

10. Bake in the preheated oven for about 20 minutes.

NOTE: *Believe it or not, this was served in the famed Gundel Restaurant as a regular dish on the menu. Nobody was rushing, however, to catch a plane. The dish did not wait for you—you had to wait for it.*

Part Three { *Recipes* }

CROQUETTES À LA PALOTA

Palotai ropogós   *16 to 20 croquettes*

6 tablespoons butter	Pinch of ground pepper
2 tablespoons plus ½ cup flour	Pinch of paprika
¾ cup milk	¾ pound cooked lean veal
2 egg yolks	½ pound boiled ham
½ pound mushrooms, cleaned and sliced	2 whole eggs, beaten
	1 cup white bread crumbs
Salt	1 cup vegetable oil

1. Melt 3 tablespoons of the butter. Add 2 tablespoons flour and stir for a few minutes; the *roux* should not brown. When it is hot, add milk and whip until smooth. Let the sauce cool for a few minutes.

2. When the sauce is warm—but not hot—whip in the egg yolks. Put the sauce aside.

3. Melt the rest of the butter and cook the mushrooms with a little salt, the pepper and paprika for 2 minutes. Set aside to cool.

4. Cut the veal and ham into pieces and put through the grinder together with the cooled mushrooms.

5. Combine ground mixture with the cooled sauce and let everything rest in the refrigerator for a couple of hours.

6. Form little sticks, 4 inches long and 1 inch wide, out of the mixture. Dip them into remaining flour, then into beaten whole eggs, finally into bread crumbs. Make sure not to ruin the shape of the little sticks.

7. Heat vegetable oil to frying temperature and gently place the breaded croquettes in it. Fry over *low* heat.

8. When croquettes are golden brown, remove them with a slotted spoon and drain on a triple layer of paper towels. Serve with any mayonnaise-based sauce such as tartar sauce or green sauce.

Serve as an appetizer, as a garnish for a fish course instead of potatoes, or as a main course for about 4 people.

CALVES' TONGUES WITH CHESTNUTS AND RAISINS

Mazsolás és gesztenyés borjúnyelv   *4 servings*

2 calves' tongues	¼ pound raisins
Salt	1 tablespoon butter
1 pound chestnuts	1 tablespoon flour

240

1. Cook tongues in water until they are soft. Drain. When tongues are cool enough to handle, pull off skin and membranes. Put tongues in 2 cups lightly salted water.

2. Cook chestnuts in 1 quart of water; peel them.

3. Add peeled chestnuts and the raisins to the tongues. Cook over low heat for 15 to 20 minutes.

4. Meantime make a light *roux* with the butter and flour. Dilute it with ½ cup cold water and whip the mixture till smooth.

5. Pour thickening over the simmering tongues. Cook for 5 more minutes, and the dish is ready to serve. Accompany with steamed rice or buttered noodles.

SALON-LUNG

Szalontüdő   *4 servings*

2 pounds calf lung and heart	1 teaspoon minced parsley
3 onions	6 tablespoons lard
3 bay leaves	4 cubes of sugar
2 garlic cloves	⅔ cup flour
1 lemon	1 teaspoon prepared mild
1 teaspoon capers	mustard
2 anchovy fillets, minced	1 teaspoon white vinegar
½ gherkin, minced	Salt
½ teaspoon minced tarragon	

1. If you don't have a close relationship with your butcher, you must clean the lung quite thoroughly yourself.

2. Chop 1 onion fine, add 1 bay leaf, and cover with water. Cook for 30 minutes. Add heart and cook for about 30 minutes, then add lung and cook for about 30 minutes longer, until both are tender.

3. Remove the cooked meat from the water and cut it into very fine strips. Place strips in a cooking-serving casserole. Reserve the cooking liquid.

4. Chop the other 2 onions and the garlic till the pieces are very fine. Grate the rind of the lemon. Mix onions and garlic, lemon rind, capers and minced anchovies, gherkin, tarragon and parsley.

5. Melt lard. Crush and dissolve the sugar cubes in it. Add the flour. Stir constantly over very low heat while browning this *roux*.

6. Add the mixture assembled in step 4 plus the remaining 2 bay leaves to the *roux*. Again stir constantly with a wooden spoon over low heat for another 3 or 4 minutes.

7. Add ¼ cup cold water to the thickened mixture and vigorously whip it. Then add about 1 cup of the liquid in which the lung was cooked; use as much as needed to make a heavy, creamlike sauce. Bring to a boil.

8. Adjust the flavor of the sauce with lemon juice, mustard, vinegar and salt to taste. The sauce can be sharp or sweet or piquant according to the way you adjust the taste at this point. Pour the sauce over the meat strips in the casserole, bring it to a boil, and serve. If you like, sprinkle the top with Paprika Essence (page 343) and minced parsley.

NOTE: *Although it seems illogical to add an extra step by using cubed sugar instead of granulated, it is much safer this way. If the melted fat is too hot, some of the granulated sugar would burn.*

About the curious name of this recipe, the only feasible answer I found was the remark of a Hungarian colleague who said that up to the middle of the nineteenth century lung was eaten only by very poor people. Some unsung genius introduced it—probably in a coffeehouse—with the above recipe; he named it szalonképes tüdő—"a lung dish that belongs in the drawing room"; or as one could say it now, "a lung stew with a college education."

✦ 18 ✦

BEEF
(MARHA)

SPICY BEEF ROULADES

Legénysült   2 *large servings, or*
4 *average servings*

1 pound beef flank steak, sliced crosswise	2 tablespoons red-wine vinegar
¾ pound leg of veal	1 bay leaf
¾ pound lean pork	Pinch of cayenne pepper, or 1
Salt and pepper	dried or fresh cherry pepper,
1 medium-sized onion, minced	or any other type of hot
2 tablespoons lard	pepper
	¼ cup sour cream

1. Have butcher cut each meat—beef, veal and pork—in a large thin slice, all the same size. Pound the meats, or have butcher do it, to make the slices thin, almost like butterfly steak. Salt and pepper the meats.

2. Place the pork slice and the veal slice on the beef. Roll up the meat tightly and tie with string.

3. Cook the onion in the lard for a few minutes. Add meat roulade and brown on all sides.

4. Mix vinegar with 1 cup water, and pour it on the meat. Add bay leaf and cayenne pepper. Cover the pot and cook till the meat is done. If necessary add more water, but always little by little.

5. Take roulade out of pan. Remove bay leaf. Add sour cream to juices remaining in pan.

6. Slice meat across. Pour sauce over meat slices. Serve with Potato Cream (page 328) or Baked Egg Barley (page 297).

NOTE: *The literal translation of the name of this dish is a puzzle. Legény means a lad. Sült means a roast. Everyone can advance his own pet theory to account for the name, since it isn't a roast and no country lad can afford the expensive ingredients.*

This is a very spicy dish, but you can eliminate all the spices and make it into a tame meat roulade.

BEEF STUFFED WITH PORK

Húsos tekercs   *4 to 6 servings*

1 large and 1 small onion, both chopped fine	inches and ½ inch thick (bottom round or flank steak)
1 tablespoon salt	
1 garlic clove, crushed	6 hard-boiled eggs
½ tablespoon freshly crushed black pepper	1 tablespoon lard
	1 teaspoon paprika
½ pound lean pork, ground	2 tablespoons tomato juice
3 slices of beef, each 9 by 6	1 green pepper, sliced

1. Mix the chopped small onion with ¼ teaspoon salt, the garlic, black pepper and ground pork. Divide it into 3 portions.

2. Spread each portion on top of a beef slice and place 2 hard-boiled eggs on top of each. Roll the packages and tie with white string.

3. Use a heavy Dutch oven with a tight-fitting lid. Wilt the large onion in lard till colored but not dark. Place meat rolls in the pot and cook, covered, for 5 to 10 minutes.

4. Add 1 cup water, the paprika, tomato juice and sliced green pepper. Continue cooking, still covered, over very low heat for about 1½ hours.

5. When meat is done remove it. Force the rest of contents through a sieve, or purée in a blender, and add the rest of the salt.

6. Remove strings from meat rolls and put meat back into the sauce. Cook over low heat for 5 to 10 minutes.

7. Slice the rolls slantwise before serving. Serve with new potatoes if in season, or with rice.

SLICED BEEF AS IN TÁPÉ

Marhaszelet tápéi módra 4 to 6 servings

1 tablespoon lard
1 medium-sized onion, cut into
 rough pieces
2 to 2½ pounds top round, tied
 as for roasting
1 medium-sized ripe tomato,
 peeled

2 garlic cloves, crushed with
 salt
1 tablespoon paprika
1 tablespoon salt
1 green pepper, sliced

1. Melt lard in a heavy casserole and add onion. Cook onion over low heat for 15 minutes.

2. Put in the beef and brown all sides over high heat for a few minutes. Push onion away from meat to the sides of the pan so meat can directly touch bottom of the casserole.

3. Add cut-up tomato, garlic and enough water to cover meat. Cook, covered, over very low heat, until meat is done.

4. Take out meat. Add to the cooking liquid the paprika, salt and green pepper. Reduce over high heat, without a cover, for 10 minutes. Make sure that the sauce does not burn. Then pass it through a sieve or purée in a blender.

5. Slice the meat and arrange it on a heatproof serving platter. Pour sauce over it. Return it to the heat for another 5 to 10 minutes, then serve.

LEMON BEEF

Citromos marhahús 4 servings

2 pounds lean beef chuck, cut
 into 1-inch cubes
1 cup beef broth
4 slices of lean bacon
1 tablespoon bacon drippings
1 tablespoon flour

1 cup sour cream
1½ tablespoons lemon juice
1 teaspoon fine-grated lemon
 rind
½ teaspoon sugar
1 tablespoon chopped tarragon

1. Cook cubed beef in beef broth until tender. Use a heavy Dutch oven or similar pot with a cover so you will not have to add more liquid. Remove meat from the pot and cool the broth.

2. In a frying pan fry the sliced bacon until crisp. Remove bacon and crumble but leave the drippings in the pan.

3. Add beef to hot drippings and cook, covered, for 5 minutes.

4. In a separate frypan make a *roux* with 1 tablespoon bacon drippings and the flour. Stir constantly and cook to a golden brown. Whip the cooled broth into the *roux,* then whip in sour cream, lemon juice, lemon rind, sugar and tarragon.

5. Pour the lemon sauce on the meat, and place in a serving casserole. Sprinkle it with the crisp bacon.

MOCK VENISON

Hamis őztokány   *10 to 12 servings*

1 trimmed whole beef tenderloin, 5 to 6 pounds	2 bay leaves
¼ pound double-smoked bacon, cut into little strips	2 medium-sized onions, peeled and minced
1 small knob celery	1 teaspoon and 2 tablespoons lard
2 parsnips	2 tablespoons flour
2 carrots	1 tablespoon sugar
½ cup wine vinegar	1 tablespoon prepared mustard
½ cup red wine	1 tablespoon lemon juice
Grated rind of ½ lemon	½ cup sour cream
10 peppercorns	

1. Start this recipe 2 or 3 days before you plan to serve it. Lard the beef with little strips of bacon.

2. Peel knob celery, parsnips and carrots; cut into small pieces. Mix 3 cups water, the vinegar and wine in a large roasting pan (not aluminum). Add the vegetables and bring to a boil.

3. Put in the beef, grated lemon rind, peppercorns and bay leaves. Put in the refrigerator to marinate for 2 or 3 days.

4. When you are ready to cook, wilt the onions in 1 teaspoon lard over very low heat; do not let the onions brown.

5. Remove beef from marinade and place it on top of onion. Cook meat for 2 or 3 minutes on each side.

6. Pour marinade over meat and cook, covered, over low heat until meat is almost cooked, for 2 hours or more.

7. Take out meat and cut into ½-inch-thick slices.

8. Use the 2 tablespoons lard and the flour to make a *roux;* when properly golden brown, pour in ½ cup cold water and whip until smooth.

9. Force vegetables and broth in which meat cooked through a sieve, or purée in a blender, and pour into the diluted *roux*.

10. Brown the sugar in a small frying pan until caramelized. Add 3 tablespoons cold water and cook for a few minutes till sugar melts. Whip in the mustard. Pour the caramel and mustard into the puréed sauce.

11. Add sliced meat; try to keep the slices whole. Cook at a slow simmer for another 10 to 15 minutes to allow sauce to permeate the meat.

12. Finally, mix in lemon juice and sour cream. Serve with White Bread Dumplings (page 300).

NOTE: *This recipe is from the National Casino, where using the most expensive meats was the rule of the past century. You can use other cuts for this, such as top round or chuck, with great success.*

The desired sweet and sour taste of this dish varies from household to household. You may adjust it by using more sugar and less lemon juice, or the other way around.

BEEF TENDERLOIN RAGOUT

Vesepecsenye becsinált   *4 or 5 servings*

2 pounds beef tenderloin	1 bay leaf
1 medium-sized onion, minced	6 tarragon leaves
2 tablespoons lard	½ pound uncooked macaroni
2 cups beef broth	Salt
1 tablespoon flour	

1. Trim beef of membrane and cut into ½-inch pieces.

2. Wilt the onion in the lard in a large braising pot.

3. Add beef. Reduce heat to the lowest possible. Cover the pot and cook; add a little broth as needed. When meat is done, carefully let the liquid evaporate and fry the meat in the fat that remains (see method on pages 271–72).

4. Dust meat with flour, stir flour into pan juices, and add remaining broth, the bay leaf and tarragon. Bring to a boil. Simmer for 15 minutes.

5. Break macaroni into small pieces and cook it in salted water. Drain it when *al dente* (cooked till it still has a little bite). Rinse with cold water.

6. Remove the bay leaf and tarragon leaves. Pour the ragout into a serving dish and surround with macaroni.

NOTE: *To an American cook the use of beef tenderloin for stew is probably sacrilegious, but in big households in Hungary they used the center cuts for tournedos-type preparations, and the ends for this recipe. Of course you can prepare this dish with less expensive beef cuts.*

It may not be easy to buy a portion of a tenderloin. If you buy a whole tenderloin (5 to 6 pounds after trimming), you will have enough meat for 4 filets mignons *and enough in addition for this recipe.*

TENDERLOIN OF BEEF BRAISED IN MUST

Mustos pecsenye   *6 or 7 servings*

2 tablespoons chopped beef suet	2 hot cherry peppers
1 whole beef tenderloin	Bouquet of flat parsley
1 carrot, peeled and sliced	½ pound Virginia ham, sliced
1 knob celery, peeled and sliced	2 cups strong beef broth
1 parsnip, peeled and sliced	3 cups sweet unfermented must
1 large onion, peeled and cut	Salt
into small chunks	1 teaspoon arrowroot

1. Render the beef suet in a roasting pan. Add the whole tenderloin of beef and brown it fast on all sides.

2. Strew all the vegetables, the cherry peppers, parsley and ham around the beef. Pour in the broth and the must. Cover the pan and braise the beef on top of the stove, or in a 325°F. oven, for 1 hour.

3. When beef is done, you should have about 2 cups of liquid left over. Strain the liquid. Adjust salt (use very little because the Virginia ham probably has enough salt), and bring to a boil.

4. Dissolve arrowroot in 1 tablespoon of cold water and whip it into the simmering stock. Serve the sauce with the beef.

5. The ham is usually discarded, but you may set it aside to use another day, to make a vegetable soup for instance.

NOTE: *The original recipe, which is just about 200 years old, uses sugar and additional must if needed. This was probably a grape-harvest dish for the very wealthy lord of the vineyard, since must is generally not available except in wine country during grape-harvest time. If you can buy a white grape juice in a German grocery store, you probably would get a similar result.*

If you don't like spicy dishes, eliminate the cherry pepper.

TRANSYLVANIAN BANDITS' MEAT WITH PULISZKA

Erdélyi zsiványpecsenye puliszkával   4 to 6 servings

1½ pounds beef tenderloin,
  sliced ¼ inch thick
½ tablespoon paprika
Salt

½ teaspoon pepper
½ pound double-smoked
  bacon, cut into thin slices
2 tablespoons lard

1. Gently pound the meat slices, making sure you do not ruin the texture; tenderloin of beef is very fragile. Sprinkle the slices with paprika, salt and pepper on one side. Roll slices lengthwise into little sausage shapes and wrap with bacon slices.

2. Heat lard in a frying pan and fast-brown meat roulades on all sides.

3. Reduce heat. Continue cooking, covered, over very low heat, until meat juices evaporate and meat cooks in its own fat. By that time it should be done.

4. Serve it with Cornmeal Dumplings (page 303).

NOTE: *I wonder where the name comes from . . . considering this is a very fast-fried dish, and speculating on the way bandits live in Transylvania. Obviously it must have been "orchestrated" by one of the better restaurants there.*

LEMON TRIPE HANGLI

Citromos pacal Hangli módra   4 to 6 servings

3 cups beef broth
3 tablespoons flour
4 tablespoons butter
4 egg yolks
Juice of ½ lemon

Salt
2 tablespoons minced parsley
3 pounds *hot, cooked*
  honeycomb tripe, cut into
  julienne strips

1. Bring the beef broth to a boil.

2. Knead together flour and butter until the mixture sticks together, then whip it rapidly into the boiling broth. Lower the heat and simmer until the broth reaches the thickness of a light cream.

3. Whip in the egg yolks and continue whipping for about 5 minutes, or until the liquid reaches the texture of a sauce. Add lemon juice and salt to taste. Mix in the parsley.

4. Add the tripe. Make sure the tripe is hot when you add it, because you cannot cook this sauce further—unless you want to make scrambled eggs.

After this you are ready to serve an army, or at any rate gastronomic adventure-seekers wanting to taste something different from the *tripes à la mode de Caen.*

NOTE: *In almost every civilized country you can buy cooked tripe. If your home town is an exception, you have to do this chore yourself. Cook it in plenty of salted water, which may take hours, depending on the disposition of the animal.*

This recipe is a heritage from the days of Turkish occupation.

ROSTÉLYOS

Rostélyos is one of the national foods of Hungary, although similar dishes exist in many other countries. The small differences in the Hungarian methods and ingredients, however, make it distinctly Hungarian.

Rostélyos can be a simple braised steak, or a stuffed and rolled steak. Also there are the regional specialties and inventions of chefs.

In the provinces you will find individual preparations of this dish, and with a little knowledge you can guess some of the local history and the characteristics of the region. The Esterházy *rostélyos,* for instance, is from Transdanubia, bearing the name of the uncrowned king of yesteryear from this area, Miklós Esterházy, who built Esterháza, a "Hungarian Versailles." His court chef created this specialty, which became the favorite of the entire region.

And isn't *debreceni rostélyos,* made with onion, green pepper, tomato, caraway seeds and the spicy paprika of the area, typical of the sunburned lowlands where much of the romance of the Pusztas is still alive?

The word *rostélyos* in Hungarian indicates (as shown in illustrated eighteenth-century cookbooks) that originally it was a grilled meat; only toward the end of the nineteenth century was it transferred to a frying pan or braising pot.

The cut of meat used can be any beef cut that is neither too fatty nor too dry. One can use a top sirloin, an unopened butterfly steak, a sirloin steak, T-bone steak, shell steak, etc. If you are going to make a stuffed *rostélyos,* obviously you cannot use anything with bone in it.

Many recipes call for dipping meat slices into flour before frying. This is not in the Hungarian style, and when you examine it, it does not seem logical either. In other nations' braised-meat cookery, the flour is needed to give some body to the gravy, but in the Hungarian *rostélyos* preparations there are always other ingredients that will thicken the liquid.

Variations are many, depending on the stuffing, sauce or spicing you want to use. In Szeged, for instance, they cook *csipetke* (see page 178) in the basic recipe.

French cuisine is known for its sophisticated and boundless variations on a single theme; Hungarian cuisine relies mostly on sure-fire formulas. *Rostélyos,* together with cabbage dishes and *gulyás,* are the exceptions to this rule. Each of these has as many as 10 to 50 variations. Here are a few of the more interesting ones.

PANFRIED ROSTÉLYOS

Serpenyős rostélyos   *6 servings*

6 slices of beef, each ½ pound
   and about ½ inch thick, or
   six ½-pound club steaks (see
   Note)
Salt
2 tablespoons flour
¼ pound lard
1 large onion, peeled

1 garlic clove, crushed
½ teaspoon caraway seeds
1 tablespoon paprika
2 pounds potatoes, peeled and
   diced
¼ pound green pepper, diced
¼ pound tomato, diced

1. Pound the beef slices well and thin them to about half of original thickness. Sprinkle with salt, then with flour on both sides.

2. Heat lard in a frying pan and brown meat on both sides over high heat for a few minutes. Remove meat and put aside.

3. Cut onion into rough pieces and wilt it in the same fat over low heat for about 15 minutes. Add crushed garlic, caraway seeds and paprika. Stir the mixture and add 2 cups cold water.

4. Place beef slices in a single layer in the same pan. Cover the pan and cook over very low heat. If you use low heat and a heavy cast-iron pan with a tight-fitting lid, you probably will not have to add any more water. If the sauce thickens too much, add a small amount of water to prevent burning.

5. When beef begins to soften, add diced potatoes, green pepper and tomato, and enough water to barely cover potatoes. Cover the pan and cook over very low heat until the meat is done.

NOTE: *You may use the same preparation for lamb steak, leg of wild boar, or venison.*

In the finest restaurants a côte de boeuf *cut is used for this.*

LORD'S ROSTÉLYOS

Mágnásrostélyos   *6 servings*

Ingredients for Panfried   ½ cup dry white wine
    Rostélyos (page 251)   ¼ cup white vinegar
½ pound bacon, sliced thin

1. Proceed exactly as in the basic recipe, through step 2.
2. After the meat is browned, line a heavy braising pot with slices of bacon. Place meat on top of bacon.
3. Cook wilted onion, tomato and paprika in the wine and the vinegar for 15 minutes.
4. Add seared steak slices, cover the pot, and finish as in the basic recipe.

NOTE: *The name comes from the fact that originally tenderloin was used for this type of* rostélyos, *which was so expensive a cut that only a lord could afford it.*

     Bacon for this should be Hungarian or German smoked bacon; or if neither of these is available, use Irish smoked bacon.

BRAISED STEAK IN CHEF CSÁKI'S MANNER

Csáki rostélyos   *6 servings*

6 slices of beef, each ½ pound   5 eggs
    and about ½ inch thick   2 tablespoons flour
Salt   2 tablespoons lard
¼ teaspoon pepper   1 green pepper, diced
¼ pound double-smoked meaty   1 tomato, diced
    bacon   1 tablespoon paprika
2 medium-sized onions, peeled   1 tablespoon tomato purée
    and minced   ¾ cup sour cream
1 cup *Lecsó* (page 315)

1. Pound the beef slices till they are quite thin. Salt and pepper them, and put them aside.
2. Cut bacon into small dice and render it in a frying pan. Add 1 minced onion and brown it fast.
3. Add *lecsó.* Stir and cook for another few minutes.
4. Beat eggs and 1 tablespoon of the flour until slightly thickened. Add to bacon and *lecsó* to make the filling.

5. Place 1 tablespoon of filling on each beef slice, or more depending on the size of slices, and press it down hard. Try to fold the sides over and then roll each side to a tube shape. Tie the rolls with string.

6. Melt lard in a heavy pot. When hot, add beef rolls and brown in a 500°F. oven for 15 minutes.

7. Remove beef rolls from the pot and reduce heat to 300°F.

8. Put the second minced onion in the pot and brown it fast. Add diced green pepper and tomato, the paprika and tomato purée. Stir well.

9. Replace beef rolls in the pot and add water to barely cover meat. Cover the pot and cook the meat slowly either in the oven or on top of the stove for about 1 hour, or until done.

10. Mix sour cream and remaining 1 tablespoon flour. Add this to the sauce and mix well. Cook it over *very low* heat for another 10 minutes.

11. Place beef rolls in the center of a platter and pour sauce on top. Serve with buttered Egg Dumplings (page 297).

NOTE: *This dish was named in honor of the famous Hungarian chef of the beginning of the twentieth century.*

The ideal cooking vessel is a cast-iron, copper or cast-aluminum oven pot of about 1-quart capacity, very wide rather than deep.

ESTERHÁZY ROSTÉLYOS

6 servings

6 slices of beef, each ½ pound and about ½ inch thick	½ teaspoon pepper
	½ lemon
¼ pound lard	⅛ pound butter
1 large onion, peeled	1 tablespoon prepared mustard
2 carrots, peeled	1 tablespoon flour
2 knobs celery, peeled	1 cup sour cream
2 parsnips, peeled	1 tablespoon fine-chopped flat
1 bay leaf	parsley
1 teaspoon salt	

1. Pound the meat well. Melt lard in a large frying pan. When lard is very hot, brown beef on both sides over high heat for 1 or 2 minutes. Remove meat and put it aside.

2. Take all the onion and half of the other vegetables, and cut them into thin slices. Fry them in the hot fat for a few minutes.

3. Add 2 cups water, the bay leaf, salt and pepper. Grate the lemon rind of

the ½ lemon and add the rind to the vegetables. Squeeze the juice of the lemon and set it aside.

4. Return beef slices to pan and cook it all over very low heat until meat is done.

5. Cut the rest of the vegetables into long matchstick shapes.

6. Melt butter in another pot and cook matchstick vegetables, covered, adding very little water when needed.

7. When meat is done, remove it from the pan. Purée the broth and its vegetables in a blender, or force through a sieve. Add mustard, the lemon juice, and the flour mixed with 3 tablespoons water. Finally, add the sour cream.

8. Put meat back into the puréed sauce and cook it for a few minutes.

9. Place meat slices neatly on a serving platter. Pour sauce over, then top with the matchstick-cut vegetables. Sprinkle with the chopped parsley.

ÖRKÉNYI ROSTÉLYOS

6 servings

6 slices of beef, each ½ pound and about ½ inch thick
1 teaspoon salt
¼ pound double-smoked bacon, sliced thin
1 pound sauerkraut
½ pound smoked pork sausage, sliced thin
2 cups sour cream
3 tablespoons lard
1 large onion, peeled and chopped

1 tablespoon paprika
1 very ripe large tomato, peeled and chopped
Pinch of dried marjoram, or ½ teaspoon chopped fresh marjoram
1 garlic clove
¼ cup light cream
1 tablespoon flour
⅓ cup white wine

1. Pound beef slices well and sprinkle salt on both sides. Pound the bacon slices well to flatten as much as possible. On top of each beef slice, place 1 bacon segment.

2. Wash sauerkraut, then squeeze it. Divide the sauerkraut into 6 portions and place one on top of each bacon-beef slice. Top sauerkraut with sausage slices. Spoon 1 cup of the sour cream evenly on top of the sausage layer.

3. Carefully roll up each beef slice with its topping; make sure none of the filling falls out. Tie each roll with string.

4. Use a large frying pan. Heat half of the lard and fast-fry the meat roulades on all sides.

5. Brown chopped onion in remaining lard in a heavy stewing pot; sprinkle paprika in, stir, and immediately add chopped tomato and 1 cup water. Place the browned roulades next to each other in the tomato mixture. Sprinkle with salt. Add marjoram and garlic, and cover the pot with a heavy lid.

6. Cook this dish over very low heat. Make sure you do not stir it, but grab both sides of the pot by the handles and make fast quarter turns if necessary to keep meat from sticking or burning.

7. When meat is done, remove from the pot and let stand for 5 minutes, then cut strings.

8. Cook the liquid in the pot until it becomes as thick as a sauce. Mix remaining sour cream, the light cream and flour, and stir into the gravy; bring to a boil and simmer for 5 minutes. Remove garlic. Force the sauce through a sieve or purée in a blender.

9. Pour sauce back into the pot, add white wine, and bring again to a boil. Simmer for a couple of minutes.

10. Place the rolled *rostélyos* on a serving platter and pour the sauce on top.

STUFFED ROSTÉLYOS À LA KASSA

Kassai töltött rostélyos   *6 servings*

Ingredients for Örkényi
  Rostélyos (page 254),
  omitting bacon, sauerkraut,
  sausage, 1 cup sour cream,
  fresh tomato and wine
¼ pound boiled ham, ground
¼ pound Virginia or

Westphalian ham, or
  prosciutto, ground
2 tablespoons light cream
1 tablespoon flour
1 egg
2 tablespoons tomato purée

Follow the same preparation as for *Örkényi rostélyos*, except make the filling of ground ham mixed with light cream, flour and egg. Cook the filling, stirring constantly, until the egg is scrambled.

Use tomato purée instead of fresh tomato.

LAMB AND MUTTON
(BÁRÁNY ÉS ÜRÜHÚS)

LAMB is not as popular in Hungary as other meats. Little Cumania, part of the Great Plains, is the only section where lamb is regularly eaten. Otherwise this meat is used only at Eastertime.

LAMB AND SPINACH STEW, BÁNÁT STYLE

Bánáti kapama   6 *servings*

2½ pounds lamb stew meat, cut into 1-inch dice	1 teaspoon hot paprika
	Salt
½ cup flour	1½ pounds spinach, washed
¼ pound lard	¼ cup ricotta cheese
1 large onion, peeled and sliced	½ cup sour cream

1. Roll meat in flour, and fry in hot lard till it reaches the color of a seared steak. Remove meat.

2. Fry onion slices in lard remaining in the pan till slices become golden.

3. Remove onion from fat with slotted spoon and put in a heavy casserole. Add paprika and salt to taste; mix.

4. Place fried meat and spinach in the casserole with the onion; add ½ cup water. Cook, covered, over a very low heat for 1 hour or longer, until lamb is tender. Check several times to see if additional water is necessary, but each time only add ¼ cup water.

5. When meat is cooked and spinach becomes totally disintegrated, like a

sauce, mix in ricotta and sour cream. Simmer for a few minutes. Serve with rice pilaf.

NOTE: *In South Hungary, where both Serbs and Hungarians cook this dish, they use sour cream made of sheep's milk and, in the springtime when they have no spinach, they substitute scallion greens.*

LEG OF LAMB WITH PICKLE SAUCE

Báránycomb uborkamártással   *6 to 8 servings*

1 very young leg of lamb, 4 to 5 pounds	⅛ pound butter
¼ cup coarse salt	3 sprigs of rosemary
Grated rind of 1 lemon	Bouquet of flat parsley
	Pickle Sauce (page 342)

1. Pound leg of lamb to make it somewhat flatter than it is. Rub it with coarse salt and let it stand for 2 hours.

2. Preheat oven to 325°F. Place lamb in a roasting pan, sprinkle with lemon rind, and rub with the butter. Put rosemary and parsley in the roasting pan.

3. Roast the lamb, covered, in the preheated oven for 1 hour. Baste several times while roasting.

4. Place lamb on a serving platter. Add any juices from the roasting pan to the pickle sauce, and mix well. Serve sauce separately.

NOTE: *This is a Vasváry recipe, dated 1830.*

SHEPHERD'S MILLET

Juhhúsos köleskása   *8 servings*

1¾ pounds lean lamb, cut into ½-inch dice	½ teaspoon black pepper
Salt	Pinch of marjoram
1 large and 2 small onions, peeled and chopped	1 tablespoon hot red paprika
¼ pound lard	1 pound uncooked millet
1 garlic clove, crushed	2 to 2½ cups beef or lamb broth

1. Bring meat to a boil in 1 quart water with 1 teaspoon salt and cook over low heat for about 1 hour. Drain the meat, saving the broth.

2. Wilt the onions in lard in a large pot over low heat for 10 to 15 minutes.

3. Add drained meat to the onions. Add garlic, pepper, marjoram and paprika. Cook for 1 minute, stirring well.

4. Add ½ cup of the broth the meat was cooked in. Cover the pot with a tight-fitting lid and cook the meat till it is almost done, for 30 minutes to 1 hour.

5. At that point pour in the millet and enough meat broth to cover it. Put back the lid and turn down heat to very low. Add extra broth if necessary. Cook until meat and millet are completely done, for 15 to 30 minutes longer. Adjust salt if necessary.

VARIATION:

Harvest kása: *Make the dish with either lamb or beef, adding plenty of diced carrots and parsnips. Replace half of the meat broth with dry white wine. Dice ¼ to ½ pound double-smoked bacon. Sauté the bacon dice until nearly cooked and pour them on top of the finished dish just before serving.*

NOTE: *This is an ancient Hungarian food, perhaps somewhat strange and certainly very hearty. Use the same method to cook goose.*

The closest English equivalent for the word kása is "porridge," but porridge suggests something quite different. The word is Slavic in origin; according to a Russian proverb, "We all consider kása a mother." The Near East also eats this type of dish. Basically, kása is a stone-ground or rough-ground cereal cooked in milk, water or other liquid. It can be sweet or it can be salty. The grain can be cracked barley, millet, semolina, rough-ground cornmeal, or other broken cereals. Kása can be served as a main course with a lot of onion and bacon slices, or with pork cracklings. When it is served with cottage cheese made of sheep's milk, it is considered a king among grain dishes. Kása can be served as a dessert, cooked in milk with honey and butter or other adornments. An amusing dish from the County of Vas is the "pushing-out kása" (kitoló kása); the last dish at a wedding feast is this version of kása; the sweetened dish is topped with pretzel-shaped cakes, indicating: "This is the final dish, and now in God's name go home, please. . . ."

MUTTON CHOP À LA TORDA

Tordai ürücomb   6 *servings*

2 pounds leg of mutton,
  without bones
Salt and pepper
1 garlic clove, split
3 tablespoons lard
½ cup beef or chicken broth
2 pounds Savoy cabbage, sliced
1 medium-sized onion, stuck
  with 2 cloves
2 carrots, peeled and sliced

2 parsnips, peeled and sliced
1 slice of peeled knob celery
½ pound double-smoked
  bacon, diced
1 pound potatoes, cut into large
  dice
6 pieces of Hungarian Debrecen
  sausage, ¼ pound each
2 tablespoons minced parsley

1. Sprinkle mutton with salt and pepper. Rub with cut side of garlic. Brown the meat in 2 tablespoons lard in a large pot.

2. Add a few tablespoons of broth, cover the pot, and simmer the meat for about 1 hour.

3. Cook Savoy cabbage in salted water for about 3 minutes and the rest of the vegetables 10 to 15 minutes; drain.

4. Uncover the meat and surround it with the cooked Savoy cabbage, the onion, and the sliced carrots, parsnips and knob celery. Add diced bacon. Pour in remaining broth and cover the pot again. Cook over very low heat until the meat is almost done.

5. Add potatoes to meat and finish cooking.

6. Meantime, sauté Hungarian sausages in remaining 1 tablespoon lard; split them lengthwise.

7. Slice the mutton on a cutting board. Place the slices in the middle of a large serving platter. Surround with the rest of the ingredients from the pot. Top with sausages, and sprinkle with parsley.

NOTE: *In Transylvania the same method is used for the entire hind leg of the mutton.*

This dish won't be very popular with people who eat fruit salad for dinner, but it would be welcomed by the shepherd of whom this story is told:

One of the Prince Esterházys once boasted before an English lord how much one of his shepherds could eat. He brought out a whole calf for him for lunch, but to make sure he wouldn't get bored with it they cooked the different parts in various ways—stewed, baked, fried, etc. When they put the last portion in front of him he wiped his mouth and said: "Your Excellency better bring that calf now because I'm getting sort of full. . . ."

✡ 20 ✡

GAME BIRDS AND GAME
(VADMADARAK ÉS VADAK)

HUNGARY is a game paradise. Venison, roebuck, wild boar, fallow deer and a great variety of game birds can be found in season. Hunters from all parts of the world come to bag *fogoly* (partridge), *szalonka* (snipe), *fácán* (pheasant), *fenyvesmadár* (field fare), *császármadár* (grouse), *fürj* (quail), *kertisármány* (ortolan), *vadliba* (wild goose) and the *tuzok,* one of the species of the bustard-plover families.

Be it a Russian premier or an English prime minister, you'll find his picture on the pages of international magazines when he is posing with the tusk of a huge wild boar (undoubtedly shot by one of the professional hunters in the party), with the imposing mountains of the Börzsöny patiently providing the background. In 1971, 40,000 hunters came to participate in a Hunters' World Congress.

Hare is very plentiful and the best are to be found in the Great Plains. This rich stock is maintained with well-organized winter feeding and spring breeding.

Although the game recipes that follow use a variety of fats, there are houses where butter is exclusively used for game birds. This is an unexplainable remnant of the Middle Ages, when almost everything was cooked with lard except game birds.

PHEASANT AS IN SZABOLCS

Fácánsült szabolcsiasan　　　　　　　*2 servings*

1 young pheasant, about 1½
　pounds
¼ pound smoked bacon, cut
　into little sticks
1 teaspoon salt

½ pound thin sheets of salt
　pork fat
1 medium-sized onion, sliced
　thin
3 tablespoons sour cream

1. Soak pheasant in cold water for a few hours.

2. Pound pheasant with mallet, then pull the outer membrane off the skin. (Pheasant skin is not like chicken skin, but has a covering film.)

3. Using the point of a knife or a larding needle, make incisions in fleshy parts of the pheasant, and insert the little bacon sticks. Salt pheasant inside and outside.

4. Wrap the sheets of salt pork fat tightly around the pheasant. Place it in a covered roasting pan and bake in a 450°F. oven for 10 minutes.

5. Remove the pan from the oven and arrange the sliced onion and sour cream on the bird. Again cover the roasting pan and return it to the oven. Reduce heat to 375°F. and roast for an additional 35 minutes.

NOTE: *Adjust the roasting time according to the age and size of the bird. The time given here is for an average bird.*

PHEASANT AS COOKED BY THE VINTNER'S WIFE

Fácán vincellérne módra　　　　　　*6 to 10 servings*

6 very young pheasants, 1 to
　1½ pounds each
1 pound cured-cooked meaty
　bacon (*Kaiser Fleisch*)
Salt
¼ teaspoon ground cloves
1 tablespoon chopped fresh
　marjoram
¼ pound butter
About 30 perfect grape leaves,
　washed
1 bay leaf, crumbled
1 teaspoon grated lemon rind

1 teaspoon black peppercorns
10 tarragon leaves
3 pounds white seedless grapes
½ bottle red Burgundy-type
　wine
Cream Sauce (see below)
Liver Purée (see below)
Croutons (see below)
¼ cup brandy
1 teaspoon currant jam
1 tablespoon lemon juice

1. Preheat oven to 350°F. Clean, wash, and dry the pheasants.

2. Cut half of the bacon into little sticks and use to lard the pheasants. Salt the birds inside and outside and rub the cloves and marjoram in the cavity.

3. Spread the butter in an ample-sized roasting pan, and line it with half of the grape leaves. Place the pheasants on their breasts in the pan.

4. Meantime chop the rest of the bacon. Fry it, and pour bacon bits and fat over the pheasants.

5. Sprinkle the bay leaf, lemon rind, peppercorns and tarragon around the birds. Cover top with the rest of the grape leaves.

6. Place the roasting pan in the preheated oven and roast the birds for 40 minutes.

7. Remove pan from oven. Remove the top layer of grape leaves. Pull half of the grapes from the stems and add to the pheasants; leave the rest of the grapes in little bunches or clusters. Return pan to oven and brown the birds at 475°F. for 5 minutes.

8. Set roasting pan on top of the stove, add half of the red wine, and baste pheasants for 5 minutes.

9. Meantime, prepare the cream sauce, liver purée and croutons.

10. Add brandy to the ready pheasants, and ignite. When flames die out, remove the pheasants from the pan.

11. Add to juices remaining in the pan the currant jam, remaining wine and the lemon juice. Bring to a boil. When the sauce reaches a gravy thickness, strain it and skim off fat. Put it aside and keep warm.

12. Cut off legs and breasts of pheasants and place on a serving platter. Decorate with little bunches of remaining grapes. Pour the gravy over the grapes.

13. Spread warm liver purée on warm croutons. Serve the croutons separately to accompany the pheasant. (This is different from the French style of service, in which the croutons would be placed underneath the birds.)

14. Serve Vintner's Rice (page 330) or a pile of straw potatoes with this dish.

CREAM SAUCE

1 tablespoon butter   ¼ cup hot milk
1 tablespoon flour

Melt butter, add flour, and stir with a whip over low heat for a few minutes. Add the hot milk and keep whipping. When the sauce is thickened, take off the heat. If it is too thick, add a little more milk and whip it in.

LIVER PURÉE

4 tablespoons butter	¼ cup brandy
Livers of the pheasants, sliced	2 egg yolks
Pinch of ground pepper	½ teaspoon juniper berries,
Salt	crushed
Cream Sauce (above)	1 teaspoon tarragon leaves

1. Melt the butter in a frying pan. Add the sliced livers, sprinkle with pepper and salt, and brown them on both sides over high heat.

2. Immediately force through a sieve, or purée in a blender. Then whip the purée with the cream sauce and brandy.

3. Add egg yolks and whip for a few more minutes.

4. Add juniper berries and tarragon leaves, adjust salt, and whip the purée well. Set it aside but keep it warm.

CROUTONS

5 hard rolls	½ cup melted butter

Cut the hard rolls into halves, then into triangle shapes. Sauté them in the melted butter. Keep them warm.

NOTE: *Grape clusters can also be baked with the gravy for about 10 minutes, and then placed on the platter.*

PARTRIDGE IN ASPIC

Kocsonyázott fogoly   *4 servings*

4 partridges	1 tablespoon lemon juice
1 teaspoon lard	2 tablespoons brandy
1 carrot, peeled and sliced	1 hard-boiled egg
20 capers	
1 envelope of unflavored	
gelatin	

1. Cut off legs and breasts of the partridges and put them into a pot. Set aside the rest of the birds.

2. Add enough water to legs and breasts to reach 2 inches above them. Cook, covered, until meat comes off the bones.

3. Remove partridge pieces from broth; discard skin and bones; strain the broth.

4. Brown remaining parts of the birds in the lard, together with carrot slices. Cook till nice and brown.

5. Add strained broth to partridge and carrot and cook over low heat for 10 more minutes. Keep skimming the broth to remove all fat. Let it cool.

6. Remove any last remaining fat from cooled broth. Bring again to a simmer, and add capers.

7. Soften the gelatin in ¼ cup cold water. Add ⅓ cup hot broth and stir until gelatin is dissolved. Add enough more of the hot broth to make 2 cups liquid aspic. Mix in the lemon juice and brandy.

8. Use 4 individual serving dishes or soup plates. On the bottom of each place 2 breasts and 2 legs and a slice of hard-boiled egg. Ladle enough liquid aspic over quail and egg to cover. Let it cool, then chill until jelled.

9. When the aspic is firm, decorate it as you like; or leave it plain, as the wife of the hunter did. Serve with a bottle of Debrői Hárslevelű wine.

WILD DUCK WITH QUINCES

Vadkacsa birsalmával   *2 servings*

1 young wild duck, 3 to 4 pounds, dressed	6 quinces
	¾ cup melted butter
Salt	½ cup dry white wine

1. Preheat oven to 300°F. Wash the duck as little as possible. Just clean inside and outside with a moist cloth. Salt well inside and outside.

2. Peel quinces and cut into segments. Stuff them into the cavity of the duck.

3. Place duck in a roasting pan and pour melted butter over the bird. Roast in the preheated oven for about 10 minutes.

4. Pour the wine on top of the duck and put it back in the oven. Continue to roast the duck, basting all the time with the butter and wine in the pan, until it is almost done. This will be 1 hour, or less.

5. Increase oven heat to 500°F. and roast for 3 or 4 minutes longer, until skin is crisp.

6. Total roasting time for a young wild duck depends on how bloody you like it. In Hungary they prefer it well cooked. Serve with a *risotto* made with the giblets of the bird, and with braised red cabbage.

NOTE: *Only the breasts of wild duck are used, since the legs are tough. As a result the duck will make only 2 servings.*

BRAISED WILD GOOSE WITH DUMPLINGS AS IN DEBRECEN

Debreceni párolt vadliba gombóccal   *about 6 servings*

¼ pound double-smoked
  bacon, chopped fine
¼ pound lard
1 medium-sized onion, sliced
1 parsnip, peeled and sliced
1 carrot, peeled and sliced
1 knob celery, peeled and sliced
1 garlic clove, mashed
1 wild goose, 7 to 8 pounds
2 tablespoons flour

1 teaspoon paprika
2 cups chicken broth
1 small bay leaf
1 teaspoon fresh marjoram, or
  a pinch of dried marjoram
10 black peppercorns
¾ cup Riesling wine
Juice of 1 lemon
1 teaspoon prepared mustard
½ tablespoon sugar

1. Preheat oven to 500°F. In a large roasting pan cook the bacon over low heat and then add the lard.

2. Add onion, parsnip, carrot, knob celery and garlic. Cook over low heat for a few minutes.

3. Wash and dry the goose and put it on top of the vegetables. Place the pan in the preheated oven for 20 minutes.

4. Remove goose and sprinkle flour on the vegetables. Mix well, then add paprika and chicken broth. Bring broth to a boil and let it simmer slowly.

5. Meantime, divide the goose, separating drumsticks and breasts. Add these together with the other parts to the vegetables and sauce. Add the bay leaf, marjoram, peppercorns and wine. Cover the pan and cook over very low heat on top of the stove till goose is done.

6. Remove goose and force everything else through a sieve. Taste the purée and add half of the lemon juice, mustard and sugar; bring to a boil. Then taste it again and adjust salt, sugar, lemon juice and mustard. Sauce should be on the piquant side.

7. Put goose back into the sauce and simmer for a few more minutes so goose will absorb the flavors of the sauce. Serve with White Bread Dumplings (page 300).

NOTE: *Wild duck can be prepared in the same way. In both cases you must pick a young bird, otherwise it will be very fishy-tasting.*

According to the taste of some circles, to serve a perfectly cooked wild game bird, let it fly through the hot kitchen. This is not the Hungarian ideal. Hungarians want to taste the bird's meat and skin, not the blood.

HARE BRAISED WITH JUNIPER BERRIES

Borókás nyúl   *4 to 6 servings*

4 juniper berries (see Note)
Salt
3 pounds hare meat, without
   bones
¼ pound smoked bacon, cut
   into strips

1 medium-sized onion, peeled
   and minced
2 tablespoons butter
1 cup sour cream
2 tablespoons flour

1. Crush juniper berries, and together with some salt sprinkle them on the hare. Cover the meat and place in the refrigerator for 2 or 3 days.
2. Lard the hare with strips of bacon. Sprinkle it with minced onion.
3. Heat butter in a braising pan. On top of the stove brown the hare and onion, making sure that the meat is turned to brown all sides.
4. Sprinkle meat with 2 tablespoons hot water, shake the pan and cook, covered, over low heat for about 45 minutes (see Note). Keep looking at it and add some water if there is no more in the bottom of the dish.
5. When meat is tender, take it out of the pan. Strain the broth.
6. Mix sour cream with flour and whip it into the strained broth. Bring to a boil, then reduce heat to very low and cook for a few minutes. Adjust salt. Spoon sauce over the hare and serve.

NOTE: *It is difficult to tell the exact length of time you need for a hare to cook, because the age and type of hare can make enough difference for the time to range between 30 minutes and 2 hours.*

Use whole sections of meat for a more attractive service. If you cut the meat into pieces, it is more appropriate for an informal luncheon.

In most vineyard areas red wine is used instead of water. Try this for an excellent variation.

Since juniper berries are rarely used in the United States, there is a fair chance that the berries you buy may be several years old. Try to get them from a place specializing in spices, where turnover is greater and the chances for fresh spice are better.

PIQUANT HARE LIVER

Pirított citromos nyúlmáj   *2 servings*

¼ cup hare fat or butter
Livers of 2 hares
Salt

Pinch of pepper
¼ cup strong stock or broth
2 teaspoons lemon juice

266

1. Render the hare fat, or melt the butter.

2. Put in the livers, and sprinkle them with salt and pepper. Cover the pot and cook livers on both sides for a few minutes.

3. Drain off the pan juices and mix them with the stock and lemon juice.

4. Put livers in a baking-serving platter and pour the liquid mixture over them. Bring to a boil, then serve immediately. Do not continue to boil because livers would toughen. Serve with White Bread Dumplings (page 300).

CHOPPED HARE STEAK

Vagdalthús nyúlból   *4 servings*

1½ pounds boned hare meat	Pinch of ground cloves
¼ pound lean pork	Dash of pepper
2 onions	1 teaspoon salt
½ pound double-smoked bacon	2 tablespoons lemon juice
3 rolls	2 eggs
½ teaspoon minced fresh gingerroot, or pinch of ground ginger	3 tablespoons lard
	½ cup strong broth

1. Grind the hare and pork together with one of the onions, half of the bacon and the rolls which have been soaked in water and squeezed.

2. Add gingerroot, cloves, pepper, salt, lemon juice and one of the eggs. Mix well and form into the shape of a loaf of bread.

3. Brush a baking pan or baking-serving platter with lard, and place the meat loaf on it. Brush the meat with more lard and then with the remaining egg, beaten.

4. Cut the second onion into thin crosswise slices and place the slices on the loaf. Chop the rest of the bacon and sprinkle it too on top of the loaf. Cover the pan.

5. Place the loaf in a 375°F. oven and bake for about 1 hour. As it bakes, baste it often with a few tablespoons of the broth. Replace cover after basting; this is one of the tricks in cooking this properly. Uncover the pan for the last 10 minutes to brown the top of the loaf.

6. Serve lingonberries with this luncheon dish, and a mushroom *risotto*.

SMOTHERED VENISON CUTLET AS IN MÁTRA

Mátrai szarvasszelet seprenyősen   *4 servings*

1½ pounds boneless leg of
   young venison
1 teaspoon salt
½ teaspoon freshly ground
   black pepper
2 tablespoons lard
1 large onion, peeled and diced

½ teaspoon caraway seeds
1 teaspoon paprika
2 medium-sized ripe tomatoes,
   sliced
2 pounds potatoes, peeled and
   cut into long segments
3 green peppers, sliced

1. Slice meat into 4 cutlets. Pound them to make flat cutlets. Sprinkle with salt and pepper.

2. Heat 1 tablespoon lard in a frying pan and brown meat on both sides over high heat. It shouldn't take more than a few minutes on each side.

3. In a separate pot melt the rest of the lard and brown diced onion in it. Then add caraway seeds, ½ cup cold water and the paprika. Cook covered for 2 minutes.

4. Pour onion mixture on top of fast-fried venison slices. Add another ½ cup water and cook covered over very low heat. Add a little water each time it appears to be evaporated.

5. When meat is almost done, add tomatoes, potatoes and green peppers and continue cooking, covered, over low heat until meat and potatoes are done.

6. Adjust salt and serve.

NOTE: *Hungarian venison or roebuck is much more tender than the American equivalent. However, by treating the game this way, you will not have to premarinate American venison either to make it tender.*

SLICED WILD BOAR IN THE BAKONY MANNER

Vaddisznószelet bakonyi módra   *4 servings*

1½ pounds fillet or 2 pounds
   chops of wild boar
Salt
¼ cup flour
¼ pound lard
2 small onions, minced

1 tablespoon paprika
½ cup meat stock
   (approximately)
1 pound wild mushrooms
3 tablespoons sour cream

1. If you use the fillet, cut it into 1-inch-thick slices. If you use chops, make about 4 double cutlets. Sprinkle the slices with salt and dredge them with flour. (There should be about 1 tablespoon flour left.)

2. Melt lard in a frying pan and fast-fry the venison slices on both sides. Place the fried slices on the bottom of a heavy casserole and set aside.

3. Fry onions in the same frying pan till golden in color. Then add 1 tablespoon cold water and the paprika. Cover the pan and cook till liquid is evaporated.

4. Add cooked onions to the meat and pour in 2 or 3 tablespoons of meat stock. Cover tightly and cook over low heat till boar is half done. Add more stock if needed.

5. Clean wild mushrooms but leave whole. Cook in the same lard in the same frying pan for 1 minute. Remove mushrooms with a slotted spoon and add to meat casserole. Cover casserole again and cook for 30 minutes longer.

6. Mix remaining 1 tablespoon flour with sour cream and mix into meat casserole. Simmer for a few minutes longer.

7. Serve accompanied with rice or Egg Dumplings (page 297).

NOTE: *This recipe can be used for venison, beef or lamb, but the cooking time will, of course, be different.*

If you cannot get wild mushrooms, soak 2 ounces dried mushrooms in cold water and add them to the meat at Step 4. Slice ¼ pound cultivated mushrooms and proceed as in Step 5.

✸ 21 ✸

TRADITIONAL STEWS (HAGYOMÁNYOS RAGÚK): GULYÁS, PÖRKÖLT, PAPRIKÁS & TOKÁNY

THE four pillars of Hungarian cooking are *gulyás, pörkölt, paprikás* and *tokány.*

GULYÁS A strange thing has happened to Hungarian *gulyás.* According to a 1969 Gallup Poll, *gulyás* is one of the five most popular meat dishes on the American cooking scene. Of course, what is usually served under this name shouldn't happen to a Rumanian. The origin of the soup, as you've read in the beginning of our story, can be traced back to the ninth century—shepherds cut their meat into cubes, cooked it with onion in a heavy iron kettle (*bogrács*) and slowly stewed the dish until all the liquid evaporated. They dried the remnants in the sun (probably on their sheepskin capes), and then put the dried food in a bag made of the sheep's stomach. Whenever they wanted food, they took out a piece of the dried meat, added some water and reheated it. With a lot of liquid, it became a *gulyás* soup (*gulyásleves*); if less liquid was added, it became *gulyás* meat (*gulyáshús*). Even today this distinction exists, probably to mystify foreigners and foreign cookbook writers.

The more parts of beef and beef innards are used, the better the *gulyás* will be. Of course, lard and bacon (either one or both) and chopped onion are absolute musts, just as you will find they are in the other three dishes.

Never use any flour. *Never* use any other spice besides caraway. *Never*

Frenchify it with wine. *Never* Germanize it with brown sauce. *Never* put in any other garniture besides diced potatoes or *galuska*. But many variations are possible—you may use fresh tomatoes or tomato purée, garlic, sliced green peppers, hot cherry peppers to make it very spicy, and so on.

An interesting technique was suggested by Mrs. Mariska Vizváry and originally published in the early 1930's. She added *grated* raw potatoes in the very beginning, presumably to give body to the soup, and she cooked bones and vegetables separately to make a strong broth with which to strengthen the *gulyás* soup at the very end.

PÖRKÖLT   The literal translation of this word is "singed," and the Hungarian word does not relate to accepted cooking terms. I suppose the closest equivalent would be "dry-stewed." The meat for this stew should *always* be diced, but in somewhat larger pieces than for *gulyás*. Paprika, lard or bacon are mandatory.

Of course onion is required, too. The Hungarian writer Julius Krúdy, who was especially fond of *pörkölt*, mused: "Onion, the apple of the earth, is able to emit such scents as women meeting their lovers do. Hot bacon dripping, the lover of the onion, keeps asking sizzlingly from the top of the stove: why was I born?—The onion, then, passionately explains everything. . . ."

Matters of opinion: whether the onions are chopped or sliced; whether to use fresh tomatoes, tomato purée, or none; sliced green peppers or none; whether to add salt for the last 10 minutes or in the usual way; to brown the meat after the onion is golden, then add paprika and water, or to add water and meat right after onion has been sautéed and sprinkle it with paprika toward the last stages.

PAPRIKÁS   The chief difference between *pörkölt* and *paprikás* is that *paprikás* is usually finished with sweet or sour cream, sometimes mixed with a little flour, but always stirred in just before serving. You may never use cream of any kind for *gulyás* or *pörkölt!* Also beef, mutton, game, goose, duck and pork are most popular for *pörkölt;* veal and chicken for *paprikás*.

TOKÁNY   The word *tokány* comes from the Rumanian *tocana,* meaning ragout. The Hungarians in Transylvania developed the ragout into an interesting formula with many variations.

The meat is cut into pieces 1½ inches by ¼ inch, long pieces in comparison to those for the other stews. The cooking method is based on the Mongolian waterless braising technique, in which the meat cooks in its own juice. The meats used are most often beef or lamb, but veal, chicken or even game can be used. Generally only black pepper is used, but in addition marjoram, or in Transylvania summer savory (*csömbér*), can be added for flavoring. In the older versions a variety of herbs was used. Onion is always used, but it is usually scantier than in the other stews. Garlic is sometimes added.

At first paprika was never used for this ragout; in the past 75 years this spice has been added to *tokány* also, but in much smaller amounts than for *pörkölt* or *paprikás*. If it is used, it should be a very small amount.

I. *Berbécstokány* (mutton) Cut leg of mutton into little *tokány* pieces and sear in a little lard. Then sprinkle with plenty of black pepper and cook, covered, over low heat till the meat is almost soft. If the mutton is old, a little water will have to be added. Measure onions equal to half the weight of the meat and slice thin. In the last half hour, mix onions with meat and cook together until the stew is done.

II. For a Transylvanian version, add some summer savory and just before serving mix in cottage-fried potatoes. Sour cream is optional.

III. Mushroom and beef *tokány* is made with summer savory and red wine.

IV. *Gambrinus tokány* is a basic *tokány* with beer added.

V. Debrecen beef *tokány* has onion and garlic fried with smoked bacon pieces. It is cooked with *lecsó* (see page 315) plus Debrecen sausage.

VI. Another category is the sour-cream *tokány*. Perhaps the most famous are the *herány* (see page 280) and the *hétvezér* (seven chieftains), which is made with beef, veal, pork, fried onions or smoked bacon, *lecsó* and sour cream.

VII. One of the most interesting versions of *tokány* is the ancient dish of sour *vetrece* (*savanyú vetrece*), which was already mentioned as a part of the dinners of King Matthias in the fifteenth century. In this type of ragout, beef is cooked with smoked bacon, garlic and black pepper; later bay leaves, mustard, lemon juice, vinegar, sugar and grated lemon rind are added, and finally sour cream. The only flavors lost over the centuries are mace, ginger and saffron. In the dining rooms of the Transylvanian gentry, paper-thin slices of peeled lemon were served on top of this more sweet than sour dish.

The variations of *tokány* are limitless. In Transylvania they serve a dill *tokány* with sour cream, accompanied by *puliszka* (see page 303); in the Kunság region there is an interesting mutton version cooked with beans, bacon and tomato; and one of the most delicious is the suckling-pig *tokány* with *tarhonya* (see page 296) from the Great Plains.

Tokány sauce should have the thickness of a ragout, somewhat thicker than the sauce of *pörkölt* or *gulyás,* but not as heavy as a cream sauce, and it should not be thickened with flour. Remember that there are definite rules, but there is no single "holy authority."

KETTLE GULYÁS

Bográcsgulyás 8 *servings*

2 medium-sized onions
2 tablespoons lard
2½ pounds beef chuck or
    round, cut to ¾-inch cubes
½ pound beef heart (optional),
    cut to ¾-inch cubes
1 garlic clove
Pinch of caraway seeds
Salt

2 tablespoons "Noble Rose"
    paprika
1 medium-sized ripe tomato
2 green frying or Italian
    peppers
1 pound potatoes
Little Dumplings (page 178)

1. Peel onions and chop into coarse pieces. Melt lard in a heavy 6- to 8-quart Dutch oven. Sauté onions in lard. Heat should be low in order not to brown the onions.

2. When onions become glossy, add beef and beef heart. Stir so that during this part of the process, which should last for about 10 minutes, the meat will be sautéed with the onions.

3. Meanwhile, chop and crush the garlic with the caraway seeds and a little salt; use the flat side of a heavy knife.

4. Take kettle from heat. Stir in paprika and the garlic mixture. Stir rapidly with a wooden spoon. Immediately after paprika is absorbed, add 2½ quarts *warm* water. (Cold water toughens meat if you add it while the meat is frying.)

5. Replace covered kettle over low heat and cook for about 1 hour.

6. While the braising is going on, peel the tomato, then cut into 1-inch pieces. Core green peppers and slice into rings. Peel potatoes and cut into ¾-inch dice.

7. After meat has been braised for about 1 hour (the time depends on the cut of the meat), add the cut-up tomato and green peppers and enough water to give a soup consistency. Add a little salt. Simmer slowly for another 30 minutes.

8. Add potatoes, and cook the *gulyás* till done. Adjust salt. Add hot cherry pepper pods if you want to make the stew spicy hot.

9. Cook the dumplings in the stew.

10. Serve the *gulyás* steaming hot in large extra-deep bowls. The meat should be tender, but not falling apart.

VARIATIONS: *I. Some housewives start with small pieces of smoked bacon instead of lard.*

It is possible to omit the tomato and green peppers and instead add a ready-made lecsó *during the last 5 minutes.*

There are many variations even on the basic ingredients. Some people use different types of meat, including pork, veal and sausages. Some add other vegetables like carrots, green beans, kohlrabi, etc.

As far as the spicing is concerned, some cooks add a small amount of black pepper in addition to paprika; others add marjoram or bay leaf; some use a little more onion and no garlic at all. Particularly in the southern section of Hungary, fresh or dried cherry peppers are added, which puts the crown on this glorious soup for the Hungarians. For a non-Hungarian, in this case, the crown is white-hot.

II. Palóc *Soup: The city cousin, a creation of Gundel's, is the* palóc *soup. This is a mutton* gulyás *with a lot of green beans and sour cream (see page 275).*

III. Pörkölt: *This stew was born out of the same love affair. If you eliminate most of the liquid and cook meat down to its fat you get* pörkölt. *You should end up with about 1 cup of rich sauce.*

If you are able to get wild boar meat, make a pörkölt *with it. Only use a young animal, so you don't have to marinate the meat.*

IV. Beer Gulyás: *Make the same way as Kettle* Gulyás, *but use beer instead of water in Step 4.*

V. Strained Gulyás *Broth* (Derített gulyásleves):   *For a formal dinner prepare a rich* gulyás *without potatoes or dumplings. When finished, strain. Serve the broth in soup cups. Use the meat to stuff green peppers (see page 307).*

VI. Kolozsvári gulyás: *This is the brother-in-law of the* székelygulyás; *it is made with beef and fresh cabbage. Follow the recipe to Step 8; when you add the potatoes, also add 1 medium-sized fresh cabbage cut to 1-inch chunks. Omit the little dumplings. Adjust salt before serving.*

NOTE: *The meat can be an inexpensive cut. It is a waste of money to use steak or tenderloin. The more different cuts you use, the better tasting the stew will be.*

The paprika must *be Hungarian "Noble Rose." Spanish paprika and other types are only coloring agents.*

MUTTON GULYÁS

Ürügulyás   6 *servings*

1 large onion, minced
1 tablespoon lard
1 tablespoon hot paprika (If
   you haven't got it, mix sweet
   paprika with cayenne, or
   throw in a dried cherry
   pepper.)
2 pounds mutton bones
3 pounds stewing mutton

1 tablespoon salt
¼ teaspoon caraway seeds
2 garlic cloves, crushed
5 medium-sized potatoes, peeled
   and diced
2 green peppers, diced
2 medium-sized very ripe
   tomatoes, diced
Little Dumplings (page 178)

1. Brown onion in lard in a heavy kettle. Remove from heat and stir in paprika. Immediately add ½ cup water.

2. Put back on the heat and add bones and stewing meat. Sprinkle with the salt, caraway seeds and garlic. Cook covered over very low heat until the stew is almost done, about 2 hours.

3. Add diced potatoes, green peppers and tomatoes, and another ½ cup water. Cook till done.

4. Make little dumplings and put them into the soup.

VARIATIONS: *I. Mutton* Paprikás *with Cabbage* Kúnsági bürgepaprikás káposztával: *This ancient method uses diced bacon instead of lard, mutton or sheep ribs, and instead of green peppers a small head of cabbage cut into 2-inch dice, and 2 or 3 pods of hot pepper. Old shepherds' descriptions always mention that this must be very fat "to be proper."*

II. Szüreti ürügulyás: *This is the vineyard cousin of mutton gulyás; it is served during the wine harvest. Dry white wine is used instead of water.*

NOTE: *The problem is to have just enough liquid but not too much. You may have to add more than the additional ½ cup during the cooking, but always add it little by little.*

In Hungary they used to use a castrated ram for this ancient stew. To remove the odor, the meat was usually boiled for a couple of minutes and drained-dried before being added to the stew pot.

CHICKEN PÖRKÖLT

Pörkölt csirke   *5 or 6 servings*

1 stewing chicken, 3 to 4 pounds
3 medium-sized onions, diced
1 tablespoon lard
1 tablespoon sweet paprika
1 tablespoon tomato purée
1 garlic clove, crushed in salt

1 teaspoon salt
2 medium-sized ripe tomatoes,
  peeled, seeded and cut into
  pieces
2 green peppers, diced

1. Cut chicken into serving pieces. Fry onions in lard until they are transparent.

2. Add chicken pieces, paprika, tomato purée, garlic and salt. Cover and cook for 15 minutes.

3. Add tomatoes and diced peppers. Cook until chicken is done. Make sure it is not cooked in a lot of liquid, but steamed in its own juice and fat. When the chicken is done, only the "angry" red, rich sauce remains under the chicken.

4. If the chicken is young, it will cook in a much shorter time; in that case you must precook the onions. Cook the browned onions with paprika in a little water, covered, for 20 minutes before you put in the chicken.

NOTE: *The large amount of onion is not a mistake. You need more than for other dishes because this preparation is not finished with sour cream; therefore the onion purée must provide the necessary juice.*

Although everyone thinks that a stewed chicken can be kept for a long time before serving (as long as it is kept hot), actually the taste is so delicate that for each minute you delay after it is ready you have lost more and more of the taste and aroma.

VEAL PÖRKÖLT

Borjúpörkölt   *4 to 6 servings*

2 pounds young veal, cut from
  the leg or leaner part of the
  breast and shoulder
2 tablespoons lard (amount
  depends on fattiness of meat)
1 large onion, minced
1 heaping tablespoon paprika

1 garlic clove, chopped and
  mashed (optional)
1 scant teaspoon salt
1 medium-sized very ripe
  tomato, or 2 drained canned
  Italian tomatoes
1 green pepper, cored and diced

276

1. Cut the veal into 1-inch dice.

2. Melt the lard in a heavy stewing casserole or Dutch oven and fry onion till it is light brown.

3. Remove from heat and mix in paprika, garlic (if used), salt and veal. Cover, and start cooking over very low heat.

4. The simple but tricky secret of this dish is to let the meat cook in the steam from its own juices and the juices of the onion. Just before the stew starts burning, add a few tablespoons of water; repeat this during the first 10 minutes of cooking whenever liquid evaporates.

5. Meantime, blanch tomato, peel, and dice.

6. When meat is beginning to get soft, in 10 to 15 minutes, add tomato and green pepper. Cook for another 10 to 20 minutes, depending on the age of the veal. Continue to add water bit by bit whenever the moisture evaporates.

7. When meat is done, let the liquid reduce as much as possible without burning it. At that point you should have a rich dark red and gold sauce-gravy, neither too thin nor too heavy, somewhat like a good American beef stew, but the texture must be achieved without any thickening.

8. Serve with Little Dumplings (page 178), Baked Egg Barley (page 297), or rice.

VARIATIONS: *I. Try this dish once without adding any tomato.*

II. To make veal paprikás, *reduce paprika to ½ tablespoon and use a small onion and no garlic. When meat is almost done, let the liquid evaporate so the meat is seared in remaining fat. Mix 1 cup sour cream with 1 tablespoon flour and stir into stew. Cook covered over very, very low heat until the meat is cooked. This dish should have a much milder, gentler taste than* pörkölt, *almost like a feminine version of it.*

III. Use any red meat, including game, for pörkölt *or* paprikás *made according to this recipe.*

NOTE: *The character of this dish derives from the careful addition of liquid —no more than ½ cup at a time for this amount of meat. Also the meat must be cooked just as the last of the liquid is evaporated so that the meat is "singed" in the last few minutes.*

CARP PÖRKÖLT

Pontypörkölt   *6 servings*

4 pounds carp	1 teaspoon paprika
1 teaspoon salt	½ pound green peppers
2 medium-sized onions, minced	1 medium-sized tomato
1 tablespoon lard	

1. Clean the carp, cut into about 12 pieces, and salt.
2. Fry onions in lard. Sprinkle with paprika and add a little water.
3. Cut each green pepper into 4 pieces, and peel and slice the tomato. Add to the stew and bring to a boil. Cook for 20 minutes.
4. Place pieces of carp in the pot and cook for 5 to 8 minutes, or until done. It takes very little time for fish to cook.

NOTE: *In the Great Plains, in Transdanubia and in Budapest, carp is prepared as described in this recipe and that for Paprika Carp (page 279), but around and in the city of Szeged cooks prepare a fishermen's broth with very little liquid, without frying the onions in lard as the first step.*

PAPRIKA CHICKEN

Paprikás csirke   4 servings

2 medium-sized onions, peeled and minced
2 tablespoons lard
1 plump chicken, about 3 pounds, disjointed, washed, and dried
1 large ripe tomato, peeled and cut into pieces
1 heaping tablespoon "Noble Rose" paprika
1 teaspoon salt
1 green pepper sliced
2 tablespoons sour cream
1 tablespoon flour
2 tablespoons heavy cream
Egg Dumplings (page 297)

1. Use a 4- or 5-quart heavy casserole with a tight-fitting lid. Cook the onions in the lard, covered, over low heat for about 5 minutes. They should become almost pasty, but definitely not browned.
2. Add chicken and tomato and cook, covered, for 10 minutes.
3. Stir in paprika. Add ½ cup water and the salt. Cook, covered, over very low heat for 30 minutes. In the beginning, the small amount of water will create a steam-cooking action. Toward the end of the 30-minute period, take off lid and let the liquid evaporate. Finally let the chicken cook in its own juices and fat, taking care that it does not burn. (If the chicken is tough, you may have to add a few more tablespoons of water.)
4. Remove chicken pieces. Mix the sour cream, flour and 1 teaspoon cold water, and stir in with the sauce till it is very smooth and of an even color. Add green pepper, replace chicken parts, adjust salt. Put lid back on casserole and over very low heat cook until done.
5. Just before serving whip in the heavy cream. Serve with egg dumplings.

NOTE: *The combination of sour cream and heavy cream is the almost forgotten, but ideal way to prepare this dish. Today, more often than not, the heavy cream is omitted. In Hungary, the lily is gilded by spreading several tablespoons of additional sour cream on top of the chicken in the serving platter.*

PAPRIKA CARP

Paprikás ponty   *4 servings*

1 carp, 6 to 7 pounds	¾ cup fish stock
1 teaspoon salt	1 cup *lecsó* (page 315)
½ cup whole-wheat flour	1 tablespoon flour
¼ cup lard	3 tablespoons sour cream
1 medium-sized onion, minced	Green pepper rings
1 tablespoon paprika	

1. Cut 4 slices from the carp, each weighing ½ pound. Use the rest of the fish to make the fish stock.

2. Sprinkle salt on fish slices, then dip the fish into whole-wheat flour. Shake off excess.

3. Heat lard to frying temperature in a large frying pan. Brown fish for 2 to 3 minutes on each side. Place browned slices in an ovenproof casserole.

4. In the same frying pan used for the fish fry onion until it turns light brown in color.

5. Remove from heat, mix in paprika, and immediately add ½ cup cold fish stock. Add *lecsó,* bring to a boil, then mix in flour and sour cream. Simmer for a few minutes.

6. Strain the sauce on top of the fish slices in the casserole. The sauce should have the texture of a thin cream sauce.

7. Cover casserole and bake the fish in a 400°F. oven for about 20 minutes. When the stew is finished, the sauce must be quite rich and thick, somewhat like the sauce for paprika chicken.

8. Put very thin-sliced green-pepper rings on the fish before serving. Accompany with rice mixed with chopped flat parsley, or with Little Dumplings (page 178).

NOTE: *Although there is sour cream in this recipe, some Hungarians believe that only heavy sweet cream, never sour cream, should be used for fish preparations.*

A nice addition to this stew is some milt and roe, if you can get them. Allow only 5 to 8 minutes to cook either.

HERÁNYTOKÁNY AS IN MAROSSZÉK

Marosszéki heránytokány   *4 to 6 servings*

1 pound stewing beef	marjoram, or ¼ teaspoon
1 pound lean pork	dried
¼ pound double-smoked bacon,	Salt
diced	1 cup dry white wine
1 medium-sized onion, minced	1 tablespoon lard
1 tablespoon paprika	¼ pound mushrooms cut in
Pinch of black pepper	chunks
Pinch of caraway seeds	1 cup sour cream
½ teaspoon chopped fresh	1 tablespoon flour

1. Cut beef and pork into strips 3 inches long and ½ inch thick.

2. Render the bacon. Add onion and wilt it over low heat for about 5 minutes.

3. Add paprika and ½ cup water and simmer for a few minutes.

4. Add beef, spices, marjoram, ½ teaspoon salt and half of the wine. Cover and cook for 30 minutes.

5. Add pork and remaining wine. Cover and cook over the lowest possible heat until meat is tender. If necessary, you may add a little more wine. Adjust salt.

6. About 10 minutes before meat is tender, melt lard in separate frying pan and fry mushrooms for a few minutes. Then add to cooking stew.

7. Just before serving, mix sour cream with flour and stir into stew. Bring to simmer, but do not cook it further.

NOTE: *Transylvania is inhabited by Rumanians, Germans and Hungarians. Although the Hungarians from Marosszék argue that this is a purely Hungarian stew, both the word* tokány, *which is of Rumanian origin, and the first word, which probably comes from the German herein, indicate that this stew is a joint venture of the three ethnic groups. Some sections omit paprika and increase the black pepper; many others add sliced pork kidney to the mushrooms.*

✳ 22 ✳

POTTED CABBAGE:
PICKLED OR OTHERWISE
(KÁPOSZTÁK MINT FŐÉTELEK)

EVERY small nation must be chauvinistic in order to survive. There was a Hungarian professor, one Horváth by name, who carried this chauvinism to the extreme of trying to show that everything originated in Hungary, including Paradise. He even tried to provide a native etymology for cabbage, and that is not too strange when one considers that Hungary has probably invented more ways to prepare cabbage than any other nation. However, the Hungarian word for cabbage comes from the Latin *caput,* meaning "head."

The most popular cabbage dish in Hungary is sauerkraut. Elek Magyar, the knowledgeable and witty journalist-cookbook author, has described, from his childhood memories, a day when boats and ships filled with tons of cabbages arrived at the Budapest wharf on the Danube. The local sailors ran out of their taverns to unload the vessels, and shortly, as a result of their work, cabbage mountains broke the skyline of the city. Waiting around were the big mustachioed cabbage-cutter specialists, and after a sale was completed a cutter went home with the buyer. The cutter got to work with his tool in the family's kitchen; adjusting his blade so that the cabbage would be cut just right, he cleaned and sliced the huge pyramid rapidly.

In the center of the kitchen stood the enormous hard-scrubbed white-oak barrel with a screw top, and surrounding it in separate piles were sliced quinces, horseradish roots, ground salt, whole black peppercorns, caraway seeds, tarragon leaves and sprays of dill.

Since the only way to make good sauerkraut is to stomp it like grapes, someone of considerable weight would get in the middle of the barrel and walk around slowly with deliberate steps, not omitting a single inch. When the father of the house got tired, usually the son took over. When the first stomper got into the barrel, he found already a handful of horseradish, quince slices and a foot-high layer of shredded cabbage. While stomping he threw in a handful of salt, caraway seeds and peppercorns. Slowly, from the action of the salt, the cabbage began to emit some juice. The flavoring ingredients were added until all the cabbage was used. In between they threw in a few whole cabbage heads also, so when they made a stuffed cabbage it would not be without "cover." The core was cut out, leaving a little cabbage around it; this core was called *cika* and was eventually eaten with roast or fried pork, as a relish.

The barrel was now full, with the salty juice reaching the top, and the tired trampler got out and covered the barrel with a piece of white linen. Then the cover, which was made of two pieces, was put on and the screws tightened. The barrel was rolled down to the basement and put on a stand so the bottom would not touch the earth. The tired people returned to the kitchen to eat their well-deserved stuffed cabbage, made from last year's batch, with ribs of pork, followed by *túróscsusza.*

The good day's hard work was amply rewarded a few months later on a snowy winter Sunday when the family sat around the table to enjoy the aroma, color and taste of a Transylvanian cabbage made with perfectly pickled sauerkraut.

To face the multitude of potted cabbage preparations would make skilled statisticians weep. It is the duty of this book to come to the aid of seekers after cabbage information. After looking over, by actual count, more than 800 such recipes, I reduced the entire list to four basic categories with a few separate specialties. The only problem I still face is that sometimes the same name is used for different preparations, depending on the age of the recipes and the area where they come from.

STUFFED CABBAGE—cabbage leaves, generally pickled, stuffed and cooked or baked together with sauerkraut.

SZÉKELYGULYÁS, sometimes called *székelykáposzta* or Székely cabbage— basically a pork *pörkölt* baked with sauerkraut and sour cream.

LUCSKOSKÁPOSZTA, sloppy cabbage.

LAYERED CABBAGE, *rakott káposzta,* most commonly called *Kolozsvári* cabbage—layers of sauerkraut, rice, sausage and meats. A subdivision in this category would be stuffed cabbages made with fish or fish roll and other ingredients, with sauerkraut as a base, following the same method of preparation.

One word of advice: in the Hungarian names for cabbage dishes there is rarely any indication whether the recipe uses fresh cabbage or sauerkraut. The name for sauerkraut is either "sour cabbage" or "barrel cabbage." However, the word "sour" or "barrel" is generally left out. A cabbage *aficionado* would know which is used by the rule generally followed in each dish. It is safe to say that most Hungarian cabbage casserole recipes use sauerkraut or whole cabbage leaves from cabbage heads pickled like sauerkraut.

STUFFED CABBAGE, BASIC RECIPE

Töltött káposzta   6 *to 12 servings*

¼ cup uncooked rice
1 pound lean pork, ground
½ pound lean beef, ground
2 garlic cloves, mashed
2 medium-sized onions,
   chopped fine
1 egg
1 tablespoon salt
½ teaspoon black pepper
2 tablespoons paprika

1 head of fresh cabbage (see
   Note)
2 pounds sauerkraut (see Note)
½ cup tomato juice
½ pound smoked pork butt,
   sliced
2 tablespoons lard
2 tablespoons flour
½ cup sour cream

1. Cook rice in ½ cup water for 10 minutes. Drain.

2. Thoroughly mix the ground pork and beef with garlic, half of the onion, the egg, salt, pepper, 1 tablespoon of the paprika and the drained rice. Put stuffing mixture aside.

3. Core the cabbage and cook the cabbage head in enough water to cover it for 10 to 15 minutes.

4. Gently take apart the cabbage, leaf by leaf. Cut out heavy veins if any.

5. Use a large oval casserole, about 6 inches high, 16 inches long and 8 to 10 inches wide, or a round one of similar size. Put sauerkraut in the casserole with tomato juice and sliced pork butt in enough water to cover. Bring to a boil, then lower heat and cook for 5 minutes.

6. Fill cabbage leaves with the stuffing mixture; with well-floured hands form rolls. Do not make the rolls too tight, for the stuffing will expand in cooking. Pinch the ends of the rolls together to seal them. (Leftover stuffing can be made into meatballs.) Cut remaining cabbage leaves into fine shreds and add to the casserole.

7. Make room in the sauerkraut with a wooden spoon, and place the cabbage rolls in it. Cook covered over very low heat for 1 hour.

8. Meantime, make a *roux* out of hot lard, flour and remaining chopped onion. Cook it for about 10 minutes, until golden yellow. Turn off heat, stir in 1 tablespoon paprika, and whip it up with 1 cup cold water.

9. Very gently remove the stuffed cabbage rolls from the casserole. Take out a ladleful of sauerkraut broth and whip it into the *roux*. Return this liquid thickening to main casserole, stirring it well. Bring to a boil.

10. Put back the stuffed cabbage leaves, cover the casserole, and finish in a 350°F. oven for 15 minutes.

11. Before serving, pour sour cream over the casserole, making sure not to break cabbage leaves.

NOTE: *This basic recipe uses a fresh cabbage head, since the United States housewife will not be able to find whole sour cabbage heads, except possibly in New York's Lower East Side.*

If you must use canned sauerkraut, always remember to eliminate its cooking time from these recipes, since canned sauerkraut is already cooked.

VARIATIONS:

I. Fry 1 chopped onion in ¼ pound diced bacon for 5 minutes. Sprinkle with a pinch of marjoram, then proceed to mix with other stuffing ingredients.

II. Start with roux; add sauerkraut, and slowly cook it for 15 minutes. Proceed preparing the stuffed leaves and cook as directed above.

III. Fry 1 chopped onion in 1 tablespoon lard for 5 minutes. Add sauerkraut, 1 tablespoon paprika and the stuffed leaves. When cooked, mix sauerkraut with sour-cream and flour mixture.

IV. In Transylvania they often add a handful of fresh dill and a glass of white wine in addition to the usual ingredients.

V. Hajdúkáposzta

1. Use 1 pound ground pork; 1 chopped small onion, fried; 1 tablespoon paprika; 1 tablespoon minced fresh marjoram; 1 egg and some salt for stuffing. Fill sour cabbage leaves.

2. Fry another chopped small onion in 3 tablespoons lard; add 1 pound sauerkraut and the stuffed leaves. Add enough water to cover.

3. Top with 1 pound meaty smoked slab bacon and 1 pound smoked Debrecen sausage and possibly a smoked rack of pork. Sprinkle with sour cream when serving. The important ingredients here are the Debrecen sausage and the smoked meats.

22. Potted Cabbage: Pickled or Otherwise

VI. Stuffed Cabbage as in Szabolcs (Szabolcsi töltött káposzta)

1. Fry 1 large onion in lard; add paprika, sauerkraut and ½ pound diced smoked bacon. Add enough water to cover.

2. Make round, peach-sized stuffed cabbage leaves, with stuffing of 1 pound ground pork, 1 tablespoon chopped dill, rice, garlic, raw egg, salt and paprika as in basic recipe.

3. Cover and cook, together with rest of ingredients, on top of stove. When almost ready (about 1½ hours) remove stuffed cabbage leaves and keep them hot.

4. Grate 3 medium-sized potatoes. Boil in 1 quart water for 10 minutes, and drain. Add to sauerkraut, and mix in.

5. About 15 minutes later pour sauerkraut over the stuffed cabbage leaves and serve. Decorate with thin-sliced ham and green-pepper rings.

VII. Stuffed Whole Cabbage (Egész káposztafej töltve)

1. Cook a firm 2-pound cabbage in salted water for 5 minutes. Remove. Gently ease off outer 8 or 10 leaves. With a very sharp knife cut-scrape out the inner part of the head, making a cabbage basket out of it. Make sure to leave bottom of core intact.

2. Chop 1 small onion and sauté it in 1 tablespoon lard. Add 1 pound ground pork, 1 tablespoon bread crumbs and 1 raw egg. Sauté for 15 minutes. Add 1 tablespoon sour cream and ½ cup cooked rice. Mix it well and stuff the hollow cabbage with it. Reshape cabbage to original form and tie it.

3. Line bottom of a deep casserole with ½ pound very thin bacon slices. Put stuffed cabbage on it. Cross the cabbage head with 2 slices of bacon.

4. Meantime sauté 1 small onion in 1 tablespoon lard. Add 2 pounds squeezed-out sauerkraut to onion and cook for 1 hour. Place sauerkraut around stuffed cabbage head in pot. Sprinkle with 1 tablespoon paprika and pour 2 glasses of wine or meat stock over it.

5. Cover the casserole and put it in a 350°F. oven for 1 hour. Remove lid; put an additional ½ cup sour cream on top of cabbage and cook it, uncovered, for 10 minutes.

VII. Hargitai Stuffed Cabbage (Hargitai töltött káposzta)

1. Sauté 6 boneless pork chops in 1 tablespoon lard till brown on each side. Remove.

2. Chop 1 small onion and sauté in the same pan for a few minutes, then add ¾ pound of ground not-too-lean pork and cook it, stirring, for another 10 minutes.

3. Cut ½ pound sausage into very thin slices and sauté them for a couple of minutes only.

4. Blanch a cabbage and remove 12 large cabbage leaves. Spread a pork

285

*chop with ground pork, topped with a few sausage slices, and wrap in 1
or 2 cabbage leaves. Tie with string.*

*5. Fry another small onion in ¼ pound diced smoked bacon. Add 2
pounds sauerkraut. Top with wrapped pork chops. Pour 2 to 3 cups meat
stock over chops. Cover and bake in a 350°F. oven for 1¼ hours.*

*6. Remove wrapped chops. Mix 1 tablespoon flour with 1 cup sour cream;
mix into the sauerkraut; adjust saltiness. Simmer for 10 minutes. When serving, sprinkle with dill.*

*IX. **Stuffed Grape Leaves** (Tötike): Use grape leaves tied with a bunch
of grape tendrils instead of cabbage, and fill with the basic stuffing. Byzantine
influence in Transylvania produced this dish, which has precious little to do
with dolma.*

*X. **Stuffed Cabbage with Fresh Sausages** (Disznótoros káposzta):
During pig-killing time farmers cook sauerkraut with fried pork sausage. You
can buy this sausage in Hungarian-Czechoslovakian stores. The sausage is put
into the sauerkraut instead of the stuffed cabbage rolls of the basic recipe.*

INCES' STUFFED CABBAGE

Incéék töltött káposztája   6 to 8 servings

(Stolen from the secret files of Peggy and the late Alexander Ince)

1 head of fresh cabbage	1 tablespoon paprika
¼ cup uncooked rice	2 pounds sauerkraut
½ cup beef broth	1 tomato, sliced
2 medium-sized onions, chopped	2 smoked pig knuckles
3 tablespoons bacon drippings	1 pound fresh sausage
½ pound lean pork, ground	½ pound oxtails
½ pound beefsteak, ground	1 pound *dagadó* (see Note, page
Dash of freshly ground pepper	229), or smoked spareribs
½ teaspoon salt	1 cup sour cream
1 raw egg	¼ cup heavy sweet cream
3 tablespoons flour	Paprika Essence (page 343)

1. Separate the cabbage leaves and place in hot water to make them limp
enough not to crack when rolled.

2. Cook rice in beef broth for 10 minutes.

3. Fry 1 onion in 1 tablespoon bacon drippings for 5 minutes. Mix ground
meats with fried onion, pepper and salt, ½ cup water, 1 egg and the semicooked rice.

4. Place mixture in separated cabbage leaves, and roll or squeeze together

in clean napkins so the rolls won't come apart when cooking.

5. Fry the other chopped onion in remaining drippings for 5 minutes. Add flour, stir, and cook for 5 or 6 minutes. Add paprika and 1 cup cold water, whip, and pour over sauerkraut.

6. Line the bottom of a large casserole with the stuffed cabbage leaves; put sauerkraut layer over. Add tomato and 2 cups water, or enough to cover the sauerkraut layer. Top with meats, neatly arranged. Cook it over very, very low heat for 2 to 2½ hours. Lift cover as few times as you can.

7. Take a huge, low-sided casserole or platter. Put sauerkraut on bottom. Place stuffed cabbage leaves around and the meats cut into individual portions in the center. Sprinkle with sour cream mixed with sweet cream and the paprika essence.

NOTE: *I've eaten this superb dish cooked by Sándor Incze, whose spirit, I hope, lingers over this book!*

SZÉKELY CABBAGE

Székelygulyás or *Székelykáposzta*   6 servings

1 large onion, peeled and chopped	2 tablespoons tomato purée
⅛ pound lard	2 pounds sauerkraut
1½ pounds lean pork, diced	½ teaspoon caraway seeds
1 tablespoon paprika	Salt
	½ cup sour cream

1. Wilt onion in lard in a heavy Dutch oven. Add pork, mix well, and cook covered for 5 minutes.

2. Add paprika, then the tomato purée; mix well. Add just enough water to cover everything. Cook over very low heat till meat is almost done.

3. Squeeze sauerkraut well. Add it to the meat with the caraway seeds, and cook for another 10 to 15 minutes. Salt should be added only at this point if you think, after tasting, that it is needed.

4. Spoon sour cream on top, and serve.

VARIATIONS:

I. Mix 1 cup sour cream with 1 tablespoon flour. Mix it into the casserole 10 minutes before it is finished.

II. Dribble Paprika Essence (page 343) on top, or save out 2 tablespoons of the pork gravy and spread that over the top.

III. Carmelize 1 tablespoon sugar in a pot, then add sauerkraut; mix well. Cook sauerkraut for 1 hour before adding it to the pork stew.

IV. If you want to cook this dish in the Hungarian peasant style, get fatty pieces of pork belly with the pork skin on; boned knuckle cut into pieces; ribs cut to small pieces. Use these to make the pörkölt.

V. By cooking the meat completely at the end of Step 1, you would have pork pörkölt (disznópörkölt).

VI. Poor people make this without meat. Sprinkle 3 tablespoons flour on the sauerkraut 10 minutes before it is cooked, and mix well. It tastes surprisingly good.

NOTE: *Hungary, in my student days, was still called a kingdom, with an admiral as its governor, even though it had ceased to be a kingdom generations before that and had no ocean.* Székelygulyás *was named with the same approach to logic. It is a cabbage dish that is not Transylvanian and was not created by the inhabitants there, the Székelys, and it is not even a gulyás. According to a letter in the magazine of the Hungarian restaurateurs guild, it happened this way: In 1846 the librarian of Pest County came too late to a little restaurant, Zenélö Óra (the musical clock), to choose from the menu. The librarian, whose name was Székely (a rather common Hungarian name), asked the owner to serve the leftover sauerkraut and pork* pörkölt *together on the very same plate.*

The improvisation was so good that the great poet Petöfi, who was nearby within hearing distance, the following day asked the restaurateur to give him Székely's gulyás, meaning the same mixture Mr. Székely got the previous day. This time the owner topped it with sour cream and the dish, together with its name, became part of the everyday repertoire. By now even the Transylvanians think this dish is their invention.

SLOPPY CABBAGE

Lucskoskáposzta   6 servings

1 medium-sized, very tight cabbage
Salt
1 pound *dagadó* (see Note, page 229) or spareribs, sliced
1 pound corned beef
3 thick slices of double-smoked bacon with the skin on
1 small onion, chopped fine
1 teaspoon whole black peppercorns

15 leaves of fresh or marinated tarragon
15 leaves of summer savory, or 1 teaspoon dried
3 to 5 sprigs of fresh dill, or 1 teaspoon dried dillweed
¼ cup sour cream
1 tablespoon flour
1 egg yolk
1 teaspoon white-wine vinegar

1. Clean the cabbage, then cut into strips ¼ inch wide. Boil in salted water, then drain and put aside.

2. Boil the pork ribs and corned beef in salted water until they are almost done, about 1 hour. Save meat cooking liquid.

3. Put the bacon slices flat on the bottom of a large baking-cooking casserole. Put over medium heat. When bacon renders some fat, add onion. Turn heat to low, to wilt onion.

4. Start the layers in the casserole with a little of the cabbage. Sprinkle it with a few peppercorns. Put the corned beef on top, then again more cabbage. Put in the herbs tied together in a bouquet (or if dried, placed in a cheesecloth bag). Put rest of meat, cabbage and pepper on top, then pour on the liquid in which the meat cooked; it should almost cover the contents. Cook over low heat till done.

5. Mix sour cream with flour, egg yolk and vinegar. Take out a ladleful of the cooking broth, mix it well with sour-cream mixture, then put it into casserole and slowly simmer for another 5 minutes.

NOTE: *This is a Transylvanian dish. The juices should remain quite thin, as the title indicates; it is just a little short of being a so-called "soup-stew."*

On special occasions this is topped with separately fried slices of pork.

You can also make this out of Savoy cabbage, just as you can all the other cabbage casserole recipes.

LAYERED CABBAGE, BASIC RECIPE, OR KOLOZSVÁRI LAYERED CABBAGE

Rakottkáposzta vagy Kolozsvári rakott káposzta   6 *servings*

1½ pounds sauerkraut
½ cup uncooked rice
1 cup meat broth
1 large onion, chopped fine
2 tablespoons lard
1 pound lean pork, ground
1 tablespoon paprika

2 garlic cloves, crushed
¼ pound smoked bacon, cut into small dice
½ pound smoked sausage, sliced
1 cup sour cream
¼ cup milk

1. Preheat oven to 375°F. Squeeze sauerkraut well, and wash it in cold water if it is too sour. Add 1 cup water and cook sauerkraut for 15 minutes.

2. Meantime, cook the rice in the meat broth for 10 minutes.

3. In a separate frying pan fry onion in hot lard for about 5 minutes.

4. Add ground pork, stir it well, and cook for another 15 minutes, breaking up the pork well. Remove from heat and mix in paprika and garlic.

5. Cook bacon dice for a few minutes. Add sliced sausage just to shake it together. Remove both with a slotted spoon.

6. In the bottom of a baking-serving casserole put fat from bacon and spread it all over the inside. Put one third of the sauerkraut in the bottom. On top of sauerkraut place half of the ground pork, then half of the rice and all the sausage and bacon. Sprinkle with half of the sour cream mixed with milk. Cover with the second third of the sauerkraut, remaining meat and rice, and finally the third part of the sauerkraut. Pour rest of sour cream and milk over, and spread it on top.

7. Bake the casserole, without a cover, in the preheated oven for 1 hour.

VARIATIONS:

I. 1. Use sweet cabbage only, and blanch the head to separate leaves. Mix well ½ pound raw veal; 1 pound goose liver, diced (substitute chicken liver if you must); ½ roll soaked in cream, then squeezed and chopped; 1 tablespoon chopped flat parsley; 3 egg yolks; 5 grinds of black pepper; 2 tablespoons sour cream.

2. Butter well an ovenproof pottery mold. Line it carefully with cabbage leaves, spread with some of the filling, and alternate until you come to the top. Finish with cabbage leaves.

3. Stand the dish in a water bath. Bake in a 375°F. oven for 45 minutes. Turn it out onto a serving platter.

II. Top the casserole with thin-sliced pork chops, fried. Some cooks thicken this with 3 tablespoons flour and 2 tablespoons lard cooked to a roux and diluted with ½ cup cold water.

III. Line a larded baking mold with sliced boiled ham (freshly made, of course). Fill with sliced hard-cooked eggs, rice and ground pork stuffing, alternating with sauerkraut and sour cream. Bake in a water bath, then turn out on a serving platter.

IV. The oldest recipes use black pepper and white wine with pork and pork sausage. No sour cream or paprika is mentioned.

V. Teleki Layered Cabbage (Rakottkáposzta Teleki módra): *Cook sauerkraut with smoked pork chops, smoked goose breast, meaty slab bacon, whole onion, cloves, and sour cream with flour stirred in. Just before serving, fry fresh pork chops separately and put on the serving platter with the finished dish. (Probably first served in Gundel by Chef Rákóczy, and named after the gourmet aristocrat.)*

LAYERED CABBAGE AS IN MÓR

Móri rakott káposzta   *6 to 8 servings*

2 pounds sauerkraut
1 small onion, cut into very fine slices
2 tablespoons flour
2 tablespoons bacon drippings
½ cup uncooked rice
1 scant cup meat broth
2 pounds pork, ground
3 egg yolks

2 tablespoons lard
½ pound pork belly with ribs (flank), cut into pieces
1 pound smoked bacon, cut into thin slices
1 cup Riesling wine
1 teaspoon whole peppercorns
Salt
1 cup sour cream (optional)

1. Rinse the sauerkraut and cook with 1 cup water for 15 minutes. Drain, saving the liquid.

2. Place on a kitchen table the drained sauerkraut, the onion, flour and 1 tablespoon bacon drippings. Work together well by hand.

3. Sauté rice in 1 tablespoon bacon drippings for a few minutes, then add the meat broth and cook for 10 minutes.

4. Mix semicooked rice with ground pork and egg yolks to make a stuffing.

5. In a separate pan melt the lard and brown pork belly pieces for 5 to 10 minutes. Add ½ cup water and cook, covered, for 30 minutes.

6. Preheat oven to 375°F. Use a large low-walled casserole like a *lasagna* pot or a *moussaka* pan, so you don't make an unsightly mess when serving. Line the bottom of the casserole with bacon slices, then put in a quarter of the sauerkraut. On top of this place the stuffing, then cover the stuffing with another quarter of the sauerkraut. Put in the pork belly pieces and sauerkraut liquid and cover with remaining sauerkraut. Pour on the Riesling and 1 cup water. Add the peppercorns and salt to taste.

7. Bake in the oven for 1 to 1½ hours. If the liquid evaporates add more wine-water mixture. During the last 10 minutes, spread top with sour cream.

VARIATIONS:

I. Make a pork pörkölt *(page 271) out of 2 pounds pork meat, and use it instead of the pork belly and ground raw pork.*

II. Fry chopped onion, garlic and sugar, and add sauerkraut. Then add 1 large ripe tomato, 1 tablespoon paprika and 2 pounds cooked smoked pork, sliced. Cook for 1 hour. Add 4 potatoes, peeled and sliced, and 2 sliced green peppers. Cook till done.

III. Another possibility is to add the nose, ears and tail of the pig. In this variation omit the flour thickening. You can also add good sausage, chicken pieces, or smoked pork chops.

IV. Some people fry the rice and ground veal, then mix it with egg-yolk mixture, before using it in the casserole.

V. You can make your own variations using different kinds of pork, smoked, roast or raw, or beef. For any variation, line the bottom of the casserole with thin slices of meaty smoked bacon.

NOTE: *This remarkable dish can not only be eaten but also used as a hot water bottle. Housewives usually began preparing it on Saturday morning; toward evening, when it was ready, they wrapped it neatly in a clean cloth and tucked it in at the foot of someone's bed. It served as a remarkable foot-warmer throughout the winter months, at the foot of the bed under the goose-down comforter. On Sunday it was eaten and the leftover was tied up in the same manner and again laid in bed. Usually it lasted for quite a few days, both in bed and on the table. It was never boiled, only reheated in the oven. The odd thing about this dish is that it gets better as it ages. As a matter of fact many people prepare it purposely at least the day before, to reheat on the day when they want to serve it.*

PIKE IN SAUERKRAUT

Savanyú káposzta csukával　　　　　　　　　　　*6 servings*

2 pounds sauerkraut	1 tablespoon flour
3 cups meat or chicken broth	1 pike, 3 to 4 pounds
1 cup wine	1 cup bread crumbs
1 tablespoon goose or chicken fat	¼ pound butter
1 small onion, chopped fine	1 cup sour cream (optional)

1. Cook sauerkraut in broth and wine for 1 hour.

2. Heat fat in a separate pan. Add onion and sauté it slowly for 10 minutes. Then add the flour; stir it for a few minutes but do not brown. Dilute with ¼ cup water, whip till smooth, and mix in with sauerkraut. Simmer for an additional 10 minutes.

3. Remove head and liver from pike and cut remaining pike into serving pieces. With a wooden spoon, make space for each piece of pike in the sauerkraut. Place liver and head in the center (so you can find it easily). Pour bread crumbs over and dot with butter.

4. Bake it in a 375°F. oven for about 30 minutes, or until fish is done but

not overdone. Do not stir. If you think the sauerkraut is sticking on the bottom of the pot, grasp handles of pot and make a fast twist-turn.

5. For traditional serving, put the liver in the mouth of the fish head, and put the head on top in the center of the platter. (This can be omitted for the squeamish.) Sour cream on top is optional.

NOTE: *The same dish is made with* harcsa, *a species of catfish found in the Danube, or with fish roe.*

Csík was a kind of small river eel which is almost impossible to find any more, but in most of the old cookbooks you find this dish cooked with csík. *I have tried it with Long Island eel cut into 4-inch pieces, and found it excellent.*

The dish belongs to the Layered Cabbage family. To make it more elaborate at some private dinners in the past, 2 different kinds of fish plus fish liver, fish milt and fish dumplings (quenelles) *were used in the same preparation. No wonder our ancestors didn't really mind Lent.*

LAYERED CABBAGE AS IN BÁCSKA

Bácskai rakott káposzta   *8 to 10 servings*

4 pounds sauerkraut
¼ pound lard
2 onions, minced
1 dried cherry pepper, freshly
  crushed
½ teaspoon crushed black
  peppercorns

½ pound fresh salt pork, cut
  into ½-inch dice
1 duck, cleaned, left whole
1 fresh pork shoulder
Salt

1. Preheat oven to 350°F. Squeeze sauerkraut till quite dry.

2. Melt lard and sauté minced onions in it for 5 minutes.

3. Add sauerkraut to onions. Mix well and cook for 10 minutes. Sauerkraut should be golden fried but not burned. Remove from heat.

4. Mix crushed cherry pepper and black peppercorns into sauerkraut and stir well. Add 1 cup water and stir again.

5. In a deep oblong ovenproof casserole place diced salt pork and sauerkraut. Put duck and fresh pork shoulder on top and cover the pan.

6. Cook in the preheated oven until duck is done, about 2 hours. Every 20 minutes or so stir the sauerkraut and turn the meats over. If necessary add a little water. Usually you don't have to add salt; nevertheless, taste it in case some is needed.

7. For the last 10 minutes, increase oven heat to 450°F. Scrape off cabbage from top of meat so meat can brown.

8. Serve in the baking casserole, but cut the meat into serving pieces and arrange pieces on top of sauerkraut.

NOTE: *This is a dish which the Hungarians in the southern part of the country learned from the Serbs, who called it* podvaruk.

In the old (now nonexistent) Hungaria Hotel's Restaurant, the same recipe was made with pheasant browned in a 500°F. oven for 5 minutes, then cooked following this method, but without the cherry pepper and with 1 tablespoon paprika added.

❅ 23 ❅

DUMPLINGS
(TÉSZTÁK)

A FRIEND visiting Hungary recently wrote to me that he had always thought that dumplings were used to repel the Turks in the Battle of Buda, but after sampling them he was sure that even a fool would not have thrown such admirable food.

There is such a vast selection of dumpling recipes that I had a difficult time to limit them to so few. The Hungarian housewife uses dumplings for many occasions: as luncheon dishes, as desserts, as part of a dinner, even as a snack. And of course some are used as soup garnishes, as you have already seen. Some of these are not true dumplings, but only a fusty statistician would object to grouping them together.

Flour, wheat, rye and all other types of cereal are truly the staff of life in Hungary. Hungarians used these grains to develop the dumpling family to a bewildering variety. Monsieur L. Saulnier, the Frenchman who wrote *La Répertoire de la Cuisine,* would have had a great time categorizing them according to shapes, sizes, kinds of flour, fillings, types of dough, cooking methods, etc. Here are some of the basic varieties.

GALUSKA   This bite-sized dumpling can be made of rough-textured cereals or fine-ground flour as well. City folk and upper classes generally ate *galuska* as an accompaniment to stews, but among village folk these dumplings were more often a main course. An interesting method is practiced in Göcsej, where they toast the flour before making a dough of it.

GOMBÓC   This has no equivalent word in English, but basically it is a large round dumpling, often stuffed with cottage cheese, plums, jams or meat. More often than not the flour is mixed with potatoes. *Gombóc* can be used for soup, but mostly it is used as a sweet main course or dessert.

KÁSA   This grain dish is of porridge-like texture in contrast to the cut-off pieces or shaped dumplings. For an example, see Shepherd's Millet (*Juhhúsos köleskása*, page 257).

SHAPING AND COOKING DUMPLINGS

Necessary equipment: a board that can be handled easily, at least 11 by 14 inches but not much larger or the board would be too heavy to hold; a slotted large spoon; a pot for cold water; a large pot for boiling water or broth; a knife or spoon.

In dumpling-eating nations there is a gadget that has appropriate holes and fits over the pan in which the dumplings will be cooked. Outside of these Middle European nations, it is easiest to use a small carving board. Before starting the cooking, wet the board and your hands, to prevent sticking. With a cutting and then a scraping motion quickly cut the dough and scrape it off the top of the board directly into the boiling water or broth. As you work over the boiling liquid, you will need to keep dipping your hands into the pot of cold water.

If you make the small-sized *csipetke* (page 178) of the *galuska* family, pinch it off with thumb and index finger. Liver, semolina (*dara*) and a few other dumplings are cut with a spoon instead of with a knife.

When you cook dumplings, always make a "trial balloon." If the trial dumpling falls apart, add some flour or bread crumbs to the dumpling mixture. If the mixture is too stiff, add some milk. The entire procedure must be done very speedily, otherwise the dumplings will be overcooked. You should also be careful not to drop too many dumplings into the broth at the same time, to prevent their sticking together.

When you finish boiling dumplings, generally sauté them for a few seconds in lard, as in the Hungarian provinces, or in goose or chicken fat, or, for certain dishes, in butter.

EGG BARLEY, HOMEMADE

Tarhonya készítés   *about 20 servings*

7 eggs   **2 pounds flour**
1 tablespoon salt

1. Mix eggs with 1 cup water and the salt.
2. Pour the flour into a large mixing vessel (a wooden salad bowl is ideal).

Little by little add the egg mixture, mixing it in with a rubbing motion. Keep rubbing your open palms till the mix becomes little uneven pieces of dough.

3. Rub the dough through a large-holed metal sieve.

4. Spread out a tablecloth, and place the egg barley on it, in a very thin layer so all the pieces can be in contact with air. It will take 3 to 4 days to dry, and the little pieces will become almost pebble-hard.

5. During this time, you should mix it up several times to make sure that every little piece is exposed to air and is becoming completely dry.

6. You will have some large pieces left over when you've finished sieving the dough. Sprinkle these with 2 tablespoons water and knead the dough again. Put it through the sieve and continue the same procedure.

NOTE: Tarhonya *will keep in a jar or box for years, just as it did for the ancient Hungarians.*

BAKED EGG BARLEY

Tarhonya főzés   6 servings

½ cup dried homemade   1 teaspoon salt
 tarhonya (page 296)   1 tablespoon paprika
3 tablespoons chicken fat or
 lard

1. Brown the egg barley in the fat in a casserole for about 5 minutes. Stir several times.

2. Add salt, paprika and water to cover. Cover the casserole and put it in a 375°F. oven. Cook until done. Usually, just about the time the water is absorbed, the egg barley is cooked. Depending on the coarseness of the "grain" and its age, it will take 40 minutes to 1 hour.

3. Use instead of rice, noodles or potato with many dishes.

EGG DUMPLINGS

Galuska   4 servings

1 egg   1 teaspoon and 1 tablespoon
3 tablespoons lard   salt
⅓ cup water   1½ cups flour

1. Mix egg, 1 tablespoon lard, ⅓ cup water and 1 teaspoon salt. Mix in the flour lightly. Do not work the mixture too much, just enough to give it an even texture, about 3 minutes. Let it rest for 10 minutes.

2. Bring to a boil 3 quarts water with 1 tablespoon salt. Dip a tablespoon into the boiling water (to prevent sticking) and with the spoon tear pieces out of dumpling mixture, dropping the pieces into the boiling water.

3. When the dumplings have all surfaced to the top of the water, turn off heat and remove them with a slotted spoon. Rinse them with cold water and drain.

4. Heat remaining 2 tablespoons lard (or chicken or goose fat) in a frying pan and lightly toss the completely drained dumplings in it for a few minutes. Sprinkle with salt to taste.

5. Serve as a garnish for traditional stews or with other main dishes with sauces.

VARIATION: *Scrambled Egg Dumplings* (Tojásos galuska) *Break 4 eggs on top of this, mixing them in quickly, to make a main course out of it. Serve as a luncheon dish, accompanied by a salad.*

NOTE: *These are somewhat like* gnocchi, *which are the fifteenth-century ancestor of this dish. Both the Hungarian and German names come from this root (see page 41).*

This dumpling is different from the galuska used for soup garnishes, because it has water in the mix and is sautéed after being cooked in water.

POTATO DUMPLINGS WITH SHEEP'S-MILK CHEESE

Dödöle   *6 to 8 servings*

Salt
1½ cups grated raw potatoes
¾ cup flour
1 tablespoon lard or bacon
   drippings

½ cup sheep's-milk cheese
   (Liptó or Brindza)

1. Fill a 3- or 4-quart pot with water and add 2 tablespoons salt. Bring to a boil.

2. Mix the grated raw potatoes with flour and a pinch of salt.

3. Place the mixture on a small wooden board and with the help of a spoon tear off walnut-sized pieces, dropping them gently into the boiling water. Cook them for 10 minutes.

4. Remove the pieces with a slotted spoon and rinse them with cold water.

5. Place the lard or bacon drippings in a frying pan. Put the little dumplings and the mashed or sieved cheese together in the pan and gently cook and stir for a few minutes. Serve immediately.

VARIATION: *Shred a small head of cabbage, or chop ½ pound sauerkraut. Cook covered in ⅛ pound butter. Mix into the dumplings. Sprinkle with additional melted butter.*

NOTE: *This dish comes from the northern section (Slovakia) of Hungary, where they call it* strapacka, *but almost the same dish is also made in Transylvania.*

POTATO DUMPLINGS IN BREAD CRUMBS

Morzsázott krumplis gombóc   *4 to 6 servings*

4 medium-sized potatoes	2 eggs
2 tablespoons plus ¼ pound butter	Pinch of salt
	1 cup bread crumbs
2 heaping tablespoons flour	

1. Boil unpeeled potatoes in plenty of water. When done, peel them and purée while still warm.

2. Add 2 tablespoons butter, the flour, eggs and salt. Mix the batter and put it on a floured kneading board. Knead it well to get a good dough.

3. Cut golf-ball-sized pieces of dough with a spoon. Dip your hands into flour and roll the pieces of dough into dumplings.

4. Bring 4 quarts water to a boil. Drop dumplings into the water and boil for about 5 minutes. Taste a dumpling to see if it is done. Remove cooked dumplings with a slotted spoon.

5. Melt remaining butter in a frying pan. Brown bread crumbs lightly, then add drained dumplings and keep rolling them over very low heat.

6. Serve as a separate course, sometimes even as the entire meal. Or you can serve them also as an accompaniment to meat.

VARIATION: *By putting a little jam in the center of each dumpling before boiling, you can make a good and substantial dessert.*

WHITE-BREAD DUMPLINGS

Zsemlegombóc   6 *servings*

2 white rolls, or 3 slices of
  white bread
3 tablespoons lard, melted
2 eggs
½ teaspoon and 1 tablespoon
  salt

2 cups flour
1 tablespoon lard or bacon
  drippings

1. Cut white rolls or white bread into small dice and sprinkle with 3 tablespoons melted lard. Shake well to mix and place in a 500°F. oven. Bake until the cubes are golden brown. Let them cool.

2. Mix eggs, ¾ cup water and ½ teaspoon salt. Stir in the flour.

3. Mix in the cooled toasted bread cubes, then let the mixture stand for 30 minutes.

4. Put 2 quarts water in a 3-quart pot, add 1 tablespoon salt, and bring to a boil. Dip a tablespoon into hot water, scoop up a spoonful of the dumpling mixture, and drop it into the water. Continue with the rest of the mixture, dipping the spoon into hot water each time. Stir every now and then to make sure dumplings do not sink to the bottom. Cook for 5 or 6 minutes. Drain dumplings and rinse with cold water.

5. Place 1 tablespoon lard or bacon drippings in a frying pan. When it is hot, put in the dumplings. Shake the pan quickly to turn the dumplings in the fat. Serve with wild game, cabbage dishes, and such.

WINTER VEGETABLE DUMPLINGS

Téli zöldséggombóc   8 *servings*

1 small knob celery
1 small carrot
4 tablespoons butter
¼ head of cauliflower, or ½
  head of a small one, chopped
  fine
3 mushrooms, chopped

4 stale white rolls
⅔ cup milk
2 eggs
4 tablespoons flour
Salt
¼ cup sour cream (optional—
  see Note)

1. Peel the knob celery and carrot, then cut into small dice. Cook covered in 2 tablespoons of the butter for about 10 minutes. Every 3 minutes or so add 1 teaspoon of water, to make enough steam for the cooking.

2. After the 10 minutes add the chopped cauliflower and mushrooms; cook covered for another 10 minutes. Mushrooms will probably release enough liquid so you don't have to add more water.

3. Crumble stale rolls and soak them in milk. Squeeze when soft. Add eggs and mix. Mix with the flour and finally add the cooked vegetable mixture. Add salt and adjust to taste.

4. Bring 3 quarts of water to a boil. Make Ping-pong-ball-sized dumplings and drop them into the water. Cook them for 10 to 15 minutes.

5. Melt remaining 2 tablespoons butter, and cook the drained dumplings in melted butter for a few minutes.

NOTE: *This versatile dumpling can be served in a soup or as an accompaniment to boiled beef and sauce. Or it can be served as a one-dish luncheon with sour cream on the side. Use the last suggestion only if you invite Hungarians who really miss their homeland.*

There is also a spring vegetable dumpling which uses spring vegetables like asparagus tips, peas, etc.

MEAT DUMPLINGS AS IN SZEPES

Szepesi húsgombóc   6 servings

1 onion, chopped fine	½ teaspoon pepper
½ cup lard	1 pound pork, twice ground
1 roll	½ pound beef, twice ground
1 garlic clove, crushed	1 teaspoon salt
1 egg	½ cup bread crumbs
10 tarragon leaves, chopped, or ½ teaspoon dried herb	

1. Wilt the chopped onion in 1 tablespoon of the lard.

2. Soak the roll in water, squeeze it, and rice it. Add the wilted onion, crushed garlic, egg, tarragon, pepper, the twice ground meats and salt. Work the mixture together well.

3. Make dumpling shapes the size of apricots. Roll them in the bread crumbs.

4. Heat the rest of the lard in a frying pan. Quickly sauté the breaded dumplings till they become golden brown.

NOTE: *If you have leftover cooked meat, you can substitute it for the raw ground meat, although you get a different kind of dumpling.*

If you don't like the taste of tarragon you can eliminate it and substitute any other herb, or use none.

GRENADIER MARCH

Gránátoskocka   6 to 8 servings

1 pound flour   1 large onion, chopped fine
2 eggs   ½ cup chicken fat
Salt   1 tablespoon paprika
1½ pounds potatoes

1. Make a hard dough with flour, eggs, a pinch of salt and ¼ cup water. Work it well, stretch it thin on a floured board, and let it rest for 1½ hours.
2. Stretch the dough to a thin sheet and cut it into 1½-inch squares.
3. Boil 3 quarts water with 1 tablespoon salt. Put in the dough squares and cook them for about 5 minutes. Drain, and rinse with cold water.
4. Meantime peel potatoes and cut them into small dice. Cook until soft, and drain.
5. Brown the onion in chicken fat. Add paprika and mix with cooked potatoes. Mash them together, but leave potatoes somewhat lumpy. The mixture should not be smooth.
6. Mix vegetables with the noodle squares, and serve.

VARIATION: *Put the mixture in a baking dish with a little chicken fat, and brown it for 15 minutes.*

GRATED NOODLES WITH CALF'S-LUNG FILLING
AS IN HORTOBÁGY

Hortobágyi reszelt tészta tüdővel   8 servings

7 eggs   2 tablesepoons lard
Flour (about 1 cup)   1 pound calf's lung
4 cups milk   1 small onion, chopped fine
Salt and pepper   ½ cup sour cream
1 tablespoon chopped flat
  parsley

1. Knead 2 eggs with enough of the flour to make a very, very hard dough.
2. Grate the dough. (So far the dough is like egg barley.)
3. Bring milk to a boil and simmer grated noodles in it over low heat, stirring. Cook until the milk is absorbed. Add more milk if necessary. Add a little salt and pepper and mix in the chopped parsley. Cool to lukewarm temperature.

302

4. Mix cooled noodles with 3 egg yolks, then fold in the stiffly beaten whites of 3 eggs.

5. Grease a heavy casserole, 3- or 4-quart size, 3 to 4 inches deep, with 1 tablespoon lard. Pour the noodle and egg mixture into it and pat it down evenly.

6. Cook calf's lung for 30 minutes. Drain, and put it through the meat grinder.

7. Sauté the onion in remaining 1 tablespoon lard for about 10 minutes. Mix onion with ground lung. Add a pinch of pepper and salt to taste. Let cool.

8. When lukewarm, mix in remaining 2 whole eggs, beaten.

9. Make a hole in the middle of the cooked noodle mixture in the casserole, and pour in the lung mixture. Spread the entire top with sour cream. Bake in a 375°F. oven for 45 minutes.

NOTE: *This is a most unusual luncheon or supper dish, and it is one of those preparations that taste quite different from one's expectations.*

As a substitute for the grated freshly made noodles, one can usually purchase freshly made egg noodles at better Italian grocers. By chopping them well, you have a reasonable facsimile. Or you can use commercial egg barley.

This eighteenth-century recipe belongs, to my knowledge, to the very small category that seems to have no close parallel in other nations' recipes.

CORNMEAL DUMPLINGS

Puliszka   *4 to 6 servings*

1 cup very coarse cornmeal   5 tablespoons lard
1 teaspoon salt
2 large onions, peeled and cut
  into thin slices

1. Bring 2 cups water to a rapid boil and slowly sprinkle in cornmeal, stirring all the while. Keep stirring and cook over low heat for about 5 minutes. Add salt; adjust salt if necessary. Keep the cornmeal mush warm in a covered double boiler.

2. Fry onion slices in 2 tablespoons lard. Cook them long enough for all the water in the onions to be evaporated and the onions to be crisp.

3. Melt remaining lard. Dip a tablespoon into the hot lard and cut a dumpling shape out of the mush. Continue this, piling the little rounds on a serving platter. When you are finished making the rounds, pour the onions with their lard over the top.

4. If you serve these with meat (like the Transylvanian Bandits' Meat, page 249), instead of using the lard from the onion, use fat left over from cooking the meat, and pour that on top of the cornmeal dumplings.

5. Serve with all kinds of main courses, roasts, stews, etc. Don't worry if the dumplings break; this is supposed to be uneven looking.

VARIATIONS:

I. Cornmeal Stuffed with Ricotta (Rakott puliszka juhtúróval)
1. When you remove the mush from the heat, let it rest for 10 minutes to become quite solid, then turn pot upside down and remove the mush in a lump. With a white thread, cut it into 3 horizontal sections.

2. Spread a baking-serving dish liberally with lard. Put in the first third of the mush and sprinkle it with ½ cup ricotta; spread 2 tablespoons sour cream on top. Place second third of mush on top, add another ½ cup ricotta, and pour ½ cup warm milk over it. Cover with final third and another ½ cup ricotta, and pour ⅓ cup bacon drippings over all.

3. Bake in a 325°F. oven for about 20 minutes.

II. Cornmeal Stuffed with Pörkölt (Rakott puliszka pörkölttel)
Follow the method of Variation I, but leave out the warm milk and lard. Instead place mutton pörkölt between the layers; use half of the recipe on page 277.

NOTE: *North Hungary (the largest part is presently Slovakia) and Transylvania live on puliszka and its numerous variations. In Transylvania the same mixture is used to make a cornmeal spongecake called prósza.*

You must use a nonprepared, nonmixed, rough cornmeal, probably obtainable in German-Hungarian stores, or in Italian stores where they sell it for making polenta.

POTATO PANCAKE STUFFED WITH BUTTERED CRUMBS

Morzsás göngyöleg krumplis tésztából   6 to 8 servings

2½ pounds potatoes
1 tablespoon and ½ cup lard
Salt
1 egg
1½ cups flour

1 medium-sized onion, chopped
⅔ cup bread crumbs
½ teaspoon black pepper
Bacon drippings

1. Cook potatoes in salted water. Peel them and push through a sieve or ricer. Add 1 tablespoon lard and ½ tablespoon salt. Let cool.
2. Mix cooled potatoes with egg and flour on a marble slab. Knead the

dough, then roll out to ½-inch thickness. Cut into pieces 7 inches square.

3. Make a filling. Melt ½ cup lard in a frying pan. Wilt the onion in it over very low heat for about 15 minutes.

4. Add bread crumbs and stir for 2 or 3 minutes while they become golden brown. Add a pinch of salt and the pepper. Let the mixture cool.

5. Put some of the bread-crumb filling on each dough square and roll up. Make sure to press ends together and close all openings so the filling will not come out during boiling.

6. Heat 3 to 4 quarts of water with 1 tablespoon salt. When it boils, cook the rolled stuffed pancakes for about 6 minutes. Handle very gently so as not to damage the walls of the stuffed rolls. Remove cooked pancakes from water with a slotted spoon; drain.

7. In the same frying pan in which the onion was prepared, fry the pancakes in a little bacon dripping until the outsides are dark gold and crisp. This also can be done in the oven; in that case, you must baste the pancake rolls and turn them to brown all sides.

NOTE: *Make certain the bread crumbs are freshly made. Ready-bought crumbs are generally stale and tasteless. You can use butter to make these if you prefer.*

✦ 24 ✦

STUFFED VEGETABLES
(TÖLTÖTT ZÖLDSÉGFÉLÉK)

GREEN PEPPERS STUFFED WITH MEAT SALAD

Hideg töltött paprika   *6 servings*

6 large green peppers
½ cup white-wine vinegar
Pinch of salt and pepper
1 pound roast veal or pork,
 diced
2 hard-boiled eggs, chopped
2 medium-sized potatoes, boiled
 and riced

2 pickles, peeled and chopped
 fine
1½ cups mayonnaise
12 thick tomato slices
1 envelope of gelatin
1¾ cups hot chicken broth

1. Preheat oven to 300°F. Place whole green peppers in oven and bake just long enough so you can pull off outer skin. Make sure the peppers remain intact. Cut peppers crosswise into halves. Take out the ribs and membranes.

2. Make a marinade with vinegar, ½ cup water, salt and pepper. Marinate the pepper halves in this for 1 hour.

3. Meantime, mix meat, eggs, potatoes, pickles and mayonnaise.

4. Remove peppers from marinade and fill them with meat mixture. Arrange pepper halves along the edge of a serving platter. Place a tomato slice on each opening. Chill the platter of vegetables.

5. Soften gelatin in ¼ cup cold water and dissolve it in the hot broth. Let it cool until syrupy.

6. With a brush, glaze the peppers with liquid gelatin. Chill them in refrigerator for 15 minutes. Repeat this process.

7. Pour the rest of the gelatin into a shallow pan in a layer about ¼ inch thick. When jelled, cut it into even dice. Make certain to cut it precisely even; it will then sparkle like so many jewels. Sprinkle in the center of the serving platter so it will be surrounded by the green peppers.

NOTE: *Experiment with using a little less gelatin. Few things are as unpleasant as a rubbery aspic.*

Prepare this luncheon or supper dish when you have leftover roast meat. Try it with any type of poultry or meat, and also you may vary the stuffing.

STUFFED PEPPERS, HOMESTYLE

Töltött paprika, otthoniasan   6 *servings*

3 pounds fresh ripe tomatoes
2 small onions
1 teaspoon salt
2 teaspoons lard
½ pound veal, twice ground
½ pound pork, twice ground
1 whole egg
1 extra egg yolk
¼ cup uncooked rice
1 tablespoon chopped flat
  parsley or green leaves of
  knob celery

¼ teaspoon ground black
  pepper
6 large fleshy bell peppers, red
  ripe if possible, or 10 to 12
  Italian or frying peppers
2 tablespoons flour
½ cup tomato juice
1 tablespoon sugar
Lemon juice

1. Blanch tomatoes for a couple of minutes, and peel. Dice tomatoes and put into a saucepan with 1 onion, peeled and halved, and ½ teaspoon salt. Cook uncovered over low heat for 30 to 40 minutes.

2. Melt 1 teaspoon lard in a small frying pan. Chop the other onion and wilt in the lard for about 10 minutes. Remove from heat.

3. In a bowl mix ground veal and pork, the whole egg and egg yolk, rice, chopped parsley, ½ teaspoon salt, the black pepper and ¼ cup ice-cold water.

4. When onion is somewhat cooled, add it to the meat mixture. Stuff peppers; leave ½ inch of space at the ends so stuffing can swell during cooking. If you have leftover stuffing, make meatballs and cook them together with stuffed peppers.

5. By now tomatoes should be cooked. Discard onion halves and force everything else through a strainer.

6. Make a *roux* with 1 teaspoon lard and the flour and cook for 1 or 2 minutes to blend. Dilute with the cold tomato juice, whip the mixture, and

add to strained tomato sauce. If sauce is too thin, simmer over low heat, uncovered, until you get the consistency you want.

7. Lay the stuffed peppers at the bottom of a heavy casserole. Pour sauce over them, cover, and cook—for about 40 minutes if you use thin-skinned frying peppers, or for 1 hour if you use bell peppers.

8. When done, adjust seasoning of the sauce. Depending on the sweetness of the tomato, you may need to add the sugar or perhaps a little lemon juice to get a nice sweet-and-sour taste. Additional salt may also be necessary.

VARIATIONS:

I. For an excellent appetizer, let stuffed peppers cool, then slice crosswise into 1/2-inch-thick slices. Serve with Spicy Cold Tomato Sauce (page 340).

II. Cut the peppers lengthwise into halves and stuff them that way. Obviously, you will need a much larger pot to cook them.

III. 1. For a completely different result, make stuffed peppers as in Variation II, and put them in a well-greased ovenproof casserole.

2. Cut 3 pounds tomatoes into 1/4-inch-thick slices and a piece of smoked bacon into 3 1/4-inch-thick slices. Score the bacon cockscomb style. Mix 1 cup sour cream with 1/4 cup heavy cream.

3. Arrange tomato and bacon slices on top of peppers. Pour sour-cream mixture on top. Bake in a preheated 400°F. oven until the top of the bacon browns.

NOTE: *Many provinces in Hungary use pork exclusively, no other sweetening than the natural sugar of the tomatoes.*

In Alföld they replace 1 ounce of the pork with the same amount of chopped or ground bacon.

MUSHROOM-STUFFED PEPPERS AS IN ORMÁNSÁG

Ormánsági gombás töltött paprika   3 or 6 servings

6 pieces of dried mushroom	2 egg yolks
1 tablespoon chicken fat	2 tablespoons bread crumbs
1/2 cup cooked rice	Salt and pepper
5 fresh mushrooms, peeled and chopped	6 green peppers
1 tablespoon minced onion	2 cups tomato purée
	1/4 cup sugar

1. Soak the dried mushrooms the night before you plan to make this.

2. Drain mushrooms, squeeze, and put through a food grinder. Sauté in chicken fat over low heat for about 30 minutes.

3. Mix rice, chopped raw mushrooms, sautéed dried mushrooms, minced onion, egg yolks and bread crumbs. Add salt and pepper to taste.

4. Cut off stem ends of peppers and remove seeds and membranes. Stuff pepper shells with the rice and mushroom mixture.

5. In a separate pot mix tomato purée, 1 cup water and the sugar. Gently place green peppers in tomato sauce. Cover, and cook over low heat for about 30 minutes.

NOTE: *For a Lenten dish, use butter instead of chicken fat.*

LAYERED GREEN PEPPER

Rakott zöldpaprika 6 *appetizer servings, or*
3 luncheon servings

1 medium-sized onion, chopped fine	6 green peppers, sliced
1 teaspoon bacon drippings	1 teaspoon salt
1 teaspoon paprika	1 pound smoked sausage
1 tablespoon tomato purée	5 hard-boiled eggs

1. Fry onion in bacon drippings. Sprinkle with paprika and immediately add ¼ cup water. Cook until liquid disappears and only clear fat remains.

2. Add tomato purée and sliced green peppers. Add salt. Add sausage and cook under a heavy lid over low heat for about 20 minutes.

3. Meantime, slice hard-boiled eggs. Take the cooked sausage from the pot and slice it.

4. Place half of the green peppers in an ovenproof casserole. On top of the peppers put sliced sausage and sliced eggs. Finally cover with the rest of the peppers. Pour sauce on top.

5. Bake the peppers in a 375°F. oven for another 10 minutes, and serve.

STUFFED ONION HALAS STYLE

Töltött hagyma halasi módra 10 *appetizer servings,*
or 5 luncheon servings

10 medium-sized Bermuda onions	1 tablespoon minced flat parsley
¼ pound lard	1 teaspoon salt
1 pound cooked lean veal, diced	½ pound double-smoked bacon
1 garlic clove, mashed	1 cup sour cream
	Pinch of paprika
	Pinch of black pepper

1. Peel onions. Cut off tops in such a way that you can take out almost the entire center of each onion. Leave 2 or 3 layers remaining as a shell to contain the stuffing. Set aside the center of 1 onion. (Use the rest for another recipe.)

2. Cook onion shells in lightly salted water for about 10 minutes. Make sure they do not get too soft, because they must not collapse later. Drain onion shells and gently pat dry.

3. Chop enough of the reserved onion center to have about ¼ cup. Slowly wilt chopped pieces in most of the lard. Save 1 teaspoon lard to grease the baking dish.

4. Add diced veal, mashed garlic, parsley and salt. Cook the stuffing, uncovered, over very low heat. Add a few tablespoons of water when the mixture becomes dry. Finally, there should be no liquid left when testing with a fork indicates that the veal is cooked.

5. Cool the stuffing mixture, then grind it. Fill the cooked onion shells with the mixture.

6. Cut bacon into 2-inch squares to fit over the tops of the onions.

7. Grease a baking-serving dish with lard, and place stuffed onions in it. Pour or spoon sour cream on top of onions. Sprinkle a little paprika and black pepper on each.

8. Place onions in a 350°F. oven and bake for 25 to 30 minutes. Serve as a hot appetizer, or as a luncheon dish.

STUFFED KOHLRABI

Töltött karalábé   *3 or 6 servings*

6 medium-sized kohlrabies	⅓ cup twice-ground veal
⅓ cup fine-chopped green kohlrabi leaves	⅓ cup twice-ground lean pork
1 teaspoon sugar	⅓ teaspoon pepper
½ white roll	1 teaspoon salt
½ cup milk	½ egg
½ small onion, minced	½ cup chicken broth
2 tablespoons butter	1 tablespoon flour

1. Peel kohlrabies and scoop out centers. Place the vegetables in 1 quart salted water and boil until half done, about 25 minutes, but the time depends on age of the kohlrabies. Drain kohlrabies and save the cooking liquid.

2. Chop very fine the scooped-out centers of kohlrabies and all the chopped leaves. Add sugar and sauté the mixture for a few minutes.

3. Add 2 cups of the cooking liquid, and cook the chopped kohlrabi centers and leaves until about half done.

4. Soak the roll in the milk, squeeze roll, and chop or shred into small pieces.

5. Fry onion in butter in a separate frying pan for a few minutes. Add ground meat and sauté for 5 minutes.

6. Add chopped roll, the pepper, salt and the ½ egg. Stir well, and remove from heat. Adjust salt if necessary. Stuff this into the empty kohlrabi shells.

7. Place stuffed shells in a baking-serving casserole. Pour chopped leaf mixture around shells, and add the chicken broth if some extra liquid is needed.

8. Cook the kohlrabies over very low heat for 25 to 30 minutes, or until vegetables are done.

9. Make a thickening with flour and ¾ tablespoon cold water. Take a ladleful of liquid from the casserole, whip it into this flour-water mixture, and pour it back into the casserole. Cook for 5 minutes longer.

10. Serve 1 stuffed kohlrabi as a hot first course, or two as a luncheon main course.

NOTE: *For a gala dinner, these can be served as a vegetable garniture to accompany the roast course.*

Kohlrabies are sometimes harvested when they are quite old. The cooking time specified here is for such a vegetable. On the other hand, if you are lucky enough to get very young vegetables, the cooking time must be reduced; cook them just until done.

PÂTÉ IN SAVOY CABBAGE TORDA STYLE

Tordai kelpástétom   *4 to 6 servings*

3 pounds Savoy cabbage
½ cup uncooked rice
1 roll
½ cup milk
1¼ pounds cooked lean pork, ground
1 medium-sized onion, minced
2 tablespoons lard
1 garlic clove, crushed
2 eggs
½ teaspoon dried marjoram, or 1 teaspoon minced fresh marjoram

¼ teaspoon freshly crushed black pepper
1 teaspoon and ½ tablespoon paprika
½ teaspoon salt
4 tablespoons bacon drippings
¼ pound double-smoked bacon, sliced
½ cup chicken broth or stock
1 tablespoon flour
½ cup sour cream

1. Preheat oven to 325°F. Cut out cores of cabbage and wash the heads well. Cook in salted water until half done. Drain.

2. Separate cabbage leaves, and cut out thick ribs.

3. Cook the rice in 1 cup water. Soak the roll in milk, squeeze out, and shred.

4. Mix rice with ground pork and the shredded roll.

5. Sauté onion in 2 tablespoons lard for 5 minutes. At the last minute add garlic. Pour this into rice and pork mixture. Put in the eggs and add marjoram, pepper, 1 teaspoon paprika and the salt. Mix thoroughly.

6. Spread bacon drippings liberally in a 5-quart, fireproof, round casserole. With the largest leaves of cabbage, form a complete layer on the bottom of the casserole; use about a third of the cabbage. Place half of meat mixture on top and pat it down. Add another third of the leaves and pat down. Add the rest of meat and finally cover it with remaining cabbage leaves. Place bacon slices on top.

7. Bake in the preheated oven for 1½ hours. During baking, baste 2 or 3 times with a few tablespoons of chicken broth or stock.

8. Turn out the cooked pâté and cabbage onto a serving platter. Cut it like a cake. You may find that it is so juicy you can dispense with sauce altogether. Or you may find it easier to leave the dish in the casserole, thus not taking a chance of breaking it while turning it out.

9. If you do want a sauce, start with the drippings and juices left in the casserole. Put the casserole over heat, and scrape up the particles from the bottom. Add the flour and stir for a few minutes. Add remaining paprika and ½ cup water. Stir and boil for 5 minutes. Turn off heat and mix in the sour cream.

NOTE: *This is a most unusual dish, not really a pâté, but closer to a terrine or* chartreuse, *and actually neither. However, the Hungarians in the southeastern section, where this dish comes from, call it by this name.*

STUFFED SAVOY CABBAGE

Töltött kel rántva　　　　　　　　　　*4 to 6 servings*

3 pounds Savoy cabbage	1 garlic clove, mashed
1 pound roast veal or pork	Salt and pepper
½ roll	½ cup flour
3 tablespoons milk	3 eggs, beaten
1 small onion, minced	1 cup bread crumbs
2 cups lard or oil	

1. Boil cabbage heads in lightly salted water until done. Take cabbage heads apart, separating the leaves. Cut out thick ribs, if any.

2. Grind the meat. Soak roll in milk, squeeze, then chop. Sauté onion in 1 tablespoon lard.

3. Mix well the ground meat, sautéed onion, garlic, chopped roll, and salt and pepper to taste.

4. Put 1 tablespoon filling into each cabbage leaf. Roll the leaf lengthwise and squeeze the ends together.

5. Dip each cabbage roll in flour, beaten eggs and bread crumbs.

6. Bring the rest of the lard or oil to frying temperature in a frying pan. Fry Savoy cabbage rolls until they are done.

STUFFED MORELS

Töltött kucsmagomba　　　　*6 appetizer servings*

1 pound morels	¼ teaspoon salt
½ pound twice-ground veal	Dash of white pepper
½ roll	2 egg yolks
¼ cup milk	½ cup sour cream
½ small onion, grated	2 tablespoons white bread
¼ pound butter	crumbs
1 tablespoon chopped flat parsley	

1. Preheat oven to 375°F. Wash morels in 3 or 4 waters to make sure that all sand and grit are removed from the little honeycombs. Place morels in 1 cup boiling water for 1 minute, then drain.

2. Carefully remove stems. Chop stems very fine and mix with ground veal. Soak the roll in milk.

3. Cook onion in half of the butter, covered, for 10 minutes. Add the mixture of veal and mushroom stems, the chopped parsley, salt and white pepper. Mix it well and cook, covered, over very low heat for 10 minutes.

4. Squeeze the soaked roll, and force it through a sieve or purée in a blender. Mix it with the egg yolks and then mix it well with the cooked stuffing.

5. Carefully stuff the morels. Spread 2 tablespoons of remaining butter in a pottery baking-serving dish. Place the morels in the dish. Sprinkle with sour cream and bread crumbs. Place a tiny bit of remaining butter on top of each mushroom.

6. Bake in the preheated oven for 15 to 20 minutes, or until golden brown. Serve in same dish.

NOTE: *This recipe comes from a late eighteenth-century Hungarian cookbook, which starts with the following sentence: "Pick only even size morels for this dish." Every now and then I get morels from enthusiastic amateur mycologists, but I am sure they would be outraged by such a request. Might as well ask for equal-sized emeralds.*

* 2ʃ *

OTHER VEGETABLE PREPARATIONS
(FŐZELÉKEK ÉS KÖRETEK)

IN Hungary vegetables are not just "cooked"; they are "prepared." The difference between an American vegetable dish and a Hungarian one is similar to the difference between plain boiled meat and a meat stew.

Hungary is famed for its vegetable gardens. The Hungarian name for green peas is *cukorborsó,* which means "sugar peas," and without additional flourishes they do taste like a sugared vegetable. Yet you will rarely find a Hungarian housewife simply steaming, boiling or sautéing peas; she would consider that as only the first step. Plain boiled vegetables are incomprehensible to a Hungarian.

I am not recommending the exclusive use of this complex treatment of vegetables, but since the simple preparations are already only too familiar, I will describe the preparations I grew up with. What makes these dishes unusual is that many of them can be eaten by themselves for luncheons, and a few will serve as appetizers.

Lecsó   *4 to 8 servings*

2 tablespoons lard
1 medium-sized onion, sliced
1 pound green Italian or frying
    peppers, sliced
3 large, very ripe tomatoes,

peeled and diced
½ tablespoon sugar
½ tablespoon salt
1 tablespoon paprika

1. Heat the lard, add sliced onion, and cook over very low heat for 5 minutes.

2. Add green pepper slices and cook for an additional 15 minutes.

3. Add tomatoes, sugar, salt and paprika. Cook for 15 to 20 minutes longer. Adjust sugar and salt to taste.

VARIATION: *Put ½ pound beef tenderloin on a board. Hold it with one hand, and start scraping it with the dull edge of a strong knife (the same way you make a proper steak tartare). It will take 10 minutes to scrape the whole piece. Heat 1 teaspoon lard till very hot, coat the bottom of the frying pan completely, and throw in the meat pulp. Work very fast and squeeze-stir to make sure that within seconds, or certainly in less than 1 minute, the meat browns. Do not let it stick together; in other words don't make a hamburger out of it, but rather something more like meat crumbs. Then mix it with the* lecsó. *Adjust salt.*

This variation comes from the great chef Emil Turós.

NOTE: *This is one of the most ingeniously used vegetable dishes in the Hungarian kitchen. First of all it is used in an appetizer; for this amount ¼ cup cooked rice or ¼ pound thin-sliced smoked sausage are added; or at the last minute 4 eggs are beaten into it.*

With the same additions lecsó *can also be used as a luncheon main course, particularly if you cook it with larger sections of smoked or fresh sausage, or frankfurter (*virsli*).*

Lecsó *is also used as an ingredient for stews and other dishes, especially when no fresh tomatoes or green peppers are available in Hungary.*

Do not use bell peppers, for they have no taste to speak of. Italian frying peppers or banana peppers are better. And do not make this dish unless you have ripe tomatoes.

The sugar must be adjusted according to the ripeness of the tomatoes; if you have vine-ripened fruit you can usually eliminate sugar altogether.

Reduce salt if you use smoked sausage, for sausage is salty.

Curiously enough, this most Hungarian of dishes originated in Serbia and is very closely related to their djuvets.

TOMATO CABBAGE, SWEET-AND-SOUR

Paradicsomos káposzta   *4 to 6 servings*

3 pounds cabbage
Salt
2 tablespoons lard or chicken
  fat
1½ tablespoons flour
½ tablespoon paprika

2 quarts tomato juice
Sugar
1 green pepper, sliced
1 onion, peeled and cut into
  halves

1. Shred cabbage to a thin slaw and place it in a 4-quart pot. Cover it with water and add 1 teaspoon salt. Boil cabbage till done; drain.

2. Melt lard in a frying pan. Add flour and stir; do not brown the *roux*. Remove from heat, mix in paprika, and add some of the tomato juice. Whip the mixture to prevent lumps.

3. Pour thickening into drained cabbage in the pot, and also pour in the rest of the tomato juice. Adjust taste with salt and sugar and bring to a boil. Add sliced green pepper and the halved onion.

4. After 3 minutes remove onion halves. Simmer cabbage for about 5 minutes longer. If cabbage was underdone at the first cooking then increase the cooking time to 10 minutes.

NOTE: *By increasing the tomato juice and reducing the cabbage you can have a good soup.*

APPLE CABBAGE GÜL BABA

Gül baba almás káposztája   *6 to 8 servings*

2½ pounds red cabbage	1 cup chicken broth
Salt	2 pounds sour apples
1 small onion, minced	2 tablespoons flour
2 tablespoons butter	1 tablespoon lemon juice
1 tablespoon sugar	

1. Slice or cut cabbage to a fine slaw. Mix with 1 tablespoon salt, cover, and let stand for 2 to 3 hours.

2. Squeeze cabbage well, a little at a time, and set it aside.

3. Wilt the onion in butter for about 10 minutes. Add sugar and brown carefully so as not to burn it.

4. Mix in the cabbage and pour in ½ cup of the chicken broth. Cover and cook over low heat for 30 minutes.

5. Meantime peel the apples and cut into fine pieces. Add to the cabbage. Cook until both apples and cabbage are properly done.

6. Mix flour with remaining ½ cup chicken broth; make sure that the mixture is not lumpy. Add lemon juice and pour into cabbage.

7. Simmer cabbage for another 5 minutes. Adjust salt, sugar and lemon juice to your sweet-and-sour liking.

NOTE: *Gül Baba was a rare phenomenon: a beloved member of the occupying Turkish forces in the sixteenth century, who established rose gardens and fruit orchards in Hungary. This dish is a tribute to him; it was created in the 1920's for one of the dinners given in connection with the International Hoteliers and Restaurateurs Convention.*

SPICED RED CABBAGE

Fűszerezett vöröskáposzta   6 *servings*

3 ounces double-smoked
    Hungarian bacon, about 3
    slices
1 large onion, chopped
2 firm heads of red cabbage,
    shredded
2 garlic cloves, minced
1 tablespoon caraway seeds
Salt

¼ teaspoon ground pepper
2 large ripe pears, peeled and
    chopped
1 lemon, halved
2 cups red wine
3 tablespoons wine vinegar
6 ounces honey
Brown sugar (optional)

1. Cut the bacon into very small dice and brown it in a large heavy pot or Dutch oven until golden brown.

2. Add the chopped onion and simmer the mixture in the uncovered pot.

3. When the onion starts to shrink and turns blond, add the cabbage, garlic, caraway seeds and ½ cup warm water. Cover and cook until the cabbage starts to get soft.

4. Add 1 teaspoon salt and the pepper. At the same time add the pears, the halved lemon, the red wine and vinegar. Cook covered for 15 minutes.

5. Add the honey. From this moment on, cook over very low heat.

6. After about 30 minutes look in the pot to see how much liquid remains. If there is too much and the cabbage is "swimming," let more than half of the liquid steam away by cooking without a cover on the pot.

7. When the quantity of the liquid is just right, taste the cabbage. If it is not sweet enough, add brown sugar to achieve the sweet-sour flavor desired. Take out the lemon pieces. Cover again and cook until the cabbage is almost done. By this time the pears will have disappeared completely and the cabbage will have reduced to a third of its original bulk. Adjust salt if necessary.

8. Take from the heat. Leave the cover slightly ajar to keep the cabbage warm till serving time. Serve as accompaniment to roast pork or game.

NOTE: *This is an early nineteenth-century recipe from Sopron.*

It is better to cook this dish a day before you plan to serve it. Then heat it in a double boiler so it will not burn.

BEAN-CABBAGE AS IN ZALAEGERSZEG

Zalaegerszegi babos káposzta   *6 to 8 servings*

1 pound dried pinto beans   2 cups tomato purée
1 pound smoked spareribs,   Salt
    sliced   ½ cup sour cream
2 pounds sauerkraut, rinsed

1. Soak the beans in water overnight.
2. Drain and rinse soaked beans. Add sliced spareribs and enough water to cover. Cook until beans are done, and drain.
3. Remove spareribs, cut off meat and chop it, and discard bones.
4. In a separate pot cook sauerkraut with tomato purée; add additional water if necessary. Cook till done.
5. Put cooked beans, chopped meat and cooked sauerkraut with its juice together. Add salt to taste. Simmer for 10 minutes, then mix in sour cream and remove from heat.
6. Serve as a vegetable accompaniment to roast or fried meats, or as a winter luncheon dish by itself.

BEANS AS IN SOMOGY

Somogyi babfőzelék   *6 to 8 servings*

1 pound dried white beans   1 garlic clove, crushed
1 bay leaf   1 tablespoon vinegar
½ pound double-smoked bacon   1 teaspoon sugar
1 tablespoon flour   ½ cup sour cream
1 small onion, minced   1 teaspoon salt

1. Wash beans well and let them soak in water overnight. (If beans are several years old, add a teaspoon of baking soda to the soaking water.)
2. Add bay leaf and two thirds of the bacon in one chunk to the beans and cook all together for about 1½ hours, till beans are tender. Remove ½ cup of liquid and reserve.
3. Chop the rest of the bacon into little pieces and melt in a frying pan. Add flour, onion and garlic, and cook for a few minutes. Add cool reserved broth and stir well.
4. Drain the cooked beans and return them to the pot. Add bacon and onion mixture, stir, and cook over very low heat for 5 minutes. Add vinegar, sugar and sour cream. Add salt and adjust to taste.

5. Cut the bacon chunk that was cooked with the beans into very small dice. Mix into the beans. Cook for a few minutes longer, and serve.

NOTE: *Do not add salt while you cook beans because salt toughens the skins.*

Do not use regular American bacon because it is the double-smoked bacon that gives the taste to this dish.

In the county of Somogy and many other areas of Hungary, this could be a one-dish meal for a family. If big chunks of bacon or smoked pigs' knuckles are added, it is considered a special treat.

BUTTERED LENTILS

Lencsefőzelék   *4 to 6 servings*

1 pound dried lentils
1 medium-sized onion, minced
1 carrot, peeled and cut into
   thin slices

¼ pound butter
Pinch of ground cloves
1 teaspoon minced flat parsley
¼ teaspoon ground pepper

1. Wash the lentils and soak them in water overnight. Drain.
2. The following day sauté the onion and carrot in 1 tablespoon of the butter.
3. Add cloves, parsley, drained lentils and pepper, and enough water to cover. Cook in a large pot until done, about 1 ½ hours.
4. While the lentils are still very hot stir in the remaining butter until it is melted. Serve with game, game birds and sausages.

SQUASH SLAW WITH SOUR CREAM

Tejfeles tökkáposzta   *4 to 6 servings*

3 pounds summer squash
1 tablespoon salt
2 tablespoons butter
2 tablespoons flour
½ small onion, grated
2 tablespoons minced dill

1 cup stock or water
1 to 2 tablespoons white
   vinegar or lemon juice
1 tablespoon sugar
¼ cup sour cream

1. Peel squash and grate through the large holes of a special squash slicer or standard 4-sided metal grater. Stop grating when you get to the seeds. Or halve the squashes and remove seeds before you start grating. You should end up with a mound of matchsticks, not pulp!

2. Sprinkle with the salt, mix, and let stand under a cover for 1 hour. Squeeze squash and set aside. (To keep summer squash or other summer vegetables from becoming mushy, rinse them in vinegar for a second before you start cooking them.)

3. Meantime make a light *roux* out of butter and flour. Add onion. When onion becomes golden brown, add the dill.

4. Put the *roux* in a large pot and mix well with stock or water. Add squash slaw. Cook for 10 minutes.

5. Add 1 tablespoon vinegar or lemon juice and the sugar, and bring to a boil. Adjust sweetness or sourness to taste. Mix in sour cream and serve.

NOTE: *This is excellent as a cold vegetable or garnish during summer months. Try it with a cold roast chicken or cold sliced duck breast.*

An early nineteenth-century variation: instead of water or stock use strained pickle juice.

FRIED TOMATOES

Paradicsom rántva   4 to 6 servings

2 pounds semiripe small
  tomatoes
1 cup flour
2 eggs
½ cup milk
1 small garlic clove, well
  mashed

6 or 7 sprigs of flat parsley
  (about ¼ cup chopped)
Dash of pepper
1 teaspoon salt
1 cup lard

1. Cut each tomato into 3 fairly thick slices, about ½ inch thick.

2. Mix ⅔ cup of the flour with the eggs, milk, garlic, parsley, pepper and salt. Put remaining ⅓ cup flour on a flat plate.

3. Dip tomato slices first into the flour, then into the batter.

4. Bring lard to frying temperature in a frying pan. Fry batter-coated tomato slices till golden brown.

5. Serve with Tartar Sauce (page 338) as a hot appetizer; or serve as a garnish with roast or fried meats or fish.

YOUNG CORN IN CREAM

Fiatal tejszínes kukorica   *4 to 6 servings*

10 ears of corn, husked	2 egg yolks
⅓ cup heavy cream	½ teaspoon salt
⅛ pound butter	1 teaspoon sugar
1 tablespoon flour	

1. Cook husked cobs in lightly salted water until they are done. Depending on the age of the corn, this can be anywhere from 10 to 20 minutes. Do not overcook. With a sharp knife cut kernels off the cobs.

2. Pour cream and 2 tablespoons of the butter into a separate pot and bring to a boil. Meantime knead the rest of the butter with the flour.

3. When cream starts boiling, lower heat and whip in flour and butter mixture. Cook for 3 or 4 minutes while constantly whipping it.

4. Add the egg yolks and continue whipping for another 3 or 4 minutes. Add corn kernels and shake or stir gently. Add salt and sugar and adjust to taste.

5. Serve as a vegetable accompaniment for fried chicken.

SORREL WITH SOUR CREAM

Tejfeles sóskafőzelék   *4 to 6 servings*

1½ tablespoons lard	¾ cup sour cream
½ small onion, minced	2 tablespoons flour
2 pounds sorrel, trimmed, washed and drained	1 tablespoon sugar

1. Melt the lard in a saucepan and cook onion in it, covered, for about 10 minutes.

2. Add the drained sorrel and cook, covered, over very low heat till sorrel is almost soft.

3. Mix sour cream and flour and stir into cooked sorrel. Simmer for 2 or 3 minutes.

4. Force the vegetable through a sieve or purée in a blender. Put it back over very low heat. Add sugar and simmer for another 2 or 3 minutes.

5. If the purée is too thick, thin it with a few tablespoons of chicken broth or water. Then just before serving whip the purée to make it smooth and creamy. Serve with a simple roast or with boiled meat or poultry.

ASPARAGUS PUDDING

Spárgapudding   6 *servings*

1 pound fresh young asparagus   4 tablespoons butter
Salt   4 eggs, separated
1 roll   4 tablespoons sour cream
½ cup milk

1. Peel asparagus and cut slantwise into 1-inch pieces. Place in saucepan with 1 cup water and 1 teaspoon salt. Cook till done, but it should still be almost crunchy and not soft. Drain.

2. Soak the roll in the milk, then squeeze. Thoroughly butter a pudding mold with 2 tablespoons of the butter.

3. Whip the rest of the butter till foamy. Add the roll, egg yolks, sour cream and 1 teaspoon salt. Whip till well mixed and fluffy.

4. Whip egg whites stiff and fold them in gently with a rubber spatula. Combine the mixture with the cooked asparagus; do it very carefully so as not to break the egg-white foam.

5. Pour the mixture into the buttered pudding mold. Do not fill mold more than three quarters full. Put on a tight-fitting top.

6. Fill a 4-quart pot half full of hot water. Set pudding mold into the pot and cook, with the cover on, for 1 hour.

VARIATION: *To serve this as an appetizer sauté 1 cup bread crumbs in ¼ pound butter till golden brown; pour crumbs on top of pudding or spoon a little over each slice. You may also combine the bread-crumb mixture with grated cheese.*

MUSHROOM PUDDING

Gombapudding   4 *to* 6 *servings*

3 stale rolls   Salt
½ cup milk   5 eggs, separated
1 small onion, grated   1 tablespoon chopped flat
¼ pound butter   parsley
½ pound mushrooms, chopped   2 tablespoons bread crumbs
Pepper

1. Soak rolls in milk. When rolls are soft, squeeze them and force through a sieve.

2. Sauté the grated onion in half of the butter over very low heat.

3. After about 6 minutes add chopped mushrooms, and pepper and salt to taste; mix. After 2 minutes add ½ cup water. Cook until the water disappears. Let the mixture cool.

4. Mix together well the egg yolks, sieved rolls, parsley and remaining butter. Add cooled onion-mushroom mixture.

5. Whip the egg whites until stiff. Gently fold in the bread crumbs, and add to the pudding mixture. Pour into a well-buttered 5-inch metal pudding mold. Do not fill the mold more than three quarters full since the pudding will expand in cooking. Cover the mold tightly.

6. Make a water bath: Put 2 quarts water in a 4-quart pot. Bring the water to a boil and stand the filled pudding mold in it. Cover the water bath. Cook the pudding on top of stove for 1 to 1¼ hours.

NOTE: *The pudding mold used in Hungary has a twist-off top with a handle. Molds like it are available in most shops that sell French kitchen utensils.*

OYSTER PLANT WITH MUSHROOMS

Erdőháti feketegyökér　　　　6 to 8 servings

3 pounds oyster plant (salsify)
Salt
1 small onion, chopped
4 tablespoons butter
½ pound fresh mushrooms, wild or cultivated
1 ounce dried mushrooms
1½ cups chicken broth
1 garlic clove, crushed
Pinch of paprika
Pinch of pepper
½ cup sour cream
2 tablespoons flour
¼ cup heavy sweet cream
1 tablespoon chopped flat parsley

1. Peel oyster plant roots and cook in 2 quarts lightly salted water till done. Drain and set aside, but keep warm.

2. Meantime make the sauce: Sauté onion in butter till limp. Slice the fresh mushrooms and add to onion. Cook for an additional 5 minutes.

3. Boil dried mushrooms in the broth with crushed garlic and spices for 20 minutes.

4. Strain the liquid over the mushroom-onion mixture, and bring it to a boil. Mix in sour cream and flour. Cook over low heat for 5 minutes.

5. Stir in heavy cream. When the sauce starts simmering again, remove from heat.

6. Place the warm oyster plant on a serving platter, pour sauce over, and

sprinkle with chopped parsley. Serve as a vegetable to accompany a fish or roast.

NOTE: *Do not wash mushrooms too much because washing removes a lot of the taste. Dried mushrooms will be especially necessary if you are not using good, fresh wild mushrooms.*

The nickname often used in Hungary for this vegetable is "winter asparagus." Throughout winter and early spring you can cook oyster plant according to most asparagus recipes, hot or cold. Too bad this vegetable is so neglected in the United States.

BAKED PRUNES RADVÁNSZKY

Aszalt szilva Radvánszky módra   *5 or 6 servings*

24 prunes	½ cup sour cream
Juice of ½ lemon	¼ cup bread crumbs
1 teaspoon flour	4 tablespoons sweet butter

1. Preheat oven to 325°F. Cook prunes in lemon juice and 2 cups water until they are soft. Remove cooked prunes with a slotted spoon.

2. Put liquid over lowest possible heat and reduce it by half.

3. Stir flour into sour cream and whip the mixture into the prune liquid. Simmer together for 5 minutes.

4. Place the prunes in an ovenproof casserole. Pour thickened liquid over prunes, sprinkle with bread crumbs, and dot with pieces of butter. Bake in the preheated oven for 30 minutes.

NOTE: *This is an adaptation, with very little change, of a late fifteenth-century description, when this was served with most meats. I see no reason why it couldn't be done in our kitchens, too.*

CAULIFLOWER FRITTER BUDAFOK STYLE

Budafoki rántott karfiol   *4 to 6 servings*

1 head of cauliflower, cut into sections	¾ cup dry white wine
Salt	2 egg whites
½ cup sifted flour	1 cup vegetable oil or clarified butter for frying
1 tablespoon vegetable oil	

1. Cook cauliflower sections in water with 1 teaspoon salt, and drain.

2. Make a batter with the flour, a pinch of salt, 1 tablespoon vegetable oil and the wine. Fold in stiffly beaten egg whites. Batter should have the consistency of a pancake batter.

3. Dip the cooked cauliflower sections into the batter, then place the sections in a sieve to drain off excess batter. Heat the vegetable oil in a frying pan. Fast-fry the cauliflower pieces to a golden brown.

BREADED CAULIFLOWER WITH SOUR-CREAM SAUCE

Bundázott karfiol tejfellel   *4 to 6 servings*

1 cauliflower head, broken into flowerets	Pinch of sugar
	⅔ cup white bread crumbs
Salt	Pinch of white pepper
2 egg yolks, beaten	2 whole eggs
¾ cup sour cream	¼ cup milk
¼ cup heavy sweet cream	2 cups vegetable oil for frying
1 tablespoon lemon juice	

1. Wash the flowerets of cauliflower and let them stand in salted cold water for 1 hour. Rinse.

2. Cook flowerets in 2 quarts of water with 1 tablespoon salt until cooked but still firm.

3. Meantime make the sauce: mix beaten egg yolks, sour cream, heavy cream, lemon juice, pinch of salt and pinch of sugar; cook in the top part of a double boiler for 5 minutes, whipping constantly. Set sauce aside, but try to keep it warm.

4. Mix together bread crumbs, ½ teaspoon salt and the white pepper.

5. In a separate bowl mix together the whole eggs and the milk.

6. Dip the drained and dried cauliflower first into egg and milk mixture, then into the bread-crumb mixture.

7. Heat the vegetable oil to 365°F., then turn heat to low. Carefully put the breaded cauliflower pieces into the oil and fry slowly until golden brown. Drain on absorbent paper.

8. Put the sauce on the bottom of a serving dish and place cauliflower on top of the sauce.

NOTE: *This same sauce can be used for steamed asparagus, whole green beans and other vegetables.*

POTATO CRUST

Burgonyakéreg   *6 servings*

1 pound potatoes   1 tablespoon minced flat parsley
2 eggs   Salt and pepper
2 tablespoons butter

1. Boil potatoes in their skins. Peel potatoes and force the pulp through a sieve. Let it cool.

2. Mix into the sieved pulp the eggs, butter, parsley, and salt and pepper to taste.

3. Butter small tartlet shells or barquettes, or any little molds, and fill them with the potato mixture. Bake them in a 375°F. oven for 10 minutes. Turn out of the molds to serve. These make an excellent garnish for a roast.

VARIATION:

BAKED MEAT AND POTATO CASSEROLE

Húsos burgonyakéreg

1 pound leftover roast pork or   1 tablespoon sour cream
    veal, or a mixture, ground   Pinch of pepper
1 egg   Salt
1 tablespoon tomato purée

1. To make a good winter luncheon dish or a more interesting garnish, butter a small baking pan or ovenproof casserole. Line it with half of the potato mixture.

2. Mix the ground meat with egg, tomato purée, sour cream, pepper, and salt to taste. Pat meat mixture on top of potato layer. Cover meat with remaining potato mixture.

3. Bake in a 375°F. oven for 15 minutes, until top of potatoes is crusty.

SOUR POTATO

Savanyú burgonyafőzelék   *6 servings*

1½ pounds potatoes   1 small onion, minced
1 bay leaf   ¼ cup sour cream
¼ teaspoon black pepper   ½ tablespoon sugar
1 teaspoon salt   1 tablespoon minced parsley
3 tablespoons lard   1 to 2 tablespoons vinegar
3 tablespoons flour

1. Peel potatoes and cut into ½-inch dice. Cook in 2½ cups water with the bay leaf, pepper and salt till potatoes are half done.

2. Heat the lard. Brown the flour and onion in lard till medium golden in color. Add ½ cup cold water and stir till smooth. Pour into the pot in which potatoes are cooking and cook over very low heat till potatoes are done. Stir every now and then.

3. In a bowl mix well the sour cream, sugar, parsley, and vinegar to taste. Pour into the potatoes, bring to a boil, and serve.

VARIATION: *Substitute fresh marjoram for the parsley.*

POTATO CREAM

Tojásos burgonyapüré   *4 to 6 servings*

2¼ pounds potatoes   Pinch of ground mace
¼ pound butter, softened   Salt
4 egg yolks

1. Boil potatoes in skins. When soft peel them. Purée the pulp while still warm, and let it cool.

2. Mix into the purée the butter, egg yolks, mace, and salt to taste. Stir till well mixed.

3. If using this for a border (like duchess potatoes), bake it in a 450°F. oven for about 10 minutes. For an example, see Veal Chops à la Gundel (page 239).

4. You can make potato "biscuits" from the mixture. Drop by large spoonfuls into shallow fat—a mixture of butter and oil—and fry until brown.

NOTE: *This recipe is unquestionably the result of French influence in the early nineteenth century.*

LIPTÓ POTATOES

Liptói burgonya   6 to 8 servings

3 pounds potatoes
½ teaspoon salt
¾ pound Liptó or Brindza
    cheese

¼ pound and ⅛ pound butter
¼ pound double-smoked bacon
1 tablespoon minced fresh dill
¼ cup bread crumbs

1. Preheat oven to 350°F. Cook potatoes in 3 cups salted water until tender, but make sure you don't overcook them. Peel and cut into slices.

2. Rice the cheese. Melt the ¼ pound butter and mix with the cheese. Set aside.

3. Cut bacon into ½-inch dice, and render in a frying pan for about 15 minutes.

4. Take out the fairly crisp bacon cracklings and add them to the cheese mixture. Also mix in the dill. Then gently add the potatoes to the cheese mixture; try not to break up the potato slices too much.

5. Butter a torte pan with the ⅛ pound butter. Sprinkle bread crumbs over it. Spoon the potato-cheese mixture into the pan. Bake in the preheated oven for about 30 minutes.

6. Remove potatoes from oven. Cut and serve the dish like a torte.

NOTE: *In northern Hungary this is eaten as a one-course meal, with the bacon fat as well as the bacon cracklings used instead of butter.*

LAYERED POTATO CASSEROLE

Rakott krumpli   6 to 8 servings

3 pounds potatoes (small
    potatoes if possible)
1½ tablespoons salt
6 hard-boiled eggs
¼ pound butter

¼ pound boiled ham, sliced
¼ pound fresh sausage, sliced
1 cup sour cream
1 tablespoon paprika

1. Preheat oven to 350°F. Drop potatoes in their skins in water to cover with 1 tablespoon salt. Cook until tender.

2. Peel and slice potatoes. Do the same with the hard-boiled eggs.

3. Butter a heatproof glass dish well. Arrange a layer of sliced potatoes neatly on the bottom of the dish. Season with salt.

4. Melt the butter in the top part of a double boiler. Sprinkle a little on top

of potatoes. Cover this layer with ham slices, and top with another layer of sliced potatoes. Again season with salt and sprinkle with melted butter. Arrange egg slices and sausage slices on top. Finish with a final layer of potatoes.

5. Pour any remaining butter on top. Spread sour cream over all and sprinkle with paprika. Bake in the preheated oven for 30 minutes.

VINTNER'S RICE

Boros rízs   *4 servings*

2 tablespoons butter
1 cup uncooked rice
1 small onion, grated
¼ teaspoon white pepper
1 teaspoon salt

1 lemon, peeled and cut into
  very thin slices
½ bay leaf
1 cup dry white wine
1½ cups chicken broth

1. Preheat oven to 350°F. Melt butter in a baking casserole and sauté rice and onion in the butter for 10 minutes, while stirring every now and then.

2. Add pepper, salt, paper-thin lemon slices, bay leaf, wine and chicken broth. Bring to a boil.

3. Bake in the preheated oven for 20 minutes. Serve with fried fish or simple veal dishes.

✫ 26 ✫

SALADS
(SALÁTÁK)

LETTUCE LEAVES IN VINEGAR DRESSING

Ecetes saláta   *4 to 6 servings*

½ cup white vinegar   Dash of salt and pepper
1 tablespoon minced onion   2 heads of lettuce
½ teaspoon sugar   Sunflower oil

1. Mix vinegar, ½ cup water, minced onion, sugar, salt and pepper. Let the dressing stand for 30 minutes.

2. Separate lettuce into leaves. Mix lettuce with dressing, and let leaves stand a little longer in a cool place to absorb flavors.

3. Sprinkle with a little sunflower oil before serving.

NOTE: *This salad is different from the Western ideal; crispness is replaced with a texture like that of a cooked vegetable that has been marinated. The leaves are supposed to be limp. Try the same dressing also on crisp greens.*

CABBAGE SALAD

Káposztasaláta   *4 to 6 servings*

1 small head of cabbage   1 teaspoon salt
1 small onion, grated   ¼ cup olive oil
1 teaspoon sugar   ½ teaspoon caraway seeds

1. Cut cabbage into fine shreds. Cover with 2 quarts hot water and let stand for 30 minutes.

2. Drain cabbage well, and press out liquid.

3. In a separate bowl mix onion, sugar, salt, olive oil and caraway seeds.

4. Mix cabbage slaw and dressing thoroughly. Chill for 10 minutes before serving.

APPLE AND SAVOY-CABBAGE SALAD

Alma-kelkáposztasaláta   *4 to 6 servings*

1 small young Savoy cabbage	Pinch of pepper
Salt	3 apples
2 tablespoons sour cream	Juice of ½ lemon
1 teaspoon prepared mustard	6 fresh mint leaves, minced
1 teaspoon sugar	

1. Wash the young cabbage leaves 4 or 5 times, then cut into a thin slaw. Put in a bowl and sprinkle with salt. Place a plate on top to press it down.

2. After about 30 minutes, press out as much liquid as possible.

3. Meantime mix sour cream, mustard, sugar and pepper. Only now peel and slice the apples, and immediately mix them with lemon juice to prevent browning.

4. Mix apples with cabbage and dressing. Sprinkle salad with the mint. Serve with cold meat or poultry.

CUCUMBER SALAD

Uborkasaláta   *4 servings*

2 medium-sized or large cucumbers	Pinch of sugar
1 teaspoon salt	1 teaspoon sweet paprika
1 medium-sized onion	¼ cup white vinegar

1. Peel cucumbers and cut them into thin slices. If they are very ripe, remove seeds. Mix with the salt, making sure that every slice is salted. Add more salt if needed. Let the slices stand for 30 minutes or, if you have time, for as long as 2 hours.

2. Meantime, peel the onion and cut into hair-thin slices. Place in a mixing bowl and add the sugar, paprika, vinegar and ½ cup water.

3. By now the cucumbers will have released almost a cup of liquid. With your hand press out as much as you can from the slices. Discard the liquid.

4. Put the cucumber slices into the bowl with the onion dressing. Mix well.

Since the cucumbers have already been salted, it's possible that you won't need to add any, but if necessary add up to ½ teaspoon. Adjust vinegar and water according to your taste for vinegar.

5. Serve in individual glass or porcelain salad dishes.

NOTE: *This is exactly the way my family made cucumber salad, although many Hungarian homes mixed cucumbers with sour cream, or with oil and vinegar, or with a sweet-and-sour dressing. This is a deceptively simple recipe with a surprisingly individual taste.*

KNOB CELERY SALAD

Zellersaláta   *4 to 6 servings*

2 good-sized knob celery, or 3 smaller ones	½ tablespoon sugar
	½ tablespoon salt
1 tablespoon lemon juice	½ teaspoon white pepper
1 medium-sized onion, peeled and sliced paper-thin	½ cup white vinegar
	1 tablespoon olive oil
1 tablespoon minced flat parsley	

1. Peel the knob celery and cut into slices with a krinkle-edged knife.
2. Boil the knob celery in 2 cups water with the lemon juice till the slices are soft but not falling apart. Save the water.
3. Sprinkle the onion slices and parsley on the bottom of a shallow serving platter.
4. Bring the water in which you cooked the knob celery to a boil again, and add sugar, salt, pepper and vinegar. Pour the hot dressing over the onion and parsley.
5. Put in the cooked knob celery, very gently so as not to break the slices. Sprinkle with olive oil. Serve the salad when the liquid is cold. This salad will keep in the refrigerator for weeks.

VARIATION: *Try this without the onion; instead use green pepper cut into hair-thin slices.*

NOTE: *When you serve this with a main course, you would not generally serve other vegetables.*

As you have noticed, knob celery is as popular an ingredient in soups and stews as is the carrot in America. Also it is often served as a vegetable, either as a purée or sliced in a sweet-and-sour sauce.

At the turn of the century a few inventive cooks experimented in using knob celery as a substitute for pineapple. According to one of the recipes, the root was sliced, sprinkled with sugar, Kirschwasser and a touch of lemon juice, and marinated in a cool place overnight. In the morning it was sprinkled with a white Tokay dessert wine, and more sugar was added if needed. I have tried it; if you don't try to compare it with fresh pineapple, it can be used as an interesting relish to accompany boiled beef, roast duckling, or a curry.

BEET SALAD GELLÉRT

Gellért saláta　　　　　　　　　　6 to 8 servings

3 pounds beets
½ cup white-wine vinegar, or
　white vinegar
1 tablespoon sugar
1 teaspoon salt
1 teaspoon prepared mustard

Pinch of caraway seeds
1 tablespoon freshly grated
　horseradish (about 2 inches
　of the root, depending on
　its thickness)
1 head of lettuce

1. Cook whole beets in plenty of water. Depending on the age of beets, it will take anywhere from 30 minutes to 1 hour.

2. When beets are tender, drain and peel them and cut them into julienne strips. Mix together vinegar, sugar, salt, mustard, caraway seeds and horseradish. Adjust the sugar and salt to your own taste. Marinate beets in the dressing overnight.

3. When ready to serve, form cups out of the lettuce leaves and fill them with 3 or 4 tablespoons of the beet salad; or put the beet salad on a large platter and encircle it with lettuce leaves. Do not use the liquid.

4. For a very elegant service, use small heads of Boston-type lettuce; remove centers and fill heads with beet salad. Serve one to a person. It isn't exactly the cost of Trimalchio's feast, but for 4 persons you will need 4 heads of lettuce.

SALMAGUNDI

Csalamádé　　　　　　　　　　6 servings

1 young cucumber
2 green peppers
1 medium-sized onion
1 small cabbage head
2 medium-sized green tomatoes

Salt
½ cup white vinegar
¼ teaspoon white pepper
¼ teaspoon sugar

1. Peel the cucumber and blanch the green peppers. Remove ribs and seeds of peppers. Peel the onion, and take off the outer leaves of the cabbage. Wash and dice the green tomatoes.

2. Slice or shred the cucumber, green peppers, onion and cabbage as thin as you can, leaving them in separate piles or in bowls. Mix a sprinkle of salt with each vegetable and leave them for 1 hour.

3. Press out as much liquid as possible from the salted vegetables. Mix together and add diced tomatoes.

4. Mix the vinegar and ½ cup water with ½ teaspoon salt. Add pepper and sugar, and bring just to a boil. Remove from heat and cool.

5. When the dressing is cool, mix with the vegetables. Let the vegetables soak in the liquid for a few hours before serving.

VARIATION: *For a relish that keeps, place the vegetables layer by layer in a 1-gallon jar with a wide mouth. Use the same liquid mixture, only use more of it, and cover the vegetables with liquid. Cover the jar tightly. You can keep this relish mixture in the refrigerator for quite a few months.*

NOTE: *In our calorie-conscious age, this is a remarkably pleasant and refreshing salad or accompaniment to cold meats. It tastes very good without any oil or mayonnaise or similar ingredient.*

If green tomatoes are not available, do not use ripe tomatoes, but substitute diced cooked knob celery or kohlrabi.

GUNDEL SALAD

Gundel saláta   *about 8 servings*

1 large tomato	16 asparagus tips, each about
2 green peppers	4 inches long
3 very small cucumbers	Sugar
Salt	¼ pound young green beans
White pepper	1 small head of Boston lettuce
2 tablespoons white-wine	3 tablespoons olive oil
vinegar	½ teaspoon tomato paste (or
4 or 5 mushroom caps	less)
Juice of 1 lemon	1 tablespoon minced flat parsley

1. *Tomato:* Dip it into boiling water for a few seconds. Peel, slice, and remove seeds. Put aside.

2. *Green peppers:* Remove ribs and seeds and cut into lengthwise slices. Dip into boiling water for 30 seconds. Drain, and put aside.

3. *Cucumbers:* Peel and cut into very thin slices. Mix with ½ teaspoon

335

salt. Let stand for 1 hour, then squeeze, and discard the liquid extracted by the salt. Mix with a pinch of white pepper and the vinegar, and put aside.

4. *Mushrooms:* Peel mushroom caps and cut into thin slices. Bring ½ cup water to a boil and add half of the lemon juice and ¼ teaspoon salt. Cook mushrooms for 3 minutes. Drain, and put aside.

5. *Asparagus tips:* Clean the asparagus and cut the tips into halves. Bring 1 cup water with ½ teaspoon sugar and ½ teaspoon salt to a boil. Cook till tips are done but still crunchy. Put aside.

6. *Green beans:* Cut beans into slanted (so-called French) slices. Bring ½ cup water to boil with ½ teaspoon salt, and cook beans till they are done but not soft. Put aside.

7. *Boston lettuce:* Wash in several waters and dry leaves with paper towels. Mix olive oil, remaining lemon juice, ½ teaspoon salt, ½ teaspoon sugar, a pinch of white pepper, the tomato paste and parsley. Adjust salt and sugar to your taste. Toss lettuce leaves, taking care not to break leaves.

8. Arrange the lettuce leaves, already lightly coated with dressing, on a large flat serving platter, round or oval. Place cucumbers, asparagus tips, green peppers, beans and tomato slices in attractive separated mounds on the lettuce. Sprinkle mushroom slices over all. Chill the salad for about 30 minutes.

NOTE: *This recipe is an interesting illustration of Károly Gundel's approach to marrying the feminine French style of salad making with the masculine, and certainly less subtle, Hungarian habits.*

This is a perfect occasion for a lucky Hungarian housewife to use her Holics (*Holitsch or Hollitsch*) *or* Habán (*Habaner*) *pottery platter. Holics is a mid-eighteenth-century Hungarian faïence, mostly made in Baroque style. Habán ceramics were made by Swiss emigrants from about 1600 on; throughout the centuries they were considered more desirable than dishes made of gold.*

SUMMER PICKLE

Vizes uborka

30 even-sized cucumbers, each 4 to 5 inches long	6 tablespoons salt
1 large bunch of dill	1 scant teaspoon flour
3 garlic cloves, crushed	1 slice of rye bread

1. Wash cucumbers thoroughly; sometimes you even have to scrub them with a brush. Dry with toweling. Cut off both ends. Make a lengthwise inci-

sion in the center of each cucumber, then make a quarter turn and do the same. This way you have a crosscut so liquid can penetrate the inside. Be sure not to cut closer than 1 inch from the ends so the cucumber will not fall apart. Do this with most of the cucumbers, but leave a few with only one center cut in case you want to stuff them later on.

2. Place half of the dill in the bottom of a 1-gallon jar. Add 1 garlic clove.

3. Stand the cucumbers on end in the bottom of the jar. Fit them in as tightly as you can. After you have done one layer, add the rest of the dill and garlic and continue with the tight packing of the cucumbers.

4. Boil 4 quarts water with the salt. Caution: Stand the pickle jar in hot water to prevent cracking! Pour the hot water and salt over the pickles. Sprinkle flour on top and cover with the slice of rye bread. Cover the top with a lid, or tightly wrap a moistened cloth around the jar top.

5. Put the jar in the sun or in a warm place for 4 or 5 days. Moisten the cloth every morning and every noon. By that time the pickles should be what is generally referred to as "semi-sour."

6. Remove everything from the jar. Strain the pickle juice. Put the pickles in the jar again and pour the strained juice over them. After this, store the pickles under refrigeration.

NOTE: *Fermenting vegetables is an ancient Hungarian custom which was brought over from Asia. Although vinegar pickling is also very common, particularly for pickles put away for the winter months, natural fermentation —which scientists generally call the milk-acid type—produces a much more natural-tasting relish. When one considers how easy this is to do and the vast difference between the commercial and the homemade article, it is difficult to understand why this natural pickling is not a more common practice.*

The aroma of the fermenting vegetables is pungent. If you do this inside, use the lid rather than the cloth, but cover the jar loosely. It is better to let the pickle ferment in a sunny place of a yard or garden.

Of course you must use unwaxed cucumbers for making pickles.

For elegant dinners, these pickles are peeled and iced.

This pickle juice is a refreshing summer drink. Hungarian women swear by it as the best brew for a good complexion.

✶ 27 ✶

SAUCES
(MÁRTÁSOK)

TO understand the Hungarian eating experience is to be aware of its dislike of "put-together" cookery. French cuisine, *grande* or otherwise, makes a dazzling virtue out of the necessity that prevailed in the pre-refrigerator era, to cover the sometimes questionable condition of fish and meat.

Making a separate sauce is the exception in the Hungarian kitchen, but when it's done, it's done quickly and inexpensively. These simple preparations may not have the subtlety of French sauces, but they are just right for the dishes they are supposed to enhance.

TARTAR SAUCE

Tartármártás   *about 2 cups sauce*

3 egg yolks	1 tablespoon lemon juice
¾ cup sour cream	Pinch of white pepper
¼ tablespoon salt	2 tablespoons olive oil
½ tablespoon sugar	¼ cup heavy sweet cream
1 teaspoon prepared mustard	¼ cup dry white wine

1. Stir well the egg yolks, sour cream, salt, sugar, mustard, lemon juice and pepper.

2. Put the mixture in the top part of a double boiler over steam. When the steam starts to cook the mixture, whip with the right hand and with the left hand add the olive oil drop by drop. (If you cook this over direct heat, make sure that the heat is not too high or you will make scrambled eggs out of the

mixture.) Add the oil very slowly, otherwise the ingredients will not amalgamate.

3. While continuing to whip the sauce, add heavy cream and finally the wine.

4. Adjust the sugar and salt; Hungarians generally like this sauce much sweeter than do Western nations. Serve with various fish dishes, Breaded Veal Knuckles (page 238) and many other dishes.

GREEN SAUCE

Zöld mártás   *about 1 ½ cups sauce*

4 or 5 hard-boiled eggs
1 tablespoon prepared mustard
Juice of ½ lemon
2 cups sour cream
1 teaspoon paprika
Pinch of white pepper

5 or 6 scallions, cut into small
   pieces, or the same amount
   of chives
3 tablespoons minced flat
   parsley

1. Separate the eggs. Place the yolks in a mixing bowl. Add mustard, lemon juice, sour cream, paprika and pepper. Mash with a fork till quite smooth.

2. Add chopped scallions and parsley. Add fine-chopped egg whites. Mix well. Use just as you would use a mayonnaise.

LEEK SAUCE

Póréhagyma-mártás   *about 3 cups sauce*

2 white rolls with crust
3 hard-boiled egg yolks
4 leeks, cleaned and chopped
   fine
1 cup mayonnaise

½ cup sour cream
Juice of ½ lemon
1 tablespoon sugar
1 tablespoon salt

1. Soak white rolls in lukewarm water for 5 minutes. Squeeze them, add hard-boiled egg yolks, and force both through a sieve.

2. Cook cleaned chopped leeks in 1 cup water. Drain them and purée through a sieve or in a blender.

3. Put the sieved roll and egg-yolk mixture in a mixing bowl. Add leek purée, mayonnaise, sour cream, lemon juice, sugar and salt. Mix well.

4. Adjust salt, sugar and lemon juice to taste. Serve this cold sauce with fish, stuffed eggs, croquettes.

SPICY COLD TOMATO SAUCE

Füszeres hideg paradicsommártás   *about 2 cups sauce*

6 medium-sized, very ripe
  tomatoes
¼ teaspoon freshly ground
  black pepper
¼ teaspoon ground dried

cherry pepper
2 tablespoons oil
1 medium-sized onion, peeled
  and minced

1. Cut tomatoes into small pieces. Cook tomatoes, using only ¼ cup water at the beginning and only adding more if necessary. Cook for about 1 hour over very, very low heat. If tomatoes are completely puréed, sometimes you may have to cook them for a longer time.

2. Force tomatoes through a sieve (do not use the blender for this!) to remove skin and seeds.

3. Add black pepper and ground cherry pepper. Drop by drop whip in the oil till completely absorbed.

4. Finally, mix in the minced (almost puréed) onion, and let the sauce cool.

NOTE: *This is a South Hungarian sauce which is served with all kinds of grilled, roasted or boiled meat or poultry dishes.*

Eliminate some of the cherry pepper if you are not fond of spicy foods. In Hungary even more cherry pepper is used, and twice as much oil.

The Serbs call this sauce ljutenica.

PÖRKÖLT BROTH

Pörkölt lé   *about 1½ cups sauce*

1 medium-sized onion, minced
1 teaspoon lard
2 green peppers, sliced
2 ripe medium-sized tomatoes,
  peeled and seeded

1 cup strong chicken broth
1 tablespoon paprika
Salt

1. Cook the onion in hot lard, covered, till soft.

2. Add green peppers. Dice tomatoes and add. Cook, covered, for an additional 5 minutes.

3. Add the broth, paprika, and salt to taste. Cook till done, usually about 30 minutes. The dressing should have body; tomato should not have become completely puréed.

This dressing or sauce can be used for noodles or *tarhonya* when meat is roasted or fried and thus has no gravy.

HORSERADISH RELISH

Ecetes tormamártás   *about 1 cup relish*

1 horseradish root, peeled and grated
½ teaspoon salt

1 teaspoon sugar
1 teaspoon cider vinegar
2 tablespoons sour cream

Mix grated horseradish with salt, sugar, vinegar and sour cream.

HORSERADISH SOUR-CREAM SAUCE

Tejfeles tormamártás   *about 2½ cups sauce*

¼ pound grated horseradish
3 tablespoons butter
2 tablespoons flour
½ cup meat broth
½ cup milk
1 teaspoon sugar

1 teaspoon salt
1 to 2 tablespoons white vinegar or lemon juice
Pinch of pepper
½ cup sour cream

1. Pour ½ cup boiling water over grated horseradish. Let it stand for a couple of minutes, then drain.

2. Make a *roux* with the butter and flour. Stir, then dilute with the broth and milk. Add sugar and salt. Bring the mixture to a simmer, then let it cook over very low heat for about 5 minutes.

3. Add grated horseradish together with vinegar and pepper and cook for another 10 to 15 minutes.

4. Adjust salt and sweet and sour to your taste, with more accent on the sour.

5. Just before serving, whip in the sour cream.

PICKLE SAUCE

Uborkamártás   *about 1½ cups sauce*

10 small hard pickles	Pinch of saffron
⅛ pound butter	2 tablespoons sour cream
2 tablespoons flour	1 teaspoon wine vinegar
1 cup stock	

1. Mince the pickles. Cook them in the butter for 5 minutes.
2. Sprinkle pickles with flour and stir. Cook for another 5 minutes.
3. Add cold stock, stir, and bring the mixture to a slow boil. Add saffron and simmer the sauce for 15 minutes.
4. Turn off heat and stir in sour cream and vinegar.

CREAM SAUCE WITH GRATED CHEESE (FOR FISH)

Sajtos krémmártás (halhoz)   *about 2½ cups sauce*

⅛ pound butter	¼ cup grated Parmesan cheese
¼ cup flour	½ teaspoon salt
1 cup fish stock (see below)	2 egg yolks
1 cup heavy cream	

1. Melt butter and add flour; stir into a *roux.* Do not cook it long; you need a light *roux.*
2. Slowly add cooled fish stock, whipping the sauce constantly as you do. Add cream and continue whipping.
3. Reduce heat to very low and simmer the sauce for 30 minutes.
4. Remove from heat and mix in the grated cheese. Add salt and adjust to taste.
5. Just before serving an oven-poached or baked fish, whip ½ cup of the sauce with the egg yolks, then add the mixture to the rest of the sauce. Cook very carefully over low heat or in the top part of a double boiler for a few minutes longer, whipping the sauce all the time.
6. If you are going to use the sauce over a fish which then has to be baked in the oven, do not add the egg yolks but use as completed in Step 5.

SIMPLE FISH STOCK

Hal-alaplé   *1 cup stock*

2 pounds fresh-water fish—   2 carrots, peeled and sliced thin
  head, bones, skin (not gills)   1 small bay leaf
1 slice of lemon   1 bunch of parsley

Put all ingredients in 1 quart water in a large kettle. Cook together, without a cover, till liquid is reduced to about 1 cup of liquid. Strain through a double layer of cheesecloth and put aside.

NOTE: *This sauce is a simplification of the classic French version that is used commonly in Hungarian restaurant and hotel kitchens.*

ANCHOVY SAUCE

Ajókamártás   *about 3 cups sauce*

⅛ pound butter   1½ cups beef stock or broth
¼ cup flour   1 teaspoon lemon juice
6 anchovy fillets, puréed   Salt
½ small onion, grated   ½ cup sour cream
Handful of fine-chopped chives

1. Make a *roux* with the butter and flour, letting it brown but not burn. Add a little cold water and stir until smooth.
2. Mix in puréed anchovies, grated onion and chopped chives. Add broth and cook the sauce over low heat for 20 minutes.
3. Add lemon juice; add salt to taste. Just before serving, mix in sour cream.

PAPRIKA ESSENCE

Paprikaszín   *½ to ¾ cup essence*

1 cup lard   1 teaspoon salt
1 tablespoon paprika

1. Place the lard in a frying pan and warm it, *do not heat it.* It is most important that you do *not* heat the lard to frying temperature because the paprika would burn immediately and both color and taste would be lost. Lard should only be a little over lukewarm when you put paprika into it. Add pa-

prika. Mix well, then add ¼ cup water and the salt. Stir again and bring to a boil.

2. Turn off heat and let the mixture rest for 30 minutes.

3. Skim off the top surface, which is the so-called paprika essence. Discard the rest.

4. Use as directed in different recipes. Generally you need only 1 teaspoon or 1 tablespoon of this essence to dribble on top of *székelygulyás,* stuffed cabbage, dishes with sour cream on top, etc.

RED PEPPER JAM

Paprikalekvár   *about six 6-ounce jars*

2½ pounds ripe red peppers

1. *Warning:* Peppers should be preferably fleshy and thick, and they must be totally ripe and completely red. Wash the peppers. Split them and remove the ribs and seeds. Cook in 2 cups water till peppers become a thick purée.

2. Force the purée through a sieve or similar apparatus, but do not purée in a blender because the skins should not go into the jam.

3. Fill sterilized jars with the jam and cover openings with pergament or parchment paper. Tie the paper on tightly with string.

4. Use a large kettle for a water bath and place jars in it; add enough water to reach halfway up the jars. Cover the water bath, and steam over low heat for 30 minutes.

5. Remove jars from the water bath and let them cool. You now have one of the best food flavorings or condiments you have ever worked with, particularly good when you have no fresh green pepper or tomato and would like to perk up the taste of a soup, stew or similar dish. By adding a little of this traditional Hungarian pantry staple, you can achieve minor miracles.

❈ 28 ❈

BREAD AND BISCUITS
(KENYÉR ÉS POGÁCSÁK)

BREAD is revered in Hungary, perhaps as in no other place in the world, and country folks still call it "life." As a child, if I dropped a slice of bread, I had to kiss it before eating it.

Breads made in the provinces have the delicacy of a cake, the complexity of a sophisticated sauce and the sheen of a Chinese pottery glaze. Certain areas use hops as a yeast, which makes the bread very light, almost balloon-high. Other areas use vegetable broth instead of water. Until World War I it was possible to purchase a starter from women who made it professionally.

Potato bread was one of my mother's specialties. It's interesting to note that she got her starter from her mother in 1921, when she married my father, just as her mother must have gotten it when she married my grandfather. So the bread we ate had a micro part of the past centuries.

POTATO BREAD WITH CARAWAY SEEDS

Köménymagos krumplis kenyér   *1 loaf*

3 medium-sized potatoes
1 envelope of dry granular
  yeast, or 1 cake of compressed
  fresh yeast

2 pounds bread flour (see
  Note)
1½ tablespoons salt
½ tablespoon caraway seeds

1. Boil potatoes in their skins. Peel them, and mash through a sieve or potato ricer while warm. You should have 1 cup mashed potatoes. Let cool.

2. Place yeast in ½ cup warm (not hot) water, and mix well with 3 table-

spoons flour in a 4-quart bowl. Let the starter rise for 30 minutes.

3. Add 2 cups lukewarm water, the salt and the caraway seeds. Add the rest of the flour and the mashed potatoes.

4. Knead the dough until it separates from hands and sides of the pot. This will take from 10 to 12 minutes.

5. Let the dough rise until it doubles in bulk. Depending on the temperature, the nature of the flour and the yeast, it will take anywhere from 1 to 2 hours.

6. Preheat oven to 400°F. Place the dough on a floured board and rework it for a few minutes. Shape it into a loaf, and let it rise for about 30 minutes.

7. Dip a brush into water and brush it on the center of bread. Then make an incision in the loaf. Bake it in the preheated oven for 45 minutes, or until it is done.

NOTE: *You may be able to purchase bread flour from a local baker. For this recipe, try to get some. At least use* unbleached *all-purpose flour. Bread flour is made from hard wheat with high protein content. All-purpose flour is a blend of hard and soft wheats; while it is satisfactory for most home uses, it will give different results from bread flour.*

It is most difficult to get the texture of Hungarian homemade bread using the home oven, but following this procedure you will come very close to the type of bread that is eaten in Hungarian homes.

As a child I had two standing jobs; one was cutting little labels and writing our name on them so my mother could stick one on each of the two huge loaves baked every week. The other was delivering the loaves in their basket to the "Nyuli-Bakery." I guess I wasn't trusted with the taking-home part.

POTATO SCONE

Burgonyalángos   16 *large scones*

3 or 4 medium-sized Idaho potatoes	½ teaspoon sugar
	1⅔ cups whole-wheat flour
½ cup lukewarm milk	½ teaspoon salt
½ envelope yeast	Vegetable oil or lard for frying

1. Boil the potatoes in their skins in salted water. Peel them while still warm and immediately mash them and put through a sieve or ricer. There should be 1½ cups mashed potatoes. Let them cool.

2. Mix the lukewarm milk with the yeast, sugar and 2 tablespoons flour. Let the starter rest for 10 minutes.

3. Add mashed potatoes, remaining flour and the salt. Knead the dough well. Set the dough aside and let it double in bulk, usually about 45 minutes.

4. Roll out the dough on a floured board to ½-inch thickness. Cut it into even shapes—squares, rounds or strips—sometimes making little notches alongside the edges to provide a more interesting appearance when finished. Also, prick with a knife-point to prevent bubbling during cooking.

5. Put enough vegetable oil or lard in a frying pan to reach a depth of ½ inch. Fry the scones over low heat. Oil or lard has to be replenished sometimes, particularly if heat is too low. If heat is turned high, scones will burn.

NOTE: *Sometimes garlic is rubbed on these scones, and they may be sprinkled with additional salt and paprika of the hotter variety. This way it's called Hussar Toast.*

This is a perfect wintertime snack, fine to accompany a good glass of beer or wine.

POGÁCSA

Pogácsa roughly translated means biscuit. Once in Debrecen I was served a *pogácsa* one foot in diameter, which surely must be the Goliath of biscuits. Although there are only two basic types, salty and sweet, within these limits there are many different kinds of *pogácsa*.

BUTTER BISCUITS

Vajas pogácsa   *12 to 15 biscuits*

12 ounces flour
8 ounces sweet butter
4 egg yolks

4 ounces powdered sugar
½ teaspoon salt
1 whole egg for egg wash

1. Mix flour and butter with a pastry blender until the mixture forms crumbs. The butter particles should be about the size of green peas.

2. Add 4 egg yolks, the sugar and salt. Work the mixture together speedily, then knead for a minute or so. Roll the dough in a ball, cover with wax paper, and place in refrigerator overnight.

3. Preheat oven to 350°F. Roll out dough between 2 pieces of wax paper into a sheet 1 inch thick. Cut into rounds with a 2½-inch cookie cutter.

4. Beat the whole egg. With a knife, score a latticework pattern on top of each biscuit. Brush egg wash on top of biscuits.

5. Place biscuits on a cookie sheet, and bake in the preheated oven for 25 to 30 minutes, or until golden brown and firm in the middle.

6. Let cool completely before eating. The texture should be crumbly, almost like a shortbread.

7. These will last in a cookie jar for weeks, in the refrigerator for months and in the freezer, if properly protected, probably indefinitely. After storage, gently warm them in a 200°F. oven before serving.

NOTE: *This recipe was given to me by the owners of Paprikás Weiss, the fine Hungarian fancy food shop in New York City, after I had admired and enjoyed their butter biscuits for many years.*

LITTLE BUTTER BISCUITS I

Vajas édes pogácsa I   *30 biscuits*

½ envelope of yeast	3 eggs
¼ cup lukewarm milk	¼ pound sweet butter
3 tablespoons sugar	½ teaspoon salt
1½ cups flour	2 tablespoons sour cream

1. Soak the yeast in the lukewarm milk, together with the sugar, for 10 minutes.

2. Mix yeast with flour, 2 eggs, the butter, salt and sour cream. Knead the dough well, then let it rest for 30 minutes.

3. Roll out the dough on a floured board. Fold it and let it rest again for 30 minutes. Preheat oven to 375°F.

4. Roll out the dough again on a floured board to 1-inch thickness. With a biscuit cutter of 1-inch diameter, punch out biscuits.

5. With the edge of a knife, make crisscross cuts on top. Beat remaining egg with 1 teaspoon water. With a feather brush, spread the tops of the biscuits with this egg wash.

6. Bake in the preheated oven for 15 minutes.

NOTE: *These are an ideal accompaniment to tea. The quality of the butter is very important; if so-called "tub butter" is available, by all means use it.*

LITTLE BUTTER BISCUITS II

Vajas édes pogácsa II   *30 biscuits*

1 pound flour	1 whole egg
½ pound sweet butter	2 tablespoons sour cream
4 tablespoons granulated sugar	1 extra egg yolk
½ teaspoon salt	

1. Mix flour with butter until the mixture is crumbly. Sprinkle with sugar and salt and add the whole egg and the sour cream. Knead quickly, but don't work on it for more than a few minutes.

2. Roll out the dough on a floured board and fold it. Place it in the refrigerator for 30 minutes. Preheat oven to 400°F.

3. Repeat the kneading, rolling, folding and resting process.

4. Roll out the dough again, and cut out biscuits with a 1- or 2-inch biscuit cutter.

5. With the point of a knife score the tops of the biscuits in a lattice pattern. Beat the egg yolk with 1 teaspoon water, and brush this glaze on the tops.

6. Bake in the preheated oven for 20 minutes.

NOTE: *This is a more crumbly biscuit, and also sweeter than the first.*

All ingredients should be cold, and the utensils you use should be cold as well. You must make these fast, otherwise you'll get the wrong texture.

COTTAGE-CHEESE BISCUITS

Túrós pogácsa   *30 biscuits*

½ pound butter	½ pound cottage cheese
½ pound flour	1 egg yolk
½ teaspoon salt	

1. Mix butter, flour and salt until the mixture forms crumbs. If the butter is cold, grate it.

2. Sieve or rice the cottage cheese and combine with butter mixture. Knead it very fast; do not work it for more than a couple of minutes.

3. Roll out the dough on a floured board, and fold it. Place in refrigerator for 30 minutes.

4. Repeat kneading, rolling and resting in refrigerator twice. Preheat oven to 375°F.

5. Finally roll out the dough to 1-inch thickness. Cut it into any size rounds with a biscuit cutter.

6. With the point of a knife score the tops of the biscuits in a lattice pattern. Beat the egg yolk with 1 teaspoon water, and brush the glaze on the biscuit tops.

7. Bake in the preheated oven for 20 to 25 minutes, or until golden brown —more golden than brown. They should look like the color of 24-carat gold.

8. Serve these as a snack, or as an accompaniment to wine. If you punch them out with a small cutter, you can use them to accompany soups the way the Russians use *pirozhki.*

VARIATION: *Potato Biscuit* krumplis pogácsa: *Substitute for cottage cheese mashed potatoes made of ½ pound potatoes weighed after peeling. As you notice, the trick here is a one-one-one relationship between the ingredients; this is a traditional Hungarian formula.*

Add a good pinch of freshly ground black pepper to the dough for this variation.

CRACKLING BISCUIT

Tepertős pogácsa   *30 biscuits*

3 tablespoons milk	1 tablespoon rum
1 pound flour	1 tablespoon salt
1 envelope of yeast	1 teaspoon pepper
1 whole egg	¼ pound lard, melted
½ pound pork cracklings,	⅓ cup dry white wine
ground or chopped	1 extra egg yolk

1. Heat milk till lukewarm. Make a starter dough with the milk, 1 tablespoon of the flour and the yeast. Let the starter rise for 10 minutes.

2. Mix remaining flour with 1 whole egg, the cracklings, rum, salt, pepper, melted lard and wine. Mix in the starter, and knead well.

3. Let the dough rise in a lukewarm place until it doubles in bulk, 30 to 45 minutes.

4. Roll out the dough on a floured board and fold it. Cover it with a clean cloth and let it rest for 10 minutes.

5. Repeat the same procedure twice or three times—rolling, folding, resting. Preheat oven to 400°F.

6. Finally roll the dough to 2-inch thickness. With a biscuit cutter 1½ inches in diameter, punch out biscuits.

7. With a sharp knife score the tops of the biscuits in a lattice pattern. Beat the egg yolk with 1 teaspoon water, and brush the glaze on the biscuit tops. Let them rest until this glaze dries, about 10 minutes.

8. Bake in the preheated oven until golden brown, about 25 minutes.

Note *on Cracklings: Pork cracklings can generally be purchased in a Hungarian, Czech, German or Austrian butcher shop. If they are not available to you, take a slab bacon and leave on the skin a layer of fat about ½ inch thick. Cut the slab into 2-inch pieces. Put in a heavy pan with about 3 tablespoons water and 2 tablespoons milk. This will make it taste almost nutty. Cook slowly until most of the fat is rendered.*

With goose cracklings you use a slightly different method. When you cut off goose fat, make sure that you cut it with skin on one end and a little bit of the breast meat on the other. Make a few incisions on the inside, leaving the outside skin intact. Cut into about 2-inch squares. Put the pieces into a pot and barely cover with water. Start the cooking under a cover, over medium-high heat. When the water evaporates, remove the cover and increase the heat to render and brown the cracklings. Turn the pieces and move them around to make sure that they don't burn.

At the strategic moment, remove the pot from the heat and sprinkle it with a few drops of cold water. The best way is to dip your hands into cold water and just shake the water over the cracklings; make sure that your face is not directly above. Remove cracklings; if they still contain too much fat, gently press them with a spoon. (Save the precious fat, of course.)

When you cut pieces of pork or goose fat, try to cut them as evenly as possible so one piece will not burn before the other is done. When the color resembles the crust of a hard roll, the cracklings are generally done.

In peasant houses, where saving was vital, instead of washing out the pan in which fat was rendered, after removing the cracklings and the fat, the cook threw flour into the pan to absorb the fat remaining; the resulting mixture was then used at a later date as roux.

This crackling biscuit is another perfect accompaniment to a glass of beer. It can be made in any size. For a stag party double the size of the biscuits.

CABBAGE BISCUIT

Káposztás pogácsa   *about 2 dozen*

1 small head of cabbage	1¼ cups flour
Salt	1 teaspoon baking powder
10 tablespoons butter	1 egg yolk
½ tablespoon granulated sugar	1 tablespoon sour cream
½ teaspoon freshly ground pepper	1 whole egg

1. Shred cabbage and mix with 1 tablespoon salt. Let it stand for at least 1 hour. Squeeze it dry.

2. Melt 2 tablespoons of the butter in a frying pan and add the sugar. Brown it carefully; don't let it burn. Add the cabbage and wilt over very low heat for about 30 minutes, or until brownish and cooked. Add the pepper and mix. Remove cabbage from the frying pan and set aside to cool.

3. With a pastry blender mix remaining 8 tablespoons butter, the flour and baking powder until the mixture forms crumbs. Add egg yolk, ½ teaspoon salt and the sour cream. Knead it quickly, to make a dough. Wrap in wax paper and put in the refrigerator for 30 minutes.

4. Remove dough from refrigerator and mix in the cold cabbage mixture. Put it back into wax paper and refrigerate for another 30 minutes. Preheat oven to 375°F.

5. Remove dough from refrigerator and roll between sheets of wax paper to ½-inch thickness.

6. With a 1-inch biscuit cutter, cut out biscuits. Place them on a baking sheet.

7. Score them with a knife. Beat the whole egg with 1 teaspoon water, and brush this glaze over the biscuits.

8. Bake in the preheated oven for about 30 minutes, or until golden.

NOTE: *You must work fast during blending and even more so during kneading.*

These are perfect cocktail snacks. I even serve them with a roast as the English serve Yorkshire pudding, making them double size for this.

* 29 *

DESSERT CREAMS, SWEET SAUCES
AND FRUIT DESSERTS
(KRÉMEK, ÉDES MÁRTÁSOK
ÉS GYÜMÖLCSÖK)

APRICOT CREAM AS IN KECSKEMÉT

Kecskeméti sárgabarackkrém   *8 to 12 servings*

5 egg yolks
⅔ cup plus 3 tablespoons sugar
1 tablespoon flour
½ vanilla bean
1¼ cups milk
2 envelopes of unflavored
   gelatin

2 cups heavy cream
35 to 40 cooked apricot halves
1 cup thick apricot jam
¼ cup Hungarian apricot
   brandy

1. Mix egg yolks, ⅓ cup of the sugar and the flour. Scrape inside of vanilla bean into the egg yolks and mix well.

2. Bring milk to a boil; add to the egg yolks, and again bring to a boil, whipping all the while. Set aside to cool.

3. Mix 1 envelope of gelatin with ¼ cup cold water, then add ¾ cup hot water and stir until gelatin is completely dissolved. Cool to lukewarm, then mix with the custard.

4. Whip heavy cream and 3 tablespoons sugar till stiff. Fold into the custard and gelatin mixture.

5. Mix remaining ⅓ cup sugar and ¾ cup water, and bring to the boiling

point. Mix second envelope of gelatin with ¼ cup cold water. When gelatin is softened, mix it with the sugar and water.

6. Pour the gelatin-syrup mixture into a 2-quart mold. When the gelatin cools and starts to jell, twist and turn the mold in such a way that the mold is coated with gelatin all over the inside.

7. When almost jelled, line the mold with apricot halves.

8. Pour in the jellied custard and let it solidify for 6 to 8 hours, or overnight.

9. To unmold, dip the mold carefully into warm water, but not too long, so as not to dissolve the gelatin.

10. Mix jam with apricot brandy, and serve separately.

NOTE: *The city of Kecskemét is famous for its apricots. This dessert is always made there during summertime. To prepare the apricots, peel and pit them, and cook with ¼ pound sugar and ½ cup water until they become glossy but not soft.*

WITCHES' FROTH

Boszorkányhab   *6 servings*

4 apples   2 egg whites
1¼ cups vanilla sugar   Juice of 1 small lemon

1. Bake the whole apples. Peel them and remove cores. Sieve the pulp or purée in a blender.

2. Add vanilla sugar and egg whites to the apple purée, and whip the mixture for about 15 minutes, or until a spoon stands up in it.

3. Finally, add the lemon juice and continue whipping for a few more minutes.

4. Serve with a homemade cookie, preferably a large flat wafer (see Rolled Wafer, page 427), to use as a dipper-accompaniment.

NOTE: *When you have a heavy meal which needs the balance of a feather-weight sweet, you have the perfect choice in Witches' Froth.*

To give an extra dimension to this froth, use the juice of only ½ lemon and add 2 tablespoons apple brandy (applejack or Calvados).

WINE CREAM

Borsodó   8 *servings*

3 egg yolks
1 whole egg
½ cup sugar
1 teaspoon fine-grated lemon
   rind

¼ vanilla bean
1 cup fruity white wine—
   Riesling

1. Mix egg yolks, whole egg, sugar and lemon rind well. Scrape the inside of the vanilla bean into the mixture and add the wine.

2. Put the mixture in the top part of a double boiler and cook it over simmering water, stirring constantly, till the mixture thickens. (If you are an experienced cook, you can do this over direct heat, but you must stir the mixture all the while.)

3. Serve as a sauce for desserts, for instance Golden Dumpling Cake (page 399). Or serve as a cream dessert accompanied by little cakes or cookies.

VARIATION: *If you like a thicker mixture, mix ½ tablespoon flour with the egg yolks in the beginning. Cook the wine cream and then mix in 2 egg whites, beaten stiff.*

NOTE: *This sauce is similar to the Italian* zabaglione. *It came to Hungary with the Italian Queen to King Matthias at the end of the fifteenth century, about the same time that it reached France under the name* sabayon.

MILK AND RUM CREAM

Tejsodó   6 *servings*

1¼ cups milk
½ vanilla bean
2 egg whites
½ cup plus 2 tablespoons sugar

3 egg yolks
1 teaspoon flour
1 tablespoon rum

1. Boil the milk with the scrapings of the vanilla bean.

2. Meantime whip the egg whites with 2 tablespoons sugar till they form peaks.

3. In a separate mixing bowl mix egg yolks, ½ cup sugar and the flour. Pour into the hot milk. Stir the mixture, without stopping, over low heat until it starts bubbling. Immediately turn off heat.

4. Without delay mix in the beaten egg whites and rum. (Omit rum if you prefer.)

5. Serve with spongecake-type desserts, Golden Dumpling Cake (page 399), puddings, etc.

CARAMEL SAUCE

Karamelmártás   *3 cups sauce, for 6 servings*

½ cup sugar   1 teaspoon flour
1¼ cups milk   ⅓ cup heavy cream
3 egg yolks

1. In a heavy-bottomed pot cook the sugar till it becomes golden brown. Add milk and stir well. Cook till sugar completely dissolves.

2. Mix the egg yolks with the flour and heavy cream.

3. Pour egg-yolk mixture into the hot caramel milk. Cook over low heat, stirring constantly. When the sauce starts bubbling, take it off the heat.

STUFFED PEAR OR PEACH

Töltött körte vagy Öszibarack   *5 servings*

2 tablespoons lemon juice   1 tablespoon sour cream
½ cup granulated sugar   1 teaspoon minced candied pear
5 pears or peaches, not overripe 2 tablespoons vanilla sugar
¼ cup ground walnuts

1. Boil 2 cups water with 1 tablespoon lemon juice and the granulated sugar.

2. Peel and core the fruit, and immediately place it in the syrup to prevent browning. Cook the fruit until almost done; it should not be soft.

3. Meantime mix thoroughly the walnuts, sour cream, candied pear, remaining 1 tablespoon lemon juice and the vanilla sugar. Make little balls of the mixture.

4. Remove fruit from syrup and stuff each piece with a little ball of the stuffing.

VARIATIONS:

I. Pour a little Kirschwasser on top of peaches, or pear brandy on top of pears, and serve a glass of the same liqueur to accompany this dessert.

II. Chill fruit well, and serve with hot semisweet chocolate sauce.

356

III. With or without chocolate sauce, place the fruit in a whipped cream nest.

QUINCE PASTE

Birsalmasajt

4 pounds ripe quinces	1 cup walnut halves (optional)
7 to 8 cups sugar	

1. Peel, core, and dice the quinces. Cook them till soft. Drain.

2. Force the pulp through a sieve or purée in a blender. Weigh the purée.

3. For every pound of purée measure 2½ cups of sugar. Cook the sugar with 2 cups water until it becomes a heavy syrup. As a test dip a wooden spoon into cold water, then dip it into the hot syrup; remove. If the sugar syrup on the spoon hardens and breaks, the syrup is ready.

4. Put the fruit purée in the syrup and cook over low heat, or in a double boiler, while stirring constantly, until the paste is very thick, like a jam.

5. Cook for a few more minutes. Pour into moistened molds. If you use the walnut halves, place them in the molds first and then pour the hot paste over them. Use small individual molds, or pour into a small baking pan and then cut the paste into diamond shapes to serve.

6. This will keep for a long time in or out of the refrigerator if wrapped in foil or wax paper.

The texture should be like that of a Japanese soybean paste dessert, or like South American guava and other fruit pastes.

NOTE: *Mediterranean countries cook quinces with their skins on, but Hungarians don't care for the slightly bitter taste of the skins.*

RHUBARB COMPOTE

Rebarbarakompót   *4 to 6 servings*

2 pounds young rhubarb stalks	2 to 3 tablespoons sugar
1 tablespoon butter	Pinch of salt
½ tablespoon flour	2 tablespoons sour cream

1. Pull off the outer skin of the rhubarb. Cut stalks into 1-inch pieces. Add ¼ cup water and cook for about 20 minutes. Drain.

2. Melt the butter and mix in the flour; stir and don't let the *roux* brown.

3. Mix the *roux* with the drained rhubarb and cook it over low heat for a few minutes.

357

4. Add sugar to taste and the salt. Whip in the sour cream till smooth. Serve either hot or cold.

NOTE: *This compote can be served cold to accompany cold breast of duckling and such; when hot, it is a good accompaniment to boiled poultry or meat; it is great with boiled beef, for instance.*

You can even use it as an ice-cold dessert for a summer luncheon; serve it in a crystal glass. You may want to make it sweeter if it is to be served as a cold dessert.

LEMON CREAM FOR BREAKFAST ROLLS

Citromkrém reggeli zsemléhez   *about 2 cups*

3 eggs
½ pound sugar
Grated rinds and juice of 2
   lemons

4 tablespoons sweet butter,
   melted

1. Whip whole eggs and sugar for 5 minutes until foamy.

2. Put the mixture in the top part of a double boiler and start cooking it over hot water. (If you are experienced, you can do this over direct heat, but don't make scrambled eggs out of it.) Stir in lemon juice and rind.

3. Drop by drop add the melted butter while still stirring over low heat. Essentially this is the same method used in making a hollandaise, and cream should thicken similarly.

NOTE: *Although it is much more common today in the British Isles than in Hungary, this pleasantly different morning gem is mentioned in nineteenth-century Hungarian cookbooks. This recipe comes from Mimi Salacz (the "adopted grandmother" of my children), whose family has made this for generations.*

✡ 30 ✡

DEEP-FRIED DESSERTS
(ZSIRBAN SŰLT TÉSZTÁK)

BOWKNOTS

Forgácsfánk, or *Csöröge*   *about 16 bowknots*

1 cup all-purpose flour	1 tablespoon sour cream
4 egg yolks	Pinch of salt
½ teaspoon sugar	2 cups vegetable oil
1 tablespoon light rum	Vanilla sugar

1. Place flour, egg yolks, ½ teaspoon sugar, rum, sour cream and salt in a bowl. Mix, then place the dough on a board and knead into a hard dough. Let it rest for 15 minutes.

2. Stretch the dough into a very thin sheet. Cut it into pieces 5 by 3 inches.

3. Make a slit in the center of each piece. Pull the two diagonally opposite corners to the center and tuck them into the slit.

4. Put the oil in a deep 2-quart frying pan. Bring oil almost to the smoking point, then turn down to lowest heat.

5. Place 2 or 3 pieces at a time in the oil. Fry for 1 to 2 minutes, turning them as they become golden. Remove the pieces from the oil with a long fork and place them on absorbent paper.

6. Place on a serving platter and sprinkle with vanilla sugar. They look especially attractive when piled up in a pyramid. Serve with a little dish of jam for each person.

DEVIL'S PILL

Ördögpirulák   *20 to 22 pieces*

6 tablespoons butter
½ tablespoon granulated sugar
Pinch of salt
1 cup flour
3 eggs

2 cups vegetable oil or clarified
   butter
½ cup grated chocolate
½ cup confectioners' sugar

1. Measure 1 cup and 2 tablespoons water into a saucepan. Add butter, granulated sugar and salt, and bring to a boil. When the mixture starts boiling, add the flour and stir constantly until the batter separates from the sides of the pan. Let it cool for 10 minutes.

2. Mix in the eggs, whipping all the while, until you get a smooth dough.

3. Pour oil or clarified butter into a frying pan. Bring to frying temperature, then turn down to very low heat.

4. Take a spoonful of dough out of the pot and shape into a round ball. Shape all the dough in this way. Place in the hot oil four or five at a time.

5. Cover the pan and fry for a few minutes. Remove cover and turn the little dumplings. When both sides are golden brown, remove them with a slotted spoon and put on towels to drain.

6. Mix chocolate and confectioners' sugar. Roll the dumplings in this mixture, then place them in a pyramid on a serving platter.

VARIATION: *Use the dumpling mixture and fill with pitted sweet or sour cherries.*

1. Place a ½-inch-thick layer of the batter on a buttered baking sheet. Top it with evenly spaced cherries.

2. Cut into large ravioli squares, and pull corners together to make little pockets or dumplings, each with a cherry as the core.

3. Fry as above. When done, roll in powdered cocoa.

ACACIA OR SQUASH-FLOWER OR ELDERBERRY-FLOWER FRITTERS

Bundázott akác, tök vagy bodzavirág   *4 to 6 servings*

8 to 10 clusters of elderberry
   flowers, or 2 dozen acacia or
   squash flowers
4 eggs, separated
2 cups flour

2 cups white dessert wine
Pinch of salt
1 tablespoon vegetable oil
2 cups vegetable oil for frying
Vanilla sugar

1. If you wash the flowers, do it gently, and dry them thoroughly. Leave a few of the flowerets to use without the coating.

2. Mix egg yolks with flour, wine, salt and 1 tablespoon oil. Whip to a smooth batter, and let it stand for 1 hour.

3. Whip egg whites till stiff and gently fold them into the batter.

4. Dip the flowers into the batter and fry in the hot oil till golden brown. Remove with a slotted spoon.

5. Dust the fritters with vanilla sugar. Put the uncooked flowers in the center of a serving platter, and place the fritters around them. Serve immediately.

NOTE: *Although it sounds terribly esoteric, actually in a simplified form this was poor people's food in Hungary. I recommend it highly for an unusual, light dessert.*

CHERRIES IN RUM FRITTER

Cseresznyék rumos palacsintában   *25 to 30 pieces*

2 eggs	½ cup vegetable oil
½ cup flour	1 pound firm Bing cherries with
1 tablespoon XXX powdered	their stems
sugar	Additional XXX powdered
Pinch of salt	sugar
1 tablespoon rum	Vanilla sugar
½ cup clarified butter	

1. Mix eggs, flour, 1 tablespoon powdered sugar, salt and rum till smooth. Let the batter rest for 1 hour.

2. Heat butter and oil in a frying pan. When frying temperature is reached, turn heat to low.

3. Dip cherries into the batter and stand them up in the butter and oil. Turn them carefully by their stems to make sure they will become crisp and golden brown on all sides. Blot them in powdered sugar on paper toweling.

4. Pile up the fritters in pyramid shape. Sprinkle with vanilla sugar.

NOTE: *A fine dessert for the weeks of cherry harvest.*

✵ 3I ✵

HOT NOODLE DESSERTS
(MELEG TÉSZTÁK)

IF someone were to ask me to name the Hungarian food preparation that is most different from that of other nations, I would name without hesitation hot noodle desserts. While this term does not translate the Hungarian *meleg tészta* exactly, it will suggest the kind of dish we are considering here.

The imagination and effort the Italians put into their pasta dishes—the myriad shapes, the variety of sauces, from simple to complex—remind me very much of the way Hungarians developed so many desserts based on noodles, different from each other in shapes, flavoring and so on. In Italy pasta is a compulsory part of the meal, just as in Hungary, but there the parallel ends. While pasta is used in many ways, the pasta course always comes toward the beginning of the meal, before the meat or poultry. The hot noodle dish, on the other hand, is usually served as a dessert. Just to confuse you further, according to Károly Gundel the Hungarian classic menu should always include a *meleg tészta* course, and often it was placed before the roast course!

These noodle dishes are always served hot; they are almost always sweet, but for an exception see the recipe for *túróscsusza* (page 369); the noodles can be boiled, baked, or both; sometimes they are also *sautéed*, but they are never *fried;* the dish can be quite simple or very complex; it can be eaten by itself as a meal or can be served as a dessert.

In Hungarian homes sweet noodle dishes will be served to you at least a couple of times a week, and in the restaurants there is always at least one such specialty prepared for the day.

CHEESE DUMPLINGS

Túrós gombóc   *5 to 6 servings*

1 pound dry cottage cheese or
   pot cheese or farmer's cheese
3 eggs, beaten
3 tablespoons sweet butter
½ cup semolina
2 tablespoons flour
Salt

6 tablespoons butter for
   sautéeing
½ cup bread crumbs
½ cup sour cream
½ cup vanilla confectioners'
   sugar

1. Force cheese through a sieve. Mix well with eggs and 3 tablespoons of the butter. Add semolina, flour and a pinch of salt. Let the mixture rest for a couple of hours.

2. Put 3 quarts water in a 4-quart pot and add 1 tablespoon salt. Bring to a slow boil. Put cold water in a dish large enough to dip your hands into.

3. Wet your hands. Take 1 tablespoon of the cheese mixture and roll a round dumpling out of it. Drop it into the boiling water and cook for 4 or 5 minutes. Because semolina is different in each country, test cook the first dumpling for 5 minutes. Then cut it into halves and see if the center is cooked. Adjust the cooking time according to the test dumpling.

4. Form the rest of the mixture into dumplings; dip your hands into the cold water before forming each dumpling. When all dumplings are cooked, rinse them with cold water.

5. Make the coating: Melt 6 tablespoons butter in a frying pan. Add bread crumbs and sauté over low heat until golden brown.

6. Roll the rinsed dumplings in the butter and crumb coating, and place them on a serving platter. Spoon sour cream on top and shake enough vanilla confectioners' sugar over all to make the dumplings look "snowy."

JAM-FILLED DERELYE (FRIAR'S EARS)

Lekváros derelye (Barátfüle)   *4 servings*

2½ cups flour
2 eggs
Salt
1 cup apricot or other jam

½ cup white bread crumbs
6 tablespoons sweet butter
Vanilla sugar

1. Put the flour on a board and make a little well in it. Put 1 whole egg and 1 egg yolk in the well. (Set the egg white aside to use in Step 3.) Add ¼ cup

water and ½ teaspoon salt. Knead the mixture into a hard dough. If too dry, add a little more water. Knead until the dough is smooth and shiny. Let it rest for 15 minutes.

2. Sprinkle the board with flour and stretch the dough to a heavy noodle thickness, about ⅛ inch, and cut it into 3-inch squares.

3. In the center of each square put ½ tablespoon of jam. Brush the edges of the squares with lightly beaten egg white. Now fold each square cater-cornered, making a triangle. Pinch the edges together to seal completely so jam cannot escape; or use a pie crimper.

4. Bring 4 quarts water with ½ tablespoon salt to a boil in a large pot, and gently drop in the triangles. After 5 minutes remove them with a slotted spoon. If a dumpling is not cooked, cook for a few minutes longer. Drain completely.

5. Brown the bread crumbs in butter until light brown, not too dark, and put the drained *derelye* in the crumbs. Mix carefully, just enough to coat them well. They will never have a "breaded" texture, so don't worry if bread crumbs stick to only some parts of the dumplings.

6. Sprinkle liberally with vanilla sugar.

NOTE: *My mother used to make these much larger, using 5-inch squares, like turnovers.*

You can fill the dough squares with ground meat, chopped sweetbreads, ground stew—just about anything you like—replacing sugar with salt, of course.

On Fridays friars could eat only meatless dishes; hence the name Friar's Ears.

PLUM DUMPLING OF SZATMÁR

Szatmári szilvás gombóc   *about 4 servings*

1½ pounds potatoes	3 tablespoons sugar
1 egg	1 teaspoon ground cinnamon
½ teaspoon salt	½ cup white bread crumbs or
5 tablespoons sweet butter	ground walnuts
1½ cups flour	¼ cup vanilla sugar
16 ripe prune-plums	

1. Cook potatoes in their skins. Peel them, and rice them while still warm. Cool the purée.

2. Mix potatoes with the egg, salt and 1 tablespoon butter. Add the flour and knead the dough well.

3. Place dough on a floured board. Stretch it to ½-inch thickness, and cut it into 16 even squares.

4. Cut open the plums, remove pits, and place ½ teaspoon sugar and a pinch of cinnamon in each cavity.

5. Place a whole plum in the center of each square of dough. Pull the corners together and make a little dumpling out of each square. Be sure to cover each plum completely; do not leave an opening anywhere.

6. Fill a 4- to 5-quart pot three-quarters full of water; bring to a boil. Gently drop dumplings into the boiling water. Every now and then move them about with a wooden spoon to prevent sticking to the bottom.

7. When the dumplings come to the surface, cook for another 4 or 5 minutes. Then remove them with a slotted spoon.

8. Brown the bread crumbs in remaining 4 tablespoons butter till golden brown, or melt the butter and add the ground walnuts.

9. Place dumplings carefully in either mixture, and roll them carefully in it until coated all over.

10. Remove dumplings to a serving platter and sprinkle them with vanilla sugar.

VARIATIONS: *If you want to make these dumplings when prune-plums are not in season you can use prune jam* (szilvalekvár). *In that case simply substitute the jam for the sugar-stuffed fruit. You will need about ½ cup jam for 16 dumplings.*

If you have plum dumplings left over, don't despair. Cut the dumplings into halves, then dip each piece into egg wash (egg yolk mixed with water). Roll in bread crumbs and fry in hot fat. Sprinkle the pieces with sugar and serve with jam.

NOTE: *The county of Szatmár is where the finest freestone plums come from.*

While 4 dumplings make an average dessert serving, it's true that when I sit down with a friend we can eat the whole batch with no leftovers.

BAKED STUFFED NOODLES

Rakott metélt   8 servings

5 eggs
¼ teaspoon salt
1 pound flour
¼ pound butter, melted
½ cup sugar
¾ cup sour cream
¼ vanilla bean, pounded to a
   pulp

¼ cup white raisins
Butter for greasing pan
2 tablespoons white bread
   crumbs
¾ cup ground walnuts
½ cup thick apricot jam

1. Make a dough with 2 eggs, the salt, flour and enough water to make a medium-hard dough.

2. Stretch the dough into a thin sheet and cut it into pieces 1 by 4 inches.

3. Bring 4 quarts of water to a boil and boil the noodle pieces for 4 minutes. Drain and rinse with cold water. Preheat oven to 375°F.

4. Separate remaining 3 eggs. Beat together well the egg yolks, melted butter and half of the sugar. Add sour cream, vanilla pulp and raisins; stir.

5. Whip the egg whites and remaining ¼ cup sugar until stiff, then gently stir the meringue into the sour-cream mixture.

6. Combine rinsed noodles and sour-cream mixture. Butter a baking pan or dish 8 by 12 inches and sprinkle with bread crumbs.

7. Spread a third of the noodles on the bottom of the prepared pan. Sprinkle with the ground walnuts. Add another third of the noddles. Spread with apricot jam. Cover with remaining noodles.

8. Bake in the preheated oven for 30 minutes. Cut into large squares to serve.

EMPEROR'S CRUMBS

Császármorzsa   8 servings

4 eggs, separated
¼ pound butter, softened
¼ pound sugar
Juice of ½ lemon

Pinch of salt
1 pound flour
1¾ cups milk
2 tablespoons raisins

1. Whip the egg yolks well with half of the butter, half of the sugar, the lemon juice and a pinch of salt.

2. Mix flour and milk, little by little, into the egg-yolk mixture. Let the dough rest for a couple of hours.

3. Preheat oven to 375°F. Whip the egg whites with the rest of the sugar till they form peaks.

4. Just before baking, gently fold the egg whites and the raisins into the batter.

5. Spread the rest of the butter in a baking pan 12 by 8 inches. Heat the pan until the butter reaches frying temperature. Pour in the batter.

6. Bake in the preheated oven for 40 to 45 minutes. After about 10 minutes, when the batter begins to become solid on the bottom of the pan, scrape it and with a chopping motion slightly break the dough. You may have to do this several times to get the uneven broken-up texture characteristic of this dish.

7. Serve with Wine Cream or Milk and Rum Cream (both, page 355), or a chocolate sauce.

NOTE: *This is an Austro-Hungarian specialty, but the exact origin is unknown.*

SWEET SQUARES OF SZEGED

Szegedi édes kockák   *12 servings*

10 tablespoons butter	1 tablespoon white wine
2 cups flour	Butter for greasing pan
¼ cup confectioners' sugar	¼ cup bread crumbs
Pinch of salt	Vanilla sugar
1 egg	

FILLING

2 tablespoons semolina	3 eggs, separated
1 cup milk	1 tablespoon grated lemon rind
⅓ cup vanilla sugar	2 tablespoons raisins
2¼ cups sour cream	

1. Mix butter and flour in a mixing bowl until they form crumbs. Mix in confectioners' sugar and a pinch of salt.

2. In a separate bowl beat the egg and the wine. Pour the mixture into the flour and butter crumbs.

3. Knead the mixture on a floured board and make a dough out of it. Cut the dough into 2 pieces, making one slightly larger than the other.

4. Roll each piece of dough separately between layers of wax paper. Preheat oven to 375°F.

5. Butter a heatproof glass dish or a baking-serving pan 9 by 13 inches, and sprinkle it with bread crumbs. Stretch the larger piece of dough over the bottom and sides of the pan.

6. Make the filling: Cook semolina in milk until it is soft, 4 or 5 minutes. Cool.

7. Mix vanilla sugar, sour cream and egg yolks; whip until foamy. Add cooled semolina, the lemon rind and raisins. Whip for another few minutes.

8. Whip egg whites till peaks form and very gently fold the foam into the sour-cream mixture.

9. Spread the filling on top of the bottom sheet of dough. Cover with the smaller sheet of dough. Prick the top sheet of dough with a fork in a few places.

10. Bake the dish in the preheated oven for 30 to 40 minutes.

11. Sprinkle with vanilla sugar while the dish is still warm. Let it cool, then cut into 3-inch squares.

NOTE: *When putting raisins into a cake, roll raisins in melted butter or flour and they won't sink to the bottom of the cake.*

PÁLFFY NOODLES

Pálffy metélt   6 to 8 servings

1 cup flour	½ cup sugar
5 eggs	5 sour apples, peeled, halved
Salt	and cored
1 quart milk	¼ cup bread crumbs
2-inch piece of vanilla bean	Butter for greasing pan
6 tablespoons sweet butter	¼ cup ground walnuts
¼ pound raisins	1 tablespoon lemon juice
Rind of ½ lemon	

1. Knead a dough from the flour, 2 eggs and a pinch of salt. If eggs are large, you may have to add a little additional flour.

2. Stretch the dough into a thin sheet and let it rest for 15 minutes. Cut it into strips about ¼ inch wide, like egg noodles.

3. Bring to a boil the milk, vanilla bean, a pinch of salt and 1 tablespoon butter. Reduce heat and put in the egg noodles. Cook until the noodles absorb all the liquid, stirring often. This should take 10 to 12 minutes.

4. Mix in the raisins, remaining butter, the lemon rind, ¼ cup of the sugar and the yolks of remaining 3 eggs. Mix well. Preheat oven to 375°F.

5. In a separate pot cook the cored and peeled apple halves in 1 cup water and 2 tablespoons sugar until they are half cooked. Remove apples and pat them dry.

6. Sprinkle the bread crumbs in a well-buttered baking-serving casserole of porcelain or heatproof glass.

7. Put three quarters of the noodle mixture in the casserole and pat down evenly. Place the half-cooked apples with cavities upwards in 2 even rows. Fill cavities with ground walnuts. Cover with remaining noodle mixture.

8. Bake the noodles in the preheated oven for 20 minutes.

9. Meantime, whip the egg whites with the last 2 tablespoons sugar and the lemon juice to make a meringue.

10. Pour the meringue on the partly baked noodle casserole and bake for 15 minutes longer, till the meringue is golden brown.

NOTE: *As a shortcut you may use ½ pound packaged egg noodles.*

This Hungarian classic is the à la financière *of noodle dishes. In the past only financiers or aristocrats like Count Pálffy could afford it.*

It might interest music lovers to know that this same Count Pálffy introduced the six-year-old prodigy Mozart to the Court and the music world of Vienna.

TUROSCSUSZA — 6 servings

2½ cups flour	½ pound cottage cheese
2 eggs	½ cup sour cream
2½ teaspoons salt	¾ cup ½-inch pieces of pork
1 teaspoon lard	cracklings
4 tablespoons butter, melted	

1. Make a hard dough by mixing the flour, eggs, ½ teaspoon salt and ¼ cup lukewarm water. If eggs are large, add a little bit more flour during kneading. Knead the dough very well, and divide it into 2 loaves.

2. Place each dough loaf on a floured board and stretch into a very, very thin sheet. Let each sheet dry for 5 minutes on each side.

3. Bring 4 quarts of water to a boil. Add remaining 2 teaspoons salt and the lard (to keep dough pieces from sticking together). Preheat oven to 350°F.

4. Tear 2- or 3-inch pieces from the dough sheets and drop them into the boiling water. Cook the noodle pieces for no more than 4 or 5 minutes; avoid

a soft, sticky dough. They should be what the Italians call *al dente.* If the noodles are overcooked, the dish will become almost pasty.

5. Drain the dough pieces from the water and mix them with the melted butter in an attractive earthenware casserole. Sprinkle with cottage cheese, sour cream and cracklings.

6. Bake in the preheated oven for 5 minutes to bring to a very hot temperature. Another attractive way is to use a large round casserole, pile up the noodles, and top them with all the other ingredients. This dish must be sizzling hot!

VARIATIONS:

If fresh pork cracklings are not available, use ¾ pound double-smoked slab bacon. Cut it in ½-inch dice and fry until almost crisp. Pour both melted fat and cracklings over the noodles, sour cream and cottage cheese: or for more Americanized style, drain off the fat and add only the bacon dice to the noodles.

(It is possible to eliminate the fresh dough and use broken-up Italian lasagne *noodles. Of course the dish won't be the real thing.)*

In Hungary most families would use freshly rendered bacon drippings instead of the butter.

NOTE: *This dish is almost an obligatory second course in a traditional Hungarian meal where one starts with Fisherman's Broth (see page 203). Although this noodle dish is not sweet, but salty and swimming in bacon fat, it is still served as a dessert.*

The Hungarian name of this dish has not been translated, because "cottage-cheese noodles" is neither accurate nor appropriate. It is similar to the problem one has with cassoulet, *which should not be translated as "bean and goose casserole."*

✢ 32 ✢

PANCAKES
(PALACSINTÁK)

IF you are fond of passionate, chauvinistic fights, question the origin of the thin pancakes known as *crêpes* in France, *Palatschinken* in Austria, *palačinky* in Czechoslovakia and *palacsinta* in Hungary. If you have enough time to bone up on the subject before this four-nation Pancake Olympics, you will find that each nation can produce enough supporting data to prove that this delicacy was created by a Frenchman, an Austrian, a Czech or a Hungarian.

Actually, this pancake did not originate in any of those nations, but seems to have come from Rumania. The oldest recorded source is a Roman manuscript, which talks about *placenta,* a round cake. Roman legions invaded ancient Dacia, which was eventually conquered and became a province of the Empire. Many legionnaires stayed on to become ancestors of today's Rumanians. The flat pancake was not invented by the Romans, for the Egyptians had it before that, but we can credit those legionaries with carrying the pancake idea around Europe. Pancakes became popular in Rumania in a primitive form about a thousand years ago. In Hungary they were known considerably later, but pancake making developed into a very subtle and complex art in Hungarian and Austrian kitchens during the seventeenth and eighteenth centuries.

According to Messrs. Gunda and Bátky, Hungarian country folk for hundreds of years made a pancake batter by mixing corn flour with water. They baked the batter on an open fire, drank cabbage broth with it, and accompanied it with half-frozen pieces of bacon. During the cold winter months this provided not only food but also warmth.

Another early version was the Transylvanian pancake; the batter was half cornmeal and half wheat flour with egg, milk and honey mixed with it. These pancakes were baked on a stone greased with bacon, and the pancake was turned with a big knife.

Some of the recipes that follow were unearthed from the yellowed pages of family recipe collections and from old forgotten cookbooks. As you experiment with them, you will see how far the idea has developed from the simple mixture of grain and water baked over an open fire, and I think you'll enjoy even the failures.

BASIC PANCAKES

Palacsinta   *12 to 14 pancakes, 7 to 8 inches in diameter*

3 eggs	Pinch of salt
1¼ cups flour	1 cup carbonated water
1 cup milk	Clarified sweet butter for
1 teaspoon sugar	cooking pancakes

1. Mix eggs, flour, milk, sugar and salt to make a smooth pancake dough. Let the dough rest for 1 to 2 hours.

2. Stir in the carbonated water at the last moment, just before cooking the pancakes.

3. Heat an 8-inch frying pan. When the pan is hot, add ¼ teaspoon of the butter. Let the butter melt and cover the bottom of the pan.

4. Pour a ladle of the batter into the pan, and gently tip and twist the pan so that the batter covers the entire pan. When the top of the batter bubbles, turn the pancake over and cook for 4 or 5 seconds longer. Remove the cooked pancake.

5. Continue until the batter is all cooked; add butter before cooking each pancake.

NOTE: *If you are very skillful in twirling the pan so that a small amount of batter covers the surface of the pan, you may be able to make 14 to 16 pancakes.*

SOUR-CREAM PANCAKES

Tejfeles palacsinta   *12 to 14 pancakes*

Basic pancakes (page 372)
2 stale white rolls, peeled
½ cup milk
7 tablespoons sugar
2 whole eggs, separated

¼ pound plus 1 tablespoon
    butter, softened
½ cup plus ⅔ cup sour cream
6 tablespoons raisins
2 extra egg yolks

1. Make the pancakes and set aside until the filling is made.
2. Preheat oven to 350°F. Break up the rolls and soak them in the milk. Squeeze the soaked crumbs and put aside.
3. Whip 4 tablespoons of the sugar, 2 egg yolks and ¼ pound butter till foamy. Add ½ cup of the sour cream and whip the mixture for a few minutes more. Add raisins and soaked crumbs.
4. Whip the egg whites till stiff and gently fold them into the batter.
5. Fill the prepared pancakes with the mixture, and roll them.
6. Butter an attractive serving casserole several inches deep with remaining 1 tablespoon butter, and place the rolled pancakes in it.
7. Mix remaining 3 tablespoons sugar, remaining 2 egg yolks and remaining ⅔ cup sour cream. Pour on top of pancakes. Bake in the preheated oven for 15 minutes.

PANCAKES À LA GUNDEL

Palacsinta Gundel módra   *6 servings*

Basic pancakes (page 372)
Walnut Filling I

4 tablespoons butter
Chocolate-Rum Sauce

WALNUT FILLING I

⅓ cup light cream
½ cup sugar
2 tablespoons rum

8 ounces walnuts, ground
¼ cup chopped raisins
1 teaspoon grated orange rind

CHOCOLATE-RUM SAUCE

4 ounces semisweet chocolate
1 scant cup milk
3 egg yolks
2 tablespoons sugar

2 tablespoons powdered cocoa
1 tablespoon melted butter
2 tablespoons light rum

1. Make the pancakes and set aside until the filling is made.

2. Make the filling: Bring the cream to a simmer, and add sugar, rum, walnuts, raisins and orange rind. Simmer over very low heat for 1 minute. Adjust texture by adding a little more cream or ground walnuts.

3. Put a heaping teaspoon of the filling in the center of each pancake. Fold in four instead of rolling.

4. Sauté the folded pancakes in butter in a large shallow pan for a few minutes on each side. Arrange the pancakes overlapping in a warm serving dish.

5. Make the sauce: Melt the chocolate in the milk over low heat. Whip in egg yolks and remove from heat. Mix in sugar, cocoa, butter and rum, and stir till smooth. Adjust thickness by adding a little more milk if sauce is too thick to pour.

6. Pour sauce over the arranged pancakes, and serve at once, 2 pancakes for each serving.

NOTE: *Once, not having enough ground walnuts on hand, I mixed about half of the amount with the same quantity of canned puréed chestnuts. The result, though not according to the authentic recipe, was spectacular.*

Almost every luxury restaurant in Hungary flames this fine delicacy although Joseph Wechsberg, who wrote the definitive profile on Károly Gundel for The New Yorker, *remarked one day in Budapest that the original dish was not flambéed.*

PANCAKE TORTE

Palacsintatorta   *6 servings*

Basic Pancakes (page 372)	1½ cups sour cream
5 eggs, separated	¼ cup white raisins
¾ cup vanilla sugar	Butter for baking dish

1. Make the pancakes as usual, but be sure to use an 8-inch pan. Leave 4 pancakes whole and cut the rest into thin strips. Preheat oven to 375°F.

2. Make the filling: Whip the egg yolks with vanilla sugar till foamy. Continue whipping while adding sour cream and raisins.

3. Whip egg whites till they form peaks. Very gently fold them into the cream.

4. Gently mix in the thin strips of pancakes.

5. Butter a round 8-inch baking dish about 3 inches deep. Line it with the 4 whole pancakes so they cover the bottom and sides completely. If necessary, cut pancakes to fit the dish.

6. Carefully pour in the cream mixture. Bake in the preheated oven for 25 minutes.

7. Carefully turn the torte out onto a serving platter, and slice it like a cake. It should be creamy enough so that you won't need any extra sauce.

SLID PANCAKES

Csúsztatott palacsinta   *8 to 12 servings*

¼ cup butter	Clarified butter for cooking
1 tablespoon granulated sugar	pancakes
4 eggs, separated	¼ cup vanilla sugar
Pinch of salt	1 cup grated semisweet
½ cup milk	chocolate
3 tablespoons flour	1 cup thick jam
¼ cup heavy cream	

1. Whip together well the butter, granulated sugar, egg yolks and salt. Little by little add the milk and then the flour. Be sure to whip the mixture until it is very smooth. Finally, add heavy cream and let the batter rest for 1 hour.

2. Beat egg whites till peaks form, then fold them into the batter. Preheat oven to 350°F.

3. Place a little clarified butter in an 8-inch frying pan or a special black pancake pan, and heat it. With a ladle dip out about ½ cup of the batter and pour in onto the hot pan. With a circular motion swirl the batter so it covers bottom of the pan. Adjust the amount of batter to conform to the size of your frying pan. Fry the pancakes slowly, *but only on one side.*

4. Slide the pancake, cooked side down, into an 8-inch torte pan (heat-proof glass, metal or ceramic). Sprinkle it with vanilla sugar and grated chocolate. You can also add jam. Also you can alternate chocolate and jam with each layer, or use only one or the other.

5. When the second pancake is done, slide it on top of the other so the two uncooked surfaces will be facing. Sprinkle with more vanilla sugar and chocolate and/or jam.

6. Continue to cook the pancakes until you get to the last one. Cook the last pancake *on both sides,* and use it as a cover.

7. Place the dish in the preheated oven for 10 to 15 minutes.

8. When serving, cut the torte like a cake.

VARIATIONS:
   I. *Use ground walnuts or roasted ground almonds in the filling.*
   II. *Top the torte with a meringue: Whip 2 egg whites and 2 tablespoons*

sugar until very stiff. Cover the top pancake with this meringue. Pipe it on with a pastry tube, or spread on with a knife. Bake in a preheated 300°F. oven for 10 to 15 minutes, or until golden brown.

HALF-BALLOON PANCAKE AS IN THE CITY OF EGER

Egri félgömbpalacsinta   6 servings

PANCAKES

¾ cup flour
1 egg
1 tablespoon sugar

Pinch of salt
¾ cup milk
Clarified sweet butter for frying

FILLING

½ cup milk
½ cup vanilla sugar
1 tablespoon grated lemon rind

¾ cup ground walnuts
¼ cup raisins

2 tablespoons butter

5 cups milk

SAUCE

2 eggs
2 to 3 tablespoons sugar
1 tablespoon flour

2 cups milk
¼ vanilla bean
3 tablespoons rum

2 tablespoons ground toasted
  walnuts

1 tablespoon ground toasted
  almonds

1. Make the pancakes: Mix thoroughly the flour, egg, sugar, salt and ¾ cup milk. Let the batter rest for 1 hour. Make 12 pancakes; for method see basic recipe (page 372).

2. Make the filling: Mix ½ cup milk, the vanilla sugar and grated lemon rind, and bring to a slow simmer. Add walnuts and raisins and mix well. Turn off heat.

3. Spread out a large white unstarched napkin or small tablecloth. Butter the center of it, in about a 10-inch circle. Place the pancakes on it, one by one, spreading a little of the filling on each pancake.

4. Pick up the four corners of the napkin and pull it around the pancakes to form a balloon, tightly but without breaking the contents. Then tie the napkin with string.

5. Bring 5 cups milk and 2 tablespoons butter to a boil in a very large pot. Place the napkin-balloon in it and cook for 15 minutes.

6. Lift the napkin from the pot, cut the string, and carefully open the package. Put the pancake-balloon on a dish.

7. Keep the balloon warm: Bring a potful of water to a boil, and place the plate with the balloon on top of the pot. Cover with a large dish. The steam will keep the ballon hot without drying it out.

8. Make the sauce: Whip eggs, sugar and flour, and little by little add the milk. Add the vanilla bean. Put the sauce in the top part of a double boiler over simmering water and cook, stirring all the while. (Or cook directly over very low heat.) Then turn off heat and mix in the rum. This sauce has a tendency to become thick. If too thick, whip in a little milk or cream.

9. Just before serving, pour the sauce over the balloon, and sprinkle the toasted walnuts and almonds over all.

10. Slice as you would a cake. If you prefer, the sauce can be served separately.

NOTE: *To toast the nuts, put shelled walnut halves and shelled whole almonds in a preheated 200°F. oven and toast for 10 to 15 minutes. Then grind the nuts together.*

After many attempts, we never succeeded in keeping the balloon shape; it always became a half-balloon, that's why we gave it this name. This recipe sounds like a lot of work; it is.

PANCAKES WITH APPLE MERINGUE

Almás palacsinta   *6 servings*

1 pound apples	Basic Pancakes (page 372)
4 tablespoons butter	2 egg whites
2 tablespoons granulated sugar	5 tablespoons confectioners'
1 tablespoon and ½ teaspoon lemon juice	sugar

1. Peel and core the apples. Put the butter in a heavy saucepan. When it is melted, add the apples and sprinkle with granulated sugar. Cook, covered, over very low heat; stir often.

2. When the apples are cooked, mix in 1 tablespoon lemon juice and mash the apples with a fork, to make a spreadable but slightly lumpy sauce. Preheat oven to 300°F.

3. Make the pancakes. As each one finishes cooking on the second side, flip it out into a buttered deep baking dish (round heatproof glass is good).

Spread each one with some of the applesauce. Continue this way till pancakes and sauce are used. Leave the last pancake top plain.

4. Make a meringue: Whip the egg whites, confectioners' sugar and ½ teaspoon lemon juice till the mixture forms peaks.

5. Spread the meringue on top of the pancakes. Bake in the preheated oven for 15 minutes, or until golden brown.

PANCAKES IN SZENTGYÖRGY MANNER

Szentgyörgyi palacsinta   *makes 12 to 16 pieces*

Pancakes
4 tablespoons sweet butter
1 cup ground walnuts
½ cup confectioners' sugar
Vanilla Cream
¾ cup plus 5 tablespoons
  granulated sugar

⅔ cup white rum
½ cup ground almonds
5 egg whites
3 tablespoons apricot jam,
  softened

PANCAKES

5 whole eggs
2 cups flour
2 cups milk

1 tablespoon sugar
Pinch of salt
1 cup carbonated water

VANILLA CREAM

11 tablespoons sweet butter
5 egg yolks
1 cup sugar
2 cups milk

1 cup heavy cream
½ cup ground white raisins
1 vanilla bean

1. Make a pancake batter with the 5 whole eggs, the flour, 2 cups milk, 1 tablespoon sugar, the salt and carbonated water. For method, see basic recipe (page 372).

2. Make 30 pancakes. To do this, put a small amount of the batter in the frying pan and quickly roll it around to coat the bottom of the pan with a thin layer. Cook the pancakes in 4 tablespoons sweet butter.

3. Line an attractive ovenproof baking pan, 13 by 9 inches, with 5 pancakes.

4. Arrange 15 pancakes on the table top and sprinkle them with a mixture of ground walnuts and confectioners' sugar. Then stack them into 5 batches of 3 pancakes.

5. Roll each triple layer tightly, and cut it across to 6 pieces. Finally, you should have about 30 tightly rolled little spirals 1¼ to 1½ inches long.

6. Stand up the spirals in the pancake-lined baking pan. Fill the pan evenly. Preheat oven to 350°F.

7. Make the vanilla cream: Melt 11 tablespoons butter over very low heat or in the top part of a double boiler over simmering water. Whip in the egg yolks. Mix in 1 cup sugar, the milk and the heavy cream, raisins and scrapings from the inside of the vanilla bean. Keep whipping till you get a quite thick cream.

8. Pour the vanilla cream on top of the pancake spirals, covering them completely. Bake in the preheated oven for 25 minutes.

9. Slice the rest of the pancakes (10), and mix them with ¾ cup sugar, the rum and ground almonds. Spoon the mixture on top of the baked spirals, and bake for 10 minutes more.

10. Meantime, whip the egg whites and 5 tablespoons sugar until they form peaks and are very stiff. Very gently mix in the softened apricot jam.

11. Take out pancakes, leave oven door open for a couple of minutes to reduce heat, then set for 300°F. Spoon the meringue on top of pancakes, and "dry-bake" in the oven till the meringue is set, for 10 to 15 minutes, or until golden brown.

12. Serve in the baking pan, since removing the dessert is rather difficult. Do not try to separate the pancakes because they will have become homogeneous anyway. Cut them into 2-inch or 3-inch squares, and serve with a spatula. (It won't be easy to make exact squares.)

❅ 33 ❅

STRUDELS
(RÉTESEK)

THIS delicacy was brought into Hungary by the Turks in the sixteenth century. The pastry is similar to the *filo* or *phyllo* pastry that is still used in the Middle East. However, the Hungarian product is as little related to this as is, let us say, the *Pannequet Soufflé au Grand Marnier* to the ancient Egyptian pancake. A strudel sheet 11 by 14 inches is so thin and light that one can blow it away with a puff of air.

In Hungary strudel is a village specialty, and even in luxury restaurants it's always a farmer girl from the provinces who is hired to make it.

I was fortunate enough to be invited to a little shop where they make strudel exclusively. I watched two girls start with a fistful of dough and within minutes pull it with the backs of their hands to such a thinness that a woman of ancient Rome could have worn it as a cloak. With an almost magic dexterity one of them tore off the edges with a continuous spiral movement of her wrist, sort of rolling up the pastry, using her arm as the spindle. Then came the lifting of the tablecloth to roll the already stuffed strudel, suddenly making it look like a huge boa constrictor. During this process the large ceiling fan, reminiscent of those you see in Southern towns, was whirling away to speed up the drying of the stretched strudel dough.

As the "closing act," the girls performed the Paganini "Twenty-fourth Caprice" of the strudel repertoire, the *vargabéles,* which had been invented by the Varga Restaurant some seventy-five years ago, in the city of Kolozsvár. Many experienced recipe readers can imagine tastes, but I doubt that anyone could fully imagine the subtle taste and texture of this queen of strudels, with its delicious noodle and cheese filling and the crispness of the many-layered pastry.

The only difference between the Paganini piece and the *vargabéles* is that for the Paganini you applaud the virtuoso when he is finished, but after the *vargabéles* you applaud Juliska when you are finished. With the pastry, of course . . .

BASIC STRUDEL DOUGH

Rétestészta   *2 strudel strips,*
                                                  about 16 servings

1¼ cups all-purpose flour (see   Pinch of salt
   Note)   ¼ pound butter or lard, melted
¾ cup instantized flour   (see Note)
1 egg   Flour
1 teaspoon vinegar

1. Sift both flours onto a board. Make a well in the center, and pour in a mixture of 1 cup lukewarm water, the egg, vinegar and salt. Knead well. You should knead and beat this dough for as long as 10 minutes until you get a smooth, puckery dough. A good workout for the dough is very important because this is what makes it stretchable.

2. Make a round loaf out of the dough, put it on a floured board, spread it with some of the butter or lard, and cover it with a pot. Let it rest for 30 minutes.

3. Cover a large table with a clean white tablecloth and sprinkle it well with flour. Gently lower the dough onto the table. Carefully stretch it from all sides, *using the backs of your hands.* Form the dough into a longish shape. Keep going around the table. Put your hands under the dough, and keep stretching it without making a hole.

4. Cut off uneven edges with kitchen shears and sprinkle lukewarm water on dough. Knead it again into the same loaf shape. Spread it with butter or lard, and let it rest again, covered, for another 30 minutes.

5. Again start stretching it with the backs of your hands, and cut off edges with shears.

6. Leave the dough for 10 minutes to dry a little so it won't stick when you roll it. (Some Hungarian cooks speed this process by using an electric fan.) Preheat oven to 375°F.

7. Sprinkle the dough with melted butter or lard. (By this time you will have prepared the filling of your choice.)

8. Place the filling mixture on one third of the dough sheet. Hold the edge of the tablecloth with both hands; gently lifting it upwards, roll the strudel dough into a roulade shape. Cut it according to the size of your baking pan.

Place it in the greased pan and spread the top with more of the melted butter or lard.

9. Bake the strudel in the preheated oven.

NOTE: *One of the secrets of a paper-thin strudel dough is the use of the right flour. Hungarian housewives use, first of all, flour that is not freshly milled. Furthermore, they will mix at least two kinds of flour: one that will give body and the other with a very high gluten content to make the dough almost rubbery. Hungarian flour and Canadian flour have the highest gluten content, and they are ideal for strudel making. You can buy flour from an Italian bakery; they generally use flour with a very high gluten content. If you find a shop (perhaps a health-food store) that sells both hard and soft flours, mix the flours half and half for strudel.*

Lard is used to spread over the dough in Steps 2, 4, 7 and 9 except when making a strudel with cottage cheese in the filling. In that case use butter.

In Budapest, where they have stores that specialize in strudels, I learned that in the wintertime they use warm water, and at other seasons lukewarm water.

Don't be surprised at vinegar as an ingredient; this helps to activate the dough.

COTTAGE-CHEESE FILLING

Túrós töltelék

3 eggs, separated	Grated rind of ½ lemon
4 tablespoons butter, softened	Pinch of salt
¾ cup vanilla sugar	1 pound cottage cheese
½ cup sour cream	1 tablespoon coarse-ground
1 tablespoon flour	semolina
¼ cup raisins	

1. Whip the egg yolks with softened butter and sugar till foamy. Slowly mix in sour cream, flour, raisins, lemon rind and salt. Let the mixture stand for 15 minutes.

2. Whip the egg whites till they form peaks. Sieve the cottage cheese and gently fold into the egg whites. Mix this with the first mixture.

3. Sprinkle the semolina on the prepared sheet of strudel dough, where you are going to put the cottage-cheese filling. Place the filling on top of the semolina.

4. Roll the strudel (see basic recipe), and bake for about 40 minutes.

VARIATIONS: *An interesting trick is to use ⅚ pound of cottage cheese, and add ⅙ pound puréed potatoes. The result is a much lighter-textured cheese strudel.*

A cookbook from Alföld suggests mixing an egg yolk with ½ cup sour cream and spreading it over the top of the rolled strudel as a glaze. Do this before baking.

NOTE: *The cottage cheese you use for strudel must be without any acidity. It should be made of whole milk and as creamy as possible.*

APPLE FILLING

Almás töltelék

2 pounds apples
¼ cup chopped walnuts
¼ cup raisins
¾ cup sugar
½ tablespoon ground
    cinnamon

⅓ cup melted sweet butter
¼ cup cake crumbs
1 teaspoon fat

1. Peel and core the apples, and grate them. Mix with walnuts, raisins, sugar and cinnamon. Stir in the melted butter and blend well.
2. Preheat oven to 375°F. Sprinkle cake crumbs on the prepared sheet of strudel dough. Spread apple filling on one third of the dough sheet.
3. Roll the strudel (see basic recipe). Cut according to the size of your baking pan, and place it in the pan. Spread the top with fat.
4. Bake in the preheated oven for 40 to 45 minutes.

POPPYSEED FILLING

Mákos töltelék

¾ cup vanilla sugar
2 eggs, separated
1 tablespoon flour
Grated rind of ½ lemon
6 tablespoons sweet butter

1 cup hot milk
½ pound poppyseeds, ground
¼ cup raisins
1 apple, peeled, cored and
    grated

1. Whip vanilla sugar and egg yolks till smooth. Add flour, lemon rind, butter and finally hot milk. Bring to a simmer and mix in the ground poppyseeds.

2. When the mixture starts simmering again, turn off heat. Let the filling cool.

3. When mixture is cool, mix in raisins and grated apple. Whip the egg whites till stiff and fold them into the filling. If it is too thick, add a little cold water.

4. Place filling on top of prepared sheet of strudel dough, and proceed exactly as described in the basic recipe. Bake for about 30 minutes.

NOTE: *Although many traditional recipes mix poppyseeds with apricot jam, you will find grated apple a wonderful taste addition. For yet another variation, reduce poppyseeds to ¼ pound and instead of the apple use 1 pound pumpkin, diced and cooked. The poppyseeds must be cooked before baking so that they do not become hardened during the baking process.*

WALNUT FILLING

Diós töltelék

Proceed as directed in recipe for Poppyseed Filling, but substitute ½ pound ground walnuts for the poppyseeds.

ALMOND STRUDEL AS IN SOPRON

Soproni mandulás rétes

⅓ cup melted lard or butter	6 whole eggs, separated
¾ cup raspberry or strawberry jam	½ cup sugar
	¾ cup ground almonds

1. Let the prepared strudel dough dry for 10 minutes. Then sprinkle it with some of the melted lard or butter, and spread jam on top.

2. Whip the egg yolks with sugar. Add ground almonds.

3. Whip egg whites till very stiff, and gently fold them into the almond mixture.

4. Fill top half of strudel sheet with the mixture. Then roll the dough (see basic recipe).

5. Sprinkle the rolled dough with more of the melted fat. Place it gently and loosely, without patting it down, on the baking sheet. Bake the strudel for about 30 minutes, or till it's golden crisp.

NOTE: *You may use other jams and also different nuts.*

POTATO FILLING

Krumplis rétes töltelék

1 pound potatoes
4 eggs, separated
Grated rind of 1 lemon
¼ pound sweet butter
½ cup ground blanched
  almonds

Pinch of salt
1 cup vanilla sugar
Melted butter

1. Cook the potatoes in their skins; peel them and rice them while hot. Let the purée cool.

2. In a mixing bowl whip egg yolks till foamy. Add lemon rind and riced potatoes. Mix in the butter and the almonds. Preheat oven to 400°F.

3. Whip the egg whites with the salt and vanilla sugar till they form peaks. Just before you are ready to fill the strudel, very gently fold egg whites into the potato mixture; use a rubber spatula.

4. Sprinkle studel sheet with melted butter. Spread with potato filling, and roll up (see basic recipe).

5. Bake in the preheated oven for 35 to 40 minutes.

NOTE: *It is difficult to believe that this strudel variety is so little known, even in Hungary, except in some of the provinces. Although the lowly potato provides the filling, it is one of the best, admittedly robust, desserts in any repertoire.*

WINE STRUDEL

Boros rétes

4 tablespoons sweet butter
1 cup freshly made white bread
  crumbs
2 cups medium-sweet white
  wine

½ cup granulated sugar
1 large strudel sheet, or 2 small
  ones (page 381)
2 tablespoons clarified butter

1. Preheat oven to 400°F. Melt the sweet butter and brown the bread crumbs for a few minutes. Stir to prevent burning.

2. Add 1 cup of the wine. Remove from heat and stir in the sugar.

3. Sprinkle the stretched strudel dough with clarified butter. Put the filling on the dough and roll as usual.

4. Twist the strudel into a spiral and place in a deep baking pan. Bake in the preheated oven for 15 minutes.

5. Pour the second cup of wine over the strudel and return it to the oven. Bake until wine disappears. At that point the strudel will start crisping. When it is golden brown and crisp, in 30 to 35 minutes, remove it from the oven.

NOTE: *This has a most interesting and pleasing taste. The texture is different from the usual strudel; it is much crustier and not as delicate. The technique is not unlike the steam-baking of French bread.*

CHOCOLATE STRUDEL

Csokoládés rétes

1 large stretched strudel sheet (page 381)	½ cup ground almonds
¼ pound butter	½ cup grated semisweet baking chocolate
6 egg yolks	4 egg whites
4 tablespoons sugar	1 cup milk

1. Let the stretched sheet of strudel dough dry for 10 to 15 minutes.

2. Melt half of the butter and sprinkle it over the dough. Preheat oven to 375°F.

3. Mix egg yolks well with sugar. Then mix in ground almonds and grated chocolate.

4. Whip egg whites until they form peaks, and carefully fold into the almond and chocolate mixture.

5. Spread the filling over a quarter of the strudel sheet; roll up the dough.

6. Butter well a large baking pan with low side walls; use all the remaining butter. Coil the strudel in the pan, starting with the outside wall and coiling toward the center. Pour the milk over the coil.

7. Bake in the preheated oven for 40 to 45 minutes. When properly done the milk will have soaked into the strudel and the top of the pastry will be crisp.

VARGA STRUDEL-CAKE

Vargabéles

2 cups flour	1 cup sugar
½ pound butter, melted	½ cup sour cream
Salt	¼ cup white raisins
1 whole egg	½ vanilla bean, pulverized
1¾ pounds cottage cheese	Vanilla sugar
5 eggs, separated	

1. Prepare a strudel dough from ¾ cup flour, ¼ teaspoon melted butter, a pinch of salt and ¼ cup water. You may have to add a little more water, depending on the flour. Let the dough rest for 30 minutes.

2. Stretch the dough to a very thin sheet, and tear off the thick edges. Let the sheet rest for 15 minutes.

3. Sprinkle the dough with melted butter, then fold it carefully. Keep folding it and sprinkling melted butter on each layer until the folded oblong becomes the size of your baking pan.

4. Butter heavily the chosen baking pan, and put the folded strudel in it. Preheat oven to 375°F.

5. Prepare a noodle dough from 1¼ cups flour, 1 whole egg, a pinch of salt and 1 cup water. Knead the dough well, and roll it out quite thin. Cut it into ¼-inch strips.

6. Boil the noodles till tender, then rinse with cold water.

7. Sauté the drained noodles in 2 tablespoons butter for a few seconds.

8. Put the cottage cheese through a sieve and mix in 5 egg yolks, the sugar, sour cream, raisins, any remaining butter and the pulverized vanilla bean. Add the sautéed noodles.

9. Beat the egg whites till stiff, then fold them into the cheese mixture.

10. Pour the filling over the top of the folded strudel dough in the baking pan. Bake in the preheated oven for 45 minutes.

11. About 10 minutes after the strudel is out of the oven, sprinkle it with vanilla sugar.

NOTE: *In some households the filling is put between flat layers of dough, almost like making baked lasagna. Other housewives roll the strudel around the noodle filling the same way as with a regular strudel filling.*

POT-CHEESE STRUDEL-CAKE

Gibanica   *4 to 6 servings*

1 large stretched strudel dough (page 381)	1 pound dry pot cheese
4 tablespoons sweet butter, melted	3 eggs, separated
	Sugar or salt

1. Preheat oven to 375°F. Let the stretched strudel dough become somewhat dry, then sprinkle it with melted butter and fold it over. Again sprinkle with some of the butter. Proceed this way until you have folded the dough to a size twice as big as the baking pan you will use. Cut the dough in half.

2. Butter an oblong baking pan and place half of the dough on the bottom.

3. Sieve the pot cheese, then mix it with the egg yolks and either sugar or salt, to your taste.

4. Whip egg whites till very stiff, then very carefully mix them into the cheese filling.

5. Spread the filling evenly on the strudel dough in the pan. Then cover with the other half of the dough.

6. Brush with remaining melted butter. Bake in the preheated oven for 30 to 45 minutes, or until golden red.

7. Cut into squares for serving.

NOTE: *This is a southern Hungarian-Serbian version of the* vargabéles, *excellent, but much heartier. There the filling includes* kajmak, *which is almost like the Spanish sweet,* dulce di leche. *It is made by boiling milk until it is reduced to about one sixth of the original quantity; the creamy substance on the top is the* kajmak, *which is then skimmed off. This was a common ingredient all over the Balkans and in Greece.*

   In the south this filling is usually seasoned with salt, but some people like it with sugar. The salty version is great as an accompaniment to wine or beer.

CABBAGE FILLING

Káposzta töltelék

2½ pounds cabbage	1 tablespoon sugar
1 tablespoon salt	½ teaspoon freshly ground
¼ pound lard	black pepper

1. Cut the cabbage into fine shreds, salt it and let it stand, covered, for 2 hours. Then squeeze it well to eliminate most of the liquid extracted by the salt.

2. Heat the lard to frying temperature. Add the sugar and let it become light brown. Stir while you do this.

3. Add the drained cabbage. Stir it immediately and cook it without a cover till cabbage is golden brown.

4. Place the cabbage on top of the stretched strudel dough. Only then sprinkle the cabbage with pepper.

5. Roll up the strudel (see basic recipe), and bake for about 30 minutes.

MUSHROOM FILLING

Töltelék gombás réteshez

1 small onion, peeled and minced	Salt and pepper
6 tablespoons butter	3 eggs, separated
½ pound mushrooms, peeled and chopped	4 tablespoons bread crumbs

1. Cook onion in 2 tablespoons of the butter, covered, for about 10 minutes. Add mushrooms and salt and pepper to taste. Cook, covered, over very low heat till there is no liquid left and only the cooking fat remains. Stir often to prevent burning. Let the mixture cool. Preheat oven to 375°F.

2. Mix in egg yolks. Whip egg whites till very stiff. Mix them in, and finally mix in bread crumbs.

3. Spread filling on the stretched strudel dough, and sprinkle with remaining 4 tablespoons butter, melted.

4. Roll the strudel very loosely to leave space for the eggs to swell during cooking (see basic recipe). Place it in a buttered baking pan, 17 by 11 inches.

5. Bake in the preheated oven for 25 to 30 minutes, till crisp.

NOTE: *This versatile member of the strudel family can be eaten as a hot appetizer, or as the main course at a luncheon, or as a snack with a glass of wine.*

✳ 34 *✳*

HOMESTYLE CAKES
(HÁZI ÉDESSÉGEK)

MY MOTHER'S CHERRY CAKE

Anyám cseresznyés lepénye   *10 to 12 pieces*

1 pound fresh cherries	1 cup flour
⅜ pound sweet butter	Pinch of salt
¾ cup granulated sugar	¼ cup bread crumbs
3 eggs, separated	Vanilla sugar

1. Pit cherries, taking care not to split them. Set aside. Preheat oven to 375°F.

2. Mix butter well with half of the granulated sugar. After a few minutes of vigorous whipping add egg yolks and continue whipping. Finally add flour and salt.

3. Beat egg whites with remaining granulated sugar till the mixture is stiff and forms peaks. With a rubber spatula, gently fold it into the butter mixture.

4. Butter a baking pan 10 by 6 inches and sprinkle it with bread crumbs. Put dough in pan, and top with cherries.

5. Bake in the preheated oven for 30 minutes. Before serving, sprinkle with vanilla sugar.

NOTE: *Summer luncheons of my childhood often ended with this dessert. I was surprised when my wife, Karen, who is an excellent baker, called it "a nice coffeecake." Perhaps for daughters of rich Western nations this cherry cake is only that, but for me it's all that a cake should be.*

Since earliest times lepény has been one of the most popular Hungarian

with fruits, cottage cheese, nuts, coffee, poppyseeds,
Ages, with candied fruits, ginger and saffron.

N CAKE AS IN TRANSDANUBIA

Prósza dunántúliasan   *1 5 squares*

ground   ½ teaspoon salt
                          1½ cups milk
                          2 ounces butter for pan

tter, softened

with sugar, softened butter and salt.

a boil. Pour it on top of cornmeal mixture and mix well.
Let it rest for 2 to 3 hours. Preheat oven to 375°F.

3. Butter a baking pan 13 by 9 inches with remaining butter. Pour in the
thickened mixture. Bake to a golden-red color.

4. Cut it into squares.

NOTE: *If possible, try to purchase freshly ground cornmeal.*

*In my childhood, my mother served this as a coffeecake, but you may also
omit the sugar and serve it with game instead of polenta, or as a stuffing for
poultry or game birds.*

*Poor people made this with water instead of milk, and they drank the milk
with it, making an entire meal out of it.*

SHEET CAKE FILLED WITH APPLES

Almás pite   *6 servings*

½ pound butter
¾ pound flour (1⅘ cups)
¼ tablespoon salt
¼ pound confectioners' sugar
  (¾ cup)

3 egg yolks
1 tablespoon sour cream

FILLING

3 pounds hard baking apples
2 tablespoons flour
4 tablespoons butter, melted
¾ cup ground walnuts

½ cup vanilla sugar
¼ cup raisins
1 tablespoon lemon juice

1. Mix butter and flour till the mixture forms crumbs. Then mix salt and confectioners' sugar into it.

2. Make a well in the center, put in 2 egg yolks and sour cream, and knead it together. Leave in a cool place for 1 hour. If the sour cream is very thick, add an extra teaspoon (see Note).

3. Divide dough into 2 parts, one slightly larger than the other. The larger part will be used for the bottom crust, and it must overlap the edges slightly. Preheat oven to 375°F.

4. Roll out each piece of dough between 2 pieces of floured wax paper to make a thin sheet of dough.

5. Make the filling: Peel and core the apples, then grate them through the coarse holes of an apple grater or squash slicer.

6. Add flour and melted butter, ground walnuts, vanilla sugar, raisins and lemon juice. Mix well with your hands.

7. Line a baking pan 12 by 8 inches with the larger piece of dough. Spread apple mixture evenly on top of this bottom crust. Cover with the smaller sheet of dough, evening it out with your hand.

8. Beat remaining egg yolk with 1 teaspoon water and spread this egg-yolk glaze over the top crust. Prick with a fork at 2- or 3-inch intervals.

9. Bake in the preheated oven for 45 minutes. When cool, cut it into 4-inch squares.

NOTE: *You can use many different filling mixtures, including other fruits and nuts or cottage cheese.*

In Hungary sour cream generally has a lighter texture than the standard product available in the United States. However, from city to city it can range from moist, like yoghurt, to very thick and paste-like.

NORTHLAND SQUARE

Felvidéki pite   *about 9 pieces*

¼ pound butter	¾ cup cake flour
1 cup sugar	1 tablespoon cocoa, sieved
2 tablespoons lemon juice	¾ cup ground walnuts
5 eggs, separated	½ cup currant jam
Grated rind of ½ lemon	

1. Preheat oven to 375°F. Whip butter, ½ cup sugar and 1 tablespoon lemon juice. Add egg yolks, lemon rind and flour, and mix well.

2. Pour mixture into a baking pan 10 by 6 inches and flatten. Bake in the preheated oven for 10 minutes.

3. Meantime start whipping egg whites while adding remaining sugar little by little. When egg whites start getting stiff add the cocoa, walnuts and remaining lemon juice.

4. Take baking pan from oven and let cool for about 10 minutes.

5. Spread the partly baked layer with jam and top with walnut mixture. Put back into the oven for 30 minutes.

6. Cut into large squares when cool.

NOTE: *You can use almost any type of jam and vary the type of nuts.*

You can keep this and the Chocolate Pite for several weeks, but it should never go into the refrigerator.

LATTICED CHOCOLATE PITE

Rácsos csokoládés pite   *8 servings*

½ pound plus 4 tablespoons butter

1¼ pounds flour

1½ cups powdered sugar

Pinch of salt

Grated rind and juice of 1 lemon

4 eggs, separated

½ pound granulated sugar

½ pound almonds, blanched and ground

¼ pound chocolate, grated

¼ vanilla bean, grated

¼ cup apricot jam

1 extra egg yolk

1. Preheat oven to 350°F. Mix butter and flour until they form crumbs. Then mix in the powdered sugar, salt, lemon rind, lemon juice and 4 egg yolks.

2. Take two thirds of the dough and pat it down on the bottom of a baking sheet 8 by 10 inches. Make sure that the sides are covered also. Bake in the preheated oven for 10 minutes. Set aside to cool.

3. Make the filling: Make a very stiff froth with egg whites and granulated sugar, then very gently, so as not to break the froth, mix in almonds and chocolate. Add vanilla bean.

4. Spread jam on top of the cooled half-baked dough. Spread filling on top of jam.

5. Roll out the rest of the dough into a thin sheet and cut into thin strips. Form crisscross, diamond-shaped latticework on top of the filling for a traditional topping.

6. Beat remaining egg yolk with 1 teaspoon water. Brush latticework with this egg-yolk glaze. Return the pan to the oven for an additional 30 to 35 minutes, or until it is properly baked.

LATTICED CHEESE SQUARES

Túrós rácsos   *about 16 pieces*
(also known as *túrós pite* or *túrós lepény*)

1¼ cups plus 2 tablespoons flour
⅜ pound butter
2 egg yolks
⅓ cup granulated sugar
½ teaspoon baking powder
Grated rind of ½ lemon
Pinch of salt

1½ tablespoons sour cream
2 whole eggs, separated
½ pound pot cheese
½ cup vanilla sugar
1 tablespoon lemon juice
Flour for pastry board
1 whole egg, beaten

1. Preheat oven to 375°F. Place 1¼ cups flour in a large mixing bowl. Cut cold butter into it and mix to crumbs with a pastry blender. It will take about 2 minutes working fast.

2. Add 2 egg yolks, granulated sugar, baking powder, lemon rind, salt and sour cream. Once more mix fast with pastry blender.

3. Now dip your hands into ice water and dry them. Mix the dough well with your hands, but for no more than 30 seconds.

4. Place three quarters of the dough in a 9-inch-square baking pan. Pat it evenly. Bake in the preheated oven for 10 minutes.

5. Make the cheese filling: Beat egg whites very stiff; set aside.

6. Push pot cheese through a sieve, then add egg yolks, vanilla sugar, 2 tablespoons flour and lemon juice. Finally fold in the stiff egg whites.

7. Spread the filling evenly on the partly baked dough.

8. Flour the table with your hands. Roll out remaining quarter of dough and cut into thin strips. Place strips in latticework position on top of filling.

9. Beat remaining whole egg with 1 teaspoon water, and brush latticework strips with this egg wash. Bake the cake for 30 minutes longer.

10. When it is cool cut it into 2-inch squares.

NOTE: *This type of dough requires fast work and as little handling with hands as possible. It can be used for dozens of dessert preparations with different fillings and shapes.*

SPONGECAKE ROULADE

Piskótatekercs   *12 to 16 slices*

6 eggs, separated	Butter for pan
Pinch of salt	1 cup jam, or more
6 tablespoons sugar	2 tablespoons vanilla sugar
4 tablespoons flour	

1. Preheat oven to 375°F. Whip egg whites with salt and 1 tablespoon water till very stiff; when you turn the bowl upside down the foam should almost stay in the bowl.

2. Add egg yolks, one by one, while continuing to whip by hand or with a mixer at slow speed. It should take an additional 2 minutes to incorporate all the yolks.

3. Add sugar by the spoonful. This process should take 3 to 4 minutes.

4. Slow down the whipping and little by little add the flour. This part actually should be done by hand because overmixing is a common danger.

5. Line a baking sheet 17 by 11 inches with wax paper and evenly butter the paper. Pour in the mixture and spread it evenly.

6. Bake in the preheated oven for 12 to 15 minutes.

7. After baking, gently pull off wax paper. Measure a fresh piece of wax paper and roll up the cake in it. Cool the cake.

8. Unroll the cake, and spread it with jam; how much you use depends on how thickly you spread it. Roll up the cake again to make a tight roulade, but without breaking it. Sprinkle with vanilla sugar.

NOTE: *This spongecake mixture is the same for the Hungarian housewife as a "basic black" dress for a fashionable woman. You can use it as a base for just about any type of dessert you care to make.*

The name piskóta *originated in the time of King Matthias (see page 13); it was introduced to the language by Italian* biscotto *makers.*

HONEY-BREAD

Mézeskalács   *24 or more pieces*

½ pound honey
¾ cup sugar
4 eggs, separated
½ teaspoon ground cloves
½ teaspoon ground cinnamon
Pinch of ground cardamom
Pinch of ground coriander
Grated rind of ½ lemon

1 tablespoon rum
1 teaspoon baking powder
½ pound rye flour
1 tablespoon butter
¼ cup bread crumbs
20 whole almonds, peeled
¼ cup milk

1. Preheat oven to 350°F. Bring honey to lukewarm temperature. Add ½ cup of the sugar and the egg yolks. Beat well.

2. Remove from the heat and add spices, lemon rind and rum. Beat well.

3. Sift baking powder together with flour, and beat into the honey mixture.

4. Whip the egg whites till stiff and gently fold in.

5. Butter a baking sheet 13 by 9 inches with the butter and sprinkle with the bread crumbs. Over this spread the batter about 1 inch thick. Place almonds on top in any design you like.

6. Bake in the preheated oven for 25 to 30 minutes.

7. Remove bread from oven and brush immediately with a mixture of the milk and remaining ¼ cup sugar, which will give it a beautiful shine. The color of this ancient Hungarian delicacy should be walnut brown.

8. Store in an airtight jar and this will keep for many months. Cut into small diamonds or rectangles to serve.

VARIATION: *Try adding slivered almonds and julienne-cut orange peel to the mixture.*

YEAST-RAISED CAKES

Kalács

The word *kalács* comes from the Slavic *koláč,* which in turn comes from *kolo,* meaning circle. The word is so common that probably no one ever defined it, just as nobody would ask for a definition of bread. Actually, a *kalács* is a cake made with a yeast dough, plain, stuffed or mixed. There are special ones for weddings, holidays and other events, made with different mixtures and of different shapes and sizes. Some of them were used centuries ago by the pagan Hungarians. Woven or braided *kalács* signified the hair sacrifice to be placed in a fresh grave, and the pretzel-shaped one was buried as a symbol of a metal arm bracelet. Among the Csángó people (Moldavia) even today, this cake mixture is baked in the shape of a ring and placed on the arm of a still-born baby, so the baby can play with it when arriving in the other world. *Kürtőskalács,* "chimney cake," was rolled onto a log and baked by being turned over an ash fire. You will find here a version of this, adapted to home-oven conditions.

WHIP-BRAIDED COFFEECAKE

Ostorkalács   *2 loaves*

1 cup milk	½ teaspoon salt
1 envelope of yeast	10 tablespoons butter, melted
1 pound flour (2½ cups)	1 egg white
¼ cup sugar	¼ cup ground walnuts
3 egg yolks	

1. Heat milk till lukewarm. Then mix 3 tablespoons milk with the yeast, 2 tablespoons flour and 1 tablespoon sugar. Let this starter rest for 10 minutes.

2. Mix the rest of the milk with the 3 egg yolks, the rest of the sugar and the salt.

3. Add the yeast mixture and the rest of the flour. Make a very hard dough out of it, adding more flour if necessary.

4. Work 6 tablespoons of the butter into the dough, making a very smooth, even texture. Let the dough rise for about 1 hour. Preheat oven to 375°F.

5. Divide the dough into 4 equal long strands, cutting each the same length as the baking sheet that you plan to use.

6. Take 2 strands of the dough and braid them neatly. Make a second braid with the other 2 strands. Butter the braids with 2 tablespoons of the butter, using a pastry brush, and let them rest in a moderately warm place for 30 to 35 minutes.

7. Whip the egg white till stiff and brush tops of braids with it. Sprinkle tops with ground walnuts.

8. Use remaining butter to grease the bottom of a baking sheet, and place the prepared braids on it.

9. Bake them in the preheated oven for 40 minutes.

NOTE: *Hungarian whips used by herdsmen are usually made of elaborately braided pieces of leather; the name of this recipe is probably a reminder of this most decorative object.*

In the old cookbooks where I found it, this cake was mistakenly called "whipped strudel" (vert rétes).

BRIDAL WEDDING LOAF

Menyasszonyi lakodalmas kalács　　　　　　　　*1 loaf*

⅔ cup milk	¼ pound butter
1 envelope of yeast	3 egg yolks
3 cups flour	1 teaspoon salt
¼ cup sugar	1 whole egg, separated

1. Bring milk to lukewarm temperature. To half of the milk add the yeast, 2 tablespoons flour and 1 tablespoon sugar. Mix together well. Let this starter rest for 10 minutes.

2. Mix the rest of the flour and the butter till the mixture forms crumbs. Then add the rest of the milk and the yeast mixture with egg yolks, remaining sugar and the salt. Mix well in a bowl. Knead and mix for 10 to 12 minutes.

3. Let the dough rest till it doubles in bulk, 45 minutes to 1 hour.

4. Put the dough on a floured board and cut into 3 parts. Roll each part to a narrow strip about 15 inches long.

5. Braid the strips to form a long loaf. Put it on a buttered baking sheet 17 by 12 inches. Preheat oven to 375°F.

6. Beat the extra egg yolk with 1 teaspoon water. Brush the loaf with egg-yolk glaze, and put it aside until the glaze becomes dry, 10 to 15 minutes in a 72°F. room. Or you can put your hand on it and feel when the glaze is dry.

7. Now brush the loaf with egg white. Bake in the preheated oven for 40 minutes.

LITTLE CHIMNEY CAKES, OVEN-BAKED

Kürtőskalács, tepsiben　　　　　　　*4 to 6 servings*

1 cup milk	¼ pound sweet butter
¼ cup granulated sugar	Melted butter
½ envelope of yeast	1 whole egg
3 egg yolks	¼ cup fine-chopped or ground
1 egg white	walnuts
½ teaspoon salt	Vanilla sugar
2 cups flour	

1. Make a yeast dough with a little lukewarm milk, 1 tablespoon granulated sugar and the yeast. Let this starter mixture rest for 10 minutes.

2. Mix 3 egg yolks and the egg white with the starter mixture. Add the rest of the milk and granulated sugar and the salt. Mix with the flour.

3. Little by little work in half of the butter. Knead the dough on a floured board for about 15 minutes. Let the dough rest till it doubles in bulk. Preheat oven to 350°F.

4. Butter metal baking tubes ½ inch in diameter and about 6 inches long. Roll dough to a thin sheet and cut strips 8 inches long and ½ inch wide.

5. Roll the strips in spirals on the buttered tubes. Make as many as the dough allows. Let them rest for 10 minutes. During this rest butter the dough twice, using a brush. Beat the whole egg with 1 teaspoon water. Finally brush the dough spirals with this egg wash.

6. Roll the spirals in the chopped walnuts and bake in the preheated oven for about 15 minutes.

7. Gently pull off the cakes from the tubes and sprinkle them with vanilla sugar. Serve the cakes while hot, with jam.

NOTE: *This is one of the oldest Hungarian cakes. The original yeast dough was rolled on a log, then placed over charcoal and turned like a spit roast while cooking. This is the only relation it has to the German* Baumkuchen; *otherwise it is quite a different cake. You could also bake the dough on a buttered rolling pin. The ends of the wood might char a little, but otherwise it will be safe.*

Corn is a basic Hungarian staple, and country folk save the dried corncobs for starters when making a fire, and also for the necessary base on which to roll the little chimney cakes.

A variation that is used today commercially in Hungary: Mix the walnuts with coarse granulated sugar. This gives a nice carmelized surface.

GOLDEN DUMPLING CAKE

Aranygaluska   about 6 servings

1 envelope of yeast
1 cup lukewarm milk
2 tablespoons granulated sugar
1 pound flour
6 egg yolks
Pinch of salt
10 tablespoons sweet butter, melted

Flour for pastry board
Butter for mold
2 tablespoons cake crumbs
1 cup ground walnuts
1 tablespoon grated lemon rind
½ cup thick apricot jam
¼ cup vanilla sugar

1. Mix yeast, ¼ cup lukewarm milk, ½ tablespoon granulated sugar and 3 tablespoons flour. Let this starter mixture rest for 10 minutes.

2. Mix remaining lukewarm milk, the egg yolks, salt, remaining granulated sugar and flour. Mix well and stir into the starter dough.

3. Add 4 tablespoons melted butter, little by little, to the dough, kneading it in to make sure it is incorporated until dough becomes blistered and separates easily from hand or spoon. Let the dough rise for about 1 hour. Preheat oven to 375°F.

4. Sprinkle flour on a board. Put the dough on it and stretch it to a sheet ½ inch thick. Cut the dough into rounds with a 1- to 1½-inch cookie cutter.

5. Butter a kugelhof mold 9 inches in diameter and 4 inches high. Sprinkle it with cake crumbs. Dip the little dough rounds into remaining melted butter, and place a layer of them tightly on the bottom of the mold. Sprinkle with a mixture of walnuts and lemon rind.

6. Arrange more buttered dough rounds to make a second layer. Put ½ teaspoon jam in the center of each round. Continue this way, alternating rounds with ground walnuts and rounds with jam until the mold is filled. Cover top with remaining melted butter. You may need up to ¼ pound additional butter at this point.

7. Bake in the preheated oven for 35 to 40 minutes. Turn out of the mold, sprinkle with vanilla sugar, and serve with Wine Cream or Milk and Rum Cream (both, page 355).

NOTE: *More traditional is a shallow round baking dish, but the kugelhof mold makes a much prettier presentation.*

POPPYSEED BISCUIT

Mákos guba (bobájka)   *6 servings*

½ envelope of yeast
1½ cups lukewarm milk
1 tablespoon plus ½ cup sugar
½ pound flour
3 egg yolks
Pinch of salt
10 tablespoons melted sweet
  butter

Flour for pastry board
1-inch piece of vanilla bean
½ tablespoon grated lemon
  rind
½ pound poppyseeds, ground

1. Mix yeast, 2 tablespoons of the milk, 1 teaspoon sugar and 2 tablespoons flour. Let this starter mixture rest for 10 minutes.

2. Mix 6 tablespoons milk, the egg yolks, salt, 2 teaspoons sugar and remaining flour. Mix well and stir into the starter dough.

3. Add 2 tablespoons of the melted butter, little by little, to the dough, and knead it in until well incorporated. Let the dough rise for 1 hour. Preheat oven to 350°F.

4. Cut dough into walnut-sized pieces. Butter a large baking pan and bake these little biscuits in the preheated oven for 12 to 15 minutes, turning the biscuits to make sure all sides are brown. Set aside.

5. Bring to a boil remaining milk, butter and sugar. Add vanilla bean, lemon rind and poppyseeds; mix well.

6. Pour hot water over the biscuits. When they are softened, drain and add biscuits to the milk and poppyseed mixture. Bring it to a simmer over very low heat. Remove from heat.

7. Serve either hot or cold.

NOTE: *Another very old Hungarian recipe. These little biscuits are almost like the pilot biscuits you eat in New England with seafood, except these are sweet and softened. In northern Hungary (present-day Slovakia) where this dish comes from, the little biscuits were stored for weeks or months in muslin bags, hanging up so the air could go through, to be used on short notice.*

Improbable as it sounds, this is a recommended dish for a cold winter luncheon; very heavy to be sure, and not the thing for a contemporary business luncheon.

POZSONYI ROULADE FILLED WITH POPPYSEEDS

Pozsonyi mákos tekercs (Beigli)   *4 loaves*

POPPYSEED FILLING

½ cup granulated sugar
2 tablespoons honey
2 tablespoons butter
2 tablespoons lemon juice
½ teaspoon fine-grated lemon
  rind

½ pound poppyseeds, ground
  or crushed
Pinch of ground cinnamon
Pinch of ground cloves

DOUGH

⅓ cup milk
½ envelope of yeast
1 pound flour
½ pound butter

¼ pound sugar
1 egg yolk
Pinch of salt
1 whole egg, separated

1. Make the filling: Mix sugar with ½ cup water and cook for a few minutes until syrupy.

2. Add honey, butter, lemon juice and rind. Take off the heat and stir in poppyseeds and spices. Keep the filling warm.

3. Make the dough: Warm milk gently and dissolve the yeast in it.

4. Mix flour, butter and sugar until the mixture forms crumbs. Add egg yolk, the milk with the yeast, and the salt. Knead the mixture well and divide it into 4 portions.

5. Stretch each portion into a thin sheet. Spread one quarter of the filling on each piece of dough. Roll them up tightly and press ends to make a secure closing.

6. Beat the egg yolk with 1 teaspoon water. Brush the rolls with the egg-yolk glaze and let them rise while the egg is getting dry.

7. Place the rolls in a cool spot (refrigerator will do) for 1 to 2 hours, until firm. Preheat oven to 375°F.

8. Now brush the rolls with beaten egg white, and prick with a fork in 3 or 4 places.

9. Place rolls on a baking sheet and bake in the preheated oven for 40 minutes.

VARIATION: *Make a walnut filling in the same way, but add 2 tablespoons crumbs of spongecake or other plain cake to the filling ingredients.*

NOTE: *One of the oddities of this traditional Austro-Hungarian recipe is that first the dough rises, then it is chilled. Chilling should last for at least 1 hour, but it is possible to prepare the dough a day before and bake it the following day. Chilling will crackle the egg-yolk glaze and after baking the surface will look somewhat like a turtle. This is a difficult type of dough to make.*

There is something unexplainable about local tradition; the Sachertorte is best in Vienna, Dobos is the finest in Budapest, cheesecake is richest in New York, and this pastry and its crescent offspring were the best in the city of Pozsony, today's Bratislava. People went there for the sole purpose of eating the best of all possible walnut loaves or crescents. It is not the ingredients that make the difference in these examples but the unbroken line of tradition, passing on the trade secrets and the little tricks to the next generation.

✼ 35 ✼

TORTES
(TORTÁK)

DOBOS TORTE

Dobos torta   *8 to 10 slices*

5 eggs, separated (Use large
  but not jumbo eggs.)
Pinch of salt
½ cup plus ⅓ cup granulated
  sugar

½ cup pastry flour
Sweet butter, softened
Chocolate Filling I (below)

1. Preheat oven to 375°F. Whip the 5 egg whites with 1 tablespoon ice water and a pinch of salt until stiff.

2. Add the egg yolks, one by one, beating for 1 minute after each addition.

3. Add ½ cup of the sugar, spoon by spoon, whipping all the time. (If you are using an electric mixer, turn down to lowest speed.) Add flour, little by little, making sure that it is completely blended into the egg mixture.

4. Line a baking sheet 17 by 12 inches with wax paper, and lightly spread it with 2 tablespoons butter. Pour the batter on the baking sheet. Tap sides a few times to even it out.

5. Bake in the preheated oven for 10 to 12 minutes, until golden brown.

6. Cut the cake into 6 even pieces each 8½ by 4 inches. Pull off the wax paper. Cover the pieces with cloth or fresh wax paper while cooling in order to retain some of the moisture.

7. Make the chocolate filling.

8. Set aside the best of the 6 pieces of pastry to use for the top of the cake.

Spread a little sweet butter on a marble slab or Formica-topped table, and place the chosen cake layer on it.

9. Spread the chocolate filling on the other 5 layers; the filling layers should be about ⅛ inch thick. Put the layers together and frost the sides. Put the rest of the filling in a pastry bag.

10. Melt the ⅓ cup sugar in a heavy frying pan; stir it with a buttered spoon as it cooks over very low heat. The sugar at first will look like dirty snow, then it will dissolve into a walnut-colored shiny liquid. Immediately remove it from the heat and spoon it directly from frying pan onto the top cake layer on the marble slab. Score it to intended portion sizes with the tip of a buttered knife, then cut it all the way through with the buttered knife. You must work fast because the caramel hardens in less than a minute. Be careful not to touch sugar with your hands.

11. When the caramel is cool, put the top layer on top of the filled layers. The shiny glaze is the crowning glory of the cake. Fit a No. 6 tube to the pastry bag and pipe a decorative border of chocolate filling around the top edge of the torte.

12. Cool the cake in the refrigerator until the filling is firm, 3 to 4 hours.

13. Slice the cake with a knife dipped into hot water. Cake will keep in refrigerator for as long as 10 days.

CHOCOLATE FILLING I

2-inch piece of vanilla bean
¾ cup confectioners' sugar
6 ounces sweet butter, softened
3 tablespoons prepared strong
espresso coffee, or 3 level
teaspoons instant coffee
powder mixed with 3
tablespoons water

1 egg
3 ounces semisweet chocolate

1. Split the vanilla bean and scrape out the insides into the sugar.

2. Mix sugar with butter, prepared coffee and the whole egg. Beat into a creamy mixture.

3. Soften the chocolate in the top part of a double boiler over hot water, or in a low oven, and mix into the filling.

4. Cool the filling in the refrigerator for 15 minutes before using it.

NOTE: *You've actually made a Dobos strip. To make a torte, bake 6 or 7 layers in separate 9-inch round layer-cake pans. If your oven is big enough, do them all at the same time; if not, do them in batches. To make a 9-inch torte to give 16 slices, double the amounts given here.*

In Hungary housewives can be divided into two camps, according to whether they believe the Dobos torte should be round or oblong. It makes no difference as far as taste is concerned. For the record, the original torte made by the great Chef was round. For the story of this classic cake, see page 62.

CHOCOLATE POPPYSEED TORTE À LA KUGLER

Kugler csokoládés máktortája   6 to 8 servings

½ cup grated semisweet chocolate
¼ pound plus 1 tablespoon butter
½ cup sugar
6 eggs, separated

¼ cup white bread crumbs
¾ cup ground poppyseeds
Pinch of salt
½ cup currant jam
Chocolate Glaze II (page 418)

1. Preheat oven to 325°F. Soften the chocolate in the top part of a double boiler over hot water, and let it cool.

2. Beat together well ¼ pound butter and the sugar. Add egg yolks, one by one, beating after each addition.

3. Pour the chocolate into the butter and egg-yolk mixture. Add bread crumbs and poppyseeds. Stir gently.

4. Whip egg whites with the pinch of salt till they form peaks. Little by little mix egg whites into the batter. Use your hand to fold so as not to break the egg foam.

5. Butter an 8-inch torte pan 3 inches deep with remaining tablespoon of butter. Pour the batter into the pan and bake the torte in the preheated oven for 30 to 35 minutes.

6. Cook the torte. Then slice it into 2 layers, and fill it with jam. Cover top and sides with chocolate glaze.

NOTE: *Kugler was one of the giants of the Hungarian pastry world (see page 56). Although he was of Swiss origin and his creations were mostly elaborate cakes with fancy fillings and decorations, he used the Hungarian housewife's common ingredient—poppyseeds—to create this unusual torte.*

BEATRIX TORTE

Beatrix torta   8 *to 12 servings*

6 eggs, separated
1¾ cups plus 5 tablespoons
    granulated sugar
1 cup almonds, peeled and
    ground
¼ pound butter
4 tablespoons vanilla sugar
    made with XXX powdered
    sugar

1 tablespoon powdered cocoa
⅓ cup milk
2 tablespoons rum
20 whole almonds, peeled
7 ounces almonds, chopped and
    lightly roasted

1. Preheat oven to 375°F. Stand a mixing bowl over the bottom part of a double boiler filled with steaming water. Beat the egg whites and ¾ cup granulated sugar over steam until so stiff a spoon will stand in them. Remove from heat, and mix in the *ground* almonds.

2. Butter a 7-inch torte pan 3 inches high with 1 tablespoon butter. Dust with fine bread crumbs. Pour in the mixture. Bake the torte in the preheated oven for 15 to 20 minutes.

3. Cool the cake. Cut it into 2 layers.

4. Make the filling: Mix the egg yolks with the vanilla sugar and the powdered cocoa. Continue mixing and add milk and finally the rum.

5. Place the mixture over low heat and beat constantly until it starts simmering. Remove from heat.

6. Whip 6 tablespoons of the butter till foamy, and mix it into the egg-yolk mixture.

7. Spread some of the filling on one cake layer. Place the other layer on top, then use the rest of the filling to spread on the sides.

8. Brown 5 tablespoons granulated sugar with ½ tablespoon butter till it is caramelized. Dip the *whole* almonds into the caramel. Work very fast; use a little spoon or pincers to hold the almonds. Add 1 teaspoon butter and stir again.

9. Place 1 cup granulated sugar in a heavy frying pan and pour in 7 ounces chopped almonds. Let the sugar melt and lightly brown; then pour it on marble or on a buttered cookie sheet and let it cool. Crush the candylike sheet in a mortar; the texture should be somewhat like that of uncooked rice. Sprinkle the top of the torte with the crushed almond caramel.

10. Place almonds on top of cake, making a circular design. Keep chilled but serve at room temperature.

NOTE: *The famed Mátyás Pince restaurant in Budapest created and serves this torte. I am deeply touched and grateful that its director, Endre Papp, and the director of the Fifth Restaurant District of Budapest, Andor Szigeti, opened their files and for the first time revealed this recipe.*

CHESTNUT TORTE

Gesztenyetorta   *8 to 12 servings*

Salt | Butter
10 egg whites | Flour
¾ cup sugar | Chestnut Filling (below)
¼ cup flour | Chocolate, grated or shaved
½ cup finely ground walnuts

1. Preheat oven to 375°F. Add 1 teaspoon cold water and a pinch of salt to the egg whites. Whip egg whites until soft peak stage. Continue to beat and add the sugar, spoon by spoon until egg whites are very stiff. (A spoon should be able to stand up in the meringue if it is beaten stiff enough.)

2. Gently add the flour, walnuts and another pinch of salt. Fold in, making sure you do not break the egg-white foam.

3. Line a baking sheet 17 by 12 inches with wax paper. Butter the paper lightly and sprinkle with flour; shake off excess.

4. Spread the batter evenly on the prepared baking sheet. Bake in the preheated oven for 12 to 15 minutes, until firm and golden brown on top.

5. Cool completely with wax paper over top to keep cake from getting crusty; then cut lengthwise into 3 pieces.

6. Fill the cake layers with chestnut filling and cover sides and top with more of it. Decorate with grated or shaved chocolate. Chill in refrigerator for several hours before serving.

CHESTNUT FILLING

2 pounds chestnuts in shells, or | ¾ cup vanilla sugar
   1 pound canned Swiss or | 1 whole egg
   French chestnut purée | ¼ cup light rum
3 ounces semisweet chocolate
½ pound plus 2 tablespoons
   sweet butter

1. Cook the chestnuts, shell and skin them, and purée while still warm. You should have about 1 pound purée.

2. Soften the chocolate in the top part of a double boiler over hot water.

3. Beat together the butter, vanilla sugar, egg and rum until the mixture is very light and foamy.

4. Add the softened chocolate and the chestnut purée, and beat until thoroughly mixed.

NOTE: *This cake can be round, square or oblong. It is an easy cake to make and yet quite different from the run-of-the-mill torte. The layers have the texture of a moist spongecake. Make smaller layers and have a torte with more than 3 layers, if you prefer. If you bake a dough a little longer, you will get crisper cake layers.*

MALAKOFF CREAM TORTE

Malakoff-krémtorta　　　　　　　　　　　*12 servings*

Spongecake (page 395)	½ cup milk
1 cup plus 1 tablespoon confectioners' sugar	½ cup plus 1 teaspoon light rum
¼ pound sweet butter	1 cup heavy cream
1 cup ground almonds	20 whole candied cherries

1. Start this the day before you plan to use it. Bake the spongecake in a round 9-inch springform pan.

2. Slice spongecake into 3 layers. Place the bottom layer on a serving platter.

3. Whip 1 cup sugar with the butter till foamy, then mix in ground almonds and finally the milk.

4. Measure one third of the ½ cup rum and moisten the bottom layer of cake with it. Spread one third of the almond mixture on top.

5. Put the second layer of cake on top of this and repeat moistening with rum and spreading with almond mixture.

6. Place third layer on top. Again moisten with rum and spread with almond mixture. Let the cake rest in the refrigerator overnight.

7. Next morning whip the heavy cream with remaining tablespoon of sugar until stiff. Lightly mix in 1 teaspoon rum. Cover top and sides of entire cake with the cream. Decorate with candied cherries.

NOTE: *Like Nesselrode, named for another Russian general-aristocrat, Malakoff originated in the Russian kitchen. It was probably brought back by French chefs and then copied by other European chefs. There are at least half a dozen recipes for cooked Malakoff cream, and another half dozen for cold preparations.*

This is a friend's family recipe at least three generations old.

PULI TORTE

Puli torta   *8 to 12 servings*

6 eggs, separated   ¼ cup flour
½ cup sugar   Butter
½ cup grated semisweet   Flour
    chocolate   Walnut Filling II (below)
Pinch of salt

1. Preheat oven to 375° F. Whip the egg yolks with the sugar till foamy. Add the grated chocolate, salt and flour.

2. Whip egg whites till they form peaks. Very gently fold into the first mixture; try not to break the egg-white foam.

3. Butter a baking sheet 17 by 12 inches, and sprinkle with flour. Pour the batter on the baking sheet.

4. Bake in the preheated oven for 12 to 15 minutes. Put it aside to cool.

5. Make the filling.

6. Cut the torte into 2 pieces. Fill with some of the walnut filling, and cover top and sides with the rest.

WALNUT FILLING II

1 cup ground walnuts   1 tablespoon light rum
¼ cup milk   ½ cup vanilla confectioners'
10 tablespoons sweet butter   sugar

1. Scald milk. Remove from heat and stir in walnuts. Cool.

2. In a separate bowl beat butter, rum and vanilla sugar together till very light and foamy.

3. Put both mixtures together and blend well.

NOTE: *When scalding milk, first rinse the pot with water; then the milk will not burn on the bottom.*

STEFANIA TORTE

Stefánia torta   *8 to 12 servings*

7 eggs, separated
Pinch of salt
½ cup plus 2 tablespoons sugar
½ cup plus 1 tablespoon flour
Butter

Flour
Chocolate-Cream Filling I
   (below)
1 tablespoon powdered cocoa

1. Preheat oven to 375°F. Whip the egg whites with 1 tablespoon water and a pinch of salt to a very stiff foam.
2. Add egg yolks, one by one, and beat for an additional 3 minutes.
3. Add ½ cup sugar, spoon by spoon, and beat for 3 or 4 minutes longer.
4. Finally slowly stir in the flour till the mixture is smooth.
5. Cover a baking sheet 17 by 12 inches with wax paper and butter the paper. Sprinkle lightly with flour. Shake off any excess.
6. Pour in the batter, and bake in the preheated oven for 18 to 20 minutes, or until golden brown.
7. Cool the torte, and cut it lengthwise into 3 pieces. Spread layers with filling and put together. Spread more of the filling smoothly on top and sides.
8. Mix cocoa and remaining 2 tablespoons sugar in a fine sieve, and sprinkle over the top of the torte. Serve chilled.

CHOCOLATE-CREAM FILLING I

6 ounces semisweet chocolate,
   softened
¼ cup heavy cream
½ pound plus 4 tablespoons
   sweet butter, softened

1 egg
1 cup vanilla confectioners'
   sugar

1. Soften the chocolate in the top part of a double boiler over hot water. Cool completely.
2. Whip the cream and set aside.
3. Whip softened butter with egg and sugar till foamy, then whip in the whipped cream. Finally blend in the cooled softened chocolate.
4. Cool in the refrigerator for 15 minutes before assembling torte.

ILONA TORTE

Ilona torta   *12 or more servings*

5 ounces semisweet chocolate	Pinch of salt
1 cup sugar	1 teaspoon ice water
6 tablespoons sweet butter	Butter
8 eggs, separated	Flour
½ pound walnuts, ground	Mocha Filling I (below)
2 tablespoons white bread crumbs	2 tablespoons chopped walnuts

1. Preheat oven to 375°F. Heat chocolate with sugar and ¼ cup water. This will take 5 to 6 minutes, with constant stirring. Heat and stir till a smooth syrup is formed.

2. In a mixing bowl whip butter with egg yolks till light and foamy. Add the chocolate syrup, ground walnuts and bread crumbs.

3. Adding salt and ice water, whip egg whites till so stiff a spoon will stand in them; then very, very gently fold them into the chocolate mixture.

4. Butter a 10-inch torte pan 3 inches deep and sprinkle with flour. Shake out excess. Pour the batter into the pan, and bake in the preheated oven for 20 to 25 minutes. Cool the cake completely.

5. Make filling.

6. Cut the cooled torte into 2 layers. Fill the layers with two thirds of the filling. Use the rest as frosting. Finally, sprinkle with chopped walnuts. Serve chilled.

MOCHA FILLING I

¼ pound semisweet chocolate	2 egg yolks
¼ cup prepared very strong espresso coffee	⅓ pound sweet butter
½ teaspoon instant coffee	⅓ cup vanilla confectioners' sugar

1. Heat chocolate and coffee together for a few minutes, until chocolate is melted and the mixture is smooth. Let it cool completely.

2. In a mixing bowl whip the egg yolks with butter and sugar till light and foamy.

3. Whip in the cooled chocolate-coffee mixture.

NOTE: *This cake is perhaps closer to me than any other for the sentimental reason that it is named after my mother and my daughter, Andrea Ilona. The origin of this torte was lost in the second half of the nineteenth century, when most of these recipes were formalized and written down. It is perhaps the richest of all chocolate tortes.*

ROASTED HAZELNUT TORTE

Piritott mogyorótorta   *8 to 12 servings*

¾ cup hazelnuts
½ pound unsweetened
   chocolate
½ pound sweet butter
½ pound sugar
6 egg whites

Pinch of salt
Butter
Flour
Mocha Filling II (below)
Whipped cream, sweetened

1. Roast hazelnuts in a preheated 200°F. oven for 10 to 15 minutes. While nuts are still hot, peel them by rubbing them in a clean kitchen towel. Grind nuts to a fine, floury texture. Increase oven heat to 375°F.

2. Soften the chocolate in the top part of a double boiler over hot water. Let it cool.

3. Whip butter with sugar till foamy, then whip in the softened chocolate and hazelnut flour.

4. Whip egg whites with a pinch of salt till very stiff, then very slowly and carefully fold them into the chocolate-hazelnut mixture.

5. Thoroughly butter a baking sheet 17 by 12 inches. Sprinkle it with flour. Pour in the mixture. Bake in the preheated oven for 12 to 15 minutes.

6. Cut the torte lengthwise into 3 layers. Fill with some of the mocha filling, and spread the rest on the top and around the sides. Decorate with sugared whipped cream if you like.

MOCHA FILLING II

½ cup sugar
¼ cup prepared very strong
   espresso coffee
¼ pound semisweet chocolate,
   softened

⅓ pound butter
6 egg yolks

1. Cook sugar with coffee until syrupy, 3 to 4 minutes. Let it cool.

2. Mix in the softened chocolate and butter. While constantly stirring, add the egg yolks, one by one, and keep stirring until the filling thickens. Cool.

NOTE: *As you notice, there is no flour in this torte, which is a notable characteristic of many Hungarian torte recipes. A Hungarian housewife or pastry chef thinks of a French, Swiss or German pastry chef who uses flour for a torte like this one in much the same way as a French chef thinks of a saucier who thickens sauces with flour.*

FATHER'S FAVORITE CHOCOLATE CAKE

Apák kedvenc csokoládétortája   *12 or more servings*

6 whole eggs, separated	2 extra egg whites
¾ cup granulated sugar	Butter
½ cup ground walnuts	Flour
4 ounces sweet chocolate,	Chocolate Filling II (below)
softened	Chocolate Glaze I (below)
3 tablespoons white bread	
crumbs	

1. Preheat oven to 375°F. Whip the egg yolks together with sugar until foamy. Add ground walnuts, softened chocolate and bread crumbs.

2. Whip all 8 egg whites until they form peaks. Very gently fold the egg whites into the first mixture.

3. Butter a 10-inch torte pan 3 inches high, and sprinkle with flour. Pour the batter into the pan and bake in the preheated oven for 20 minutes.

4. After 20 minutes test with a fork; if it comes out clean, the cake is done; if not bake for a few more minutes. Cool.

5. When the cake is cool, cut it into 2 layers. Fill the cake with some of the filling and spread some around the edges, but do not put any on the top.

6. Spread the glaze on top of the torte. Place it in the refrigerator to cool before serving.

CHOCOLATE FILLING II

2 egg yolks	4 ounces sweet chocolate,
6 ounces butter	softened
½ cup vanilla confectioners'	
sugar	

Beat egg yolks, butter and sugar together until well mixed. Add the softened chocolate and blend well. Place in the refrigerator for 30 minutes before using.

CHOCOLATE GLAZE I

4 ounces sweet chocolate   1 tablespoon butter
3 tablespoons granulated sugar

Cook chocolate and sugar with ¼ cup water for 6 to 8 minutes. Take from the heat and stir in the butter until it is melted and the glaze smooth and shiny.

VARIATION: *Make double the amount of filling. Cut torte into 3 layers, and make 2 layers of filling.*

NOTE: *"Father" does not like fancy decorations, so let only the shine of the glaze give the pleasure to the eye.*

APPLE TORTE WITH LEMON GLAZE

Almatorta citromjéggel   *8 to 12 servings*

1¾ cups all-purpose flour
½ pound sweet butter
¼ pound peeled almonds,
   ground fine

¼ pound vanilla confectioners'
   sugar
Apple Filling (below)
Lemon Glaze (below)

1. Preheat oven to 375°F. Mix flour and butter with pastry blender until crumbs form. Add the almonds and sugar. Knead together well.
2. Divide the dough into 4 sections. Between two sheets of floured wax paper, roll each section into an even thin torte layer. Cut each layer to desired torte shape.
3. Put the layers on a baking sheet without sides. Bake in the preheated oven for 12 to 15 minutes, till the layers are golden brown, on the light side.
4. Carefully slide them off the baking sheet onto a rack to cool.
5. Make the filling and cool it.
6. Spread a layer of filling on each torte layer, and cover top with lemon glaze, letting it dribble down the sides. Chill overnight in refrigerator. Let the torte stand at room temperature for 45 minutes before serving.

APPLE FILLING

¾ pound sugar
1¾ pounds apples, peeled,
   cored and chopped
¼ cup almonds, peeled and
   sliced lengthwise

½ cup chopped citron
Juice of 1 lemon

Bring the sugar and ¾ cup water to a boil. Add chopped apples. A few minutes later add almonds, citron and lemon juice. Cook the mixture till it becomes like a hot jelly. Stir often. Cool before using.

LEMON GLAZE I

Citromjég I

¼ pound confectioners' sugar   Juice and grated rind of ½
1 egg white   lemon

Sift confectioners' sugar to remove all lumps. Whip egg white with sugar, lemon rind and juice, till a spoon can stand up in it.

LEMON GLAZE II

Citromjég II

¼ pound confectioners' sugar,   Juice of ½ lemon
  sifted

Combine sugar with lemon juice and 1½ tablespoons warm water. Whip till the glaze becomes brilliantly shiny like a silk satin. Use immediately.

NOTE: *For best results make this torte the day before you plan to use it, and keep it in the refrigerator till serving time.*
Both glazes can be used on top of other tortes.

DANKOVSZKI TORTE

Dankovszki torta   *12 or more servings*

7 eggs, separated   Butter
½ cup sugar   Flour
⅓ cup grated chocolate   Filbert Filling (below)
1 tablespoon white bread   12 whole filberts, toasted
  crumbs
¾ cup toasted filberts, ground
  fine

1. Preheat oven to 375°F. Mix egg yolks with sugar till foamy. Add grated chocolate, bread crumbs and *ground* filberts.
2. Whip egg whites until stiff peaks form, then very gently fold them into the first mixture.
3. Butter and flour a 10-inch torte pan 3 inches deep. Pour in the batter,

and bake in the preheated oven for 20 to 25 minutes. For testing use the fork method; gently push a fork into the torte; if it comes out clean, the cake is baked.

4. Cool the torte, then cut it into 3 layers. Fill it with the filbert filling, leaving enough to cover sides and top.

5. Decorate with the *whole* filberts and sprinkle with the somewhat lumpy remaining filbert-sugar mixture.

6. Put the torte in the refrigerator for a day to mellow, then serve this classic Hungarian torte in its full glory.

FILBERT FILLING

1 cup confectioners' sugar	4 eggs
¾ cup fine-ground toasted filberts	2 tablespoons granulated sugar
	½ pound butter

1. Brown the confectioners' sugar, stirring constantly, then add the ground filberts. Brown it all together for a few more minutes.

2. Butter a soup plate and pour the mixture in it. Let it cool.

3. Place the cooled nut and sugar mixture in a mortar and crush it with a pestle till it becomes powdery. Sieve it, and set aside the lumpy pieces that did not go through the sieve.

4. Place the eggs and granulated sugar in the top part of a double boiler and cook, stirring constantly, until the mixture becomes creamy. Cool.

5. Whip the butter till foamy. Add to the cooled egg and sugar mixture, and finally add the fine-sieved filbert mixture.

PORCUPINE TORTE

Sün torta   *8 to 12 servings*

FIRST TORTE

4 egg yolks	6 egg whites
4 tablespoons sugar	Pinch of salt
3 tablespoons flour	

SECOND TORTE

4 tablespoons butter	2 tablespoons sugar
1 tablespoon prepared very strong espresso coffee	1 tablespoon flour
2 eggs, separated	1 tablespoon powdered cocoa

Butter   ½ cup thick apricot jam
Flour   Walnut Filling III (below)
2 tablespoons rum   1 cup cake crumbs

1. Make the first torte: Whip the egg yolks with the sugar till foamy. Add flour and keep whipping.

2. Whip the egg whites with a pinch of salt till they form peaks, and gently fold them into the first mixture. Set aside. Preheat oven to 375°F.

3. Make the second torte: Mix the butter, coffee, egg yolks and sugar, whipping all the while.

4. Sieve flour and powdered cocoa together, and blend thoroughly with the egg-yolk mixture.

5. Whip the egg whites until stiff, and gently fold them into the second mixture.

6. Butter 2 torte pans, each 8 inches in diameter and 2 inches high. Sprinkle with flour. Pour each torte batter into a separate pan. Bake in the preheated oven for 15 to 20 minutes.

7. Prick the baked layers with a fork, and drop by drop moisten them with rum till they are soaked.

8. Cut the first torte, the light-colored one, into 2 layers. Place one layer, cut side up, on a cake plate. Cover the cut side with jam. On top of the jam place one quarter of the walnut filling.

9. Place the second torte, the brown one, on top, and cover it with another quarter of the filling.

10. Spread the cut side of the second light-colored layer with the rest of the jam. Place it, jam side down, on top of the filling-covered brown layer.

11. Cover top and sides of cake with the rest of the filling. Put the cake crumbs in a sieve and shake over top of cake.

WALNUT FILLING III

¼ cup milk   2 egg yolks
½ cup ground walnuts   1 tablespoon rum
¼ pound butter
½ cup vanilla confectioners'
     sugar

1. Bring the milk to a boil with the ground walnuts. Remove from heat and cool.

2. Beat butter, sugar and egg yolks together till foamy. Add the rum.

3. Combine both mixtures when the first mixture is cool.

GERBEAUD SLICE

Gerbeaud szelet   *10 or more servings*

½ cup milk
½ envelope of yeast
½ cup XXX powdered sugar
1½ cups cake flour
6 ounces sweet butter, softened

3 egg yolks
½ teaspoon salt
Walnut Apricot Filling
(below)
Chocolate Glaze II (below)

1. Warm ¼ cup of the milk to lukewarm. Mix with the yeast, 1 tablespoon of the sugar and 3 tablespoons of the flour. Let this starter rest for 10 minutes.

2. Add the rest of the flour, the softened butter, egg yolks, salt and remaining milk and sugar. Knead together quickly. Let the dough rise for 10 to 15 minutes.

3. Divide the dough into 3 portions. Preheat oven to 375°F.

4. Make the filling.

5. Stretch each portion of dough to fit a baking sheet 13 by 9 inches. Put one dough layer on the baking sheet with a ¼-inch overlap at the edges.

6. Evenly spread half of the filling on top of the dough, then cover with another thin sheet of dough. Add the rest of the filling, and cover with the last sheet of dough.

7. Bake the cake in the preheated oven for 40 minutes. Cool.

8. Make the glaze.

9. Cover the cooled cake with glaze, using a spatula or any other implement that will enable you to make it very smooth. When the glaze is dry you may slice the cake, but not before.

WALNUT APRICOT FILLING

3 egg whites
½ cup sugar

1 cup ground walnuts
3 tablespoons thick apricot jam

Whip egg whites and add sugar little by little till the mixture forms peaks. At the very end gradually add the ground walnuts and jam.

CHOCOLATE GLAZE II

¼ cup sugar
1 tablespoon powdered cocoa

3 ounces sweet chocolate
½ teaspoon sweet butter

Mix ¼ cup water with the sugar, powdered cocoa, chocolate and butter. Cook over low heat for 8 to 10 minutes, stirring all the while.

NOTE: *This biscuitlike cake was created by a famous Budapest confectioner, whose shop still exists under the name of Vörösmarty Pastry Shop (see page 56).*

Hungarian housewives always add a pinch of salt and 1 tablespoon water when whipping egg whites. The foam becomes stiffer and yet lighter. They also add a spoonful of water when whipping cream.

CARROT TORTE

Sárgarépatorta   *8 to 12 servings*

6 eggs, separated
1½ cups confectioners' sugar
1½ cups puréed cooked carrots
Grated rind and juice of ½
   lemon
1 teaspoon ground cinnamon

½ cup fine-ground hazelnuts
½ teaspoon baking powder
½ cup white bread crumbs
¼ cup flour
2 tablespoons butter

1. Preheat oven to 375°F. Mix egg yolks well with sugar.
2. Add the puréed carrots, lemon rind and juice to the egg yolks, and mix well.
3. Make a stiff foam of the egg whites and gently mix with the cinnamon, ground hazelnuts and baking powder.
4. Mix bread crumbs and flour into egg whites, and gently fold into the carrot mixture.
5. Butter a 9-inch torte pan 3 inches high with the butter, and pour in the batter.
6. Bake in the preheated oven for 20 to 25 minutes. Test with a needle to make sure the cake is cooked.

RIGÓ JANCSI

12 servings

7 eggs, separated
Pinch of salt
½ cup sugar
2 tablespoons powdered cocoa
⅓ cup flour

Butter
½ cup thick apricot jam
Chocolate Glaze III (below)
Chocolate-Cream Filling II
   (below)

1. Preheat oven to 375°F. Whip the egg whites with a pinch of salt and 1 tablespoon water till very stiff.

2. Add egg yolks, one by one, and continue to beat for about 3 minutes. Add sugar, little by little, and beat it for still another 3 minutes.

3. Sieve cocoa and flour together and mix into the first mixture.

4. Cut a piece of wax paper to fit a baking pan 16 by 12 inches. Butter the paper. Spread the batter evenly in the lined pan, and bake in the preheated oven for 12 to 15 minutes.

5. Use a fork to test if the cake is done. When it is done, let it cool.

6. Pull off wax paper. Cut cake lengthwise into 2 portions. Spread the top of one portion with apricot jam and set it aside.

7. Make the glaze, and spread it on the second layer of cake. When the glazed layer is cool, cut it into 4-inch squares.

8. Make the filling, and spread it on top of the apricot jam. Place the chocolate-glazed squares on top. Dip a slicing knife into hot water and cut the cake squares all the way through to the bottom.

CHOCOLATE GLAZE III

2 ounces semisweet chocolate	2 tablespoons powdered cocoa
½ cup sugar	½ teaspoon sweet butter

1. Melt the chocolate in the top part of a double boiler over hot water. Cool.

2. Mix sugar and cocoa with ¼ cup water. Add to cooled chocolate, mix in the butter and simmer for 5 minutes.

CHOCOLATE-CREAM FILLING II

1 envelope of unflavored gelatin	2½ cups heavy cream
2 ounces semisweet chocolate	¾ cup vanilla sugar made with XXX powdered sugar

1. Dissolve gelatin in 1 tablespoon cold water. Add 4 scant tablespoons hot water and stir well. Let gelatin cool.

2. Soften the chocolate in the top part of a double boiler over steaming water, and let it cool.

3. Whip the heavy cream till stiff and add sugar, spoonful by spoonful, while whipping all the time.

4. Add the gelatin and the cooled melted chocolate, little by little. If whipped cream is very cold, the softened chocolate should be lukewarm. If you are not very experienced, do it the other way around and add the whipped cream mixed with gelatin to the softened chocolate, and keep adding it until you get a smooth, pale-brown color.

NOTE: *The original recipe, based on information from the Hungarian Bakers and Confectioners Guild, did have apricot jam; this was forgotten in the past seven decades. Perhaps it does make the cake somewhat wet, but try it with jam and without jam to determine your own preference.*

What the original recipe did not have was gelatin, which the present recipe includes. Frankly, it is a puzzle to me how they jelled the filling, because without gelatin the filling does not quite stand up.

It is most important that the chocolate you use should be of the finest quality, the kind used by first-class professional pastry shops.

According to menus of the 1920's, the cake was also baked in a round pan. I see no reason why it shouldn't be done. In this case, of course, you should cover the sides with whipped cream and sprinkle the top with chocolate shavings.

✳ 36 ✳

COOKIES, SMALL CAKES, SMALL PASTRIES (APRÓSÜTEMÉNYEK, SZELETEK ÉS TEASÜTEMÉNYEK)

JENNY'S WALNUT COOKIES

Jennyke diós süteménye   2 dozen sandwich cookies

1½ cups flour, approximately
1 cup sweet butter
½ cup confectioners' sugar
⅔ cup ground walnuts

¼ teaspoon salt
Walnut Cream Filling (below)
Vanilla sugar

1. Preheat oven to 375°F. Mix flour and butter until the mixture forms crumbs. Add sugar, walnuts and salt. Knead well. You may have to add about ¼ cup flour so the dough will not feel sticky. It will help to put the dough in the refrigerator for 30 minutes before rolling, particularly if you are not used to pastry work.

2. Cut the dough into halves. Roll out each half between sheets of wax paper to ¼-inch thickness.

3. Cut dough with a small biscuit cutter. Place rounds on a baking sheet, and bake in the preheated oven for 12 minutes. Cookies should be only lightly browned around the edges. Cool.

4. When cookies are cool, fill them with walnut cream filling, making a kind of sandwich out of them. Sprinkle with vanilla sugar.

WALNUT CREAM FILLING

¼ cup milk
¼ cup sugar
1-inch piece of vanilla bean

¾ cup ground walnuts
2 tablespoons lemon juice
⅓ cup sweet butter

1. Bring milk, sugar and vanilla bean to a boil; do not let the mixture boil over.

2. Reduce heat. Stir in the ground walnuts and lemon juice. Let the filling simmer until thickened. Shut off heat and let the filling cool. Discard vanilla bean.

3. After filling is completely cooled, whip the butter in a separate bowl till it is foamy. Then whip in the walnut filling.

NOTE: *This cookie is a specialty of Mrs. Jenny Szemere Stratford* (see page 447).

NON PLUS ULTRA

about 3 dozen sandwich cookies

1 cup flour
¼ pound plus 1 tablespoon
 butter
1½ tablespoons vanilla sugar
2 egg yolks
Pinch of salt

1 egg white
4 tablespoons confectioners'
 sugar
½ tablespoon lemon juice
¼ cup peach or other jam

1. Preheat oven to 350°F. Using 2 knives, work together thoroughly the flour and butter. Add vanilla sugar, egg yolks and salt. Knead well but quickly.

2. Put the dough between 2 sheets of wax paper and roll it to ¼-inch thickness.

3. Punch out cookies with a 2-inch cutter. Punch out the centers of half of these rounds with a 1-inch cutter. Place them on a baking sheet and bake for 15 minutes.

4. Make a meringue: Whip the egg white till stiff, then mix with confectioners' sugar and lemon juice.

5. Spread the meringue on top of the rounds and also the rings. Place them in the warm oven, turn the heat off and bake (or almost dry) them for 30 minutes. The meringue must remain snow white. Cool.

6. When cooled, spread jam on the sides without meringue. Put them together, making little sandwiches with the meringue glaze on both outer sides, with jam showing in the center of one.

NOTE: *My maternal grandparents lived in a small town called Tolna-Tamási, and one of my fondest childhood memories is connected with their dining room, or more specifically with the credenza in their dining room. Non Plus Ultra cookies were always on the bottom shelf ready to be "sampled" or stolen as the case may be. Together with my cousin, Évi, we actually named these cookies* tamási. *I am willing to bet that they were better than Monsieur Proust's* madeleines.

WALNUT SLICE

Diós szelet   *2 dozen slices*

½ pound walnuts
½ pound confectioners' sugar
1 egg, separated
2 tablespoons plus a few drops
    of lemon juice

3 tablespoons granulated sugar
Butter and crumbs for baking
    pan

1. Preheat oven to 200°F. Grind the walnuts just before using them, and mix with the confectioners' sugar.
2. Mix egg yolk with 2 tablespoons lemon juice, then mix this with the walnut and sugar mixture.
3. Put the batter on a board and roll into a loaf 2 feet long. Slightly flatten the top to get a shape 1 inch high and 3 inches wide.
4. Beat the egg white, granulated sugar and a few drops of lemon juice until very stiff. Spread the meringue on top of the loaf.
5. Dip a knife into flour before cutting each slice, and cut the loaf into 1-inch slices. Put them on a buttered and crumbed baking pan.
6. Bake the slices, or virtually dry them, in the barely warm oven for 10 to 15 minutes. The glaze must remain white.
7. Serve with afternoon coffee, or after-dinner coffee. They taste almost like candy.

EVENING FAIRY

Estike   *4 dozen cookies*

1 tablespoon butter	Few drops of vanilla extract
¾ cup flour	Pinch of salt
2 eggs	1 tablespoon lemon juice
¾ cup sugar	1 tablespoon aniseeds

1. Butter a baking sheet with the butter, and sprinkle lightly with flour.

2. Beat the eggs, sugar, vanilla, salt and lemon juice until foamy. This should take from 10 to 15 minutes.

3. Slowly add remaining flour and beat for another 5 minutes.

4. Place teaspoons of dough on the buttered and floured baking sheet. Leave 1 inch of space between the little cookies. Sprinkle a few aniseeds on top.

5. Leave the unbaked cookies at room temperature for the night. The following day bake them at the lowest possible heat for 10 to 15 minutes, or until they are done. These have to be almost dried rather than baked, like a good meringue.

NOTE: *The name comes from the fact that these are prepared the night before.*

SWEET BULL'S EYE

Édes ökörszem   *about 30 sandwich cookies*

½ pound sweet butter	3 egg yolks
¾ pound cake flour (about 1⅘ cups)	1 tablespoon sour cream
Pinch of salt	½ cup fine-chopped almonds, approximately
¼ pound confectioners' sugar (about ¾ cup)	Sugar
Grated rind of ¼ lemon	Apricot jam

1. Preheat oven to 375°F. Mix butter, flour and a pinch of salt until the mixture forms crumbs. Add sugar, lemon rind, 2 egg yolks and the sour cream. Make a dough out of the mixture by kneading lightly.

2. Put a sheet of wax paper on a board and place half of the dough on it; top with another sheet of wax paper. Roll the dough to ¼-inch thickness.

3. Take off the top sheet of wax paper, and cut the dough with a round

cookie cutter 2 inches in diameter.

4. Roll out the other half of the dough, and cut it too with a 2-inch cookie cutter. Then for this batch only, use a smaller cookie cutter, about 1 inch in diameter, and cut out the centers, thus making little doughnut shapes.

5. Beat the remaining egg yolk with 1 teaspoon water. Brush the little doughnut shapes with this egg wash. Then dip them into the chopped almonds.

6. Place the first batch of cookies without the holes and the almond-topped little doughnut shapes on a baking sheet. Bake in the preheated oven for 15 minutes.

7. Sprinkle the baked almond-topped rings with sugar. Place jam in the center of the baked rounds (the first batch). Put almond-topped rings on the jam-topped rounds. Jam will show in the center as the "bull's eye."

NOTE: *Hungarian apricot jam is generally available at most Middle European stores, and you will find it is a much thicker and less runny jam than those usually sold elsewhere.*

If you want to reheat a cake or cookie that has no cream in it or glaze on top, put it in a wet paper bag and keep in a 250°F. oven for about 15 minutes.

WHIPPED-CREAM STICKS

Tejszínes rúdacskák   *30 cookies*

4 egg whites	1 cup flour
⅔ cup sugar	Butter
Pinch of salt	Flour
¾ cup heavy cream	

1. Preheat oven to 375°F. Beat the egg whites and sugar together until the meringue is very stiff and foamy.

2. In a separate mixing bowl, add the pinch of salt to the cream, and whip until the cream is stiff.

3. Gently combine the two mixtures. Little by little add the flour. Make absolutely sure that you don't break the foam. Place the mixture in a pastry bag fitted with a ¼-inch tube.

4. Butter a baking sheet and sprinkle it with flour. Squeeze out little sticks 4 inches long on the baking sheet, leaving 2 inches of space between them.

5. Bake in the preheated oven for 10 to 15 minutes, or until the sticks are golden brown. Remove from pan with a warm knife.

NOTE: *Have a cup of hot chocolate accompanied with these little cakes, and you are instantly carried back to "the good old days" of Franz Joseph.*

ROLLED WAFER

Göngyölt ostya   *about 3 dozen wafers*

½ vanilla bean   Pinch of salt
⅔ cup sugar   ½ cup flour
7 tablespoons butter   Butter for pan
2½ egg whites

1. Preheat oven to 225°F. Scrape inside of vanilla bean into the sugar. Whip vanilla and sugar with butter till foamy. Add egg whites and salt, and whip for 5 minutes.

2. Add flour and whip for an additional 3 or 4 minutes.

3. Thoroughly butter a baking sheet. Spread thin layers of batter, 2 inches wide and 5 inches long, on the baking sheet. Bake for 10 minutes.

4. When done, gently separate wafers with a knife. You must work very quickly in removing wafers from baking sheet because they will stick within seconds. While hot, they can be rolled on the handle of a wooden spoon. Or you can leave them flat.

NOTE: *This is not really a wafer in the sense of a French gaufrette.*

ALMOND CRESCENTS

Mandulás kiflik   *about 20 crescents*

1⅔ cups flour   Pinch of salt
½ pound butter   ½ cup confectioners' sugar
1 cup ground blanched   Vanilla sugar
   almonds

1. Preheat oven to 375°F. Mix flour and butter together till they form crumbs. Then add ground almonds, salt and confectioners' sugar. Mix well.

2. Cut dough into walnut-sized pieces and roll to form pieces 4 inches long and ½ inch thick. Twist each one slightly to make a crescent shape.

3. Place crescents on a baking sheet. Bake in the preheated oven for 12 to 15 minutes. Cool for 5 minutes.

4. While crescents are still warm, dust them with vanilla sugar.

WATER-DRAGGING BUTTER CRESCENTS

Vizen kullogó omlós kifli   *about 30 pieces*

3 cups flour	1 tablespoon cream sherry
10 tablespoons sweet butter	¼ cup ground walnuts
½ tablespoon salt	¼ cup ground hazelnuts
7 tablespoons sugar	3 tablespoons light cream
1 envelope of yeast	1 teaspoon plum jam
2 tablespoons lukewarm milk	1 whole egg
¾ cup sour cream	Vanilla sugar
2 egg yolks	

1. Preheat oven to 375°F. Mix flour with butter until the mixture forms crumbs. Add salt and 3 tablespoons sugar.

2. Dissolve yeast in lukewarm milk. Add sour cream, egg yolks and sherry. Knead together with the buttered flour and make a real hard dough out of it.

3. Line a 3-foot-square white cotton cloth with wax paper. Place dough in the middle. Bring the corners of the cloth together and tie very loosely, thus allowing ample space for the dough to expand. However, the bag must be sealed so no water can enter.

4. Take a very large dish, half fill it with warm (not hot) water, and place dough package in it. When dough rises to the surface and floats like a balloon, it has risen enough.

5. Take out the dough and gently untie it. Place it on a floured board and roll it out to ½-inch thickness. Cut into pieces 3 by 5 inches.

6. Mix walnuts, hazelnuts, remaining 4 tablespoons sugar, the light cream and plum jam.

7. Fill the centers of the pieces with the filling. Roll up each piece and twist into crescent shape.

8. Beat the whole egg with 1 teaspoon water. Spread tops of the crescents with the egg wash. Place them on a buttered baking sheet, and bake in the preheated oven for 15 minutes.

9. While still warm, sprinkle with vanilla sugar.

NOTE: *This recipe is nearly 200 years old. The curious name and the technique probably developed when houses were drafty and a yeast dough had no evenly warm place to rise. Apparently placing the dough in lukewarm water solved the problem. When the dough turned around in the water, it was ready for shaping.*

The texture is somewhat different from the usual yeast crescent. Many other fillings can be used.

MOORS' HEADS

Indiáner   *12 individual cakes*

4 eggs, separated	¼ pound sweet chocolate
Pinch of salt	1 tablespoon sweet butter
⅔ cup granulated sugar	1 cup heavy cream
⅔ cup flour	3 tablespoons vanilla sugar

1. Preheat oven to 350°F. Whip egg whites with a pinch of salt till they are foamy and stand in peaks.

2. Add the egg yolks, one by one, beating after each addition for about 2 minutes.

3. Add the granulated sugar and whip for another 2 minutes. Add flour, little by little, and stir until the batter is very smooth.

4. Butter a special *indiáner* form (or if not available, a muffin tin). Fill 12 forms to three-fourths capacity with the batter. Bake in the preheated oven for 10 to 12 minutes.

5. When the cakes are cool, cut them across into halves, and scrape out the center of each half.

6. Make the glaze: Place the chocolate in the top part of a double boiler and soften over hot water, while stirring. When chocolate is completely melted, remove from heat. When cool, whip in the butter.

7. Dip the top halves of the cakes into the chocolate glaze, and place them in refrigerator to harden.

8. Whip the heavy cream till it becomes stiff, then mix in the vanilla sugar.

9. Fill the hollowed-out unglazed halves of the cakes with the sweetened whipped cream. Place chocolate-glazed halves on top. Whipped cream should show through around the middle, resembling grinning teeth.

NOTE: *Some housewives cover both halves with chocolate glaze.*

While this may seem like a particularly rich cupcake in the United States, in Hungary and Austria it would fall in the same category as French pastry.

LITTLE FRUIT BASKETS

Gyümölcskosárkák   *12 cakes*

¼ pound butter
1¼ cups flour
7 tablespoons vanilla
  confectioners' sugar
Pinch of salt
Grated rind of ½ lemon

2 egg yolks
½ tablespoon sour cream
2 cups heavy cream
1 cup drained currant jam
  (Bar-le-Duc)

1. Preheat oven to 375°F. Mix butter and flour with a pastry blender until the mixture forms crumbs.

2. Mix in 4 tablespoons sugar, the salt, lemon rind, egg yolks and sour cream; knead till the mixture becomes a homogeneous dough. Cover it with a cloth and let it rest in the refrigerator.

3. Cut three quarters of the dough into 12 even pieces. With these line 2 ½-inch fluted round cupcake or basket molds with a thin layer of dough.

4. Cut remaining quarter of dough into 12 pieces. Stretch each piece with a rolling pin to get 6-inch pieces. Roll each piece separately and twist into a thin crescent. Make sure that the curve of the crescents is as wide as the widest part of the molds so they will fit.

5. Place the filled molds and the crescents on separate pastry sheets and bake them in the preheated oven for 12 to 15 minutes, or until they are well baked and colored.

6. Whip heavy cream with remaining 3 tablespoons vanilla sugar; gently mix it with currant jam.

7. Fill each basket with some of the cream mixture, and place a twisted crescent as the handle of the basket. The whipped cream will hold it in place.

VARIATION: *Other fillings could be fresh raspberries or wild strawberries or freshly grated chocolate mixed with whipped cream.*

PUFF PASTRY

The Hungarian name of this preparation means "leaf pastry," which is very descriptive since this marvel of unknown origin is really leaves of dough separated by layers of butter. With a formula of half flour and half butter, and with two single and two double turns, you make 288 layers or leaves.

The only thing that causes the dough to rise is the butter, since there are no chemicals, baking powder or anything else added to promote the process of rising. Escoffier said that the secret of good cooking was three secret ingredients: "butter, butter, butter." With puff pastry we should modify this to "finest butter, finest butter, finest butter." The less water and the more butter fat in the butter you use, the better chance you have for a many-layered featherlight puff pastry.

Many pastry chefs add rum instead of vinegar to help the "lift." Hungarians generally use vinegar, which to them has a less-pronounced taste.

Do not roll the pastry into too large sheets, because then the butter layers will be too thin and the pastry will not bake properly. The opposite is also true: if rolled into too small sheets, the butter layer will be too thick and the butter will run out during baking.

If the pastry shrinks while baking, the relationship between butter and dough is wrong. Either one or the other was too hard, or you did not let the pastry rest long enough between turns, or the finished pastry did not rest enough before baking. If the pastry doesn't rise, you probably made too many turns for the amount of pastry you have. If you have hard pastry with rough edges and top, you used too much flour for dusting during rolling. If butter runs out during baking, either you did not mix in enough flour or the oven is not hot enough. If the pastry collapses toward the end of baking, the oven is too hot.

PUFF PASTRY

Leveles vajas tészta

½ pound butter	½ tablespoon vinegar
½ pound flour	½ tablespoon salt

1. Knead butter with 2 tablespoons flour for about 1 minute. Set aside 2 tablespoons of this, and roll the rest in wax paper. Store in the refrigerator.

2. Take the 2 tablespoons of the mixture and mix it into the rest of the flour. Knead together with the vinegar, salt and ¾ cup water for 5 to 6 minutes, until you get a smooth, silky dough.

3. Shape the dough into a round and cut 3 or 4 incisions on top. Cover the dough with a cloth, and let it stand on the kneading board for 30 minutes.

4. Roll out the dough into a sheet 1 inch thick in the shape of a cross. Place the chilled butter from step 1 in the center of the dough. Fold over the dough flaps on all sides to cover the butter.

5. With hands and rolling pin, pat and roll out the dough-wrapped block of butter until it is doubled in size. Roll it into an oblong approximately 24 by 8 inches.

6. Fold the dough oblong in three, as if folding a letter to fit into an envelope.

7. Turn dough upside down and stretch it again. Repeat the folding process. Let dough rest in the refrigerator for 1 hour.

8. Repeat the stretching and folding, and let the dough rest again in the refrigerator.

9. Ideally, use the dough the following day, but it is possible to keep it in the refrigerator for 2 to 3 days.

NAPOLEONS

Krémes lepény   *12 to 14 pieces*

Puff Pastry (page 430)   1-inch piece of vanilla bean
3 egg yolks   2 tablespoons flour
1 whole egg   ⅓ cup sugar
½ tablespoon butter, softened   Powdered sugar
1¼ cups milk

1. Prepare the puff pastry. Preheat oven to 400°F. Roll the dough to fit a baking sheet 10 by 15 inches. With a warm knife cut off the edges of dough. With a fork, prick holes in a few places.

3. Bake in the preheated oven for 10 to 15 minutes. Cool the pastry. Cut it into halves and put it aside.

4. Make the filling: Beat egg yolks and whole egg together with the softened butter, milk, vanilla bean, flour and sugar.

5. At first cook the filling over high heat, then reduce heat. While continuing to beat, cook the filling till it thickens. (If you are not an experienced hollandaise maker, do this over furiously boiling steam in a double boiler rather than over direct heat.) Remove the vanilla bean. Cool the filling.

6. When both puff pastry and filling are cool, spread the bottom sheet of pastry with filling. Cover with the top sheet. Sprinkle with powdered sugar through a fine sieve.

7. Cut the pastry with a very sharp, serrated slicing knife. Use a very decisive motion, without pressing, otherwise you have a disaster on your hands.

NOTE: *This is a little different from the traditional French Napoleon, but I think even the French would exclaim, celebrating this difference. Perhaps I should mention that this is actually an Italian pastry; the original name, Na-politana, was changed some 75 years ago.*

WHIPPED-CREAM ROULADE

Tolóka levelestésztából   *12 to 15 pieces*

Puff Pastry (page 430)   ¼ cup vanilla confectioners'
1 whole egg   sugar
1½ cups heavy cream   ¼ cup ground roasted almonds

1. Make the puff pastry. Preheat oven to 400° F.
2. Roll the pastry to as thin a sheet as you can make. Cut it to strips 14 by 2 inches.
3. Beat the egg to make egg wash and brush it over the strips.
4. Use special metal tubes 6 inches long, 1 inch wide at the thicker end and ¾ inch wide at the smaller end. Starting at the thicker end of the tube, wrap each tube with a dough strip, thus forming a loose spiral of dough.
5. Place the wrapped tubes 2 inches apart on a baking sheet. Bake in the preheated oven for 12 to 15 minutes.
6. Carefully remove metal tubes and let the pastry cool.
7. Mix heavy cream with vanilla sugar and whip it until stiff. Fill pastry tubes with whipped cream, using a pastry bag.
8. Dip the ends of the filled pastry tubes into almonds. Because of the whipped cream, quite a lot of almonds will stick.

NOTE: *The Hungarian name means "little push-out," indicating the process of removing the metal tube.*

PASTRY HORNS MADE WITH LEAF LARD

Hájas szarvacskák   *12 to 15 pieces*

½ pound fresh leaf lard   2 eggs
½ pound flour   ½ cup piquant jam
1 teaspoon plain lard   ½ cup *ground* walnuts
½ teaspoon salt   ½ cup *chopped* walnuts
1 teaspoon granulated sugar   ½ cup vanilla sugar
1 teaspoon sour cream

1. Force the leaf lard through a sieve, or purée in a blender, and whip it till foamy, about 10 minutes.

2. Mix flour with 1 teaspoon lard, the salt, granulated sugar, sour cream and 1 egg. Add about 1 cup of water. Knead for 10 to 15 minutes, till the dough puckers and is quite silky on the outside. Let it rest for 30 minutes.

3. Roll out dough into a ¼-inch-thick sheet. Spread it with one third of the whipped leaf lard. Fold over the dough like puff pastry.

4. Roll out the dough again and spread it with second third of the leaf lard. Repeat the folding.

5. Roll out again, and spread with the rest of the lard. Fold over once again and let the dough rest in the refrigerator for 1 hour.

6. Stretch the dough to a very thin sheet, less than ¼ inch. Cut it into 4-inch squares.

7. Put 1 teaspoon of jam and 1 teaspoon ground walnuts in the center. Starting with one corner, roll up the square with the jam inside to make a horn. Fill and roll all the squares.

8. Beat the second egg for glazing, and brush egg over the tops of all the horns. Dip them into the chopped walnuts. Sprinkle them with vanilla sugar.

9. Bake for 15 to 20 minutes.

NOTE: *Leaf lard is the inner lining of the ribs of the pig. It's soft and not unlike the yellow chunks of fat in fat chickens. It must be fresh or it will not act as a quasi-chemical ingredient to raise the pastry layers.*

This same dough can be used without sugar and with more salt just like conventional puff pastry, for a great variety of hot appetizers.

✡ 37 ✡

CONFECTIONS
(ÉDES CSEMEGÉK)

THE following five recipes bring to mind the afternoon teenager parties, the *zsúr* of yesteryear's Hungary. The repertoire is vast, and there are several books that deal exclusively with these sweets. The common characteristic is that none of these is baked; they are either cooked on top of the stove or mixed together in various ingenious ways. These could be called *mignons*, or *les frivolités*. Served with other baked small sweets, they make a delightful addition to the *compotier* served after dinner or with your afternoon coffee.

CHOCOLATE MIGNON TOPPED WITH RUM CHERRY

Csokoládés csemege rumosmeggyel   *20 pieces*

¾ cup sugar   1 cup grated walnuts
½ cup grated semisweet   2 tablespoons dark rum
  chocolate   20 cherries in rum

1. Boil ½ cup of the sugar with ¼ cup water. Mix in the grated chocolate and simmer for 2 minutes. Remove from heat.

2. Add grated walnuts and the rum, and work them in well.

3. Make about 20 little balls and roll them in remaining sugar. Make a little hole in the top of each ball and place a rum cherry in it.

4. Put them into fluted little *mignon* cups. Store them in the refrigerator.

COFFEE MIGNON

Kávécsemege   *24 pieces*

¾ cup plus 2 tablespoons sugar   1 cup ground walnuts
⅓ cup prepared strong espresso   2 tablespoons roasted coffee
  coffee   beans, crushed or ground fine

1. Combine ¾ cup sugar and the liquid coffee, and simmer until the mixture becomes quite syrupy.
2. Add walnuts, mix, and remove from heat.
3. When cool enough to handle, make little balls of the mixture. Mix ground coffee beans with 2 tablespoons sugar and roll the balls in it.
4. Place the balls in fluted little *mignon* cups. Store them in the refrigerator.

ALMOND ROULADE

Mandulás szalámi   *24 to 30 pieces*

6 tablespoons butter   1 cup ground almonds
½ cup granulated sugar   ½ cup chopped almonds
1 tablespoon powdered cocoa   3 tablespoons rum
1½ cups ground tea   ½ cup XXX powdered sugar
  biscuits or plain cookies

1. Soften the butter and mix it with the granulated sugar, powdered cocoa, cookie crumbs, ground almonds, chopped almonds and rum.
2. Roll the mixture in wax paper to the shape of a roulade, about 2 inches in diameter. Then roll it in the powdered sugar. Wrap in wax paper and store in the refrigerator until firm.
3. When the roll is firm, slice it. Slice only as much as you will use, and store the rest in the refrigerator.

NOTE: *It is very important that the* ground *almonds be almost as fine as* flour, *and the* chopped *almonds be in quite rough pieces.*

HONEY POPPYSEED SALAMI

Mézes szalámi mákkal   *24 to 30 pieces*

1½ cups honey   Pinch of ground cloves
¾ cup ground poppyseeds   ½ teaspoon ground cinnamon
1½ cups ground walnuts

1. Bring honey to a boil; the easiest way, even if fairly slow, is to do it in a double boiler.

2. Remove honey from heat and mix in the poppyseeds, walnuts and spices. Mix well, and let the mixture cool.

3. Place the mixture on a marble slab or wet board and shape it into a salami-shaped cylinder. Roll it in wax paper and store in the refrigerator overnight.

4. Cut into slices just before serving.

SWEET CHESTNUT PÂTÉ

Édes gesztenyés pástétom   *24 to 30 pieces*

1 pound whole chestnuts in
  shells
10 tablespoons sweet butter
1¼ cups vanilla sugar made
  with XXX powdered sugar

3 tablespoons rum
½ cup currant jam, softened
½ pound sweet baking
  chocolate

1. Cook the chestnuts in their shells. When soft, peel them and purée them while still hot. There should be 1¼ cups purée.

2. Cream butter with sugar till foamy. Add rum and keep creaming the mixture. Add puréed chestnuts and mix well (possibly on a marble slab).

3. Line a small pâté mold with wet wax paper. Press the purée into it, and put it in the refrigerator.

4. Next day, with the help of the paper, gently remove pâté from the mold and discard paper. Carefully spread softened jam on top.

5. Soften the chocolate in the top part of a double boiler over steam. When properly soft, spread it evenly on top of the pâté. Put pâté back in the refrigerator to harden.

6. When serving this, dip a knife into warm water before each slice is cut.

☀ 38 ☀

REGIONAL MENUS, SPECIALTY DINNERS AND FEASTS FOR RED-LETTER DAYS (TÁJI ÉTRENDEK, KÜLÖNLEGES VACSORÁK ÉS ÜNNEPI LAKOMÁK)

TRANSDANUBIA (DUNÁNTÚL)

PÉCSI CIRFANDLI	Roast Goose Liver, served cold
	Sült libamáj
	Guinea Hen Potage as in Csurgó
	Csurgói gyöngytyúkleves
AKALI OLASZRIZLING	Esterházy Rostélyos
	Egg Barley
	Tarhonya
BADACSONYI OTTONEL MUSKOTÁLY	Golden Dumpling Cake with Wine Cream
	Aranygaluska borsodóval
	Seasonal Fruits
BLACKBERRY BRANDY	Black Coffee

THE GREAT PLAINS (NAGY-ALFÖLD)

Lebbencs Soup
Lebbencsleves
HOMOKI EZERJÓ Duckling in Rice as in Alföld
Alföldi rizses kacsa
NEMESKADARKA Mutton Paprikás with Cabbage
Kunsági bürgepaprikás káposztával
Wine Strudel
Boros rétes
Fruit
APRICOT BRANDY Black Coffee

NOTE: *The Hungarian dishes in these menus can all be found in the recipe chapters. Consult the Index for pages.*

NORTHERN HUNGARY (ÉSZAK-MAGYARORSZÁG)

Hare Soup
Felvidéki finomnyúlleves
CSEMŐI RIZLING Potato Dumplings with Sheep's-Milk Cheese
Dödöle
Smothered Venison Cutlet as in Mátra
Mátrai szarvasszelet seprenyősen
Northland Square
Felvidéki pite
PLUM BRANDY Black Coffee

SOUTHERN HUNGARY (DÉL-MAGYARORSZÁG)

Serbian Bean Soup
Szerb bableves
Serbian Carp
Rácponty
BÁNÁTI RIZLING   Layered Cabbage as in Bácska
Bácskai rakott káposzta
Pot-Cheese Strudel Cake
Gibanica
Black Coffee

TRANSYLVANIA (ERDÉLY)

Fresh Dill Soup
Friss kaporleves
CSONGRÁDI KADARKA

Heránytokány as in Marosszék
Marosszéki heránytokány
Transylvanian Bandit's Meat with Cornmeal
Dumplings
Erdélyi zsiványpecsenye puliszkával
Cabbage Salad
Káposztasaláta cikával
Liptó Cheese Spread with Green Peppers
Körözött juhtúró
GREEN WALNUT BRANDY

Varga Strudel-Cake
Vargabéles

LENTEN DINNER

OLASZRIZLING
     Stuffed Eggs Casino
   Töltött kaszinótojás zöldségsalátával
      Spawn Soup
     Böjti halikraleves
VILLÁNYI HÁRSLEVELŰ
  Mushroom-Stuffed Peppers as in Ormánság
   Ormánsági gombás töltött paprika
      Carp Pörkölt
      Pontypörkölt
     Pálffy Noodles
     Pálffy metélt
     Oranges, Figs
      Cheeses
     Black Coffee

A GAME DINNER

    Lentil Soup with Partridge
    Lencseleves fogolyhússal
TOKAJI HÁRSLEVELŰ Piquant Hare Liver
    Pirított citromos nyúlmáj
SOPRONI KÉKFRANKOS
  Hare Braised with Juniper Berries
      Borókás nyúl
    Pheasant as in Szabolcs
    Fácánsült szabolcsiasan
     Apple Cabbage
   Gül baba almás káposztája
      Potato Crust
     Burgonyakéreg
     Slid Pancakes
    Csúsztatott palacsinta
PEAR BRANDY   Black Coffee

441

Part Three [*Recipes*]

MIDDAY MEAL IN A FISH CSÁRDA

SZEKSZÁRDI KADARKA   Fishermen's Broth
Halászlé
Túrós csusza
Fresh Fruit

A REPAST ON PIG-KILLING DAY
(DISZNOTOROS VACSORA)

Orja Soup
Orjaleves
VILLÁNYI SILLER   Hot Liver Sausage
Májas hurka
Homemade Sausage
Házi kolbász
DEBRŐI HÁRSLEVELŰ   Pork Flekken
Sertésflekken
Salmagundi
Csalamádé
Cottage-Fried Potatoes
Stuffed Cabbage as Made on Pig-Killing Day
Disznótoros káposzta
SZILVÓRIUM
(PLUM BRANDY)   Bowknots
Forgácsfánk

442

DINING IN THE EIGHTEENTH-CENTURY MANNER

Herb Soup
Füvesleves
SOMLÓI FURMINTOS Fish Sausage as in Rábaköz
Rábaközi halkolbász
Tenderloin of Beef Braised in Must
Mustos pecsenye
White-Bread Dumplings
Zsemlegombóc
Stuffed Morels
Töltött kucsmagomba

TOKAY SWEET
SZAMORODNI Water-Dragging Butter Crescents
Vizen kullogó omlóskifli
Wine Cream
Borsodó
Fruits

HUNGARIAN PEACH
LIQUEUR (Possibly Coffee)

Part Three [*Recipes*]

AN ELEGANT DINNER *ANNO* 1900

CSOPAKI OLASZRIZLING   Stuffed Eggs in Pastry
Tésztában sült töltött tojás
Strained Gulyás Broth
Derített gulyásleves
TOKAY SZAMORODNI   Roast Fogas
Roston sült fogas
VILLÁNYI BURGUNDI
Braised Steak in Chef Csáki's Manner
Csáki rostélyos
Potato Cream
Tojásos burgonyapüré
Apple and Savoy Cabbage Salad
Alma-kelkáposztasaláta
APRICOT BRANDY

Apricot Cream as in Kecskemét
Kecskeméti sárgabarackkrém
Hungarian Cheeses
Fruits
Black Coffee
TOKAY ESZENCIA   Cookies and Little Cakes
Aprósütemények

A GUNDEL BANQUET, BASED ON HIS RECIPES

Palóc Soup
Palócleves
BADACSONYI   Fogas à la Gundel
SZÜRKEBARÁT   *Fogas Gundel módra*
MÓRI EZERJÓ   Layered Cabbage Teleki
Rakottkáposzta Teleki módra
TOKAY ASZÚ   Pancakes à la Gundel
Palacsinta Gundel módra
EGRI BIKAVÉR   Fresh Fruits and Cheeses
COGNAC   Black Coffee

A NOTE ON SIX POEMS BY *JÓZSEF BERDA*

POETRY has been a popular pastime in Hungary for over a thousand years. Hungarians love food and wine and the pleasures of the table. If you put these two facts together it must be quite obvious that the choice of poems dealing with the subject is nearly unlimited.

Hungarian cuisine—as I hope this volume amply demonstrates—contains nearly every hue of the taste-rainbow with complexities and subtleties comparable to any cuisine. Yet I feel that the quintessence of it is the enjoyment of robust foods and wines, the passion for earthly pleasures and the praise of nature's heavenly gifts. No one wrote about these with as much gusto and Walt Whitmanish understanding as József Berda.

My great and good friend Paul Tabori, in the spirit of true friendship toward Berda, who was a friend of his, and toward me and toward the non-Hungarian world, translated them, performing the miracle of transplantation and transformation.

THANKSGIVING

THE very first step toward writing a worthwhile book is to get the right people to help you. I'd like to give credit to:

Ferenc Aczél, editor of Corvina, for his tireless search for hidden illustrative treasures.

Iván Boldizsár, writer, editor, raconteur, for many of the historical notes.

Dr. Tibor Borza, director of the Hungarian Restaurateur's Museum, for allowing us to dig into their priceless material, as well as his successor Dr. Balázs Draveczky.

Iván Engel-Teván, the sensitive artist, whose drawings appear in many of the chapters.

Harry Ford, art director.

Milton Glaser, the eminent artist, for his friendship and for the image of the definitive goose.

Imre and Ferenc Gundel, for valuable information on the Gundel family.

Zoltán Halász, editor-author, who contributed valuable information to many chapters.

Kate Hartson, editorial director of Wings Books, for her creative ideas.

Gyula Illyés, "the conscience of Hungary," whose wisdom (or at least a small particle) I hope was successfully transplanted to some of the pages.

Zoltán Kenderessy, executive pastry chef, for his superb recipes.

Inez M. Krech, for going through the recipes with a high-powered microscope.

Dorothy Parker, editor, who shaped the first edition of this book with loving care.

Erzsi Rusznyák, for the gastronomic map.

Etel "Mimi" Salacz, for her ancestral recipes.

Mrs. Jenny Szemere Stratford, who enjoyed, suffered, puzzled and triumphed over the testing of the recipes for several years.

A special thanks to Paul Tabori, novelist, scholar, journalist, for many, many things, including his father Kornél's priceless gastronomic picture collection, and for advancing theories and emendations of the manuscript.

Amerigo Tot, the great sculptor, for his illustration.

Master chef József Venesz, the dean of the Hungarian restaurant industry, for gracing this book with his introduction and for an overview of the entire subject.

Joseph Wechsberg, for his preface, his understanding and many evenings of symposiums.

Lojos Zilahy, noted Hungarian novelist, for sharing with me his ancestor, Ágnes Zilahy's book, and for his description of the ox-roasting.

And my gratitude to many others, including:
István Bart, president of Corvina Publishing, Budapest
Mr. and Mrs. Gyula Bandl
Maria Cochetti, curator of the Bibliotheca Casanetense, Rome
Egon Eigen, executive chef
Otto von Habsburg
Reverend Andrew Hamza
Richard Hosking, curator of the British Museum
Peggy Ince
Paul Kovi
Doe Lang
Zoltan Syposs
Robert O'Brien
György Rózsa, curator of the Hungarian National Museum
Miklós Vajda, editor of *The New Hungarian Quarterly*

SELECTED BIBLIOGRAPHY

A Divatújság főzőkönyve. Budapest, 1909.

A Hét szakácskönyve. Budapest, 1902.

A New Yorktól a Hungáriáig. Budapest, 1965.

Ambrózy, Ágoston. *Tokaj-Hegyalja néhány szellemtörténeti vonatkozása.* Budapest, 1932.

Apor, Péter. *Metamorphosis Transylvaniae.* N.p., 1736.

Bálint, Sándor. "Adatok a magyar búcsújárás néprajzához." *Ethnographia,* 1939.

Balla, Vilmos. *A kávéforrás.* Budapest, 1927.

Ballai, Károly. *A magyar kocsmák és fogadók a XIII–XVIII században.* Budapest, 1927.

————. *A magyar vendéglátóipar története.* Budapest, 1943.

————. *Magyar-francia gasztronómia.* Budapest, 1938.

Barczay, Oszkár. *A régi magyar konyháról.* Budapest, 1893.

Barczi, Géza. *A magyar nemzeti nyelv életrajza.* Budapest, 1966.

Bátky, Zsigmond. *A magyar konyha története.* Budapest, 1937.

————. *Ettek-e a honfoglaló magyarok nyereg alatt puhított húst.* N.p., 1903.

Bel, Matthias. *Ad Paratus Historiam Hungariae.* Posonii [Bratislava], 1735.

Bertrandon de la Brocquiere utazása. N.p., 1933.

Bevilaqua Borsody, Béla. *A budai és pesti mészáros céhek ládáinak okiratai.* Budapest, 1939.

Bevilaqua Borsody, Béla, and Mazsári, Béla. *Pest-Budai Kávéházak.* Budapest, 1935.

Blaze de Bury. *Voyage en Autriche et Hongrie.* Paris, 1851.

Boldényi, J. *La Hongrie Ancienne et Moderne.* Paris, 1853.

Bright, Richard. *Travels from Vienna Through Lower Hungary.* Edinburgh, 1818.

Browning, H. Ellen. *A Girl's Wandering in Hungary.* N.p., 1896.

Bruyerius, Campegius. *De Re Cibaria.* N.p., 1600.

Clusius. *Curae Posteriores,* N.p., 1611.

Csapó, József. *Új Füves és Virágos Kert.* Budapest, 1775.

Csepka, L. *A budapesti pincérek 50 éves története.* Budapest, 1885.

Czeglédi, Károly. *A kunok eredetéről.* Budapest, 1949.

Czifrai, István. *Magyar nemzeti szakácskönyv,* 1st ed., Pest, 1826; 3rd ed., Pest. 1829.

Dezséry, László. "Dobostorta/Emlékezés." *Vendéglátás,* April, 1962.

Dittmayer, Andor. *Szakácsművészeti szakkönyv.* Budapest, 1935.

Dobos, József. *Magyar francia szakácskönyv.* Budapest, n.d.

Dömötör, Tekla. *Naptári ünnepek.* Budapest, 1964.

Duby, Károly. *Magyar-francia szakácskönyv.* Budapest, 1883.

"Egy lakoma/A nemzeti Casinóról," *Budapesti Hírlap,* May 26, 1907.

Fábián, Gyula. *A mézeskalács/Néprajzi Értesítő.* Budapest, 1913.

Fehér, Géza. *A bolgár törökök szerepe és műveltsége.* Budapest, 1940.

Fingerhut. *Monographia Generis Capsici.* Düsseldorf, 1833.

Fodor, Ferenc. *A jászság életrajza.* Budapest, 1942.

Fornády, E. *Szőlőművelés.* Budapest, 1949.

Glück, Frigyes, and Stáder, Károly. *Az inyesmesterség könyve.* Budapest, 1889.

Greguss, Ágost. *Az étkezés aesthetikája.* Budapest, 1899.

Gundel, Károly. *A vendéglátás művészete.* Budapest, 1934.

Hagn, Károly. *Cukrászat.* Budapest, 1943.

Halász, Zoltán. *Hungarian Wines Through the Ages.* Budapest, 1958.

Hangay, Octáv. *A paprikáról.* Budapest, 1887.

Harsányi, Adolf. *Kávésok, pincérek, kávéfőzők.* Budapest, 1909.

Hegyesi, József. *Előételek.* Budapest, 1895.

———. *Legújabb házi cukrászat kézikönyve.* Budapest, 1893.

Hering, G. E. *Sketches on the Danube.* London, 1838.

Herman, Otto. *A magyar halászat könyve.* Budapest, 1914.

Hóman, Gyula, and Szekfű, Gyula. *Magyar történelem.* Budapest, 1936–1939.

Horn, J. *Hazai vadnövényeink konyhai felhasználásáról.* N.p., 1916.

Horvát, Henrik. *Zsigmond király és kora.* Budapest, 1937.

Hutas, Magdolna. *A főzés eszközei és műveletének nyelvi kifejezése.* Budapest, 1951.

———. *Szakácsok, régi ételek. A szakácsok szervezete.* Budapest, 1953.

Ilk, Mihály. *A Nemzeti Kaszinó százéves története.* Budapest, 1927.

Illyés, Gyula. *Kháron ladikján.* Budapest, 1969.

Katona, Imre. *Sárköz.* Budapest, 1962.

Katona, József, and Dömötör, József. *Magyar borok, borvidékek.* Budapest, 1963.

Kemény, György. *Mézeskalácsosok.* Budapest, 1925.

Kertész, Manó. *Szokásmondások.* Budapest, 1922.

Kesselbauer, K. *Észrevételek a tokaji borról.* Kassa [Kosice], 1835.

Kettner. *Book of the Table.* London, 1887.

Kisfaludy, Sándor. *Regék a magyar előidőből.* Buda, 1818.

Kiss, Lajos. *A Szegény ember élete.* Budapest, 1939.

Kömlei, János. *Szükségben Segítő Könyv.* Budapest, 1907.

Közlemények a debreceni Kossuth Lajos Tudományegyetem Néprajzi Intézetéből. Budapest, 1958.

Kugler. *Szakácskönyv.* Budapest, 1900.

László, Gyula. *A Honfoglaló Nép Élete.* Budapest, 1944.

László, Péter. *Kurtakocsma.* N.p., 1949.

Lorincze, Lajos. *A régi pásztorok eledeléről.* Szentgál, Veszprém m., n.d.

Lővy, Náci. *Elmult éjszakák: Anekdóták kávéházakból.* N.p., n.d.

Magyar, Elek. *Pesti Históriák.* Budapest, 1920.

Magyar Szállodás és Vendéglős, 1896–1943. N.p., n.d.

Malortie, Ernst von, *Das Menu.* Hannover, 1888.

Marencich, Ottó. *Négynyelvű ételszótár.* Budapest, 1957.

Márki, Ferencz. *I. Ferencz József.* Budapest, 1907.

Márki, Sándor. *Mátyás király kora.* Budapest, 1902.

Márkus, Mihály. *A bokortanyák népe.* Budapest, 1943.

Matyus, István. *Ó és új dianetetica.* Pozsonyi [Bratislava], 1737.

Mazsáry, Béla. *Társadalmi élet a vendéglőkben.* Budapest, 1939.

Miskolcy, István. *Magyarország az Anjouk korában.* Budapest, 1923.

Nagy, Miklós. *Mult és jelen a Marosszögben.* Budapest, 1947.

Nagy Czirok, László. *Pasztorélet a Kiskunságon.* Budapest, 1959.

Negyven év a magyar szállodás és vendéglőipar életéből. Budapest, 1939.

Newnham-Davis, N., *The Gourmet's Guide to Europe.* New York, 1908.

Poltz, Johann Moritz. *Ein Klein Ungarisches Chronicon.* N.p., 1685.

Proháczik, János, and Csáki, József. *A konyhamészáros kézikönyve.* Budapest, 1959.

Radvánszky, Béla. *A magyar családélet és háztartás a XVI és XVII században.* Budapest, 1897.

———. *Régi magyar szakácskönyvek.* Budapest, 1893.

Rákóczi, J. *Szakácskönyv.* Budapest, 1964.

Rapaich, Raymund. *A kenyér története.* Budapest, 1934.

Ravasz, László. *Árúismeret cukrászoknak.* Budapest, 1961.

Régi pesti kávéházak. Budapest, 1927.

Reső Ensel, Sándor. *Magyarországi népszokások.* Pest, 1867.

Révai Nagy Lexikona. Budapest, 1916.

"Roger mester siralmas éneke" [13th-century manuscript].

Schnitta, Sámuel. *Étlapszerkesztés.* Budapest, 1966.

Szalay, József. *A Magyar nemzet története.* N.p., 1897.

Szadeczky, Lajos. *Az iparfejlődés és a céhek fejlődése.* Budapest, 1913.

Sztáray, Zoltán. *Haraszthy Ágoston.* [California], 1964.

Szomaházy, István. "Beszélgetés egy öreg huszárral és kormornyikkal a Nemzeti Casinó régi életéről." *Pesti Napló,* October, 1924.

Tábori, Kornél. *A magyar vendéglátás irodalma.* Budapest, 1924.

Torbágyi-Novák, L. *A barackpálinkáról.* Budapest, 1943.

Török, Károly. *Lakodalmi szokások as Alföldön.* N.p., 1864.

Tóth, Béla. *Magyar ritkaságok.* Budapest, 1899.

Townson, Robert. *Travels in Hungary.* London, 1797.

Trócsányi, Zoltán. *Kirándulás a magyar multba.* Budapest, 1937.

Turós, Emil, and Turós, Lukács. *A mi szakácskönyvünk.* Budapest, 1961.

Ukers, H. William. *All About Coffee.* New York, 1935.

Universal Lexikon der Kochkünste. Leipzig, 1913.

Vajkai, Aurél. *Balatonmellék.* Budapest, 1964.

Vajtai, István. *Homokországban.* Budapest, 1947.

Vendéglátóipari konyhatechnológia. Budapest, 1956.

Venesz, József. *Az ételkészítés technikája.* Budapest, 1964.

————. *A magyaros konyha.* Budapest, 1965.

Veres, Péter. *Szűk esztendő.* Budapest, 1942.

Viski, Károly. *Hungarian Peasant Customs.* Budapest, 1932.

Zilahy, Lajos. *The Dukays.* New York, 1949.

Zolnai, Béla. *Hajdúk.* Budapest, 1951.

Zsemlyei, Oszkár. *A magyar sütő, cukrász és mézeskalácsipar története.* Budapest, 1940.

For the final authority on Hungarian spelling *Helyesírási tanácsadó szótár,* 3rd ed. (Budapest, 1967), was used.

INDEXES

I PEOPLE, PLACES, EVENTS

III HUNGARIAN INDEX

(BETŰRENDES RECEPTMUTATÓ)

Index